Power and Illicit Drugs in the Global South

More than a hundred years have passed since the adoption of the first prohibitionist laws on drugs. Increasingly, the edifice of international drug control and laws is vacillating under pressures of reform. Scholarship on drugs history and policy has had a tendency to look at the issue mostly in the Western hemisphere of the globe or to privilege Western narratives of drugs and drugs policy. This volume instead turns this approach upside down and makes an intellectual attempt to redefine the subject of drugs in the Global South. Opium, heroin, cannabis, hashish, methamphetamines and khat are among the drugs discussed in the contributions to the volume, which spans from Sub-Saharan Africa to Southeast Asia, including the Middle East, North Africa, Latin America and the Indian Subcontinent. The volume also makes a powerful case for an interdisciplinary approach to the study of drugs by juxtaposing the work of historians, political scientists, geographers, anthropologists and criminologists. Ultimately, this edited volume is a rich and diverse collection of new case studies, which opens up venues for further research.

This book was originally published as a special issue of *Third World Quarterly*.

Maziyar Ghiabi is Lecturer in Modern Iranian History at the University of Oxford, UK, and Titular Fellow at Wadham College, University of Oxford. Prior to this position, he was a Postdoctoral Fellow at the Paris School of Advanced Studies in Social Sciences (EHESS), France, and a member of the Institut de Recherche Interdisciplinaire des Enjeux Sociaux (IRIS), France. Maziyar obtained his Doctorate in Politics at the University of Oxford (St Antony's College) where he was a Wellcome Trust Scholar in Society and Ethics (2013–2017). Besides working on drug policy, Maziyar has published on urban ethnography and history from below.

ThirdWorlds

Edited by Shahid Qadir, *University of London, UK*

ThirdWorlds will focus on the political economy, development and cultures of those parts of the world that have experienced the most political, social, and economic upheaval, and which have faced the greatest challenges of the postcolonial world under globalisation: poverty, displacement and diaspora, environmental degradation, human and civil rights abuses, war, hunger, and disease.

ThirdWorlds serves as a signifier of oppositional emerging economies and cultures ranging from Africa, Asia, Latin America, Middle East, and even those 'Souths' within a larger perceived North, such as the U.S. South and Mediterranean Europe. The study of these otherwise disparate and discontinuous areas, known collectively as the Global South, demonstrates that as globalisation pervades the planet, the south, as a synonym for subalterity, also transcends geographical and ideological frontier.

Corruption in the Aftermath of War
Edited by Jonas Lindberg and
Camilla Orjuela

Everyday Energy Politics in Central Asia and the Caucasus
Citizens' Needs, Entitlements and Struggles for Access
Edited by David Gullette and
Jeanne Féaux de la Croix

The UN and the Global South, 1945 and 2015
Edited by Thomas G. Weiss and Pallavi Roy

The Green Economy in the Global South
Edited by Stefano Ponte and
Daniel Brockington

Food Sovereignty
Convergence and Contradictions,
Condition and Challenges
Edited by Eric Holt-Giménez,
Alberto Alonso-Fradejas, Todd Holmes and
Martha Jane Robbins

The International Politics of Ebola
Edited by Anne Roemer-Mahler and
Simon Rushton

Rising Powers and South-South Cooperation
Edited by Kevin Gray and Barry K. Gills

The 'Local Turn' in Peacebuilding
The Liberal Peace Challenged
Edited by Joakim Öjendal,
Isabell Schierenbeck and Caroline Hughes

China's Contingencies and Globalization
Edited by Changgang Guo, Liu Debin and
Jan Nederveen Pieterse

The Power of Human Rights/The Human Rights of Power
Edited by Louiza Odysseos and
Anna Selmeczi

Class Dynamics of Development
Edited by Jonathan Pattenden,
Liam Campling, Satoshi Miyamura and
Benjamin Selwyn

Third World Approaches to International Law
Edited by Amar Bhatia, Usha Natarajan, John Reynolds and Sujith Xavier

Fragility, Aid, and State-building
Understanding Diverse Trajectories
Edited by Rachel M. Gisselquist

Rural Transformations and Agro-Food Systems
The BRICS and Agrarian Change in the Global South
Edited by Ben M. McKay, Ruth Hall and Juan Liu

Sustainable Development in Africa-EU relations
Edited by Mark Langan and Sophia Price

New Mechanisms of Participation in Extractive Governance
Between Technologies of Governance and Resistance Work
Edited by Esben Leifsen, Maria-Therese Gustafsson, María Antonieta Guzmán-Gallegos and Almut Schilling-Vacaflor

The Development Dictionary @25
Post-Development and its Consequences
Edited by Aram Ziai

Power and Illicit Drugs in the Global South
Edited by Maziyar Ghiabi

For more information about this series, please visit: https://www.routledge.com/series/TWQ

Power and Illicit Drugs in the Global South

Edited by
Maziyar Ghiabi

LONDON AND NEW YORK

First published 2019
by Routledge
2 Park Square, Milton Park, Abingdon, Oxon, OX14 4RN, UK

and by Routledge
52 Vanderbilt Avenue, New York, NY 10017, USA

First issued in paperback 2020

Routledge is an imprint of the Taylor & Francis Group, an informa business

Foreword © 2018 Philippe Bourgois
Introduction, Chapters 3-4, 7-11 © 2019 Global South Ltd, www.thirdworldquarterly.com
Chapter 2 © 2017 James Mills. Originally published as Open Access.
Chapter 5 © 2017 Dennis Rodgers. Originally published as Open Access.
Chapter 6 © 2017 Maziyar Ghiabi. Originally published as Open Access.

With the exception of Chapters 2, 5 and 6, no part of this book may be reprinted or reproduced or utilised in any form or by any electronic, mechanical, or other means, now known or hereafter invented, including photocopying and recording, or in any information storage or retrieval system, without permission in writing from the publishers. For details on the rights for Chapters 2, 5 and 6, please see the chapters' Open Access footnotes.

Trademark notice: Product or corporate names may be trademarks or registered trademarks, and are used only for identification and explanation without intent to infringe.

British Library Cataloguing in Publication Data
A catalogue record for this book is available from the British Library

ISBN 13: 978-0-367-58518-1 (pbk)
ISBN 13: 978-1-138-32354-4 (hbk)

Typeset in Myriad Pro
by RefineCatch Limited, Bungay, Suffolk

Publisher's Note
The publisher accepts responsibility for any inconsistencies that may have arisen during the conversion of this book from journal articles to book chapters, namely the possible inclusion of journal terminology.

Disclaimer
Every effort has been made to contact copyright holders for their permission to reprint material in this book. The publishers would be grateful to hear from any copyright holder who is not here acknowledged and will undertake to rectify any errors or omissions in future editions of this book.

Contents

Citation Information	ix
Notes on Contributors	xi
Foreword: Decolonising drug studies in an era of predatory accumulation *Philippe Bourgois*	1
1. Introduction – Spirit and being: interdisciplinary reflections on drugs across history and politics *Maziyar Ghiabi*	15

Part I: Genealogies of Drugs

2. Decolonising drugs in Asia: the case of cocaine in colonial India *James Mills*	26
3. A diplomatic failure: the Mexican role in the demise of the 1940 Reglamento Federal de Toxicomanías *Isaac Campos*	40
4. Drugs of choice, drugs of change: Egyptian consumption habits since the 1920s *Philip Robins*	56

Part II: Ethnographies of Drugs

5. Drug booms and busts: poverty and prosperity in a Nicaraguan narco-*barrio* *Dennis Rodgers*	69
6. Maintaining disorder: the micropolitics of drugs policy in Iran *Maziyar Ghiabi*	85
7. 'We Will Revive': addiction, spiritual warfare, and recovery in Latin America's cocaine production zone *Pablo Seward Delaporte*	106

Part III: Comparative Perspectives on Drug Wars

8. Fighting crime and maintaining order: shared worldviews of civilian and military elites in Brazil and Mexico 122
   Anaís M. Passos

9. Turning deserts into flowers: settlement and poppy cultivation in southwest Afghanistan 139
   David Mansfield

10. Quasilegality: khat, cannabis and Africa's drug laws 158
    Neil Carrier and Gernot Klantschnig

11. Why do South-east Asian states choose to suppress opium? A cross-case comparison 174
    James Windle

    Index 193

Citation Information

The chapters in this book were originally published in *Third World Quarterly*, volume 39, issue 2 (February 2018). When citing this material, please use the original page numbering for each article, as follows:

Foreword
Decolonising drug studies in an era of predatory accumulation
Philippe Bourgois
Third World Quarterly, volume 39, issue 2 (February 2018), pp. 385–398

Chapter 1
Introduction – Spirit and being: interdisciplinary reflections on drugs across history and politics
Maziyar Ghiabi
Third World Quarterly, volume 39, issue 2 (February 2018), pp. 207–217

Chapter 2
Decolonising drugs in Asia: the case of cocaine in colonial India
James Mills
Third World Quarterly, volume 39, issue 2 (February 2018), pp. 218–231

Chapter 3
A diplomatic failure: the Mexican role in the demise of the 1940 Reglamento Federal de Toxicomanías
Isaac Campos
Third World Quarterly, volume 39, issue 2 (February 2018), pp. 232–247

Chapter 4
Drugs of choice, drugs of change: Egyptian consumption habits since the 1920s
Philip Robins
Third World Quarterly, volume 39, issue 2 (February 2018), pp. 248–260

Chapter 5
Drug booms and busts: poverty and prosperity in a Nicaraguan narco-barrio
Dennis Rodgers
Third World Quarterly, volume 39, issue 2 (February 2018), pp. 261–276

Chapter 6
Maintaining disorder: the micropolitics of drugs policy in Iran
Maziyar Ghiabi
Third World Quarterly, volume 39, issue 2 (February 2018), pp. 277–297

Chapter 7
'We Will Revive': addiction, spiritual warfare, and recovery in Latin America's cocaine production zone
Pablo Seward Delaporte
Third World Quarterly, volume 39, issue 2 (February 2018), pp. 298–313

Chapter 8
Fighting crime and maintaining order: shared worldviews of civilian and military elites in Brazil and Mexico
Anaís M. Passos
Third World Quarterly, volume 39, issue 2 (February 2018), pp. 314–330

Chapter 9
Turning deserts into flowers: settlement and poppy cultivation in southwest Afghanistan
David Mansfield
Third World Quarterly, volume 39, issue 2 (February 2018), pp. 331–349

Chapter 10
Quasilegality: khat, cannabis and Africa's drug laws
Neil Carrier and Gernot Klantschnig
Third World Quarterly, volume 39, issue 2 (February 2018), pp. 350–365

Chapter 11
Why do South-east Asian states choose to suppress opium? A cross-case comparison
James Windle
Third World Quarterly, volume 39, issue 2 (February 2018), pp. 366–384

For any permission-related enquiries please visit:
http://www.tandfonline.com/page/help/permissions

Notes on Contributors

Philippe Bourgois is Professor of Anthropology and Director of the Center for Social Medicine at the Semel Institute at the University of California, USA. He has conducted long-term fieldwork in Central America and the US inner city, and has published over a dozen books, edited volumes and special issues of journals, and approximately 150 articles.

Isaac Campos is Associate Professor of History at the University of Cincinnati, USA. He holds a PhD in History from Harvard University. His prize-winning book *Home Grown: Marijuana and the Origins of Mexico's War on Drugs* (2012) explored the development of drug policy and drug war ideology in Mexico between the sixteenth century and 1920. His current project examines illicit drugs in Mexico, and to some extent greater North America, between 1912 and 1940.

Neil Carrier is Lecturer in Social Anthropology at the University of Bristol, UK. He has for many years researched the anthropology and political economy of drugs in Africa and beyond, as well as the social underpinnings of Somali global trade networks. His works include *Kenyan Khat: The social life of a stimulant* (2007) and *Africa and the War on Drugs* (with Gernot Klantschnig, 2012).

Maziyar Ghiabi is Lecturer in Modern Iranian History at the University of Oxford, UK, and Titular Fellow at Wadham College, University of Oxford. Maziyar obtained his Doctorate in Politics at the University of Oxford (St Antony's College) where he was a Wellcome Trust Scholar in Society and Ethics (2013–2017). Besides working on drug policy, Maziyar has published on urban ethnography and history from below.

Gernot Klantschnig is Senior Lecturer in Social Policy/Crime and Director of the MA in Global Crime and Justice at the University of York, UK. His research focuses include the politics of drugs and their control. His publications include *Crime, Drugs and the State in Africa: The Nigerian Connection* (2013) and *Drugs in Africa: Histories and Ethnographies of Use, Trade and Control* (edited with Neil Carrier and Charles Ambler, 2014).

David Mansfield is a Senior Fellow at the London School of Economics, UK. He has been conducting research on rural livelihoods and poppy cultivation in Afghanistan for 20 consecutive growing seasons. He is the author of *A State Built on Sand: How Opium Undermined Afghanistan*. He has worked for the Afghan Research & Evaluation Unit since 2005.

James Mills is Professor of Modern History and was founding Director of the Centre for the Social History of Health and Healthcare (CSHHH), at the University of Strathclyde, UK. His publications include *Cannabis Nation: Control and Consumption in Britain, c.1928–2008*

(2012), *Cannabis Britannica: Empire, Trade and Prohibition, 1800–1928* (2003) and *Drugs and Empires: Essays in Modern Imperialism and Intoxication* (edited with Patricia Barton, 2007).

Anaís M. Passos is a doctoral candidate in the field of Comparative Political Sociology at Sciences Po Paris, France. Her thesis deals with the role that military forces in Brazil and Mexico have undertaken in domestic security in democratic regimes. She also is a Researcher at the *Observatoire Politique d'Amérique Latine and Caraibe* (OPALC), France.

Philip Robins is Professor of Middle East Politics and Fellow of St Antony's College at the University of Oxford, UK. His most recent book is *Middle East Drugs Bazaar* (2016), which was a 10-country study of illicit drugs in the Middle East. He has also published widely on drugs in Afghanistan and Pakistan, as well as Egypt, and is a renowned scholar of Turkey.

Dennis Rodgers is Professor of International Development Studies at the University of Amsterdam, the Netherlands, and a Research Associate in the Centre on Conflict, Development and Peacebuilding at the Graduate Institute, Switzerland. An anthropologist by training, his research focuses broadly on issues relating to the political economy of conflict and violence in cities in Latin America (Nicaragua, Argentina) and South Asia (India).

Pablo Seward Delaporte is a NSF-funded PhD student in the Department of Anthropology at Stanford University, USA. His doctoral work focuses on urban poverty, structural violence, and addiction in Peru and Chile.

James Windle is Lecturer in Criminology at University College Cork, Ireland. His research focuses on illicit drug markets, illicit enterprise and street gangs. He is the author of *Suppressing Illicit Opium Production: Successful Intervention in Asia and the Middle East* (2016) and co-editor of *Historical Perspectives on Organised Crime and Terrorism* (Routledge, 2018).

FOREWORD

Decolonising drug studies in an era of predatory accumulation

Philippe Bourgois

ABSTRACT
The cultural and political-economic valences of psychoactive drugs in the Global South offer critical insights on local and international fault lines of social inequality and profiteering. Historically, in a classic primitive accumulation process the trafficking of industrially produced euphoric substances across the globe have wreaked havoc among vulnerable populations while extracting profit for the powerful. The complex flows of capital generated both by illegal addiction markets and also by the mobilisation of licit public funds to manage their mayhem, however, suggest the contemporary utility of the concept of 'predatory accumulation'. The Enlightenment-era concept of 'primitive accumulation' usefully highlighted state violence and forcible dispossession in the consolidation of European capitalism. A contemporary reframing of these processes as predatory accumulation, however, highlights contradictory, nonlinear relationships between the artificially high profits of illegal drug sales, repressive governmentality and corporate greed. It sets these patterns of destructive profiteering in the context of our moment in history.

The powerful pharmacological characteristics of psychoactive drugs mobilise culturally constructed meanings that are shaped by even more explosive political-economic forces. This makes studying industrially produced and illegally marketed mind-altering drugs incredibly challenging, interesting and important if we are to comprehend the stakes of our contemporary globalised era of devastating narcotics profiteering. The complexity of the pharmacological/cultural/political-economic mesh may also explain why we understand so little about drugs despite their powerful effect on shaping inequality, cultural conflict and the omnipotence of capitalism across the world.

As historians of colonialism and globalisation have repeatedly documented (often only from the margins of their discipline), ever since the rise of merchant capitalism and the expansion of European colonial conquest, the trafficking of industrially produced pleasurable substances has often wreaked havoc. It also created the modern phenomenon of 'addiction' among vulnerable populations across the globe.[1] Arguably the course of these wide-ranging regional and micro-local 'epidemics' represent canary-in-the-mine bellwethers that can help us identify the fault lines of suffering both within a society, a city or a rural village, and across continental divides. They expose the violent contradictions of power, social inequality, vulnerability and resistance both within local communities and across large-scale social formations.

If one approaches illegal drugs and their use – or abuse – empathetically with a strong dose of anthropology's hermeneutic of 'cultural relativism', they are also capable of revealing – or rather grasping at – a tantalising, but hard-to-define, glimpse of human strivings for utopian dreams and social solidarity, even as they expose us to the brutal reality of the vicious depths of human greed and self-interested cynicism. Repeated historic attempts to experiment with, as well as to repress, drugs demonstrate the fraught potentials of human creativity and dogmatic normativising intolerance. Similarly, contradictorily, a close documentation of epidemics is simultaneously capable of evoking both a faith in the human universal search for dreams or happiness, and a confirmation of the symbolic ideological violence of individual agency and self-control that justifies repression and victim-blaming.

On an embodied level, 'narcotic' drugs – whatever 'narcotic' really means, aside from being judged illegal and immoral by state authorities[2] – are simultaneously capable of relieving and producing physical/psychic pain, anxiety and depression. They promote dialectics of social generosity and cruel, self-interested greed – creativity and stupor, as well as revolt and domestication. As this collection of articles on drugs in the Global South demonstrates, the effects and trajectories of drugs on individuals and societies often appear exceedingly familiar, but simultaneously prove themselves to be shockingly socially labile or mysterious. In distinct settings and moments of history, they have alternatively been objectively harmless, essentially irrelevant, ecstatically fun or brutally destructive and cruelly manipulable.

The intellectual poverty of public health-dominated drug studies

Unfortunately, most of the well-funded researchers who have studied mind-altering psychoactive illicit drugs over the past half century have been concentrated in public health, which is the only major academic discipline to have a large, thriving subfield devoted to their study, currently referred to – somewhat politically correctly and moralistically – as 'substance-use-disorder prevention research'.[3] This research is disproportionately funded by the US government through its multiple National Institutes of Health – especially the Institutes on 'Drug Abuse', (NIDA), 'Alcohol Abuse' (NIAA) and 'Mental Health' (NIMH). Behavioural psychologists dominate the field of public health, and this young, insecure and largely soft-money-funded discipline tends to mimic, for its survival and legitimacy, the rigour of quantitative methods and the technical determinism of the laboratory sciences.[4] The lion's share of the funding targets applied solutions to complex social problems through the prolonged scientific Rorschach of the human genome or through massive investment in often for-profit random-controlled trials that test magic-bullet pharmacological antagonist synapse blocks to the brain's pleasure receptors, or through individual-level psychological therapeutic interventions administered in a socially decontextualised vacuum.

'Harm reduction' has managed to establish a liberal hegemony over the applied topic of substance abuse and HIV prevention, but this approach, which thinks of itself as being non-judgmental and strives to meet users on their own terms to reduce chronic suffering, is, in fact, a jumble of inconsistent contradictions. It is dominated by biomedicine's hyper-sanitary population-level gaze and, despite its good intentions, often morphs into a pathologising left hand of the state inadvertently at the service of social control. Harm reduction is also subject to the blinders of public health's narrowly conceptualised middle-class fantasy world that celebrates individual agency and normativity in an unrealistic social power vacuum. It is hegemonized by a naïve conviction that democratic access to 'objective knowledge' will drive conscious individual behaviour change, one person at a time, on a population level. Harm reduction represents an almost textbook case of a classic mechanism of governmentality, illustrating Foucault's[5] passive/aggressive conception of the quasi-omnipotence of 'biopower' as a 'positive' discourse in the 'knowledge/power apparatus'. It saves life while stripping human subjectivity of its capacity for autonomous creativity in the name of civilisation and responsible modernisation. As Ghiabi's[6] provocative ethnographic deconstruction of repression and compassion in Iran's national policies towards drug control, in this special issue, illustrates, harm reduction travels problematically. It is a slippery, culturally constituted, humanitarian scientific approach buffeted by overlapping contradictory ideological, religious and secular values that congeal in the all-too-practical state priorities of managing social crisis and maintaining control of unruly non-normative populations. Harm reduction everywhere – not just the notably contradictory case of Iran – is capable of melding scientific therapeutic efficiency and empathetic ethical tolerance with ideological righteousness and even brutal repression, despite simultaneously quasi-politically carving out temporarily semi-safe shared public spaces[7] for vulnerable populations.

The prohibitionist imperial power stigma of drug use

The ebbs and flows of regional, global and local tastes and preferences for specific drugs repeatedly catch us by surprise even when they are simply repeating forgotten patterns that may have occurred only two, three or four generations earlier. Drug-use fashions almost inevitably generate moral panics and predictably mobilise nationalist xenophobic, messianic and socio-biological racist discourses even though the epidemics will be ultimately tamed or will simply burn out by themselves and fade away. To be fair, anyone who has experienced on an embodied level the mystery of 'addiction', whether personally through uncontrollable emotional cravings or manic ecstatic/soothing epiphanies followed by torturous withdrawals, or through the loss of a family member or loved one, knows how seriously one has to take the pharmacological power of drug effects. Unfortunately, the socio-cultural and political-economic 'determinants' of drug effects are much harder to see. When one does ethnographic work in settings dominated by drug trafficking and drug use, the everyday emergency and high stakes of money, violence and damaged health can overwhelm one's capacity for the larger, longer term perspective offered by Rodgers'[8] analysis in this issue of life history outcomes in a formerly crack- and gang-ridden, barrio in Managua, Nicaragua.

The poverty in academic, policy and popular thinking about drugs and the underdevelopment of theory in much of the academic literature probably have something to do with the stigma that surrounds drug use. It may, more politically, be the historical effect of the unevenly and hypocritically enforced long-term prohibitionist global era whereby the most imperially powerful nations have fitfully attempted to criminalise or contain psychoactive drug use, even as they have also been the protagonists in promoting industrial drug trafficking over the past two centuries in their ongoing internecine struggles for global dominance of foreign markets, territories and natural resources. The United States, not surprisingly, has for well over a century been the leading hypocritical gendarme of prohibitionist drug policies. US officials have repeatedly intervened directly in the internal sovereign public policy affairs of countries, as Campos[9] documents in this issue with his 1940 case study of the US government's sabotage of Mexico's attempts to medicalise and decriminalise illegal use of drugs to diminish their harmful effects. Simultaneously, the United States throughout the Cold War and continuing now through the War on Terror-for-Oil has repeatedly fomented, or at least tolerated, industrial-level cultivation and processing and it even sometimes facilitated the consolidation of mafioso/cartel/paramilitary/gang organisations that have promoted the trafficking of drugs – especially heroin and cocaine – in order to finance counterinsurgency guerilla fighters serving US interests across the globe. This has been most dramatically well documented in South-east Asia during the Vietnam War[10] and in Central America during the revolutionary decade of the 1980s.[11] Historians, political scientists, anthropologists and investigative journalists have repeatedly documented these cynical imperial state power plays, but their scientific or journalistic muck-raking publications tend to be treated as bizarre, ultra-leftist conspiracy theories simply because they document outrageous political excesses and unethical interventions. Their inconvenient facts tend to be 'doxically'[12] swept under the rug of historical memory.

The critical theoretical potential of drug studies

From a safer theoretical distance, longue durée historians of globalisation, and occasional anthropologists in indigenous settings have provocatively suggested that the human appetite for altered states of consciousness has been a driving force for exploratory travel, international trade, conquest, colonialism and imperialism.[13] Anthropologists working in more 'traditional' stateless societies have repeatedly documented the centrality of psychoactive drug use in rituals buttressing social cohesion, personal and community health, and age-graded socialisation processes and hierarchies.[14] Again, it is the industrial production and trafficking of psychoactive substances – including alcohol, of course – that most disrupts a society's ability to harness psychoactive drug use. This has been occurring unevenly all across the world with the expansion of the market demand for psychoactive drugs among vulnerable lumpenised populations. In fact, a review of the literature documenting the hyper-profitable traffic in psychoactive substances that has accompanied most cultural, economic and military contact throughout history suggests that drugs and alcohol have been a crucial component of Marx's[15] somewhat ambiguous and polemical concept that he ambivalently referred to as 'so-called primitive accumulation'. The flooding of industrially processed drugs and alcohol into vulnerable non-capitalist social formations violently unleashed the market demand along with the labour force willing to work for wages. It facilitated dispossession from land and natural resources, enabling the consolidation of the transition from merchant agricultural to industrial capitalism. Arguably, drugs have become even more crucial for extending our current transition to a high-tech-, digital- and finance-driven neoliberal version of predatory speculative and, ironically, state-subsidised, corporate capitalism.

This special issue, with its broad spectrum of social science and historical approaches to the topic of illegal psychoactive drugs in the Global South which explore the lessons that can be learned from a decolonising emphasis, highlights the exciting power of interdisciplinary international comparative case studies, but also brings home how little we actually know. Methodologically, the papers draw from a combination of ethnographic methods (Carrier, Ghiabi, Passos, Rodgers, Seward), social historical and diplomatic archival excavation

(Campos, Ghiabi, Mansfield, Mills, Windle) and voluminous grey and popular press literature documentation (Carrier, Ghiabi, Passos, Windle). The critical insights of social scientist drug researchers and the unorthodox combination of qualitative and grey literature documentation, however, tends to be relegated to the margins of both academic and public policy discourse. It is no coincidence, for example, that a disproportionate number of the authors in this special issue – including me – are located within awkward or opportunistic and fragile interstitial academic research, policy and applied biomedical settings. Hopefully, following Bourdieu's[16] critique of academic orthodoxy or Foucault's – again passive/aggressive – celebration of the 'specific intellectual',[17] the collective cross-fertilisation of our marginal academic locations may facilitate critical, heterodox insights on misrecognised processes of social inequality and coercive normativity. The papers also provocatively reveal the limits of our ability to document taboo facts on the ground, as well as our analytical understandings of the distinct commonalities and disjunctions of the effects of drugs across distinct geographical and historical settings. They challenge us to push our field forward further. There are clearly some dramatic regional/continental patterns as suggested by the strong contingent of individual case studies in this issue, from Latin America (Campos, Passos, Rodgers, Seward) and the Middle East/Central Asia (Ghiabi, Mansfield, Robins) as well as the more synthetic solo articles on South-east Asia (Windle) and sub-Saharan Africa (Carrier), supplemented by a detailed social history and decolonising historical case study of the South Asian demand for industrially produced cocaine in the early twentieth century (Mills). Pointedly, there are, however, just as many dramatic local regional discontinuities; hence the issue's topical rather than more traditional geographical or historical organisation. The challenge for us is to raise even more ambitious critical questions around what new perspectives on illegal psychoactive drugs in the Global South can reveal about our moment in history – or dare I say the essences of human ways of being in the world, as Ghiabi writes in his introduction to this special issue.

Predatory accumulation across the Americas

My participant-observation anthropological (and my more technocratic 'specific-intellectual' applied public health) work on drugs has all been in the Americas at the retail endpoint of the multi-billion dollar cross-continental narcotics industry primarily in what I call the Puerto Rican–US inner city colonial diaspora,[18] as well as in multi-ethnic homeless shooting encampments stranded in vacant lots or under urban freeways.[19] Having spent so much of my life befriending often-violent sellers and street-based injectors and abusers and users of heroin, cocaine and fortified liquor in US inner cities, I may be overrating the importance of illegal narcotics, but I think they represent an extreme version of a more widespread pattern of 'predatory accumulation' that has increasingly shaped the global economy since the 1980s, when the right-wing populist politicians Ronald Reagan and Margaret Thatcher rose to power in the United States and England and aggressively instituted the neoliberal policies that have dramatically increased social inequality and augmented corporate power both locally and cross-continentally.[20]

In an effort to make sense of and lay blame for the attraction, destructiveness and enduring mesmerising power of drugs among the most vulnerable poor, I am revisiting Marx's 200-year-old concepts of 'lumpen [populations]'[21] and 'primitive accumulation'[22] to adapt them to our unfortunate historical era. This helps me explain the economically irrational brutality of the US state's response to the human collateral fallout from the rising rates of unemployment, racist segregation and economic inequality that its prohibitionist and neoliberal policies have propagated. This predatory era has been especially violent, innovative and transformative across the Americas, generating tremendous levels of human suffering among displaced peasants and vulnerable shantytown dwellers as well as humongous profits for oligarchs, multi-national corporations and lumpen drug dons.[23] The profitable illegality of narcotic drugs has also spawned flexibly adaptive de-territorialised networks of organised crime. Drug cartels have been capable of establishing vertical monopolies over the cultivation, production and marketing of psychoactive drugs. Ironically, following the licit economy's notoriously undercapitalised export platform maquiladora factory logistics that proliferated across the Global South outside of sovereign state control since the US pioneered the model during the Korean War in its Caribbean colony of Puerto Rico,[24] the illicit economy is producing heroin, cocaine, crystal methamphetamine and synthetic opioids primarily for US and European consumption. Narcotics laboratories hidden in remote jungle and desert settings thrive across the Global South and increasingly the Global East precisely because these regions suffer from inadequate public- and private-sector investment and from corrupt legal infrastructures. Ironically, this innovative 'post-colonial' mode of predatory production of a handful of globally illicit agricultural consumption items – heroin from poppies and cocaine from coca leaves[25]– has inverted the directionality of the abusive Global South-to-North terms of unfavourable trade and capital flows for export agricultural products that have historically favoured the more industrialised Global North.

The illicit predatory economy

Contemporary addiction markets for illegal psychoactive drugs arguably, at first sight, represent a more classic example of a primitive accumulation industry. The hyper-profitability of exporting laboratory-processed pure heroin, cocaine, methamphetamine and synthetic opioids requires the artificial regional advantages of coercive state policies of illegality and public-sector dysfunctionality in select countries of both the Global North and South. They also produce ever-larger reservoirs of lumpenised populations across the world. The narcotics industry is not capable of reproducing itself through licit productive processes of stable, exploitative surplus-labour extraction through legal mechanisms. Instead, these addiction markets have to rely on brute force to administer themselves and extract their monopoly profits. In an abusive form of lumpen accumulation, they routinely kill off or maim a large proportion of their customers and most of their entry-level labour force – including their administrators. Contradictorily, however, contra Marx's insightful analysis of how colonialism and the slave trade spawned Europe's transition from mercantile to industrial capitalism, and contra Rosa Luxemburg's[26] critique of industrial capitalism's need to expand markets through imperial conquest, the destructive global trade in narcotics has been able to capitalise the hitherto unusable labour of increasingly lumpenised populations expelled from the licit economy in both the Global North and South. Again, piggy-backing on global financialisation and flexible maquila export-platform production techniques, they hitch-hike rides on the transport routes of shipping containers, commercial airplanes, speedboats, light aircraft, digital bank transfers, tax shelter schemes and – presumably in the future – drones. Ironically, they have managed to re-energise the market consumption power of the younger generations who lost their footing in the post-industrial labour force of the North even as they maim or kill off that generation. They innovatively produce cyclically changing menus of psychoactive products – 'speed', 'dope', 'crack', 'weed' – that creates a profitable inelastic compulsively fetishistic demand for their exports. The only subsidy they require from the state is that these products remain illegal; otherwise their profits would plummet to the levels of coffee, sugar, tea and tobacco commodity exports.

International banks and financial service companies – generally the same ones that cater to dictators and Mafioso-style racketeers – have been laundering the dirty dollars that US addicts spend on illicit agricultural and synthetic products, channelling them southward since at least the 1980s. A substantial amount of that illicit cash has been reinvested productively in the licit economy – especially in Colombia and Mexico – in a more classic productive process of primitive accumulation. In fact, even relatively minor, sideshow transshipment territories such as the Dominican Republic have cashed in productively on the global narcotics industry. Agricultural rural and informal urban shantytown economies have been unevenly capitalised by remittances from the criminal diaspora. Dirt-poor peasant villages in the Dominican Republic, in the remote provinces of Northern Mexico, and even in the indigenous Miskitu territories of Honduras and Nicaragua, have sprouted brand new multi-story cement houses, cell phone towers and clandestine airport runways. Almost half a dozen Caribbean island nations and, not coincidentally, most of the still-really-existing colonies from the trans-Atlantic slave trade era – especially the British Virgin Islands, Aruba, Cayman Islands, Curacao and Sint Maarten – have morphed into mini-outlaw finance service economies that launder cash from international narcotics sellers and assorted racketeers.[27]

Southward narco-capital flows to Latin America from the Global North, however, come at a tremendously destructive cost of corruption and paramilitarisation. Most Latin American countries – with the exception of Venezuela, Argentina and Brazil – were too poor to become endpoint markets for smugglers. By the late 1990s, however, a multitude of new internal domestic addiction markets had exploded throughout Latin American countries – especially Central America and the Caribbean. This explosion in local narcotics consumption – cocaine rather than heroin – in so many large and small cities, as well as remote rural villages of Central America, the Caribbean and northern Mexico, is simply the geographical accident of a few crumbs of the much larger narcotics trade spilling over en route before they reach their more-profitable final destination in the United States. To lower production and transport costs, the cartels pay local processors and smugglers at transit points in-kind with a small sample of the product they are producing or transporting rather than in cash. These local subcontractors then take it upon themselves to violently flood their impoverished villages with cheap cocaine products in the form of crack ('roca', 'piedra', 'patraseado') or even more toxic precursor substances from the cocaine production process ('basuco' in Colombia, 'paco' in Argentina, 'base' in Ecuador) to convert their in-kind payments into cash.

Again, in a pattern consistent with colonial-era primitive accumulation dynamics, the diffusion of these addiction markets to exceptionally remote locations and vulnerable populations in Latin America has been the product of the ratcheting up of state coercion and legal repression generated by the escalation of the US wars on terror and drugs. Traffickers responded to the intensified monitoring of US airspace after 9/11 by multiplying short-legged international transport layovers along diversified airborne, overland, underground and aquatic routes. This proliferation of transshipment points diversified and expanded local tributary markets that became incubators for interpersonal and gang violence. Firearm imports flow along narcotics export routes, and the rising demand for heroin, cocaine, methamphetamine and marijuana in North America, as well as the US government's dogged commitment to domestic repressive prohibition drug policies and weak gun control laws, have skyrocketed the rates of firearm murder across much of Latin America and the Caribbean since the 1990s.[28] During the 2000s, seven Latin American countries had the highest per-capita rates of 'peace-time homicide' in the world. Seventeen Latin American countries found themselves in the ignominious United Nations tally of the 20 most murderous states on Earth in the 2010s.[29]

Contra the more classic trajectory of primitive accumulation that channels violently expropriated subsistence and communal resources into the productive licit private market economy, the easy undocumented cash of illegal narcotics distorts national patterns of economic development in producer nations.[30] It curtails investment in human capital and stymies opportunities for employment in more diversified economic sectors that are not linked to the easy money of narcotics production. Again, I find it more useful to conceive of it as 'predatory accumulation' whereby disjointed economies, dependent on an exceptionally profitable extractive resource like oil or diamonds, lumpenise disproportionately large sectors of their populations, and administer themselves through violence rather than market forces. The influx of US addiction-dollars also distorts the consumption patterns of narco-elites. They squander their cash on the conspicuous consumption of fetishised foreign import luxuries, reversing the southward flow of the capital they manage to capture at such a high human cost. More importantly, the Southward flood of narcotics cash corrupts politicians and spawns warlord-controlled fiefdoms. Entire nations morph into narco-states, institutionalising the interface between the state and organised crime. Impunity becomes routinised, thriving off of incompetent administrative bureaucracies that fail to deliver services to the licit economy. In the most affected nations (Honduras, Guatemala and large regions of Mexico in the 2000s–2010s), the justice apparatus and some of the highest executive politicians and ministers can be bought for an insignificant fraction of the narco-dollars accumulated by nouveau-riche local drug bosses. This, in turn, spawns further investment in hyper-profitable extractive illegal natural resource depredation – especially mining and rainforest clear-cut lumbering – initiating new cycles of ongoing predatory accumulation that destroys the environment and dispossesses indigenous populations. The only requirement is that the state be weak, cheap and illegitimate.

Licit predatory economies and special interest groups inside the US

Ancillary predatory licit special interest groups and micro-industries have also exploded at the impoverished retail endpoints of the global narcotics industry in the US inner city, where the premature die-out and incarceration of an ever-larger and younger generation of licitly unemployable addicts is occurring. Most street-corner drug lords do not have the legal cultural capital to operate outside their impoverished ghettoized neighbourhoods, and the minimal amount of illicitly generated capital they begin to accumulate becomes visible and is often channelled back into the mainstream licit economy through criminal justice fines, civil forfeiture asset seizure laws and rapacious lawyers. The size of this legal syphoning of capital out of the illegal narcotics markets is massively augmented by the mobilization of a completely licit taxpayer-financed public subsidy of punitive and therapeutic service providers to manage the victims of predatory accumulation.

The punitive right hand of the US states' almost fivefold increase of its incarcerated population between 1980 and 2010[31] has exploded public budgets for law enforcement, criminal justice and medical emergency.[32] This gold rush of public tax dollar subsidies for the administration of punishment bloats the unionised overtime pay of police officers and prison guards, inflates the salaries of lawyers and judges and multiplies the lucrative contracts available to ancillary correctional administration industries and construction firms. As a police officer quipped to me, 'The War on Drugs put my daughter through college'; and a lawyer acknowledged, 'Zero tolerance [police enforcement] pays my mortgage'. Civil-asset-forfeiture mechanisms and court fees and fines are the most blatant and purposeful mechanism for extracting visible capital from inner-city drug markets. They enable the legal expropriation of both legally and illegally generated accumulations of capital and property so long as the funds or property are reinvested in law enforcement.

The politically weakened left hand of the state also, largely unwittingly, participates in this predatory accumulation that mobilises taxpayer resources off of the destruction of lumpenised populations. Massive amounts of tax dollars are transferred to clinicians and social service providers through the allocation of physician-mediated disability subsidies.[33] Even well-intentioned criminal justice alternatives to incarceration such as the expansion of court-mandated drug and mental health treatment become cash cows for a slew of private for-profit and non-profit social service agencies.

The profitable mesh of poverty, unemployment, racism, hyper-incarceration and plentifully accessible drugs in the US inner city is by no means monolithic or conscious of itself. For the most part, it is inadvertent and opportunistic. This does not mean, however, that specific special interest groups are not conscious of their self-interests. Notably, the stock value of the private, for-profit corrections corporations was the first to skyrocket the day after the right-wing billionaire Donald Trump unexpectedly won the US presidential elections on 7 November 2016. A generation earlier, the prison guard union took advantage of Reagan's opportunistically punitive right-wing charisma and, by the mid-1980s, had already become the second largest political lobby in the state of California. It pushed that state to pioneer the nation's enactment of draconian zero-tolerance drug laws. California led the United States with the fastest rise in incarceration rates of any state for almost two decades, setting the model for the historical phenomenon of mass incarceration – or, more precisely, the 'hyper-incarceration' of poor African Americans and Latinos.[34]

The licit pharmaceutical multinational corporations arguably represent the deadliest special interest addiction micro-industry. The producers of cold remedies lobbied politicians to allow them to maintain pseudoephedrine (a precursor for methamphetamine) in their multi-billion dollar over-the-counter products for colds, and spawned the rural speed epidemic of the late 1990s and early 2000s.[35] Simultaneously, the licit pharmaceutical producers of prescription pain pills initiated a long-term propaganda campaign putting scientists and government bureaucrats on their payroll. They managed to persuade medical associations across the United States to declare pain to be the 'fifth vital sign'. Researchers publishing in the most prestigious US medical journals sloppily began citing a 101-word-long letter to the editor about low rates of substance abuse disorder among terminally hospitalised cancer patients as definitive, scientific proof that 'opioid therapy rarely resulted in addiction'.[36] Pharmaceutical companies deployed an army of marketeers and lobbyists to knock on doors inside hospitals and US Congress. Pathetically, US doctors were boondoggled into massively overprescribing opioid pills.[37]

Purdue Pharma spearheaded this national opioid orgy timing it to coincide with the release of its newly patented OxyContin pill in 1996.[38] Purdue even managed to infiltrate the bureaucracy of the Federal Drug Administration (FDA), the US government agency responsible for testing drug safety and efficacy, and arranged for an official, Dr Curtis Wright, to officially declare OxyContin 'safer than rival painkillers.' In fact, however, Purdue scientists had pharmacologically engineered OxyContin's high-dosage time-release formula to increase the potential for consumers to develop a compulsive craving for opiates.[39]

The explosion of the national opioid pill addiction epidemic from the mid-1990s through the late 2010s adroitly tapped into public-sector subsidies for health insurance for retired and disabled people as well as into the market for legally insured – primarily white – unionised blue-collar public- and private-sector workers. A disproportionately high number of the legally employed – primarily white – consumers of these initially medically prescribed pills lost their footing in the legal labour market once they became physically addicted, creating a nefarious – but again completely unintended – feedback loop of additional disposable consumer demand for illegal heroin. It also created a niche market for discounted counterfeit synthetic opioid pills made from fentanyl powder produced and marketed by diversified Chinese and Mexican cartels. US heroin and opioid pill overdose mortalities skyrocketed to record levels in the second half of the 2010s.

Ironically, since the 2000s, some of the processing and marketing cartels – especially in Mexico, China and Colombia – have increasingly proved themselves capable of outcompeting the traditional licit industrial behemoth of pharmaceutical multi-national corporations headquartered for the past century in Europe and the United States. This first occurred when Mexican cartels began importing precursor chemicals from China to produce crystal methamphetamine for the US market, shortly after 2006 when the US politicians were finally forced by a muckraking press to oblige the licit pharmaceutical corporations to remove pseudoephedrine (a precursor for methamphetamine) from over-the-counter cold remedies.[40] In the early 2010s, these flexibly morphing cartels took advantage of the market demand created by the Big Pharma opioid producers to synthesise much more deadly and innovative clandestine laboratory-produced fentanyl and fentanyl-related opioid compounds.

Big Pharma's and organised crime's predatory accumulation through addiction markets pale in comparison to the cynical and purposeful manipulation of the compulsive qualities of the licitly industrially marketed products created by 'Big Tobacco' and 'Big Food'. Both those industries hired scientists to carefully maximise the addictive appeal of their products. The industrial food industry titrated relative contents of sugar, fat, salt, textural composition and colour to over-stimulate pleasurable taste receptors, thereby setting off a global obesity, diabetes and cardiovascular disease epidemic. The fake science of the US-based tobacco companies is legion,[41] but the cynicism and racism of the production and marketing of menthol cigarettes is less well known. Mentholated cigarettes pharmacologically increase the psychoactive release and intensity of delivery of nicotine to the brain's synapses because of menthol's affinity to the nicotinic receptors when it is combusted. Furthermore, they targeted these mentholated products to African American youth – concentrating billboard advertisements around segregated high schools. As a result, African American men have the highest rates of death from lung cancer of any group in the United States. This racist targeted marketing to vulnerable youth, however, is minor compared to their subsequent investment in massifying the distribution of cheap industrially packaged cigarettes to the much larger Chinese and African international markets that are creating huge future die-outs from lung disease.[42] Similarly, the Big Pharma opioid producers are seeking out new global markets in the face of the US backlash against the rising overdose rates they caused.[43] These diverse corporate predatory lumpenised accumulation processes operate all over the world, but they tend to pioneer them in the United States. Their brutal macro-level effect can already be measured epidemiologically by the 'mystery' of the historic reversal of modern secular demographic trends in life expectancy since 1997[44] among poor whites in the United States. Maybe we are nearing the end of the post-enlightenment era of biopower.

Disclosure statement

No potential conflict of interest was reported by the author.

Funding

This research was supported by NIH grant number UL1TR001881, with comparative contextual data from AA020331, DA037820, DA038965, DA010164.

Notes

1. Courtwright, *Forces of Habit*; Schivelbusch, *Tastes of Paradise*.
2. Bourgois, "Disciplining Addictions."
3. National Institute on Drug Abuse (NIDA), "Drugs, Brains, and Behavior," 5.
4. Porter, *Trust in Numbers*?
5. Foucault, *Discipline and Punish*; Foucault, *History of Sexuality*.
6. Ghiabi, "Maintaining Disorder."
7. Zigon, "An Ethics of Dwelling."
8. Rodgers, "Drug Booms and Busts."
9. Campos, "A Diplomatic Failure."
10. McCoy, *The Politics of Heroin*.
11. Scott, "Cocaine, the Contras, and the United States."
12. Bourdieu, *Outline of a Theory of Practice*, 159–70.

13. Schivelbusch, *Tastes of Paradise*; Eber, *Women & Alcohol*; Courtwright, *Forces of Habit*.
14. Goodman and Lovejoy, *Consuming Habits*.
15. Marx, *Capital*, 872–942.
16. Bourdieu, *Homo Academicus*.
17. Bourgois, "Disciplining Addictions"; Messac et al., "Good-Enough Science-and-Politics."
18. Bourgois, *In Search of Respect*.
19. Bourgois and Schonberg, *Righteous Dopefiend*.
20. Harvey, *A Brief History of Neoliberalism*.
21. Bourgois, "Lumpen Abuse."
22. Bourgois and Hart, "Pax Narcotica."
23. Bourgois, "Insecurity, the War on Drugs."
24. Ibid.
25. It is surprising that khat has not followed the profitable trajectories of poppies and coca leaves.
26. Luxemburg, *Accumulation of Capital*.
27. US Department of State, *International Narcotics Control Strategy Report*.
28. Bourgois, "Insecurity, the War on Drugs."
29. United Nations Office on Drugs and Crime (UNODOC), *Global Study on Homicide*.
30. Bourgois, "Insecurity, the War on Drugs."
31. Kaeble and Glaze, *Correctional Populations in the United States*.
32. American Civil Liberties Union, "Combating Mass Incarceration."
33. Hansen and Bourgois, "Pathologizing Poverty."
34. Wacquant, *Punishing the Poor*.
35. Reding, *Methland*.
36. Leung et al., "A 1980 Letter."
37. Quinones, *Dreamland*.
38. Keefe, "The Family That Built an Empire of Pain."
39. Ryan, Girion, and Glover, "More than 1 Million Oxycontin Pills."
40. Reding, *Methland*.
41. Proctor, *Golden Holocaust*.
42. Novotny, "'Ultimate Prize' for Big Tobacco."
43. Lopez, "Painkiller Companies."
44. Case and Deaton, "Mortality and Morbidity in the 21st Century," 63.

Bibliography

American Civil Liberties Union. "Combating Mass Incarceration: The Facts." American Civil Liberties Union, 2011. https://www.aclu.org/

Bourdieu, Pierre. *Outline of a Theory of Practice*. Translated by Richard Nice. Cambridge: Cambridge University Press, 1977.

Bourdieu, Pierre. *Homo Academicus*. Stanford, CA: Stanford University Press, 2008.

Bourgois, Philippe. "Disciplining Addictions: The Bio-Politics of Methadone and Heroin in the United States." *Culture, Medicine and Psychiatry* 24, no. 2 (2000): 165–195.

Bourgois, Philippe. *In Search of Respect: Selling Crack in El Barrio*. 2nd ed. New York: Cambridge University Press, 2003.

Bourgois, Philippe. "Lumpen Abuse: The Human Cost of Righteous Neoliberalism." *City and Society* 23, no. 1 (2011): 2–12.

Bourgois, Philippe. "Insecurity, the War on Drugs, and Crimes of the State: Symbolic Violence in the Americas." In *Violence at the Urban Margins*, edited by Javier Auyero, Philippe Bourgois, and Nancy Scheper-Hughes, 305–321. Oxford: University of Oxford Press, 2015.

Bourgois, Philippe, and Laurie Hart. "Pax narcotica: Le marche de la drogue dans le ghetto portoricain de Philadelphie." *Homme* 219–220 (2016): 31–62.

Bourgois, Philippe, and Jeff Schonberg. *Righteous Dopefiend*. Berkeley: University of California Press, 2009.

Campos, Isaac. "A Diplomatic Failure: The Mexican Role in the Demise of the 1940 Reglamento Federal De Toxicomanías." *Third World Quarterly*. doi:10.1080/01436597.2017.1389268.

Case, Anne, and Angus Deaton. "Mortality and Morbidity in the 21st Century." *Brookings Papers on Economic Activity* 2017 (2017): 397–476.

Courtwright, David T. *Forces of Habit*. Cambridge: Harvard University Press, 2009.

Eber, Christine Engla. *Women & Alcohol in a Highland Maya Town: Water of Hope, Water of Sorrow*. Austin: University of Texas Press, 1995.

Foucault, Michel. *Discipline and Punish*. 2nd ed. Vintage Books, 1977.

Foucault, Michel. *The History of Sexuality*. Translated by Robert Hurley. New York: Vintage Books, 1988.

Ghiabi, Maziyar. "Maintaining Disorder: The Micropolitics of Drugs Policy in Iran." *Third World Quarterly*. doi:10.1080/01436597.2017.1350818.

Goodman, Jordan, and Paul E. Lovejoy, eds. *Consuming Habits: Drugs in History and Anthropology*. London: Routledge, 2006.

Hansen, Helena, and Philippe Bourgois. "Pathologizing Poverty: New Forms of Diagnosis, Disability, and Structural Stigma under Welfare Reform." *Social Science and Medicine* 103 (2014): 76–83.

Harvey, David. *A Brief History of Neoliberalism*. Oxford; New York: Oxford University Press, 2005.

Kaeble, Danielle, and Lauren Glaze. *Correctional Populations in the United States, 2015*. Washington, DC: US Department of Justice, Bureau of Justice Statistics, 2016.

Keefe, Patrick. 2017. "The Family That Built an Empire of Pain." *New Yorker*, October 30: 32.

Leung, Pamela T. M., Erin M. Macdonald, Matthew B. Stanbrook, Irfan A. Dhalla, and David N. Juurlink. "A 1980 Letter on the Risk of Opioid Addiction." *New England Journal of Medicine* 376, no. 22 (2017): 2194–2195.

Lopez, German. "Painkiller Companies Are Now Globally Exporting Addiction for Profit – Just like Big Tobacco." Vox.Com, December 22, 2016. https://www.vox.com/science-and-health/2016/12/22/14039122/opioid-epidemic-oxycontin-mundipharma

Luxemburg, Rosa. *The Accumulation of Capital – An Anti-Critique*. Translated by Kenneth J. Tarbuck. New York: Monthly Review Press, 1973.

Marx, Karl. *Capital: A Critique of Political Economy*. Translated by Ben Fowkes. vol. 1. London: Penguin Books, [1867] 1990.

McCoy, Alfred W. *The Politics of Heroin: CIA Complicity in the Global Drug Trade*. Chicago, IL: Lawrence Hill Books, 2003.

Messac, Luke, Dan Ciccarone, Jeffrey Draine, and Philippe Bourgois. "The Good-Enough Science-and-Politics of Anthropological Collaboration with Evidence-Based Clinical Research: Four Ethnographic Case Studies." *Social Science & Medicine* 99 (2013): 176–186.

National Institute on Drug Abuse. "Drugs, Brains, and Behavior: The Science of Addiction." (2014): 1–38. https://www.drugabuse.gov/publications/drugs-brains-behavior-science-addiction.

Novotny, Thomas E. "The 'Ultimate Prize' for Big Tobacco: Opening the Chinese Cigarette Market by Cigarette Smuggling." *PLoS Medicine* 3, no. 7 (2006): e279. doi:10.1371/journal.pmed.0030279.

Porter, Theodore M. *Trust in Numbers?: The Pursuit of Objectivity in Science and Public Life*. Princeton, NJ: Princeton University Press, 1995.

Proctor. *Golden Holocaust: Origins of the Cigarette Catastrophe and the Case for Abolition*. Berkeley: University of California Press, 2012. http://www.myilibrary.com?id=358734.

Quinones, Sam. *Dreamland: The True Tale of America's Opiate Epidemic*. New York: Bloomsbury, 2015.

Reding, Nick. *Methland: The Death and Life of an American Small Town*. New York: Bloomsbury, 2009.

Rodgers, Dennis. "Drug Booms and Busts: Poverty and Prosperity in a Nicaraguan Narco-Barrio." *Third World Quarterly*. doi:10.1080/01436597.2017.1334546.

Ryan, Harriet, Lisa Girion, and Scott Glover. "More than 1 Million Oxycontin Pills Ended up in the Hands of Criminals and Addicts: What the Drugmaker Knew." *LA Times*, 2016. http://www.latimes.com/projects/la-me-oxycontin-part2/.

Schivelbusch, Wolfgang. *Tastes of Paradise: A Social History of Spices, Stimulants, and Intoxicants*. Translated by David Jacobson. New York: Vintage Books, 1993.

Scott, P. D. "Cocaine, the Contras, and the United States – How the U. S. Government Has Augmented America's Drug Crisis." *Crime, Law and Social Change* 16, no. 1 (1991): 97–131.

United Nations Office on Drugs and Crime (UNODOC). *Global Study on Homicide 2013*. Vienna, Austria, 2014. https://www.unodc.org/documents/gsh/pdfs/2014_GLOBAL_HOMICIDE_BOOK_web.pdf.

United States Department of State, Bureau for International Narcotics and Law Enforcement Affairs. *International Narcotics Control Strategy Report. Volume II: Money Laundering and Financial Crimes*. Washington, DC: State Department Bureau Report, 2014.

Wacquant, Loïc. *Punishing the Poor: The Neoliberal Government of Social Insecurity*. Durham, NC: Duke University Press, 2009.

Zigon, Jarrett. "An Ethics of Dwelling and a Politics of World-Building: A Critical Response to Ordinary Ethics." *Journal of the Royal Anthropological Institute* 20, no. 4 (2014): 746–764.

INTRODUCTION

Spirit and being: interdisciplinary reflections on drugs across history and politics

Maziyar Ghiabi

ABSTRACT
Few commodities are as global as drugs. Cannabis, opium, heroin, amphetamines, lysergic acid diethylamide (LSD), khat, psychedelic cacti and mushrooms as well as an interminable list of other natural or synthesised substances travel and are consumed around the globe for all possible reasons. Human migration, trade, cultural trends, medical practice, political repression: together they constitute the drug phenomenon today – and indeed in much of human history. In this, drugs are spirit-like commodities, their value resting upon a fundamental ambiguity made up of individual, psychological, social, cultural, economic and medical circumstances. Defining a drug is an attempt at defining a spirit on the edge, which metamorphoses in time and space. At the same time, drugs remain a fundamentally political object. They are substances controlled by states, through mechanisms of policing, legitimated by judicial and medical evaluation, condemned often on moral grounds. Situated between a fluid social existence and a static legal dimension, drugs can become inspiring hermeneutic objects of study.

Alternative interpretations of misery and oppression need to re-channel the debates around culture and poverty to more exciting theoretical arenas that reframe material reality's relationship to ideology and redefine how social process emerges in the confrontation between structure and agency.

Bourgois, "Just Another Night in a Shooting Gallery," 43.

Few commodities are as global as drugs. Cannabis, opium, heroin, amphetamines, Lysergic acid diethylamide (LSD), khat, psychedelic cacti and mushrooms as well as an interminable list of other natural or synthesised substances travel and are consumed around the globe for all possible reasons. Human migration, trade, cultural trends, medical practice, political repression: together they constitute the drug phenomenon today – and indeed in much of human history. In this, drugs are spirit-like commodities, their value resting upon a fundamental ambiguity made up of individual, psychological, social, cultural, economic and medical circumstances. Defining a drug is an attempt at defining a spirit on the edge, which metamorphoses in time and space. At the same time, drugs remain a fundamentally political object. They are substances controlled by states, through mechanisms of policing, legitimated

http://orcid.org/0000-0002-2171-2811

by judicial and medical evaluation, condemned often on moral grounds. Situated between a fluid social existence and a static legal dimension, drugs can become inspiring hermeneutic objects of study.

Yet academe has systematically left scholarship dealing with drugs to a corner of the whole, especially in the social sciences. Drug scholarship is met with curiosity and anecdotal interest. These feelings are a reflexive spasm at the heart of which stands a formalistic understanding of social sciences and humanities, one that narrows the scope of social and political phenomena to univocal manifestations. The ambiguous nature of drugs in the modern world and their transversal effect are seen as dispensable oddities in a world made up of institutional records, leadership personalities, econometric stats and epidemiological surveys. Can social scientists and humanities scholars dispense drugs as a side note of bigger questions around the social and the political?

In October 2016, 12 scholars coming from different disciplinary backgrounds gathered in Oxford at St Antony's College to test the potentials and perils of interdisciplinarity in drug research. The event, sponsored by the Wellcome Trust Small Grant for Society & Ethics, took the form of a symposium titled 'Drugs, Politics and Society in the Global South', which later gave the name to this special issue. The primary objective was not that of simply producing new analytical and descriptive knowledge to be added to the annals of drug studies. The goal, instead, was to build through an interdisciplinary platform fresh insight into the study of the modern and contemporary world. Historians, political scientists, urban and cultural anthropologists, geographers, criminologists and medical anthropologists enlivened the discussion for two days. Rather than gathering a list of the usual suspects working on drugs, the symposium enabled a venue for the encounter of a unique blend of multiple disciplines. The blending of these different approaches resulted in a polyvocal and multi-faceted engagement around and within the phenomenon of drugs. Drugs became a frame, a lens, through which one could interpret and relocate broader historical and epistemological questions.[1]

On the benefits of interdisciplinarity, academic departments have long been informed. The consumed edge of disciplines is often where new knowledge is produced, but there is more in sight for the heterodox seekers. It is the intellectual encounter, even when rowdy and disharmonious, between different disciplines that salutes the production of episteme and the unleashing of new interpretations. The fields opened up by this volume remain *in fieri*: made of multiple disciplinary approaches, this volume hands the reader and the researcher a rich basket of primary material. The archival notes of Indian, Mexican and Egyptian narcotic officials and medical practitioners are prelude to the field notes in rehabilitation and treatment centres in contemporary Iran and Peru and to the interviews with poppy cultivators in Afghanistan, the khat and cannabis consumers in East and West Africa and gang dealers in Nicaragua, as well as to the geospatial images of cropped lands in Central Asia and the prohibition dictums in the south-east. This unparalleled methodological landscape speaks firmly about the plurality of the drug phenomenon and on the open-ended horizon in front of those willing to engage with it. In this sprit, the contributions that propped up the symposium aim at integrating drugs – and their annexed realities – within the social sciences and humanities, by addressing larger questions around history, power, society and life. After all, how can one pretend to understand contemporary drugs policy and drug worlds without acknowledging the historical dimension of drug phenomena? Or else, how can we realistically speak of drugs in modern cities if we do not look at the life of drug use(rs) in praxis?

Before introducing the volume's contributions, I would like to direct the readers' attention towards a few contextual and theoretical particulars that animate this special issue.

What is the drug situation?

'Farcical' and 'delusionary' are two ways that one could describe the ways governments, throughout the twentieth and twenty-first centuries, attempted to counter the market of illicit drugs or to depict drugs as essentially and exclusively evil.[2] The latter of these attempts is readily provided by the 2017 World Drug Report, published by the main United Nations (UN) anti-narcotic body United Nations Office on Drugs and Crime (UNODC), where it is argued that 'the magnitude of the harm caused by drug is underlined by the estimated 28 million years [sic!] of "healthy" life … lost worldwide in 2015 as a result of premature death and disability caused by drug use'.[3] The data is intended to produce a state of alertness in the reader and to convince them that drugs are a serious cause of danger and harm in today's world. That said, a few pages onwards the report dedicates a small section to incarceration and the institution of prisons. It says that of the many millions of people who are incarcerated every year around the world, around 20% of them use drugs,[4] with drug use in prison being notoriously more dangerous due to riskier modes of consumption (ie injection). This said, one is invited to ponder about drugs being a serious danger for people in prison, which they effectively are. Yet a second thought is indispensable: isn't drug crime a primary cause of incarceration worldwide?[5]

This model of thought, which by 2017 has developed a certain level of sophistication – exemplified by the provision of complex data on 'life loss', for instance – remains at the heart of knowledge production about drugs in governmental institutions. After more than a hundred years since the first Opium Control conventions in Shanghai (1909) and The Hague (1911), drugs policy and, with it, drug scholarship has gone through a moment of reflection and transformation – perhaps the transition to a new cultural era about drugs. A consensus has been reached, rather unanimously, on the failure of the status quo: the legitimacy of prohibition of drugs, as enunciated by North American officials in the 1960s and 1970s with Richard Nixon and, with greater emphasis, in the 1980s with Ronald Regan, has expired. For those who had announced the crumbling of the prohibitionist regime,[6] Uruguay's president Pepe Mujica's bold steps towards legal regulation of cannabis in Uruguay symbolised a *sui generis* Judgement Day. Contextually came also the recreational and medical cannabis laws in the northern part of the Americas, which so far has resisted the regressive tide embodied by Donald Trump's election to the US presidency in 2016. Variants of these examples are in progress in other parts of the globe, including Europe where the Portuguese government had led the drug decriminalisation camp since the late 1990s. Other cases may be less obvious: the Islamic Republic of Iran, which is discussed in the special issue, has opened up discussions about the possibility of managing drug consumption through state intervention and is currently introducing 'safe injection rooms' for heroin users; Latin American heads of state, from Colombia and Mexico to Bolivia and Guatemala, have expressed support for an alternative model to the US-led 'War on Drugs'. If there is a time for renewal of policy models vis-à-vis drugs, it ought to be the coming decade.

Reform of international strategy towards illicit drugs does not exhaust the rationale behind its discriminating power. At the other end of the spectrum of reform stands the militarisation of drugs policy to which the United States has historically been faithful and which has recently enlisted among its ranks the Philippines' president Rodrigo Duterte. The latter has manifested his auspices of nothing short of the physical cleansing of 'drug addicts' from the face of the Earth. To do so, he has legitimated law enforcement to shoot on sight suspected drug users and drug dealers. If not taken down, drug criminals are taken to overcrowded prisons, where they exist in degraded human conditions. The result is several thousand cadavers, including dozens of teenagers.[7] His vision is not exceptional, even though his means may be for now. Being tough on drug users is a policy position hard to reform after several decades of systemic demonisation of drugs in the modern world. Evidence of this is given by drug reformers themselves. Proponents of cannabis regulation and legalisation are often forgetful that cannabis represents a small share in the economy of punishment of drug prohibition. Especially in the West, cannabis represents the bourgeois milieu of consumption, the one affected less systematically by policing and prison. Were cannabis legalised, the core of prohibition, its assemblage of crime/punishment, would remain in place, perhaps even more powerfully against vulnerable social classes, and categories already the object of criminalisation.

War on drugs is no metaphor. Fought with weapons, armies, police and an array of media, medical and justice tools, this war has nonetheless an allegorical dimension. It is not a war *on* drugs as most of the governments and international agencies involved in it declare. The objective of the combat is other than the chemical substance or the psychophysical state the substance induces. The targets of this system are the categories deemed worthy of punishment. With some generalisation: Black and Hispanic people in the United States; Arabs and Africans of the suburbs in Europe; poor, rural, indigenous and marginal populations in Latin America; proletariats and precariats in Africa and Asia – transversally poor, marginal, unorthodox, subaltern groups of humans around the globe. The rich and bourgeois classes are practically left untouched by the 'War on Drugs', unless they feel emotionally involved in some narco-saga on Netflix.

To this institutional violence produced by state enforcement of drug laws, there are other competing forms of violence. One is the violence of criminal organisations and drug traffickers. This violence is largely symbiotic and contextual to the 'War on Drugs', as it is reproduced within ecologies of contention between state and criminality. The other side of drug violence is that of 'addiction'. An object of caricature in state-led discourse and propaganda, addiction remains both a governmental concept[8] and a biomedical(ised) datum. Its violence is intimate and diffused at the same time, as it touches upon individual psyche and familiar/societal lived experience. Yet its violence is rendered more dramatic by the encounter with a system of prohibition which outlaws the biomedical existence of the condition itself: a drug user dependent on a certain illegal substance suffers from his/her condition and, simultaneously, from that of illegality (with its more nefarious consequences: police, prison and punishment). These different forms of violence all fall within a line of continuity; indeed, they belong to the same line of existence, which the special issue discusses in its plurality.

The insistence on the multidimensionality of the drug phenomenon is a key component of the following contributions. After all, what is a drug and what is addiction remain questions with unclear answers. The definitions of drug and addiction are not only tied to a political, legal interpretation; they are also connected to the ambivalent boundaries of medical knowledge. One should carefully evaluate the pharmacological determinism of medical production on drug use, as it exhausts drugs of their social value and place. In this respect, the line of legality and illegality is blurred as much as that of use and abuse. This is acknowledged in a clumsy way by public authorities, their reaction dwindling between a totalitarian discretion, as in the UK ban of all substances with mind-altering effect (with the commercially wise exceptions of alcohol, coffee, tea and sugar), or in the holistic ambiguity of anti-narcotic policing across the globe, which makes the crime at the discretion of law enforcers.

The holistic engagement with the matter of drugs in this special issue is contextualised within a geographical political space, itself the choice of an epistemological evaluation. The contributions of this volume provide analyses on the Global South. They do so not because they deem this space, the South, exceptional and differing. On the contrary, the contributions take regions other than the West as a site of investigation of global history, cultural phenomena, political paradigms and social theories, eventually to integrate knowledge across space.

'Global South' defines a region that encompasses the southern hemisphere of the globe. It is heir to the categories of 'Third World' and 'Developing World', both of which have reached, in the eyes of many, an ethical and political bankruptcy. Seeing drugs from the South, thus, enables a reconfiguration of established scholarly narratives on the subject. Ideas and practices in this field are not simply imitated and univocally spoken by non-Western populations; they are often the result of localised dynamics, themselves moving across borders, in time and space. More specifically, the special issue has the objective to prioritise those areas of the world that have been left beyond scholarly gaze, despite drugs being a salient element in their history and politics. Might it be the case that empirical cases emerging from the South inform the hermeneutic effort of those studying similar phenomena in the North?

The contributions

All in all, the special issue has three main purposes, which I tried to explore in the first part of this introduction. One is of a conceptual type and is concerned with situating 'drugs' within the study of history and society in the contemporary world. This means that the way the contributions discuss the issue of illicit drugs is one that invites complementarity, rather than exclusivity and exceptionality, in the context of larger-than-drugs questions. Another principal question which drives this volume is that of methods and disciplines. Interdisciplinarity and multidisciplinarity are fully explored here, with a rich range of different methodologies and theories at play. Drugs being a polymorphic question, they deserve pluralistic methods. Finally, the special issue invites exploration of areas and worlds that have been off the radar of drug scholars. With this, it also incites scholars to turn upside down established assumptions about the place of drugs in the social sciences, *sensu lato*, suggesting that we may understand the history of drugs more aptly *from the (Global) South*.

The special issue is divided into three main sections. Following this introduction, three articles constitute the section titled *History and Genealogy of Drugs*. Here James H. Mills tackles the coming of age of cocaine use, a drug regarded as modern and Western, in the Indian subcontinent. Through this case, the author recasts assumptions about the Orient and its drug culture, showing through detailed historical narratives how cocaine was indigenised and not simply imposed by Western market forces. A derivative of the coca plant cultivated in the Andean region, in the early nineteenth century cocaine was the emblem of the emerging Western pharmaceutical industry. In Mills' account, one can see how this substance travelled across the globe not so much as a colonial product (to say it with Antonio Gramsci, *as hegemony*) imposed on the colonised, but rather as a commodity to which the local population bestowed new social and cultural meaning.

The second contribution is that of Isaac Campos: his study of the Mexican state's attempt at regulating opiate distribution through state-led programmes. If one expected India to be the setting for cannabis and opium use, and found that Jim Mills discussed cocaine, the Mexican case has little connection to *marijuana*, the quintessential Mexican drug. Instead, opiates and opiate maintenance programmes occupy the historical stage. The article opens with a vignette in which the Mexican government takes steps to regulate narcotic drugs in order to eradicate the role and influence of criminal organisations, which corrupt the institutions of the state. One is led to think that it is Mexico City in 2018. Instead, it is 1938!

Campos's article convincingly demonstrates how forms of governance of 'addiction' and illegal drugs have not unilaterally descended from the north of the border, the United States, to Mexico. The Mexican case tackles this in two moments: firstly, with the proposition of maintenance programmes for drug users by the Mexican official Salazar Viniegra (a character himself worthy of great interest); and secondly, with the withdrawal of this same programme in favour of prohibitionist policies. All of this is, using the title of Campos' earlier book, *home grown*.[9]

The last piece of this section is about Egypt. Philip Robins, a scholar of politics, provides a detailed account of the Egyptians' taste for drugs in modern times. The article follows the vicissitudes of hashish users and haphazard efforts by the state to counter its trafficking and mass use up to the 2011 popular uprising. By then Egypt's drug culture had dramatically changed, with an increase in Tramadol consumption, a sign of changing social and political conditions in the country. The political deadlock brought in following the Arab Spring might have engendered a changing perception of historical time among young Egyptians.[10] With its attention to historical continuity and the place of formal politics in shaping anti-narcotics, the article stands out as one of the few contributions on drugs history and policy in the modern Arab world.

The historical and genealogical inquiry is followed by the second section, titled *Ethnographies of Drugs*. Ethnographic knowledge lives in symbiosis with in-depth, bottom-up historical research. As a method, a tool of action, ethnography is a premium approach for public engagement.[11] Because of its use of narrative, often told in an accessible language, and the portrayal of situations of ordinary life, knowledge conveyed through this methodology speaks more directly to a broader audience. It also enriches theoretical knowledge with empirical details, which when juxtaposed can facilitate transversal understanding – in our case, of global drug situations.

Dennis Rodgers, who is the author of the first piece of this section, writes in an ethnographic style rich in colourful conversations and (extra)ordinary episodes. This total immersion in the field, supported by untranslated Spanish expressions, follows the highs and lows of local drug entrepreneurs, through a long-term ethnographic study of a *barrio* in Managua, Nicaragua's capital. This longitudinal perspective has obvious sociological value, but its insights are greater than that. It describes with acumen the economic options of drug criminals, their investments, venture failures and success in an ecosystem that changes rapidly and, very often, with drama. But a dramatic conclusion is not the fate of all drug dealing. Contrary to much of the scholarship, which holds that drug traffickers eventually fail in their business model – being killed, imprisoned and/or taken over by competitors – Rodgers shows how the trajectory of drug dealing is not set a priori. Indeed, it is open-ended and the result of multiple factors, made up of individual as well as structural conditions. Unemployed drug dealers often develop 'alternative occupational trajectories' and investments, which enables them to cease or alternate their involvement in the illicit – and dangerous – trade. In line with the vision of the special issue, the author invites us to understand the narcotic issue holistically.

This invitation is taken up by the second article, which focuses on the Islamic Republic of Iran. Maziyar Ghiabi's piece identifies an apparent paradox in Iran's drugs policy, the coexistence of draconian measures for drug traffickers and welfare-oriented policies for drug users. Paradoxes are rich interpretative moments and the Iranian case is intended as a window through which one can observe broader political questions around power and illegality. By using ethnographic vignettes from different settings of Iran's drug world, the article shows how state-led and civil society programmes work along a continuum, at times hardly distinguishable. The reader is taken through the author's field notes on plain-air drug-using hotspots in Tehran, in-flat female rehab centres in Arak and illegal treatment 'camps' through the country. This micropolitical approach suggests that the Islamic Republic does not adopt strict ideological and hierarchical lines of control over the enforcement of order. Instead, power operates by *maintaining disorder* and through grassroots authoritarianism. The text opens up a new venue for studies of drugs policy in Iran, a country that tops rankings of drug confiscation, drug consumption and medical support for drug users. It also paves the ground for scholars in politics who are keen to adopt ethnographic methods, thus setting a new horizon both for interdisciplinary studies of politics and grounded political analysis.[12]

The third and last article of the ethnographic section is that of Pablo Seward, on a Pentecostal ministry acting as a rehabilitation facility for drug addicts. Parallel to Ghiabi's findings, the author shows how recovering drug users adopt the 'war rhetoric' of anti-narcotics in treating addiction. Seward, however, is not interested in the political dimension of recovery, but mostly in its spiritual one, which adds up to the literature on global Pentecostalism and faith-based recovery. Based on three months' immersion in a Pentecostal addiction treatment ministry in the Upper Amazon, Peru, the article looks at how individual transformation occurs through conversion and recovery among coca paste users. The social abandonment is juxtaposed to the promise of miraculous recovery, and social re-integration. This narrative proceeds with great attention to the contextual world of the 'War on Drugs' and its structural burden. The three ethnographic pieces bind together, painting a polymorphous phenomenon, that of drugs, which overarches crime, health, power and spirit.

The third section that concludes the special issue is made of *Comparative Perspectives on Drug Wars*. Here the reader encounters a truly varied set of contributions, from those of geographers to criminologists, and political scientists to cultural anthropologists. The trait d'union among these four contributions is the incitement to comparison. Broadly speaking, this occurs in two ways: classically, through the comparison of two different countries, as in Anais Pessoa's article, between Brazil and Mexico; otherwise, as in David Mansfield's contribution, it occurs through the juxtaposition of two domestic cases in Afghanistan, or through a multi-case study or transnational look as in James Windle's as well as Neil Carrier and Gernot Klantschnig's articles, respectively.

In brief, Anais Passos takes into consideration two distinct military operations deployed in Rio de Janeiro, Brazil, and Tijuana, Mexico. The period under analysis is 2007 to 2015, one in which anti-narcotics played a key role in national politics both in Brazil (in view of the Olympic Games) and in Mexico (in light of the cartels' hyper-violent activities). Based on dozens of interviews with top officials in the police and military, the author investigates the transition to a militarised approach to drug control in the two countries. Brazil and Mexico represent two important cases in drug scholarship, yet comparative approaches have been scant thus far. In its argument, this study describes how militarisation produced increased violence and high human costs, all of which fomented rather than quieting state–cartel confrontation.

David Mansfield studies Afghan opium with the aim to reassess the 'balloon effect', a major theory arguing that eradication of drugs in one area prompts increase in another. His objective is, firstly, to go beyond the anecdotal and unsystematic claims in favour of this theory. Based on a combination of in-depth fieldwork and high-resolution geospatial imagery, in more than 20 sites divided between two formerly desert areas, the author brings new light on the dynamics of crop cultivation in the world's opium hub, Afghanistan. The article provides unparalleled details about poppy crop dynamics, making use of a comparative approach between two different Afghan regions.

Neil Carrier and Gernot Klantschnig's article considers the legal status of cannabis and khat, two of the most popular drugs in the African continent. Their objective is to demonstrate that legal ambiguity matters, something they name 'quasilegality'. In this endeavour, they re-interpret Lee Cassinelli's original work on khat[13] and situate it in a transnational comparative perspective. They describe how a commonly legal substance, such as khat, is publicly regarded as illegal, whereas cannabis, which is illegal with no exceptions, is used and tolerated almost as a legal drug. Both substances, thus, exist in a condition of 'quasilegality'. This condition bears dangers and opportunities, and one wonders whether they are peculiar to Africa or can actually be meaningful in interpreting drug laws in other contexts around the globe.

The final article of the comparative section is James Windle's contribution on South-east Asia. The author is concerned with the rationale behind the adoption of prohibition in Thailand, Laos and Vietnam. By providing a catalogue of different factors, such as economic, security, national, ethnic and religious, the article sets a taxonomy of motivations behind prohibitionist policies. This dispels the argument about prohibition being simply an imported ideological object, while reassessing the importance of political economy and security for drugs policy.

History, ethnography and comparative approaches build an arc of knowledge that covers – or hopes to cover – the long spectrum of social and cultural manifestations of drug worlds.

Conclusion

Drugs are an epiphenomenon of secular processes of social and political formation. They affect and are affected by larger historical dynamics, their value in today's world being tied to a political category, that of illegality. One could recount innumerable episodes where enforcers of drugs policy – police, justice, prison and welfare/medicine – impinged upon the existences of people using, or dealing with, drugs. It goes from the pharmaceutical opiate epidemic in the United States, where patients on prescription painkillers are forced to rely on illegal opiate supplies once their prescription expires, with the high risk of overdose (eg 60,000 deaths only in 2016);[14] to young men from former colonies being the object of systematic police searches in the Parisian suburbs; or the impoverished, plebeian groups of opiate and amphetamine users in Iran, Afghanistan and Pakistan, who circulate among prison, rehab centres and the cities' outskirts; or the gang members dealing in drugs for wealthier consumers and being arbitrarily shot down by militarised police in Brazil and the Philippines; or those who have developed a dependency on a chemical substance, it being heroin, meth, crack cocaine, methadone or fentanyl, who perish from overdose due to adulteration of the drug they purchased, illegally, in the street; or the human misery caused by chemical crop eradication plans across the planet. All these episodes have a common theme, that of violence engendered by a systemic exclusion. This makes drugs policy, essentially, a global policy of *means without ends*.[15]

Besides the imposition of policy upon people's lives, drugs constitute also social life in the Global South (and, in different ways, everywhere else). They are a source of sociality among people who share a taste for a common substance (eg khat chewers, cannabis smokers, heroin users, etc.). Pleasure remains a key aspect of drug use, one that is often overlooked in drug studies, including partly in this special issue. Hence, they have also a deep-seated cultural value and belong to a dynamic body of traditions (eg opium use in the Middle East and North Africa [MENA], coca in the Andean region, cannabis in Africa and the Indian subcontinent). In the guise of religious practice this happens with hashish among Sufis in Western Asia and North Africa; but it occurs also through the birth of new traditions, for instance in the rave culture of Western capitals and their use of psychoactive substances such as LSD, amphetamine-type stimulants (ATS) and psychedelic cacti; or through the ayahuaska tourism to which bourgeois cosmopolitans sign up for therapeutic purposes.[16] Their economic value is key to drug producers as much as in communities in which drug dealing often secures the means of sustainment. Indeed, drugs partake in the production of social life in ways that go far beyond chemical intervention on the brain.

This condition of drugs in the modern world informs everyday life in the South as much as in the North of the globe. Of course, as this special issue describes, circumstances change, means of intervention vary, political gestures elapse and cultural values shift, but a common frame can be ascribed globally. The phenomenon of drugs, whether consumption, dealing, cultivation or repression, deserves inclusion in the treatment and study of the modern world. It does so through the acknowledgement of its multidimensionality, which in return invites interdisciplinary passion. With this in mind, the special issue invites researchers to embrace that, as sometimes in everyday life, trespassing is key to any advancement.[17]

Disclosure statement

No potential conflict of interest was reported by the author.

Funding

This work was supported by the Wellcome Trust [grant number 202095/Z/16/Z], [grant number WT101988MA].

Notes

1. A description of the symposium can be accessed here: http://www.area-studies.ox.ac.uk/symposium-drugs-politics-and-society-global-south The participants in the symposium were: Dennis Rodgers (Amsterdam), Gernot Klantschnig (York), Giulia Zocatelli (King's College London), Isaac Campos (Cincinnati), James Mills (Strathclyde), James Windle (East London), Maziyar Ghiabi (Oxford), Neil Carrier (Oxford), Orkideh Behrouzan (King's College London), Pablo Seward (Stanford), Saeyoung Park (Leiden) and Anais Medeiros Passos (SciencesPO – Paris).
2. Levine, "Global Drug Prohibition."
3. UNODC, *World Drug Report 2017*, 9.
4. Ibid., 13.
5. Alexander, *The New Jim Crow*; Dikötter and Brown, *Cultures of Confinement*.
6. Quah et al., *Ending the Drug Wars*.
7. Al-Jazeera, "Thousands Demand End to Killings."
8. Seddon, *A History of Drugs*.
9. Campos, *Home Grown*.
10. Brownlee and Ghiabi, "Passive, Silent and Revolutionary."
11. Fassin, "Why Ethnography Matters."
12. Auyero, "Introductory Note to Politics under the Microscope."
13. Cassanelli, "Qat: Changes in the Production."
14. CNBC, "US Drug Overdose Deaths Topped 60,000 in 2016."
15. Agamben, *Means without End*.
16. Labate and Cavnar, *Ayahuasca Shamanism in the Amazon*.
17. Cf. Wacquant, "Towards a Reflexive Sociology."

Bibliography

Agamben, Giorgio. *Means without End: Notes on Politics*. Vol. 20. London: University of Minnesota Press, 2000.

Alexander, Michelle. *The New Jim Crow: Mass Incarceration in the Age of Colorblindness*. New York: The New Press, 2012.

Al-Jazeera. "Thousands Demand End to Killings in Duerte's War on Drugs." 2017. Accessed August 17, 2017. http://www.aljazeera.com/news/2017/08/thousands-demand-killings-duterte-drug-war-170821124440845.html

Auyero, Javier. "Introductory Note to Politics under the Microscope: Special Issue on Political Ethnography I." *Qualitative Sociology* 29, no. 3 (2006): 257–259.

Bourgois, Philippe. "Just Another Night in a Shooting Gallery." *Theory, Culture & Society* 15, no. 2 (1998): 37–66.

Brownlee, Billie Jeanne, and Maziyar Ghiabi. "Passive, Silent and Revolutionary: The 'Arab Spring' Revisited." *Middle East Critique* 25, no. 3 (2016): 299–316.

Campos, Isaac. *Home Grown: Marijuana and the Origins of Mexico's War on Drugs*. Chapel Hill: University of North Carolina Press, 2012.

Cassanelli, Lee. "Qat: Changes in the Production and Consumption of a Quasilegal Commodity in Northeast Africa in the Social Life of Things Commodities in Cultural Perspective." In *The Social Life of Things: Commodities in Cultural Perspective*, edited by A. Appadurai, 236–257. Cambridge: Cambridge University Press, 1988.

CNBC. US Drug Overdose Deaths Topped 60,000 in 2016, with more Potent Illicit Drug use on the Rise, 2017. Accessed October 27, 2017. https://www.cnbc.com/2017/10/27/us-drug-overdose-deaths-topped-60000-in-2016.html

Dikötter, Frank, and Ian Brown. *Cultures of Confinement: A History of the Prison in Africa, Asia and Latin America*. Ithaca, NY: Cornell University Press, 2007.

Fassin, Didier. "Why Ethnography Matters: On Anthropology and Its Publics." *Cultural Anthropology* 28, no. 4 (2013): 621–646.

Labate, Beatriz Caiuby, and Clancy Cavnar, eds. Ayahuasca Shamanism in the Amazon and beyond. Oxford: Oxford Ritual Studies, 2014.

Levine, Harry G. "Global Drug Prohibition: Its Uses and Crises." *International Journal of Drug Policy* 14, no. 2 (2003): 145–153.

Quah, Danny, John Collins, Laura Atuesta Becerra, Jonathan Caulkins, Joanne Csete, Ernest Drucker, Vanda Felbab-Brown, et al. *Ending the Drug Wars: Report of the LSE Expert Group on the Economics of Drug Policy*. London: LSE Ideas, 2014.

Seddon, Toby. *A History of Drugs: Drugs and Freedom in the Liberal Age*. London: Routledge, 2009.

United Nations Office on Drugs and Crime. *World Drug Report 2017*. New York: United Nations Publications, 2017.

Wacquant, Loic. "Towards a Reflexive Sociology: A Workshop with Pierre Bourdieu." *Sociological Theory* 7, no. 1 (1989): 26–63.

ᵃ OPEN ACCESS

Decolonising drugs in Asia: the case of cocaine in colonial India

James Mills

ABSTRACT
This article examines a drugs trade in Asia that has been largely forgotten by historians and policy-makers, that in cocaine. It will briefly trace some of the contours of this commerce and the efforts to control it. It will also assess how successful these efforts were. The article is designed to contribute fresh perspectives on recent controversies in the historiography of drugs in Asia to argue that the agendas and agency of consumers are central to understanding why markets have formed there for psychoactive substances in the modern period.

Introduction

After a surveillance operation that had started in January of that year, Bombay Excise Inspector P. J. Hudson decided that he had enough evidence on 7 April 1934 and ordered a raid. The premises in Ghati Gully seemed to be at the centre of an illegal cocaine trade, with the drug stored at one property and sold from another to customers who consumed on the spot after handing over their payment. A posse of officers and constables was dispatched together with an informant and a bogus customer. The plan worked well at first as the 'customer' successfully purchased the drug and gave the signal. The posse charged onto the scene and attempted to grab those inside the building only to meet fierce resistance. Gang members responded quickly, and set about the officers with bamboo lathis and broken bottles. The official account in the Bombay Police Gazette noted that 'the constables, realising the position, undid their belts and started defending themselves. The Inspector and the Sub-Inspector, who were concealed … went to the rescue of the men'. Newspaper accounts were more dramatic, and *The Statesman* reported that 'overwhelmed by numbers, the small excise party were forced to beat a retreat with four of their men injured'.[1]

This episode points to a drugs trade in south Asia that has been largely forgotten by historians, that in cocaine. The significance of this trade lies in its potential to provide new perspectives on a range of issues in the history of intoxicants, drugs and medicines in Asia. Consumers of intoxicants and narcotics there were certainly the reason for the establishment and early development of today's international drugs regulatory system, as the 1909 Shanghai Opium Conference lead directly to the establishment of the Opium Advisory

---

ⓘ http://orcid.org/0000-0001-9384-2087

This is an Open Access article distributed under the terms of the Creative Commons Attribution License (http://creativecommons.org/licenses/by/4.0/), which permits unrestricted use, distribution, and reproduction in any medium, provided the original work is properly cited.

Committee and the Permanent Central Opium Board at the League of Nations.[2] It was Asian consumption of local drugs, opium and to a lesser extent cannabis, which drove these processes and historians have therefore focused on these.[3] By examining the rapid emergence of a market for cocaine, that most modern of pharmaceutical products in 1900, this article promises to produce a more complex picture of Asia's drugs consumers. It will challenge accounts written by historians that have assumed that suppliers drove markets, an argument that first emerged in Western imaginations in the nineteenth-century.[4]

To do this, the article therefore also addresses suppliers of cocaine to south Asia in this period. The initial sources of the drug lay outside of Asia, in Holland and Germany, while Japan later established itself as a producer. Answering the question of who transported cocaine into the region will provide important new conclusions about the global circulation of drugs and medicines. In the history of intoxicants in Asia, the focus has been on the supply of opium by Western imperialists to China and East Asia. As recently as 1999, Carl Trocki restated the view that the colonial regime in India, for example, was 'a global drug cartel which enslaved and destroyed millions and enriched only a few'. Studies by Bello and by Kingsberg have shown that Asian states were equally active, as those in Central Asian kingdoms and in imperial Japan sought to profit from Asian consumers of intoxicants.[5] The story of cocaine there promises to force a rethink. It is clear that Western colonial governments were quick to prohibit cocaine use in their territories, so the large market in Asia was established despite their policies rather than because of them. The suggestion is that private entrepreneurs, rather than colonial states, became involved in large-scale movements of psycho-active intoxicants and medicines much earlier than the 1940s as previously thought.[6]

A clearer picture of how the market for cocaine was supplied in Asia also promises insights that go beyond the debates about the history of intoxicants there. Studies by Chakrabarti and Attewell of the flow of medicines from Asia have shown that the region had long been the source of medicinal substances for those elsewhere and that exports grew in the nineteenth century.[7] Other work has suggested that migration from India in this period stimulated the flow of Asian medicines around the world as migrants took their medications with them.[8] This article provides glimpses of the reverse flow, in order to better understand the arrival of Western medicines in Asia. Much of the work that addresses that process has looked at the impact of state-sponsored colonial medicine in forcing Western ideas and products on local societies as 'tools of empire'.[9] By looking at a medicine that arrived in Asia despite the efforts of colonial governments to prevent it, the study promises to reshape ideas so that pharmaceutical companies, medical entrepreneurs and local commercial interests are placed at the heart of accounts of the ways Asia took to Western medicines in the early twentieth-century.

Finally, the story at the start of this article suggests that government struggled to control flows of cocaine. Throughout the nineteenth and early twentieth centuries administrations in Asia lead the way in debating how intoxicant-consuming societies could and should be governed. Historians have argued that their positions were diverse, ranging from efforts to prohibit consumption altogether, to excise regimes that raised revenue from the markets for intoxicants and medicines.[10] This diversity survived into the twentieth-century and yet by 1910 unanimity had rapidly been established across British territories in Asia that cocaine ought to be prohibited for anything but strictly medical or scientific purposes. Explaining this, and tracing government responses elsewhere in Asia to cocaine in these decades, will provide a clearer and more detailed understanding of a period and a place in which modern systems of governing narcotics markets were established and in which drugs crises were framed for the first time.

Cocaine consumption in India

In 1902 the *British Medical Journal* printed a report by an Indian doctor, Kailas Chunder Bose, which concluded that:

> Besides the use of cocaine hydrochlorate as a therapeutic agent its consumption as a drug for intoxication is so great in Calcutta that unless stringent measures be adopted to control its sale I have reason to fear that its demoralizing effects will soon spread amongst the juvenile members of respectable families and that at no distant date special asylums will be required for the safety and treatment of cocaine inebriates.

He went on to detail 10 cases of cocaine use that he had encountered in the city. The first was L.B.M. 'a promising boy aged 20, very respectably connected [who] fell into bad company and contracted the habit of taking opium and bhang [cannabis] in their various forms'.[11] In an effort to give up opium he took to cocaine and before long was taking 30 grains a day (equivalent to about 2 grams). After consuming nothing nutritional but milk he suffered diarrhoea and died. The second case was of a Sanskrit scholar and priest in his forties who was advised by a 'learned Pundit' to use cocaine to help him fast. He increased his daily doses and Bose noted that 'he has given up his priestly duties and mixes freely with low-class people. He lives entirely upon the charity of his neighbours'. Another story merited its own subtitle 'Cocaine in the Zenana'. Its central figure was 'a healthy-looking Hindu girl, aged 16 [who] contracted the cocaine habit under peculiar circumstances':

> An elderly woman living in the same house advised her to take cocaine to get rid of dysmenorrhoea which she was subject to. She also cited instances where cocaine proved a sovereign remedy for removing sterility. The foolish girl followed her advice and took cocaine every day clandestinely in 1 gr. doses for six weeks. She then increased the daily dose and one day she took 10 gr [about a half gram]. Half an hour after she had taken the dose she complained of a choking sensation and soon became unconscious. At this stage I was summoned to see her. The patient had all the symptoms of hysteria and I prescribed for her accordingly ... at about 10am the following morning marked improvement was noticed in her general condition ... at about 1 pm she became very cross and wanted to go to the adjoining room where she had her box containing betel leaves and spices ... on opening the folded betel leaf cocaine was discovered and then on being questioned the girl made a clean breast of the whole thing and further said that there were three more girls under the same roof who were taking cocaine in pretty large doses.

The author reported that 'information has also reached me that women dealing in fancy goods who have access into private houses carry cocaine clandestinely and sell it to girls who take it in small doses with betel leaves'. This was a reference to paan, the popular Indian refreshment in which a number of leaves from the betel creeper are smeared with a variety of ingredients and then formed into triangular shaped parcels. The content of each paan is different according to the preferences of the customer. Common ingredients include areca nut, catechu (from the heart wood of the katha tree) and betel-oil. Once folded into the leaves the parcel is placed in the mouth and chewed. Evidently cocaine had found its way into the list of ingredients.[12]

The *British Medical Journal* was sufficiently intrigued by this that it devoted an editorial piece to the subject. It alleged that 'the drug is imported in ounce bottles by certain Mohammedan and Marwari dealers. These bottles are sold for 2½ rupees each but the material is more usually put up in small packets costing 1, 2 and 4 pies and retailed by the sellers of betel, the leaf of which is so universally chewed by Indians ... unfortunately it appears that some of those addicted to the vice have obtained their supply from dispensaries and even from medical men ... the habit is a costly one and this will probably prevent its spread among the lower classes in India'. The editorial concluded that 'repressive measures must, therefore, be far-reaching as well as drastic if the evil is to be adequately dealt with'.[13] A half decade later, G. F. Ewens wrote in 1908 that 'of late years a new habit, that of cocaine taking either by mouth or as snuff or hypodermically has sprung up'. However, he remained convinced that 'it is an expensive habit and the sufferers are consequently well-to-do and frequently medical men'. As Superintendent of the Lahore Lunatic Asylum his observation was based on patients who had been brought to the hospital.[14]

A report another half decade later painted a different picture of India's users. Chunilal Bose's 1913 report to the *British Medical Journal* observed that 'not many years ago cocaine was a drug hardly known to the people of India outside the medical profession and now, sad to reflect, it has taken a vigorous hold of a certain class of people in this country both in town and village. In Calcutta ... there is reason to believe that the cocaine habit has much increased and is rapidly spreading'. Bose had served in the Chemical Examiner's Department of the Government of Bengal for 27 years, so was well-placed to chart changes in drugs markets as his office was responsible for analysing samples of substances seized by the police and excise officers. His report included details of those though to have died from cocaine consumption thanks to post-mortem reports passed on by a colleague in the police. The first case was B.D., a Hindu male, aged about 23 years, a resident of Calcutta and by occupation a 'pressman' [i.e. he worked a press of some sort]. Bose noted that the individual was 'addicted to alcohol and to cocaine' before recounting the following story:

> On May 28th 1912 he played cards with his friends up to a late hour of the night and distributed pan (betel) with cocaine to his companions taking the largest share himself. He left the place soon after and at 2.30am on May 29th he was found lying unconscious and groaning at a neighbour's doorway. Medical aid was summoned, the man was removed to hospital, but died on the way there.

Bose noted that the man's body was poorly nourished and that he detected cocaine in the bowels and urine of the corpse. His second example was of 'a woman of the town ... in the habit of taking cocaine'. Aged about 28 years of age she had left home at 1.30 am and returned five hours later. He reported that 'she was seen to be staggering while washing her mouth at a hydrant hard by. Very soon afterwards she lay down, became unconscious, and in a few minutes she died'. He noted that there were no signs of violence on her body and that there was a 'marked quantity' of cocaine in her viscera.

His final case was of a Hindu female, who lived with her husband in Calcutta, and who was on a visit to her sister-in-law on the day of her death. While there she 'offered L. some white powder which she believed to be a specific remedy for acidity and indigestion. They each took some of the powder and within half an hour they became ill and then unconscious'. The sister-in-law survived while the young wife died. Bose concluded at the end of these stories that 'the drug is very easily procurable by the common people [and] the people are getting to be more familiar with its uses'. In little more than a decade after the point that India's cocaine consumers first came to attention the evidence suggests that drug was being used by both males and females, across the country, and by those of all religions and classes.[15]

The picture remained the same in the 1920s. A. W. Overbeck-Wright was the Superintendent of the mental hospital at Agra. He reported in 1921 that:

> The habit is said to have originated in the chawls [working class tenements] of Delhi, being used there first as an application to the glans penis to delay the orgasm and increase the pleasure of

the habitués of these places. From this beginning its use has extended till now it is extensively used by debauchees of the worst description.

He included details of two consumers that he had treated in the Agra hospital. The first was a 30-year-old Patwari [keeper of land records] who was 'wild and excited in appearance and in a continuous state of restless activity'. It seems that he had been admitted by his family and that he had been using cocaine for some time. The Superintendent noted that the man was convinced that 'his wife and neighbours were in league to poison and electrify him [and] had done him out of his employment'. Overbeck-Wright's second case was a Muslim syce [groom or stableman] who was aged about 25. The doctor wrote of the patient that 'he himself had apparently been a vicious debauchee for years, addicted to cocaine and the constant companionship of prostitutes' and observed that the man was abusive and prone to aural hallucinations. Despite this, however, his case notes suggested that there was some recovery when the patient was denied the drug.[16]

It was suggested that by 1929 'somewhere between a quarter and a half a million individuals [were] taking cocaine in India'.[17] These few anecdotal accounts from the first three decades of the twentieth century do little more than provide glimpses of India's cocaine consumers, but they do suggest that the market quickly became diverse and complex and remained so. Men and women used the drug, those that did so could be rich or poor, and Muslim and Hindu were numbered among those that sought it. It was consumed for a range of purposes, from the medicinal to the recreational. What is most surprising of all, however, is that this most modern of drugs[18] was quickly domesticated through that most familiar of modes of consumption in south Asia: paan.

Control and supply

In 1906 the Council of the Governor General of India met to discuss how controls on cocaine could be imposed across all of the territories under British administration in South Asia. In the notes of the meeting it became clear, however, that efforts to ensure that cocaine could only be used for medical ends dated back to the turn of the century in some parts of India:

> Cocaine has been notified as an intoxicating drug within one or other of these Acts since 1900 in Bengal, since 1903 in Bombay and since 1905 in Madras and its sale has been confined in those Provinces to approved chemists, druggists or medical practitioners with the intention that they shall supply it only for medicinal purposes.[19]

The discussion in the council was about extending the policies of these administrations to the whole of the rest of India.[20] The Excise Act in each of those areas was to be the device used and this meant that cocaine was to be subject to the following restrictions:

> No person shall have in his possession any drugs which the Local Government has, by notification ... declared to be included in the definition of 'intoxicating drugs' except under, and in accordance with the terms of, a general exemption granted by the Local Government.

> No person shall have any quantity of any intoxicating drugs ... greater than the amount therein specified in respect of such drugs unless he is permitted to collect, cultivate, manufacture or sell the same, or holds a pass therefore from the Collector or some other officer empowered by the Local Government to grant such passes.[21]

Excise Acts were the device by which the colonial government sought to raise revenue by taxing the trade in a variety of products but it was made clear that in the case of cocaine an income was not the intended purpose. The Council of the Governor General of India concluded that in Bombay, Bengal and Madras 'its sale has been confined ... to approved chemists, druggists or medical practitioners with the intention that they shall supply it only for medicinal purposes. It is now most desirable that similar action should be taken ... which applies to the rest of India'.[22] The Bill was approved by the Governor-General on 10th August 1906 and by the India Office back in London on 4 September, so by Autumn 1906 all of the colony was subject to laws that were aimed at suppressing the use of cocaine for anything but medicinal purposes.

It is worth drawing attention to the date, as this action makes the Government of India the first in the world to attempt such a geographically comprehensive ban. In the US individual states imposed restrictions from 1887 onwards[23] but it was only in 1914 that the Harrison Narcotic Act saw the 'introduction of national drug prohibition'.[24] In the UK cocaine possession was first controlled in 1916 through the wartime Defence of the Realm Act 40B but these temporary regulations were placed on a sounder legislative footing only in 1920 with the Dangerous Drugs Act.[25]

When the order from the Council of the Governor-General was presented to the regional governments the message clearly got through. A member of the Legislative Council in the United Provinces, for example, declared that 'in order to make it clear that in this legislation there is no question of raising revenue I may say that it has been decided that no fees will be taken on licences or passes'.[26] An Indian member of the same Legislative Council noted that 'there is no desire on the part of the Government, as I believe is the case, to derive any revenue from the sale of this most injurious drug'.[27] The President of the Council insisted that 'the object of this legislation is to put a stop to the cocaine habit ... licences would only be given to persons who sell cocaine as a medical drug and the sale of it as an intoxicant would be absolutely prohibited'. Elsewhere he reiterated that 'the Government proposes to make rules of such stringency as will prevent the sale and possession of cocaine except for bona fide medical purposes'.[28]

While this article started with a story from Bombay in the 1930s that showed that efforts to enforce these rules could be fiercely resisted, it did not take three decades before the authorities realised that their efforts at control were failing. As early as 1907 a letter from the Collector of Customs in Bombay to the Commissioner of Customs, Salt, Opium and A'bkari argued that 'cocaine is smuggled to a very considerable extent. As the result of searches made at my request by the Postal authorities 44 packages containing cocaine were found in one mail's delivery at Delhi, and 47 in the registered post between Aden and Bombay ... the difficulty of checking its importation is great since it can be conveyed in a very small compass by letter or book-post and a large quantity could be brought as personal baggage by a traveller'.[29]

This letter sparked a nationwide correspondence as the Government of India sought to establish whether this was an isolated case or whether an earlier attempt to prevent cocaine being sent through the post had failed.[30] The authorities in Burma replied that 'most of the contraband cocaine which finds its way into Rangoon is brought by the passengers and crews of Chinese steamers plying between Rangoon, Singapore, Hongkong, Swatow, Amoy and other Chinese ports'. Those in Madras reported 'that large quantities of cocaine pass through the Customs, especially at Calcutta, labelled and invoiced as "powdered Tartaric acid" or mixed with other crystalline substances from which it can be easily separated by solution and obtained pure on recrystallization' while In Bengal it had been discovered that 'the seizures made in cases of illicit possession or sale of cocaine, principally in Calcutta, go to show that the bulk of such cocaine is of German manufacture, the principal manufacturer being "Merk". Preparations also by Messrs. Burgoyne Burbidges and Borrows Welcome [sic] of London are also met with from time to time; the proportions of seizures are roughly stated as follows; "Merks" (Germany) 75 percent, Burgoyne's (London) 15 per cent and Other Makers 10 per cent'.

The Under-Secretary of the Government of the Punjab alleged in 1908 that 'it would appear that lascars [Indian merchant seamen] are possibly implicated in the contraband importation of cocaine'. Taken together, these letters seem to show that within a couple of years of the nationwide restrictions on cocaine use a number of smuggling routes into India had developed, through the post and the ports, and involving Chinese and Indian sailors.[31] However, further investigations suggested that it was not just Asian go-betweens who sought to profit from cocaine-smuggling:

> Personating a smuggler one of our Excise officers got into dealings with two European members of the crew of a ship recently in Calcutta who appear to be agents of the Glasgow firm in their smuggling trade. One of them instructed the Excise officer how to communicate with the firm and following these instructions the Glasgow firm were asked if they could supply 1000 ozs of cocaine. They have sent a reply offering the cocaine at 25 rupees an ounce … the name of the firm is Messrs Gowan and McLean, St Vincent Street, Glasgow.[32]

Duncan Gowans of the firm was questioned by the police in Scotland and confessed to an elaborate scheme whereby coded messages were sent from Calcutta where he had been supplying Johoor Ali. However, John McGimpsey, the Chief Detective Officer on the case found evidence of a more extensive trade and he concluded that 'it appears from the correspondence that Mr Wyper of the SS City of Karachi and probably other officials are mixed up with the illegal smuggling of cocaine into India'.[33]

A centralised monitoring system for cocaine was soon established and it began to show how extensive the illicit trade had become. In 1912 in Bombay Presidency over 148 lbs of the drug were seized but in Bengal the figure was 373 lbs. To put this in context legal sales of cocaine in that year amounted to just over 34 lbs in Bombay.[34] Ten years on the smuggling was still happening. In Madras it was reported that 'one case of seizure of illicit cocaine occurred during the year. The cocaine was seized on board S.S. Torilla at the Madras Port. The drug was of Japanese manufacture and the quantity amounted to 26418 grains. It was stated that the drug was obtained for sale at Kopio, Japan. The accused in the case consisted of two members of the engine crew, a Chinaman and a Chitagonian'.[35] In Bombay the authorities seized only 17 lbs while in Bengal they found scarcely more than 1197 ozs. Whether these smaller confiscations point to the success of the Government's policy or its failure is difficult to say for sure, but it was certainly the case that in some years large seizures indicated a lively traffic in the drug; towards the end of the 1920s Bengal reported that it had confiscated 146 lbs in 1928–1929 compared with 174 lbs in 1927–1928.[36] Even administrators inland worried about cocaine sales within their territories. In the same year the Government of the United Provinces of Agra and Oudh complained that:

> The nefarious traffic in illicit cocaine continued to flourish in spite of the vigilance on the part of the Police and Excise staffs and the heavy sentences which were generally passed in the cases which reached the courts. Most of the bigger cities were affected by the evil and the cocaine habit was undoubtedly wide-spread among the urban population. Very few cases were reported from rural tracts. Illicit cocaine came into the country from Germany, Japan and Holland; and smugglers in these provinces got their supplies from Calcutta, Bombay, Delhi and Ajmere. Detection was not an easy matter. The drug being odourless and small in bulk was therefore

easily smuggled. The principals engaged in the business seldom handled the drug which was hawked by hirelings for sale to the public. It was seldom therefore that organisers were caught and as the profits were large smugglers spent money readily and experienced no difficulty in securing the services of undesirable persons as carriers and agents.[37]

Clearly then, smuggling of cocaine to India continued during and after the First World War and in spite of the international control system set up in 1919.[38] However, after the First World War more cocaine seemed to be coming from Japan. This was demonstrated in a report prepared for the Government of India in 1931 by J. Slattery of the Central Board of Revenue. He noted that 'in 1929 particular attention was drawn to it [cocaine] by reason of several large seizures each of more than a thousand ounces, made at Calcutta. The total quantity seized in that year in Calcutta and Rangoon came to some 9000 oz and if that figure represented five per cent of the whole the total illicit import reached the alarming figure of 180000 oz or 11250 lbs'.[39] The cocaine seized carried the labels of the Fujitsuru, Buddha and Elephant brands but it was discovered that no legitimate pharmaceutical company produced these. The seizures were made on board ships of the British India Far East Company and the Indo-China Line of the Jardine-Matheson group. Given this information, Slattery headed for Japan and China via Singapore and Hong Kong. Conducted between January 1930 and July 1931, his survey reported corrupt officials, secretive police officers and shadowy organisations. He concluded that:

> The Chinese and Indians on the British India steamers received their supplies from different sources, the Chinese from Kwong Yee Sang etc. [at Kobe] and the Indians from Japanese traffickers, the Chinese obtaining the Fujitsuru brand and the Indians the various Japanese brands. Also seeing that the Fujitsuru brand was represented in India as being of German manufacture and so commanded a better market than the Japanese article the sources supplying the Fujitsuru variety were not open to the Indians.[40]

Slattery, however, was not telling the full story here as he had not just come across Chinese and Indian smugglers. A couple of years earlier he interviewed a British sailor named Gibson who had been arrested in Rangoon. Gibson openly admitted that 'I traded on the fact that as a British ship's officer I was above suspicion'[41] and he exploited this by purchasing cocaine in Japan and selling it in India.[42] Nevertheless, Slattery's investigation clearly shows that three decades of colonial regulations designed to 'put a stop to the cocaine habit' had succeeded only in creating complex networks that provided an illicit supply of the drug to south Asian consumers.

Conclusion

Why is the above story important for those considering the history of intoxicants, drugs and medicines in Asia? The answers lie in the challenge it presents to accounts of consumers of such substances there that have lingered ever since the nineteenth-century. As debates raged in Britain about the First Opium War, a trope emerged in which critics of the country's actions in China conjured up images of Asian opium consumers as hapless dupes of wicked British opium suppliers. The Reverend Algernon Thelwall, for example, asked indignantly in 1839 how the British government could 'stand by unconcerned, and countenance, in its enlightened and professedly Christian subjects, that system of smuggling, by which a poisonous drug is introduced into China to the ruin and destruction, moral and physical, of thousands and tens of thousands of its inhabitants'.[43] Jump forward to more recent times and Carl Trocki remains convinced that the British who traded opium between their possessions in India and the Chinese empire were 'a global drug cartel which enslaved and destroyed millions and enriched only a few'[44] while Martin Booth states simply that 'inevitably, as the availability of opium rose so did the demand for it'.[45] In between times the whole international drugs regulatory system was established in order to deal with the 'problem' of Asian consumption of opium and opiates. Supply drove demand was the underlying logic; as wily Westerners supplied, helpless Asians consumed.

Post-colonial studies provided the tools to challenge these assessments. Following Edward Said's work, scholars were more alert to the idea that easy generalisations in which Westerners were dominant and determined and Others simple and weak had their origins in the myth-making projects of colonial-era Orientalism.[46] Those influenced by the Subaltern Studies project began to study more closely the agendas and agency of groups marginalised by the colonial state and local elites and found an 'autonomous domain' in which ideas and actions often drew on neither.[47] Work on commoditization and its cultural history was also important as in drawing attention to 'the social life of things'[48] historians and anthropologists argued that individuals 'with their drive to discriminate, classify, compare and sacralize' could be active agents in attaching values to commodities.[49]

Among the first historians to provide revisionist accounts were Frank Dikötter, Lars Laamann and Zhou Xun, who challenged the idea of a nineteenth-century 'opium plague' in China as the product of the colonial era. They argued that it was the invention of Christian missionary's keen to conjure up a moral crusade to energise support for their efforts among the Chinese. It has proven remarkably durable as the Communist Party (CCP) seized on the idea that Western countries had poisoned their way to power in China as a powerful ideological image. It also featured heavily in the early stages of the establishment of the international drugs regulatory framework where US interests deployed it. In researching recently opened Chinese archives, Dikotter, Laaman and Zhou instead found sophisticated consumer cultures around opium. Different grades and a range of preparations of opium were on offer, and imported versions from India or Central Asia vied for customers with the domestic product produced across China. The elites could afford to sample whatever was on offer and incorporated their favourite types into both social events and private moments of relaxation. Others tailored their tastes to their incomes, and consumers varied from those that took opium on a daily basis to others who would try a little only at gatherings or when in company. For much of the nineteenth-century and into the twentieth, taking preparations of opium was generally considered socially acceptable in China.[50] Yangwen Zheng found similar evidence and concluded that 'opium smoking could not have come to a better place at a more opportune moment; it was a welcome addition to the Ming–Qing–Republican economy, culture and society'.[51] Such accounts 'decolonised' drugs histories in Asia by seeking to move beyond colonial-era images and constructs.

The story about cocaine in South Asia similarly challenges these colonial-era ideas. There is no well-organised supplier of the drug that might be accused of acting as the East India Company may have done with opium in China. Instead, what emerges from the records is a diverse and disparate range of opportunists who sourced batches of the drug to smuggle into India to take advantage of the prices inflated by British controls. Cocaine was produced by only a limited number of companies at this time, so the labels of such corporations as Merck and Wellcome Burroughs were often found on seized consignments. However, this was not because those corporations were themselves organising a market for their products in India, but rather because smugglers were simply buying up legal supplies in Europe (where cocaine was largely unregulated until 1917) for illegal profits in British territories in south Asia. The story of the Glasgow chemist and his Indian partners is the clearest demonstration of this tangle of relationships, as the source of the drug was a local shop in Scotland which had been approached by imperial sailors at the bidding of Calcuttans eager to exploit the market in Bengal. It is true that after the First World War Japan and its colonies seem to have become a well-organised and state directed source of cocaine.[52] By then the supplier was simply filling a gap in the Indian market left by the disruption and decline of European supplies due to the hostilities of the period. It was acting as a supplier to an existing market rather than as the force behind a new one.

If the story fails to provide any evidence of a core supplier acting consciously to create a new market it certainly does offer glimpses of a rapidly growing and increasingly powerful market. It is the complexity of the latter that is most striking and which resonates so strongly with other examples where a drug has suddenly infiltrated a society. The domestication of cocaine through its incorporation into the south Asian rituals of taking paan is significant and striking. It seems that Indians may have developed an appreciation of that most modern of drugs, but that it did so only through a traditional mode of consumption. The sources show that cocaine may well have been recommended in the first place as a medicine, and that it retained a reputation as a therapeutic thereafter. It was also purchased as an aid to recreation and relaxation and as a tonic, a pick-me-up that falls somewhere between medication and intoxication. It was consumed across India's various communities and throughout the country, in a range of social contexts, and by both genders. It sometimes appears as a solitary pursuit but often was consumed in company. Crucially this market developed despite the efforts of colonial governments to prohibit it. In India, regulation had been in place since 1900 and yet the story that opened this article shows that over three decades later both controls and enforcement mechanisms were resisted, sometimes violently.

In all of this the cocaine market in south Asia resembles opium in nineteenth century China, where the substance 'went from medicine to mass drug food [and] patterns of consumption altered, demand increased and the understanding of opium use changed'.[53] It also resembles *yaa-baa* in contemporary Thailand. There the drug was originally used as an aid to productivity by workers, but now 'consumption is indeed extremely diverse and wide-ranging, and the drug in turn proves able to satisfy the expectations of many different types of users'.[54] Among the latter can still be found labourers and office-staff, but these have been joined by groups drawn from throughout society including elite school and university students, street-children and prostitutes.

It is the Asian consumer that seems to be driving the market in all of these instances. Experimentation and innovation ensure that substances with initially limited functions, but with enticing properties, are quickly adopted for a wider set of purposes. In the examples from China and Thailand, this experimentation and curiosity on the part of individual consumers seems to be linked to social, cultural and economic change, and it was certainly the case that the decades considered here in which cocaine spread south Asia India were marked by 'severe dislocations'.[55] None of this is to deny that suppliers have a role in the development and expansion of markets once they exist, and historians are right to insist that 'one has to provide a clearer picture of the push and pull factors that are so characteristic of an illegal economy'[56] when considering the consumption of illicit drugs. It is, however, to challenge the assumptions and assertions of those who look chiefly to Western suppliers in explaining the origins of markets for intoxicants in Asia in the modern period. Cocaine may have been a thoroughly modern Western drug, the product of late nineteenth century laboratory science and of the technological processes of the maturing pharmaceutical industry as it entered the 1900s. But it was Indians who incorporated it into their rituals of consumption, their medical practices and their tastes for intoxicants, and who thereby turned south Asia into one of the largest markets for cocaine of the twentieth century. It is this conclusion that adds to the recent historiographical push to decolonise drugs and drugs consumers in Asia and to recover the agendas and agency of those using psychoactive substances there in order to provide a clearer view of the forces driving markets for them.

Disclosure statement

No potential conflict of interest was reported by the author.

Funding

This work was supported by the Wellcome Trust [grant number WT200394/Z/15/Z].

Note on Sources

IOL refers to files from the India Office Library at the British Library in London; NA signifies files from the UK's National Archives in Kew; Bombay General Files can be found in the Maharashtra State Archives in Mumbai.

Notes

1. India Office Library (British Library) IOL File L/I/1/203, 'Excise Supplement to the Bombay Police Gazette 28 February 1935'.
2. Bruun et al., *The Gentlemen's Club*; McAllister, *Drug Diplomacy*.
3. Trocki, *Opium, Empire and Political Economy*; Mills, *Cannabis Britannica*.
4. Booth, *Opium*; see also Travis Hanes and Sanello, *The Opium Wars*.
5. Bello, *Opium and the Limits of Empire*; Kingsberg, *Moral Nation*.
6. Chouvy and Meissonnier, *Yaa Baa*.
7. Chakrabarti, *Materials and Medicine*; Attewell, "Interweaving Substance Trajectories."
8. Mills, "Globalising Ganja."

9. Headrick, *Tools of Empire*. The exception is Nandini Bhattacharya's recent article which explores the multiple routes by which Western medicines found their ways to Indian markets; Bhattacharya, "Between the Bazaar and the Bench."
10. For a sense of the diversity of these efforts see the essays in Mills and Barton, Drugs and Empires.
11. Opium and cannabis ('bhang') had been popular sources of medication and intoxication for centuries in south Asia. For details see Richards, "Opium and the British Indian Empire"; Mills, *Cannabis Britannica*.
12. Extracts taken from Chunder Bose, "Cocaine Intoxication and its Demoralizing Effects."
13. "Cocainism in Calcutta," 1041–1042.
14. Ewens, *Insanity in India*, 116–118.
15. Bose, "Cocaine Poisoning," 16–17.
16. Overbeck-Wright, *Lunacy in India*, 271–273.
17. Chopra and Chopra, *Cocaine Habit in India*, 1022.
18. The alkaloid 'cocaine' was only isolated in 1860 by the German Albert Niemann and its chemical formula described in 1862; Berridge, *Opium and the People*, 217. For an overview of its manufacture see Courtwright, *Forces of Habit*, 50.
19. IOL L-PJ-6-776, File 2878, note 1.
20. The areas named are the United Provinces of Agra and Oudh, the Punjab, the North-West Frontier Province, the Central Provinces, Burma, Coorg and Ajmer.
21. IOL L-PJ-6-776, File 2878, note 2.
22. IOL L-PJ-6-776 File 2878, note 6.
23. Streatfeild, *Cocaine*, 136.
24. Spillane, *Cocaine*, 1.
25. Berridge, *Opium and the People*, 251–264.
26. IOL L/PJ/6/747 File 428, note 3.
27. IOL L/PJ/6/747 File 428, note 4.
28. IOL L/PJ/6/747 File 428, note 5.
29. IOL R-20-A-1437, File 54/1, note 12.
30. IOL R-20-A-1437, File 54/1, note 13.
31. IOL R-20-A-1437, File 54/1, note 14.
32. UK National Archives (NA) HO 45/10601/189271, note 19.
33. NA HO 45/10601/189271, note 20.
34. IOL V-25–323-13, note 15. Figures for legal sales in Bengal are not available for 1912/13.
35. IOL V-25–323-13, note 16.
36. IOL V-25–323-13, note 17.
37. Ibid.
38. McAllister, *Drug Diplomacy*, 37.
39. Slattery, *Investigation of the Problem of Smuggling*, 1.
40. Ibid., 155–156.
41. NA FO 371/14768/248.
42. Meyer and Parssinen, *Webs of Smoke*, 121–124.
43. Thelwall, The iniquities of the opium trade with China, 72.
44. Trocki, *Opium, Empire and Political Economy*.
45. Booth, *Opium*.
46. Said, *Orientalism*.
47. Guha, *Subaltern Studies*, 4.
48. Appadurai, *Social Life of Things*.
49. Kopytoff, "Cultural Biography of Things," 87.
50. Dikötter et al., *Narcotic Culture*.
51. Yangwen, *The Social Life of Opium in China, 1483–1999*, 9.
52. Karch, "Japan and the Cocaine Industry," 154–158.
53. Brook and Tadashi Wakabayashi, *Opium Regimes*, 7.
54. Chouvy and Meissonnier, *Yaa-Baa*, xx.
55. Bose and Jalal, *Modern South Asia*, 126.
56. Chouvy and Meissonnier, *Yaa-Baa*, xix.

Bibliography

Appadurai, A. *The Social Life of Things: Commodities in Cultural Perspective*. New York: Cambridge University Press, 1999.

Attewell, G. "Interweaving Substance Trajectories: Tiryaq, Circulation and Therapeutic Transformation in the Nineteenth Century." In *Crossing Colonial Historiographies: Histories of Colonial and Indigenous Medicines in Transnational Perspective*, edited by A. Digby, W. Ernst, and P. Mukharji, 1–20. Newcastle: Cambridge Scholars, 2010.

Bello, D. *Opium and the Limits of Empire: Drug Prohibition in the Chinese Interior, 1729–1850*. Cambridge, Mass: Harvard University Press, 2005.

Berridge, V. *Opium and the People: Opiate Use and Drug Control in Nineteenth and Early Twentieth Century England*. London: Free Association Books, 1999.

Bhattacharya, N. "Between the Bazaar and the Bench: Making of the Drugs Trade in Colonial India, c. 1900–1930." *Bulletin of the History of Medicine* 90, no. 1 (2016): 61–91.

Booth, M. *Opium: A History*. New York: St Martin's Griffin, 1999.

Bose, C. "Cocaine Poisoning." *British Medical Journal* 1 (1913): 16.

Bose, S., and A. Jalal. *Modern South Asia: History, Culture, Political Economy*. London: Routledge, 1998.

Brook, T., and B. Tadashi Wakabayashi. *Opium Regimes: China, Britain and Japan, 1839–1952*. London: California University Press, 2000.

Bruun, K., L. Pan, and I. Rexed. *The Gentlemen's Club: International Control of Drugs and Alcohol*. Chicago, IL: University of Chicago Press, 1975.

Chakrabarti, P. *Materials and Medicine: Trade, Conquest and Therapeutics in the Eighteenth Century*. Manchester, NH: Manchester University Press, 2010.

Chopra, R. N., and G. S. Chopra. "Cocaine Habit in India." *The Indian Journal of Medical Research* xviii, (1931): 66.

Chouvy, P., and J. Meissonnier. *Yaa-Baa: Production, Traffic and Consumption of Methamphetamine in Mainland Southeast Asia*. Singapore: Singapore University Press, 2004.

Chunder Bose, K. "Cocaine Intoxication and Its Demoralizing Effects." *British Medical Journal* 1 (1902): 1020–1022.

"Cocainism in Calcutta." *British Medical Journal* 1, (1902): 1039.

Courtwright, D. *Forces of Habit: Drugs and the Making of the Modern World*. Cambridge: Harvard University Press, 2001.

Dikötter, F., L. Laamann, and Z. Xun. *Narcotic Culture: A History of Drugs in China*. London: Hurst, 2004.

Ewens, G. F. *Insanity in India: Its Symptoms and Diagnosis*. Calcutta: Thacker Spink and Co, 1908.

Guha, R. *Subaltern Studies 1*. Delhi: Oxford University Press, 1982.

Headrick, D. *Tools of Empire*. Oxford: Oxford University Press, 1981.

Karch, S. "Japan and the Cocaine Industry of Southeast Asia, 1864–1944." In *Cocaine: Global Histories*, edited by P. Gootenberg, 146–164. New York: Routledge, 1999.

Kingsberg, M. *Moral Nation: Modern Japan and Narcotics in Global History*. Oakland: University of California Press, 2013.

Kopytoff, I. "The Cultural Biography of Things: Commoditization as Process." In *The Social Life of Things: Commodities in Cultural Perspective*, edited by A. Appadurai, 64–94. New York: Cambridge University Press, 1986.

McAllister, W. *Drug Diplomacy in the Twentieth-Century: An International History*. London: Routledge, 2000.

Meyer, K., and T. Parssinen. *Webs of Smoke: Smugglers, Warlords, Spies and the History of the International Drug Trade*. Oxford: Rowman and Littlefield Oxford, 1998.

Mills, J. *Cannabis Britannica: Empire, Trade and Prohibition, 1800–1928*. Oxford: Oxford University Press, 2003.

Mills, J. "Globalizing Ganja: The British Empire and International Cannabis Traffic c. 1834 to c. 1939." In *Consuming Habits: Global and Historical Perspectives on How Cultures Define Drugs*, edited by J. Goodman, A. Sherratt, and P. Lovejoy, 178–193. London: Routledge, 2007.

Mills, J., and P. Barton. *Drugs and Empires: Essays in Modern Imperialism and Intoxication, c.1500 to c.1930*. Basingstoke: Palgrave, 2007.

Overbeck-Wright, A. W. *Lunacy in India*. London: Bailliere, Tindall and Cox, 1921.
Richards, J. "Opium and the British Indian Empire: The Royal Commission of 1895." *Modern Asian Studies* 36 (2002): 375–420.
Said, E. *Orientalism*. London: Pantheon Books, 1978.
Slattery, J. *Investigation of the Problem of Smuggling of Cocaine into India from the Far East*. Simla: Government of India Press Simla, 1931.
Spillane, J. *Cocaine: From Medical Marvel to Modern Menace in the United States, 1884–1920*. Baltimore, MD: John Hopkins University Press, 2000.
Streatfeild, D. *Cocaine*. London: Virgin, 2002.
Thelwall, A. *The Iniquities of the Opium Trade with China*. London: Allen, 1839.
Travis Hanes, W., and F. Sanello. *The Opium Wars: The Addiction of One Empire and the Corruption of Another*. London: Robson, 2002.
Trocki, C. *Opium, Empire and Global Political Economy: A Study of the Asian Opium Trade*. London: Routledge, 1999.
Yangwen, Z. *The Social Life of Opium in China, 1483–1999*. Cambridge: Cambridge University Press, 2003.

A diplomatic failure: the Mexican role in the demise of the 1940 Reglamento Federal de Toxicomanías

Isaac Campos

ABSTRACT
In 1940 Mexico implemented a new revolutionary strategy in its fight against drug trafficking and addiction with a policy that legalized the sale of morphine to opiate addicts. While this approach to drug addiction was not entirely new or unique, it was strongly opposed by the United States, which responded by declaring an embargo on narcotic shipments to Mexico. As a result, Mexico was forced to abandon the plan just a few months after it was implemented. Often seen as a moment when Mexico might have gone in a different, less prohibitionist drug-policy direction, this episode has been overwhelmingly interpreted as an early and striking example of U.S. drug-control imperialism in Latin America. While such interpretations are not incorrect, they have missed an equally critical element of the story—a series of catastrophic diplomatic failures on the Mexican side which undermined various opportunities Mexico had to salvage the policy in some form. The episode thus stands in contrast to more well-known diplomatic challenges during the period in which Mexico's diplomats have been lauded for outmaneuvering their U.S. and European counterparts.

In Mexico, everyone knows the story. On 18 March 1938, President Lázaro Cárdenas expropriated the property of powerful foreign oil companies and nationalised the industry. Mexicans poured into the streets in celebration, marking the event, which is still commemorated annually, as the maximum triumph of Mexican revolutionary nationalism. Mexico had taken on the Great Powers and won.[1]

At almost precisely the same moment, another Mexican challenge to Great Power hegemony was being crafted, once again involving a highly valuable, nationally indispensable and globally traded commodity – narcotic drugs. In 1940, the plan was set in motion in the form of a new *Reglamento Federal de Toxicomanías* (Federal Drug Addiction Regulation). The new Reglamento created a state monopoly over narcotic distribution, and the federal government began selling high-quality morphine to opiate addicts in exchange for their submission to treatment. The original aim of the Reglamento, as conceived by its chief architect, Dr Leopoldo Salazar Viniegra, was to destroy the illicit market and wrest drug users from the 'clutches of the trafficker'. By offering for sale the highest quality drugs at wholesale prices, addicts,

Salazar believed, would inevitably buy from the state rather than from street dealers, and from there the benefits would cascade – the illicit traffickers would be run out of business, the addicts would develop ongoing and healthy relationships with physicians, and the various collateral costs of drug prohibition, like the corruption of the police and the crimes committed by addicts to afford their habits, would melt away.[2]

It was a creative and decidedly revolutionary solution to a seemingly intractable problem. It was also interpreted by US officials as a major challenge to the international drug-control system. But unlike the oil challenge of 1938, this one would end, as Salazar himself put it, in 'humiliation' for Mexico.[3] Within a week of the plan's implementation, the United States quietly cut off all narcotic exports to Mexico, jeopardising not only the viability of the Reglamento, but Mexican medical practice in general. Two months later, Mexican officials surrendered, agreeing to rescind the policy in exchange for an end to the narcotics embargo.

While the episode was a clear diplomatic defeat for Mexico, in retrospect it is often interpreted as a kind of moral victory, for history has now shown that Salazar's strategy was probably the wise one. After all, much of what he foresaw has come to pass – prohibition has indeed enriched traffickers, fomented corruption and ultimately done little to solve the problem of addiction. From an early twenty-first century vantage, with Mexico in the midst of extreme drug war-related violence, 1940 is sometimes framed as a fork in the road, when for an instant perhaps another future might have been possible. It thus continues to resonate in present policy debates.[4]

This framing of the Reglamento's demise is a product of a scholarly literature that, understandably enough, has focused overwhelmingly on the US role in quashing the policy.[5] However, Salazar himself, in a policy post-mortem written a few years later, actually argued that the US had good reason to respond as it did. Rather than emphasising the US role, Salazar blamed Mexico's 'eternal and disastrous electoral politics' for the Reglamento's downfall.[6] As with his original arguments justifying the policy, the quite brilliant, iconoclastic psychiatrist had a point, even if he did not quite recognise the full extent of the political and diplomatic breakdown that had occurred on the Mexican side.

This essay contributes to a growing body of new research on Latin American drug history by demonstrating that Mexico had significantly more agency in the outcome of these events than has been previously recognised.[7] At the same time, while scholars of US–Mexican relations have recently emphasised the coherence and effectiveness of Mexican diplomacy during these years, this case represents a significant exception to that rule.[8] Drawing on a number of previously untapped documentary sources, including the intense conversations within the Mexican policy bureaucracy in the midst of the crisis, I argue that as much as the story of the doomed Reglamento is one of US imperial exertion in Mexico, it is also one that saw numerous political, diplomatic and bureaucratic failures on Mexico's part. Simply put, Mexico was badly outmanoeuvred by its northern neighbour. The episode thus provides a stark contrast with the oil expropriation and other major diplomatic challenges of the period, along with a very different result – 'humiliation' and total defeat, when at least partial victory might have been achieved.

***

In February 1938, Dr Leopoldo Salazar Viniegra was appointed chief of Mexico's narcotics service which at the time was housed within the Department of Public Health (*Departamento de Salubridad Pública* or, simply, *Salubridad*). The 40-year-old Salazar was a brilliant, highly respected psychiatrist, with years of experience at the Federal Hospital for Drug Addicts. He taught at the National University and, over the years, held numerous important posts both professional and academic.[9] He was also an iconoclast, boldly putting forward his often-unorthodox views, and willing at times to push ethical boundaries to do so, such as when he brought a pair of opiate addicts in front of his classroom and had them inject themselves with morphine so that students might witness the effects. Or when he engaged in target practice with live firearms on the grounds of the National Psychiatric Hospital, despite requests from above that he desist, until a stray bullet entered the home of one of the employees who lived on the grounds. Or in his teaching where he had little patience for grades and thus let his students grade themselves, a policy that produced considerable friction with university authorities. Or, most importantly for our purposes, when he offered colleagues cigarettes that were supposedly filled with tobacco, but in fact were mixed with marijuana. The point was to get them to use marijuana unawares so that he could prove to them that the drug did not produce any of the negative effects popularly attributed to it.[10] It was ethically dubious but typical Salazar. He was a singular character, never afraid to challenge if not completely break the rules.

Thus, shortly after taking office, he began to craft the new Reglamento. In July 1938, the first news of it appeared in the press when *El Nacional* optimistically announced that 'the old problem of the clandestine traffic in narcotic drugs would soon be resolved'.[11] Over the coming year, he would publicise the details of the programme both domestically and internationally while, behind the scenes, he shepherded it through the vetting process at the General Health Council, the body tasked with approving the policy before it could be presented to the President of the Republic for his signature.[12]

Through all of this, and given the way Salazar framed the question, it is quite remarkable how little controversy the plan itself provoked in Mexico, a country where drugs had long been demonised for inciting crime and 'degenerating the race'.[13] Salazar repeatedly stressed the need to 'recognize the existence of incurable drug-addicts', and it was on this key point that he distinguished the Reglamento from the ambulatory maintenance system that had earlier existed in the United States. Mexico, he explained, was dispensing with the belief that the programme would actually cure addiction.[14] This in turn led to another quite radical idea: 'This new approach should also abandon the procedure of persecuting the trafficker, substituting for it competition that would make the business of illicit trafficking unprofitable'.[15] In other words, the state itself should become Mexico's most important drug dealer, selling the best possible drugs at the lowest possible prices.

In part, timing probably explains the quiet response to the Reglamento, with the raging controversy over the oil expropriation and the looming war in Europe dominating the news. But even behind the scenes, during the meetings of the General Health Council, there was near-unanimous support for the policy and virtually no concern voiced regarding the ethics of the programme.[16] It seems that the time was right in Mexico for this policy to gain approval.

The only significant public controversy regarding the Reglamento during Salazar's tenure occurred after a Mexico City addict was arrested, in March of 1939, with morphine in his possession along with a permit from Salazar to carry the drug. Typical of his general disdain for rules, Salazar had essentially put the Reglamento into effect for his own patient, though the policy had not yet been approved.[17] Afterwards, Salubridad had to assure the press that drugs had not yet been legalised in Mexico. The episode also added to the controversy and sensational headlines that had emerged from Salazar's ethically dubious marijuana research.[18]

All of this contributed to a growing sense among US policymakers that perhaps the Mexican narcotics chief was out of control.

It had not always been that way. Initially, despite serious misgivings about Salzar's ideas, some US policymakers had expressed considerable respect for his education and standing, and on at least one occasion this translated into a decided reluctance to intervene forcefully in Mexican affairs. But as events around the doctor became increasingly circus-like during the fall and winter of 1938–1939, such sympathy seemed to evaporate.[19] This was evident in the spring of 1939 when Salazar was appointed as special representative for Mexico to the League of Nations in order to present the Reglamento to the League's Opium Advisory Committee. Once in Geneva he met privately with the State Department's Stuart J. Fuller who later evinced a clear air of condescension when recounting the meeting, concluding that the Mexican psychiatrist was a bit of a charlatan. He was apparently encouraged in this view by the other (unnamed) Mexican official at the meeting. 'He is a novice and lacks experience. Manner in which he talks indicates instability of character and thought. His Mexican colleague did not seem much impressed. Said Dr S. view did not represent views of Mexican Government'.[20]

Then Salazar disappeared. Scheduled to address the Opium Advisory Committee about the Mexican programme, he suddenly took leave for unspecified reasons. As a substitute, he wrote a letter that his fellow representative, Manuel Tello, delivered, which outlined the programme and the reasons it was being pursued. US drug chief Harry Anslinger responded that he hoped Mexico would postpone the enactment of the new regulations until the committee had been given a chance to study them, for the United States might not interpret the programme as fulfilling 'a medical requirement' as was mandated by the international conventions. Referring to the March scandal with Salazar's patient, he also expressed concern that the programme had apparently already begun to be implemented. Tello promised 'to communicate to the Mexican Government the request that the promulgation of the new legislation should be deferred until it had been examined by the next session of the Committee'.[21]

The promise was never kept and it was for this reason that Salazar would later claim that the US 'rightfully' felt 'betrayed' by Mexico. He blamed this failure on the presidential politics that apparently led to his ouster in September 1940.[22] Indeed, though back in early 1938 the United States had begun lobbying for Salazar to be replaced, his removal, as Salazar claimed, appears to have been motivated mostly by the developing 1940 presidential campaign.[23] Somewhere in the transition, the message from the League meetings was lost. Salazar blamed politics for this, though, as we will see, members of the General Health Council would later complain that Salazar had vacated his post without leaving a trace of prior developments.

Whatever the case, the Reglamento, which was in the final stages of approval, would continue forward. After a few small revisions were made during the fall it was signed by President Cárdenas. On 17 February, the policy became official after its publication in the *Diario Oficial*, and, on 9 March, the first narcotic dispensary opened in Mexico City, though by that point the diplomatic missteps had already begun to mount.[24]

***

About a month after Cárdenas had signed the policy, but still a month before its full implementation, the United States issued a stern warning to Mexico. It was Laurence Duggan, the State Department's Director of the Office of American Republic Affairs, who met with the Ministerial Counselor at the Mexican Embassy, Luis Quintanilla, to express opposition to the new programme by which, as US officials understood it, 'persons who habitually and with non-therapeutic ends use narcotics could legally receive from authorized physicians and surgeons, prescriptions that gave them the right to personally obtain, from pharmacies, certain quantities of narcotics to satisfy their vice'. Duggan went on to explain that such a system 'differed completely from that which reigned in all the countries of the world', and then detailed the various ways such a programme conflicted with US law, especially the Narcotics Import–Export Act of 1922 which allowed the US to only export narcotics when these were destined 'exclusively to medical and legitimate uses'. While Mexico might consider such use 'legitimate', the United States did not, and thus would likely be forced to prohibit all narcotic exports to Mexico if the plan went into effect. On 9 February, Mexico's Ambassador to the US, Dr Francisco Castillo Nájera, penned a summary of this conversation in which he emphasised how seriously the US was taking the question: 'These objections have been presented in an absolutely friendly manner; but I can assure you that, in the case that the law … is approved, the United States would take the restrictive measures that it has cited'.[25]

Thus, more than a month in advance of the first dispensary's inauguration, Mexican officials were made aware of the potential consequences. Unfortunately, the foreign ministry, despite receiving Castillo Nájera's correspondence on 15 February, delayed nearly a month in relaying the message to Salubridad. It was a catastrophic delay in communication for which the foreign relations bureaucracy had no good excuse.[26] As a result, Mexican government officials spent a month unknowingly sending all the wrong signals to the United States.

In late February, for example, US Customs Agent Harold S. Creighton visited Mexico City to discuss various matters related to drugs, including the Reglamento. The trip was scheduled on the eve of a planned visit to Mexico by Anslinger, head of US drug control and the man who was charged with determining whether or not a given drug application was 'medical and legitimate'. Having studied the question with the help of the Treasury Department's legal counsel, Anslinger had already decided to impose the embargo if Mexico went ahead with the plan.[27] Nonetheless, he appears to have been willing to find a compromise and saw Creighton's trip as a chance to gauge Mexico's position. To this end, he sent Creighton a copy of new regulations on drug addiction promulgated by the Colombian government which he considered 'far superior to the contemplated Mexican regulations which probably attempt to accomplish the same purpose'. He hoped that Creighton would cite them in his conversations with Dr José Siurob who had headed Salubridad since the previous September's personnel shake up.[28] Since 1932, Colombian doctors had been allowed to prescribe opiates to addicts for their 'disintoxication', but there had been no limit on the amount of time that the disintoxication could entail. The programme had thus allowed for indefinite prescribing of opiates to addicts. After a few years the Colombian authorities determined that the policy had been a failure, as addicts were getting the drugs not only for their 'personal satisfaction' but also to sell on the black market. Thus, in 1939 the law was altered to allow for a three-month period of private 'disintoxication', after which the addicts would have to move on to hospital treatment.[29] Anslinger's suggestion that these regulations serve as a model for Mexico demonstrates that he was not completely opposed to private opiate prescribing as long as it was for 'disintoxication', and not for an indefinite period of time.

Unfortunately, Mexican officials, still unaware of the quiet ultimatum, made various gestures that suggested total disregard for the US position. On 23 February, Creighton, who had been invited to Mexico by Siurob, arrived to find the public health chief out of town. He was left waiting for six days. 'Up to the present time Dr Siurob has not returned to Mexico City and yet his office advises that he is expected daily'. On the 27th, the Treasury Department counselled that Anslinger cancel his March trip. On the 28th Creighton updated Washington: 'Dr Siurob … asked me to come to Mexico, for just what purpose I do not know until I see him and I shall remain until he returns to Mexico City'.[30] On the eve of his eventual departure, Creighton informed fellow customs agent Edson Shamhart that he'd been on a 'Fool's Errand', and was forced to leave the country with an 'empty basket'. He went on to refer cryptically to 'another offer' he'd made Siurob, 'but I doubt if he will ever take the d[amn] first step'. Creighton, who closed by asking Shamhart to consign the letter to his fireplace, was clearly deeply frustrated with the situation.[31]

On 9 March, the first dispensary was opened. On the same day, the US ultimatum was finally passed along to Dr Siurob. On the 12th, the General Health Council met for the first time to discuss the ultimatum, more than a month after it had been issued.

It was a packed house, with 23 members in attendance for what would be a spirited 3.5-hour session mingling indignation, bluster and some realism. The meeting began with the reading of Castillo Nájera's summary of the ultimatum, and it was established that the main conflict involved Article 3 of the Reglamento which authorised doctors to prescribe up to a month's supply of narcotics and in doses that were higher than those allowed by the National Pharmacopoeia. Siurob emphasised that Mexico's legislation was good and worthy but that the US note had to be taken seriously. The doctors Eliseo Ramírez and Ignacio González Guzmán insisted that Mexico must hold fast. A number of the physicians, including Siurob, Ramírez and González Guzman, took time to reiterate all the reasons Salazar had enumerated for the programme, in this way emphasising the apparent injustice of the US position.

Dr Alberto León then intervened decisively, emphasising that the key was for Mexico to go to the League of Nations and ask for that body's opinion on the matter 'without alluding to the received note', while also 'exchanging views with the United States and getting them to see that the principal end was not exactly to supply drugs without any control, but rather to scientifically treat the addicts like legitimate sick people'.[32] León went on to insist that Mexico must show that the drugs were not simply going to be distributed to addicts. Instead, morally upright physicians would administer the drugs directly to the patients.

León's strategy would eventually win the day, but only after considerable debate. An invited guest from the Ministry of the Interior, the lawyer and revolutionary veteran José López Lira, strongly took exception to León's position, arguing that Mexico's laws must be respected in all cases, and particularly in this instance, as this was a law that had been studied carefully over a long period and that was already in effect. He argued that, 'from a legal perspective', Mexico 'can't and should not' accept any suggestions either from the League or from a foreign government, though from a moral one it was perhaps obligated to at least give some explanation as to the ends that were being pursued with the Reglamento. Mexico, he continued, 'solves its problems in accordance with its revolutionary regime'. He went on to argue that Mexico must put the issue before the League to explain, from a scientific perspective, the advantages and 'goodness' of the Reglamento. This opinion was seconded by the doctors Francisco Bassols and Heberto Alcázar (Salazar's replacement). Siurob then asked that a committee be formed composed of González Guzman, Bassols, Alcázar and the lawyer Ramón Acevedo to study the situation and for all to return in two days for another discussion.[33]

By that meeting, on Thursday 14 March, the crisis had escalated significantly, with the US having sent notice that it was imposing the narcotics embargo. The meeting got underway at noon, would last more than five hours, and would be marked by a significantly more sombre mood. Siurob suggested that the timing of the two US notes, the embargo coming just days after the ultimatum, indicated the gravity of the situation. That of course was not how the notes had been sent, but reflected the ongoing damage from the February communication breakdown between the foreign relations ministry and Salubridad.[34]

The meeting continued with the reading of some key passages from the reigning international drug-control agreements, and Siurob asking for council opinion as to whether Article 3 of the Reglamento indeed violated these. There, Dr Francisco Pax identified some potential wiggle room, noting that while the 1931 Convention for Limiting the Manufacture and Regulating the Distribution of Narcotic Drugs did require countries to specify the quantities of drugs needed for medical and scientific needs, as well as for reserve stocks, and for exporting countries to refuse export permits to those that had already imported their yearly maximum, it also stipulated that exceptions could be made for 'exceptional cases where the export in the opinion of the Government of the exporting country is essential in the interests of humanity or for the treatment of the sick'.[35] In short, perhaps a debate at the League of Nations could do some good.

Siurob then asked the committee that he had formed two days earlier to report on what they had learned. For the committee, the dire reality of the situation seemed to be setting in. While they emphasised that the Reglamento and its legality under international law had been carefully studied prior to its implementation, they conceded that the US interpreted the Conventions differently and that the League could possibly agree with the Americans.

Unbeknownst to the committee, analysts on the US side had expressed similar uncertainty with respect to the legal question. The Treasury Department's Office of the General Counsel, which had studied the situation and concluded that the narcotics embargo was both legal and appropriate, nonetheless conceded that its interpretation of the law, 'while probably correct, is not entirely free from doubt' (a second iteration of the analysis conveniently excluded this sentence). Specifically, the counsel had recognised some ambiguity in the law with respect to the key phrase 'medical and legitimate', noting that while the US Import–Export Act referred to 'medical and legitimate' uses, what was intentioned was 'medical *or* legitimate' uses. The latter of course could potentially encompass any number of scenarios and applications. Anslinger was well aware of this ambiguity which he noted on 6 April to the State Department's Stuart J. Fuller, specifically underlining this section of the counsel's opinion.[36] In short, there was more potential for successful negotiation at the League than Mexico was even aware.

Back in Mexico, Siurob's special committee emphasised that there were 'many difficulties in facing the problem', some of which had been caused by Salazar having left the promulgation of the Reglamento pending when he was removed from his post. 'He had all of the threads of the issue in his hands and upon separating from the Department he did not leave any trace with respect to it'. However, the committee continued to emphasise the importance of making a case before the League of Nations and, given 'the indispensable need to have enough drugs in order to sustain the Reglamento', recommended cancelling the programme, 'in order to see if it is possible to change the criterion of the American Government and to take the measures that should have been adopted in advance'.[37]

Here León once again made an influential intervention, agreeing with the committee's sentiments but emphasising that it was not the Reglamento that the US objected to but rather Article 3 of the policy which authorised doctors to prescribe drugs in doses higher than those allowed by the National Pharmacopoeia. Thus, if Mexico simply changed that portion of the Reglamento, he argued, the problems with the US would be eliminated. He also urged that it was 'necessary to face reality' given that within a month Mexico's stocks of drugs would run out and there wouldn't be sufficient supply for serious medical needs. For León, it was key that Mexico take the 'legal and friendly route', which meant exchanging views with the United States on the question to see if the latter could be convinced that the legislation was 'good and appropriate'. Siurob backed this idea and emphasised that Mexico should go before the League.[38]

After considerable debate over whether it would be indecorous for Mexico to suspend the Reglamento, the above suggestions were synthesised into a definitive strategy: only those elements of the Reglamento that were in dispute would be suspended, Mexico would ask the US to lift the embargo, and Siurob was authorised to discuss the issue 'privately and thoroughly' with US Embassy personnel. Strangely, the one measure that seemingly everyone agreed upon – the need to take the case before the League of Nations – was discarded for reasons that are completely absent from the meeting minutes.[39]

That afternoon, Siurob penned a response to the US based on these resolutions. In the meantime, he also made his proposal directly and in person to State Department officials in Mexico City.[40] On the 19th Siurob followed up with a letter to Thomas Parran, the US Surgeon General.[41] Already by the 21st Anslinger had decided to reject the proposal, though the State Department would overrule him. Indeed, Ambassador Daniels went as far as to suggest that the embargo should be suspended, another indication that there was some room for negotiation if Mexico could exploit the right channels.[42]

On the 22nd, Salubridad published some rather confusing 'clarifications' on the programme in the Mexico City press. These were clearly the changes that León had originally suggested, though they made no allusion to the embargo, and instead were justified as being a necessary response to misinformation circulating in the media. The key point of emphasis among the various items was that doctors would be 'applying' – that is, injecting – the drugs directly to the patients. Siurob had specifically promised the US to make this change in his conversations with Ambassador Daniels, later pointing him to the clarifications in the press to prove he had followed through.[43] However, the 'clarifications' provided little clarity and were, as US officials would note, contradictory. While one section suspended authorisations for narcotic prescribing by personal doctors, another noted that such authorisation would only be given to doctors under the condition that they apply the drugs directly to the patients, and another that this privilege would only be given 'discretionally' to highly trained physicians of impeccable character.[44]

On 26 March, the Ministry of Foreign Relations offered its own analysis of the situation, severely criticising the new Reglamento, arguing that the new system would 'surely make more difficult the control of the illicit traffic and almost impossible the effective coordination of the treatment procedures to which the addicts should be subjected'. This conclusion was based primarily on the notion that the addicts would be able to purchase the narcotics and then do with them as they pleased. The analysis went on to point out that the Reglamento certainly seemed to violate the spirit of the international treaties to which Mexico was party, though it conceded that this point was debatable. Finally, it noted that Mexico simply did not have the resources to experiment in these matters.[45] Meanwhile the State Department responded to Siurob's entreaty, emphasising that the US would agree to talks but only of a strictly informal nature, that the US law was clear and could only be amended by an act of

Congress, and thus if Mexico wanted the US to rescind the embargo, it would have to fully repeal the Reglamento through presidential decree.[46]

On 2 April, the General Health Council met again. It was at this meeting that Siurob began to take complete control of the Mexican response. Ironically, he did so by first declaring that he and the council shared equal responsibility for the Reglamento and its future, and to this end he wanted to share Ambassador Castillo Nájera's latest communications on the matter, including the US offer to hold informal talks. The members then debated whether Mexico should suspend the Reglamento in advance of talks with the US. The letter from Castillo Nájera was read several times for correct interpretation and, ultimately, Siurob was named as Salubridad's delegate to engage in informal talks with US officials. Siurob ended the discussion by encouraging the council to maintain solidarity and high spirits, without fear, and with the confidence that the ends being pursued were noble 'and in harmony with the principles dictated by the Revolution'.[47]

In the meantime, Salubridad worked up a response to the foreign ministry's analysis, noting that if, after considering the Department's latest response, the ministry still considered the Reglamento to be violating international treaties, then Mexico would retire the Reglamento and cancel the informal discussions with the US. Salubridad insisted that the main issue – that users would be prescribed narcotics that they could take home and possibly resell – was now moot, as the clarifications made in late March required that private doctors inject the patients directly. Those regulations, it should be noted, said nothing about how the dispensaries would handle the drugs, but reports in the press did make clear that this is also how the drugs were being provided there. Salubridad's response also specifically noted that only doctors would be allowed to pick up the drugs at the pharmacies, though the clarifications of March were not nearly so specific on this point.[48] The foreign ministry found all of this convincing and insisted that these specific guidelines be officially incorporated into the Reglamento. It also noted that if the US decided to bring the issue before the League, the ministry was ready, in concert with Salubridad, to strenuously defend the Mexican position in Geneva. Mexico was ready to fight and its diplomats now believed it had a case to make.[49]

In truth, there were many factors that suggested Mexico might have been able to salvage, if not the complete Reglamento, at least some version of it. There was, as we have seen, uncertainty on the US side that the Mexican system must necessarily be interpreted as 'illegitimate' narcotics use; there was Anslinger's indication that the Colombian programme was acceptable to the US; and there were potential allies at the League. As Mariana Flores Guevara has demonstrated, relatively strong support for a maintenance approach to drug addiction had been voiced by the Polish and Swiss League delegates during the 1939 meetings.[50] Furthermore, while the British, who were in the midst of a dispute with Mexico over the oil expropriation, were unlikely to support the Mexican system, the existence of a de facto maintenance programme in the United Kingdom might have been used by Mexico to justify its programme.[51] Indeed, a key element of effective Mexican diplomacy since the Revolution had been the practice of pointing to international examples to justify its own internal policies, however radical. Furthermore, since the outbreak of the Second World War, President Franklin Roosevelt had mandated that US diplomats find solutions to outstanding disputes with Mexico so as to shore up US–Mexican relations.[52]

Unfortunately, however, a thorough discussion at the League never occurred. In May, at the next session of the League's Opium Advisory Committee in Geneva, the Mexican representative was caught completely off guard by a formal complaint from Canada that the Mexican programme had gone into effect without there having been a full discussion of it. The Canadian delegate emphasised that, a year prior, Mexico had promised to delay implementation until that discussion had occurred. Incredibly, the new Mexican representative stated that he was unaware even that the Reglamento had become law. Clearly, another total breakdown in communication had occurred.[53]

In the meantime, Siurob had travelled to the US for the informal negotiations. On Saturday 4 May, he, along with the Harvard-trained José Zozaya of Mexico's Institute of Hygiene, met in Washington DC over lunch with Anslinger, along with Stuart Fuller and H. S. Bursley of the State Department, Assistant Surgeon General Lawrence Kolb, and J. W. Bulkley of the Customs Bureau. Despite having received encouragement to fight from the foreign ministry, Siurob began the discussions in conciliatory fashion, noting that the Reglamento had been developed prior to his tenure and thus he had dutifully carried out the policy, but, in his opinion, 'the matter should have been studied more thoroughly before such action was taken'.[54] He nonetheless went on to tout the loss of business that the traffickers had already suffered given that 700 addicts had been visiting the Mexico City dispensary. Anslinger then asked him who was supplying the other 3300 addicts that Siurob claimed existed, to which he could only reply that he assumed it was the traffickers. Siurob then emphasised that the regulations had been changed so that addicts could not be prescribed drugs by doctors, but were instead required to appear at the dispensaries for their injections. He also contended, as Salazar had done on many occasions, that the punitive methods of the US clearly didn't work. To make this argument he cited the existence of roughly 300,000 addicts in New York City. Kolb and Anslinger challenged this, arguing that there weren't that many addicts in the whole country and asked where he'd gotten his statistics. Siurob said it was a journal but he couldn't remember the title.[55] Anslinger then presented Siurob with a League of Nations document the US had written up on its experience with narcotics clinics, as well as a memorandum produced by the Federal Bureau of Narcotics on the same subject, and the analysis of the legal situation done by the Treasury Department that had served as the foundation for the US embargo. The US representatives were frustrated that Siurob had never seen the League document though it had been forwarded to Mexico. The Americans urged Zozaya, who they saw as favourable to the US point of view, and who also spoke English well, to help Siurob read these documents over the weekend.

On the 7th of May the same group, minus Kolb, convened at Fuller's office in the State Department. According to the US minutes, Zozaya and Siurob explained that they had read the documents and had become convinced that 'the United States is taking the right course; that the Mexican regulations were entirely wrong'. Siurob promised to take up the matter with Cárdenas and recommend that the Reglamento be suspended immediately. 'This, he stated, would be tantamount to abandoning the regulations, or having them become obsolete. They do not wish to give any notice to the press or to make any formal statement, but merely to surrender quietly in order not to give critics anything to ridicule, particularly because there is a presidential campaign in progress in Mexico and if the public were to get the idea that this action is taken to cooperate with the United States, they stated the cry would be "the United States is dictating again."' In response, Anslinger agreed to lift the US embargo once the Reglamento was officially rescinded. Tellingly, in the original minutes, the word 'surrender' was used, but then crossed out by Bursley who replaced it with the phrase 'change the situation'. This was done, Bursley explained, in order to 'make the record more useful in case we ever want [to] show [it] to any Mexican official'.⁵⁶ On 6 June, Siurob gave Cárdenas his recommendation and the President signed the order.

Four days later, Siurob presented the General Health Council with a fait accompli, despite his earlier insistence in the midst of the crisis that he and the council had equal responsibility in the matter. In that final meeting on the subject, Siurob suddenly changed his tone on the results of the Reglamento. Now he claimed, in contrast to what he had initially argued before Anslinger, that the new Reglamento had been a failure – that while the addicts came to the dispensary, so did the traffickers, and rather than the users reducing their regular dose, they were increasing it. Where this new information came from is not clear. He continued: 'it has been observed that the only approach that bears optimal fruit is the relegation of the addicts in farms adequate for the purpose; and due to the present economic circumstances and the global situation caused by the European war, it is impossible to put this into practice, and taking into account these factors and that the treatment of addicts is inadequate and negative, and further the experience gained by the American Government, and having the clear authority in these matters given by both the Council and the President of the Republic, and without forgetting the decreed suspension of narcotics imports to Mexico', he 'thought it convenient' to have the President suspend the Reglamento. He then asked for the Council's approval of the decision that had already been made. He went on to explain that the decree was simple and should 'satisfy public opinion', by citing the European war and the consequent shortage of narcotics as the reason for the suspension. Here the State Department's Herbert Bursely, who was clearly in tune with Mexican sensibilities on these matters, was again key, for it was he who had suggested that Mexico cite the war as the reason for rescinding the policy.⁵⁷ León backed Siurob's decision, noting that the Reglamento had 'fueled proselytism, the number of addicts and traffickers … and that the scarcity of drugs is notable and that the Department exhausted its reserves having to acquire the drugs from merchants who have raised the price'. Siurob added that the issue was complicated and would have to be taken up by the League of Nations, while Alcázar noted that drug addicts could not definitively be cured. That was the extent of the debate, and the measure was passed. On 3 July, Cárdenas' order, citing the problems created by the war in Europe, was published in the *Diario Oficial*, and the Reglamento was officially dead.⁵⁸

***

The Second World War mostly benefitted Mexico. Its onset greatly aided the successful expropriation of the oil industry, international wartime demand helped jumpstart Mexico's economy, and the conflict helped repair strained US–Mexican relations. Thanks also in part to the war, Franklin Roosevelt and other pro-Mexico officials in the US became some of Mexico's greatest allies during these years.⁵⁹ But with respect to the new Reglamento Federal de Toxicomanías, wartime contraction of the global narcotics market also provided leverage for Harry Anslinger and the other US officials who favoured a narrow definition of 'medical and legitimate' narcotic use. This story thus undoubtedly remains, at least in part, one of power and timing.⁶⁰

However, Mexican diplomacy during this crisis, in contrast to other significant episodes of the era, left much to be desired. It may have been, as others have argued, that, in comparison to major questions like the oil expropriation, the issue of drug addiction was simply too inconsequential for Mexico to dedicate much political capital to.⁶¹ However, this close examination of the decision-making process suggests that the course of events on the Mexican side was driven more by disorganisation and breakdowns in communication than by rational analysis. Of course, we might still attribute this to the issue's relative low standing. Cárdenas certainly appears to have had little interest in the problem, and provided virtually no input on how it should be resolved. Thus, it was left to lower level bureaucrats, principally Siurob, to handle the diplomacy with some aid from the foreign relations bureaucracy. And it was there, between the Ministry of Foreign Relations and Salubridad, that the most significant breakdowns occurred and where, as a result, various chances to possibly salvage the policy were lost.

Disclosure statement

No potential conflict of interest was reported by the author.

Acknowledgements

Funding for this research was provided by the Charles Phelps Taft Research Center (University of Cincinnati), the David Rockefeller Center for Latin American Studies (Harvard University), and the Social Science Research Council's 'Drugs, Security, and Democracy' program. My thanks also to Maziyar Ghiabi for organising this special issue, and to the anonymous readers for their insightful comments.

Notes

1. Scholars today are somewhat less convinced that it was quite the triumph it is often assumed to have been. See Maurer, "Empire Struck Back." See also Meyer, *Mexico and the United States*; Brown and Knight, *Mexican Petroleum Industry*.
2. Advisory Committee on Traffic in Opium and Other Dangerous Drugs, "Mexican Draft Regulations for the Treatment of Addicts," 4.
3. Salazar Viniegra, Leopoldo. 1945. "Opio y política: Historia de una humiliación."[Opium and Politics: History of a Humiliation.] *Excelsior* (Mexico City), December 19. My thanks to Mariana Flores Guevara for providing me with a copy of this article.
4. See, for example, Meyer, Lorenzo. "Vivir con una soberanía relativa," [Living with a Relative Sovereignty] Terra, September. 26, 2013. https://noticias.terra.com.mx/mexico/lorenzo-meyer-vivir-con-una-soberania-relativa,c4996ea013a51410VgnVCM10000098cceb0aRCRD.html (accessed May 4, 2017); Katia D'Artigues, "El Presidente que legalizó las drogas," *El Universal*, June 11, 2015, http://www.eluniversal.com.mx/entrada-de-opinion/columna/katia-dartigues/nacion/politica/2015/11/6/el-presidente-que-legalizo-las (accessed May 4, 2017); "De cuando en México las drogas fueron legales, https://lareddeartemisa.wordpress.com/2011/06/25/de-cuando-en-mexico-las-drogas-fueron-legales/ (accessed May 4, 2017); Nancy Cázares, "Cuando el 'Tata' Cárdenas legalizó las drogas,'" *La Izquierda Diario*, May 6, 2016, http://desa.laizquierdadiario.com/Cuando-el-Tata-Cardenas-legalizo-las-drogas (accessed May 4, 2017).

5. Walker, *Drug Control in the Americas*, 122–3; Astorga, *Drogas sin fronteras*, 202–27; Flores Guevara, "La alternativa mexicana"; Pérez Montfort, *Tolerancia y prohibición*, 282–307; Enciso, "Los fracasos del chantaje," 71–3.
6. Salazar Viniegra, Leopoldo. 1945. "Opio y política: Historia de una humiliación."[Opium and Politics: History of a Humiliation.] *Excelsior* (Mexico City), December 19.
7. For an overview, see Gootenberg and Campos, "Toward a New Drug History."
8. For the argument that during the Cárdenas presidency Mexican policymakers were 'better skilled in international negotiations, more realistic in the evaluation of historical contexts, and more creative in situations of crisis than their European and US counterparts', see Schuler, *Mexico Between Hitler and Roosevelt*, 1. Dwyer, *Agrarian Dispute*, similarly argues that Mexican diplomats skilfully employed 'weapons of the weak' to outmanoeuvre their US counterparts, especially during the mid-1930s agrarian crisis. For other examples of skilled Mexican diplomacy, see Hall, *Oil, Banks, and Politics*, especially 140–4.
9. Flores Guevara, "La alternativa mexicana," 67–72.
10. For the classroom morphine experiment, see the undated transcript in Manicomio General, Expedientes de Personal, Legajo 2, Expediente 3, Archivo Histórico de la Secretaría de Salubridad y Asistencia (hereafter, MG, EP, Exp. 2, Leg. 3, AHSSA); for the target practice, see the correspondence beginning August 12, 1938, in the same file; on his grading, see Flores Guevara, "La alternativa mexicana," 73; on the experiments with marijuana see Astorga, *Drogas sin fronteras*, 205–211.
11. "El problema comercial de las drogas," *El Nacional*, July 6, 1938, p. 1.
12. Salazar Viniegra, "Exposición de motivos."
13. Campos, *Home Grown*.
14. Memcon with Dr Salazar Viniegra, May 27, 1939; File: Mexico, Dr Salazar Viniegra; Subject Files of the Bureau of Narcotics and Dangerous Drugs, 1916–1970; Records of the Drug Enforcement Administration, Record Group 170, National Archives at College Park, College Park, MD (hereafter simply "Mex-LSV, NARA"); Provisional Minutes … June 2, 1939; Mex-LSV, NARA.
15. Salazar Viniegra, "Exposición de motivos," 558.
16. Meeting minutes numbered 24–30, between October 25 and December 20, 1938, Consejo de Salubridad General, Actas de Sesión, Libros, 1 (hereafter: CSG/AS/Lbs/1), AHSSA.
17. Stewart to the Secretary of State, March 22, 1939; Mex-LSV, NARA.
18. "Se acusa al Dr. Salazar Viniegra de dar mariguana a los locos de la Castañeda" Excelsior, Nov. 1, 1938; "Médicos académicos fumaron 'Dna. Juanita," El Universal, Oct. 22, 1938; "La mariguana sí es dañosa," El Universal, Oct. 24, 1938.
19. For example, compare: Creighton to the Commissioner of Customs on June 15, 1938, and then on February 21, 1939, along with Stewart to the Secretary of State, December 12, 1938, all three in Mex-LSV, NARA.
20. Memcon with Dr Salazar-Viniegra, May 27, 1939; Mex-LSV, NARA. The other Mexican official was possibly Manuel Tello, the official Mexican representative to the League.
21. Provisional Minutes … June 2, 1939; Mex-LSV, NARA.
22. Salazar Viniegra, Leopoldo. 1945. "Opio y política: Historia de una humiliación."[Opium and Politics: History of a Humiliation.] *Excelsior* (Mexico City), December 19.
23. Flores Guevara, "La alternativa mexicana," 134–8. By May of 1938 the State Department was counselling Treasury to back off and allow events to take their own course in Mexico. Gorman to Creighton, May 17, 1938; Mex-LSV, NARA.
24. For the final council deliberations on the programme, see Actas de Sesión #61–62, November 2–3,1939, CSG/AS/Lbs/1, AHSSA. Cárdenas signed on January 5, 1940. http://www.dof.gob.mx/nota_to_imagen_fs.php?cod_diario=191983&pagina=5&seccion=1 (accessed May 7, 2017).
25. Castillo Nájera to SRE, February 9, 1940, III-2398–6, Archivo Histórico Diplomático de la Secretaría de Relaciones Exteriores, México City (hereafter, SRE).
26. Siurob to SRE, March 14, 1940, III-2398–6, SRE. For the Secretariat's decidedly weak explanation, see, in the same file, Ernesto Hidalgo to Siurob, March 15, 1940.

27. Anslinger to F. Thornton, February 3, 1940; File: Mexico, New Regulations; Bureau of Narcotics and Dangerous Drugs; Record Group 170; National Archives and Records Administration, College Park, MD (hereafter Mex-New Regs, NARA).
28. Anslinger note, dated February 1, attached to Daniels to Sec. of State, January 31, 1940, Mex-New Regs, NARA; Anslinger to Shamhart, February 15, 1940, Mex-New Regs, NARA.
29. Sáenz Rovner, "Prehistoria del narcotráfico en Colombia," 74–5.
30. Note from Treasury, February 27, 1940; Mex-New Regs, NARA.
    Creighton to the Commissioner of Customs, February 28, 1940; Mex-New Regs, NARA; Memcon by Robert G. McGregor, Jr., February 29, 1940, Mex-New Regs, NARA.
31. Creighton to 'Ed' [Shamhart], March 5, 1940; Mex-New Regs, NARA.
32. Acta de Sesión #9, March 12, 1940, CSG/AS/Lbs/2, AHSSA.
33. Ibid.
34. However, Siurob appears to have already been aware of the delay, for he immediately complained about it to foreign relations officials. Siurob to SRE, March 14, 1940, III-2398–6, SRE.
35. The meeting Minutes refer to 'Article 8' of the Convention but it was clearly Article 14 that was being referred to; http://biblio-archive.unog.ch/Dateien/CouncilMSD/C-191-M-136-1937-XI_EN.pdf (accessed May 7, 2017).
36. Anslinger to Fuller, April 6, 1940; Mex-New Regs, NARA.
37. Acta de Sesión #10, March 14, 1940, CSG/AS/Lbs/2, AHSSA.
38. Ibid.
39. Ibid.
40. Siurob to SRE, March 14, 1940, III-2398–6, SRE; Castillo Nájera to SRE, March 19, 1940, III-2398–6, SRE.
41. Siurob to Parran, March 19, 1940; Mex-New Regs, NARA.
42. From Gallardo Moreno to Siurob, March 21, 1940, Ramo Presidentes-Lázaro Cárdenas, Gal. 3, Exp. 422/3; AGN, Mexico City; Anslinger to Maxon, March 21, 1940; Mex-New Regs, NARA. Walker, *Drug Control in the Americas*, 129–30.
43. Siurob to Daniels, March 23, 1940; Mex-New Res, NARA. On the US reading of the contradictions, see documents appended to Anslinger to Fuller, April 6, 1940; Mex-New Regs, NARA.
44. "Puntos fundamentales para la aplicación Legal del nuevo Reglamento de Toxicomanías, *El Nacional* (Mexico D.F.), March 22, 1940, Section 1, 1–2.
45. "El Reglamento Federal de Toxicómanos … ," March 26, 1940, III-2398–6, SRE.
46. Castillo Nájera to Siurob, March 30, 1940, III-2398–6, SRE.
47. Acta de Sesión #12, April 2, 1940, CSG/AS/Lbs/2, AHSSA.
48. Irigoyen to Hay, April 16, 1940, III-2398–6, SRE. For the various press reports along with a translation of the regulations, see Stewart to the Secretary of State, April 2, 1940, Mex-New Regs, NARA.
49. "Sugestiones de la Secretaría … ," April 20, 1940, III-2398–6, SRE.
50. Flores Guevara, "La alternativa mexicana," 125–33.
51. On the British system see Lindesmith, "British System of Narcotics Control"; Seddon, "Women, Harm Reduction and History."
52. Schuler, *Between Hitler and Roosevelt*, 132, 199. For another example of deft use of foreign examples to justify Mexican policies, see Hall, *Oil, Banks, and Politics*, 140–4.
53. The delegates' names are absent from the minutes. Advisory Committee on Traffic in Opium and Other Dangerous Drugs, "Report to the Council," 6.
54. "Memcon of discussions … ," May 4 and 7, 1940; Mex-New Regs, NARA.
55. On the Federal Bureau of Narcotics routinely underestimating addict numbers in the US, see Courtwright, *Dark Paradise*, 110–23.
56. "Memcon of discussions … ," May 4 and 7, 1940; Mex-New Regs, NARA.
57. Walker, *Drug Control in the Americas*, 130.
58. Acta de Sesión #16, June 11, 1940, CSG/AS/Lbs/2, AHSSA; "Decreto que suspende…" *Diario Oficial*, XVVI, No. 3 (July 3, 1940).
59. Schuler, *Mexico Between Hitler and Roosevelt*, 200–1; 205–7.

60. William B. McAllister demonstrates that Anslinger utilised leverage gained from war shortages for various purposes during these years, though he also shows that the British sometimes undermined Anslinger's efforts by exporting drugs to Latin America in competition with the US. See his *Drug Diplomacy in the Twentieth Century*, 144–9. On wartime leverage see also Reiss, *We Sell Drugs*.
61. Flores Guevara, "La alternative mexicana," 156.

Bibliography

Advisory Committee on Traffic in Opium and Other Dangerous Drugs. "Report to the Council on the Work of the Twenty-Fifth Session, Held at Geneva from May 13th to 17th, 1940." *Opium and Other Dangerous Drugs* 11, no. 3 (1940): 6.

Advisory Committee on Traffic in Opium and Other Dangerous Drugs. "Mexican Draft Regulations for the Treatment of Addicts." *Opium and Other Dangerous Drugs* 11, no. 4: 3–4.

Astorga, Luis *Drogas sin fronteras*. México, D.F.: Grijalbo, 2003.

Brown, Jonathan C., and Alan Knight, eds. *The Mexican Petroleum Industry in the Twentieth Century*. Symposia on Latin America Series. Austin: University of Texas Press, 1992.

Campos, Isaac *Home Grown: Marijuana and the Origins of Mexico's War on Drugs*. Chapel Hill: The University of North Carolina Press, 2012.

Courtwright, David T. *Dark Paradise: Opiate Addiction in America Before 1940*. Cambridge, MA: Harvard University Press, 2001.

Dwyer, John Joseph *The Agrarian Dispute: The Expropriation of American-Owned Rural Land in Postrevolutionary Mexico*. Durham: Duke University Press, 2008.

Enciso, Froylán. "Los fracasos del chantaje. Régimen de prohibición de drogas y narcotráfico." [The Failures of Extortion. Drug and Drug Trafficking Prohibition Regimes.] In *Seguridad nacional y seguridad interior* [Interior and National Security], edited by Arturo Alvarado and Mónica Serrano, 61–104. Vol 15 of Los grandes problemas de México [The Great Problems of Mexico]. México, D.F.: El Colegio de México, 2010.

Flores Guevara, Mariana. "La alternativa mexicana al marco internacional de prohibición de drogas durante el cardenismo." [The Mexican Alternative to the International Framework of Drug Prohibition During the Cárdenas Years.] Bachelor's thesis, El Colegio de México, 2013.

Gootenberg, Paul, and Isaac Campos. "Toward a New Drug History of Latin America: A Research Frontier at the Center of Debates." *Hispanic American Historical Review* 95, no. 1 (2015): 1–35.

Hall, Linda B. *Oil, Banks, and Politics: The United States and Postrevolutionary Mexico, 1917–1924*. Austin: University of Texas Press, 1995.

Lindesmith, Alfred R. "The British System of Narcotics Control." *Law and Contemporary Politics* 22, no. 1 (1957): 138–154.

Maurer, Noel. "The Empire Struck Back: Sanctions and Compensation in the Mexican Oil Expropriation of 1938." *The Journal of Economic History* 71, no. 3 (2011): 590–615.

McAllister, William B. *Drug Diplomacy in the Twentieth Century*. London: Routledge, 2000.

Meyer, Lorenzo. *Mexico and the United States in the Oil Controversy, 1917–1942*. Austin: University of Texas Press, 1977.

Pérez Montfort, Ricardo. *Tolerancia y prohibición: Aproximaciones a la historia social y cultural de las drogas en México*. [Tolerance and Prohibition: Approximations to the Social and Cultural History of Drugs in Mexico]. México: Penguin Random House, 2016.

Reiss, Suzanna. *We Sell Drugs: The Alchemy of US Empire*. Oakland, CA: University of California, 2014.

Sáenz Rovner, Eduardo. "La prehistoria del narcotráfico en Colombia: Serie documental: desde la Gran Depresión hasta la Revolución Cubana." [The Prehistory of Narcotrafficking in Colombia: Documentary Series: From the Great Depression Until the Cuban Revolution.] *Innovar: Revista de ciencias administrativas y sociales* 8 (1996): 65–92.

Salazar Viniegra, Leopoldo. "Exposición de motivos para el nuevo Reglamento Federal de Toxicomanías." [Exposition of Motives for the New Federal Drug Addiction Regulation.] *Criminalia* 5, no. 9 (May 10, 1939): 555–560.

Schuler, Freidrich E. *Mexico between Hitler and Roosevelt: Mexican Foreign Relations in the Age of Lázaro Cárdenas, 1934–1940*. Albuquerque, NM: University of New Mexico Press, 1998.

Seddon, Toby. "Women, Harm Reduction and History: Gender Perspectives on the Emergence of the 'British System' of Drug Control." *International Journal of Drug Policy* 19, no. 2 (2008): 99–105.

Walker III, William O. *Drug Control in the Americas*. Revised ed. Albuquerque, NM: University of New Mexico Press, 1989.

Drugs of choice, drugs of change: Egyptian consumption habits since the 1920s

Philip Robins

ABSTRACT
Much has been written and published about the 25 January 2011 Egyptian revolution from the perspective of contemporary history and political science. Much less attention has focused on social policy. I am unaware of any scholarly material that has dealt with illicit drugs during the critical 2011–2016 period, yet increasing drugs consumption provided a social backdrop to the events of that period. This paper identifies historical trends in illicit drugs consumption over the course of the last century to the beginning of the Arab Spring. During much of this period hashish was the drug of choice. This paper argues that drug consumption was on the rise in Egypt well before the downfall of President Husni Mubarak in February 2011, but that it has grown markedly since the ousting of the former president. It will ask which have been and are the drugs of choice in contemporary Egypt. It will further ask how this composition has changed and why, giving special focus to the relatively new mass, opioid drug, Tramadol.

Introduction

Drugs have regularly featured in the social profile of consumption and leisure in modern Egypt, at least when consumers have been able to afford them. At certain times, such as in the 1920s and 1930s, the era of Egypt's 'white drugs' epidemic, the profile of the drugs in question have included heroin and even cocaine.[1] Until the approach of the millennium, however, there was arguably something close to a consensus that Egypt's drug of choice was hashish. As one fictional drugs commentator put it recently, hashish is not a drug, 'it's chocolate, the elixir of life'.[2]

Just because this has been the profile of drug use in the past – the white drugs era had effectively passed some eight decades ago – does not mean that such a situation will simply reproduce itself indefinitely. The marijuana-style drug called bango has emerged as a significant drug of choice over the last two decades, especially. This trend has also surfaced, notably in the Sinai Peninsula and the east of the country, where the authority of the state is often contested. There is strong and recurrent anecdotal evidence that bango has been grown and trafficked in the eastern governorates of Egypt. For example, *Al Masry al Youm*, one of Egypt's leading newspapers, published in January 2012 a short article reporting that four tonnes of bango had been caught being smuggled from the Sinai in a truck.[3] For a second example, a four line report in the same paper a month later refers to half a ton of bango being apprehended east of Ismailiyya, the drugs being caught in a car on the way to Sinai.[4] Egypt also developed something of a fondness for synthetic drugs, notably in the 1980s and the 1990s. It was against this background of a discernible rise in drug taking across society that a relatively little-known substance emerged rapidly to transform the market. This was a manufactured opioid, marketed under the commercial name of Tramadol. An analgesic, this has become nothing less than the 'epidemic drug' of the anti-Mubarak revolutionary period.

This paper is concerned to explore the pattern and composition of drug taking in Egypt, before, during and immediately after the period of revolutionary turmoil under President Mubarak, here defined as spanning the period between the run-up to the 25 January 2011 revolution and the restoration of a military dominated regime with the election to the presidency of Abdul Fatah al-Sisi in May 2014. In doing so, it will contextualise Egypt's experiences by introducing drug taking in historical perspective. It will make judgements about trends in the consumption of drugs, as well as when certain drugs were on the rise and others were on the wane, and explain why. The second part of the paper will focus on the transformatory impact of Tramadol. Drawing on the work of Egyptian anti-drugs epidemiologist, Professor Emad Hamdi of Cairo University, it will seek to explain the origins, impact and possible consequences of Tramadol.[5] This paper primarily uses a qualitative as opposed to a quantitative method, though it does make use of quantitative data available, primarily through the work of Professor Hamdi and his Cairo-based medical research team. The material for this paper was assembled during three research trips to Egypt during the revolutionary period of 2011–2012, with a fourth research visit taking place in July 2016. A total of 31 or more in-depth interviews were conducted with health service and policy professionals, and law enforcement personnel. In addition to these interviews, two focus groups of approximately two hours duration for each were also convened in order to test the indicative nature of the material.

Illicit drugs consumption in modern Egypt

Much of Egypt's engagement with illegal drugs has comprised an uneasy, fluctuating relationship between informal markets and formal state bodies. This has taken place against the strong yet unclear legacy of monarchical times. Latterly, there has been the spectre of a looming international control regime becoming fitfully more salient from the earliest part of the twentieth century. In many ways, the binary tensions involving the two domains continue today.

Cairo first began to address the drugs issue in 1879, with its attempt to control the public circulation of drugs. The cultivation of hashish in Egypt was the subject of a special law of March 1884. This was followed by the adoption of a law to proscribe the sale of hashish in the coffee houses of Cairo in 1895. The only existing law in Egypt which touched the question of drug trafficking was contained within the decree of 15 September 1904, which is most concerned with the regulation of pharmacies. No special mention is made in that law about types of drugs, such as cocaine, morphine and opium.

The litany above suggests that the legal infrastructure for dealing with drugs-related issues in Egypt was ragged and inconsistent to say the least. For example, the cultivation of opium poppy was prohibited in October 1918, but permitted again in 1920.[6] Otherwise, what Pino Arlacchi, former Director-General of a specialist UN agency on drugs and crime, has called an 'open availability model' typified the international drugs market Egypt included, that is to say a period of largely ineffectual control.[7]

Pressures on Egypt to intensify its engagement with the emerging multilateral drug regulatory regime received a twin boost in the 1920s. The post First World War period witnessed the influx of white drugs into Egypt at largely affordable prices. At the same time, Cairo, as with other emerging administrations in the developing world, was obliged to respond to the increasingly intrusive multilateral framework of drugs control contained within the League of Nations. So, for example, Egypt's new anti-narcotics decrees made both trafficking and the possession of drugs a criminal offence.[8]

Egypt's first anti-narcotics law was published in December 1927; it established a state body for the elimination of illicit drugs. Since then, Egypt has continued upon a spasmodic journey in the direction of the institutionalisation of anti-drugs activities. Egypt's current specialist anti-drugs police, the Anti-Narcotics General Administration (ANGA), was set up in 1976 according to Deputy Director-General, Tareq Ismael.[9] It now possesses an extensive framework comprising 11 separate departments.[10]

According to this drugs regime-in-the-making, there was no multilateral framework by which the early application of a nascent international law could be applied, even at a purely symbolic level.[11] By contrast, countries could both market and sell their drugs externally, and regulate the sale and distribution of their drugs locally. The popularity of drugs as a consumer good and as a health product ideally suited for self-medication meant that they could become a significant export market.

Over time, there were mixed feelings at the existence and operation of the open availability model. The US increasingly wanted to regulate global conduct in relation to drugs. By contrast, much of the rest of the world, especially those states involved in the cultivation of significant volumes of drugs, were content with the preceding arrangements. It was the US, as the world's emerging superpower, with a penchant for a formal legalism in international as well as its national affairs, which won the day.

The old model was superseded by the so-called 'penal control model', which, as the name suggests, was an approach more markedly interventionist and punitive than before. This philosophy would soon result in a process of institution building, in order to prompt and then expand this type of restrictive norm diffusion. Though nominally multilateral in approach, in reality the building of an international regime was largely left to the handful of global powers of the day, and their bureaucratic specialists, led by the US. By 1931 a raft of multilateralism had resulted.[12] Little of it had been driven by or was especially pertinent to contemporary Egypt.

Egypt and its drugs of choice[13]

Incremental criminalisation

As the penal control model gained greater traction in the field of multilateral interaction in general, and relations between Egypt and the US in particular, one might have expected greater bilateral tensions to begin to stoke up. This was largely not to be the case, however, at least not initially. The Egyptian side managed the potential policy dissonance between them over such matters by keeping a discrete distance. The widespread and unregulated buying and selling of drugs was discontinued. Instead, there was a tacit understanding that such trade should be largely confined to one main part of Cairo, the poorer neighbourhood of El-Batniyyah,[14] which had enjoyed an independent character since the city of Cairo was in its infancy. The material on El-Batniyyah is derived from participant observation, together with selected interviews with: a shopkeeper, whose father had run a bookshop in the drugs heyday; a group of manual workers shovelling sand at the entrance to a club; a man introduced as 'the man who really knows', whose parents had sold drugs in the area, but who had been imprisoned in the wake of the 1980 and subsequent a taxi driver plying the streets to and from the district; a member of the upper middle class, who used to buy hashish in the district.

Curiously, the area was located in a compact neighbourhood, just up the hill from the historic Islamic centre of Al-Azhar University. There were two entry points. The drugs, which included hashish, heroin and others, were sold on trestle tables, largely in the open. Most of the time the authorities left the drugs trade well alone. Occasionally, the area was visited by the police, often for purposes of their own consumption. Even when law enforcement bodies arrived with a less benign agenda little appeared actually to change, or at least no more than temporarily. Sometimes, the drugs sellers were dispersed in a token attempt to clear up an area of open criminality. This tended to be perfunctory at best. Typically, such drug peddlers would escape with their merchandise on mopeds, allowing them to navigate the narrow, winding streets with greater success than their pursuers. They would soon return to take up their activities as before. Alternatively, dealers would not even bother with such a charade. Those who felt a particular entitlement simply stood their ground and attempted to intimidate the police officers and other law enforcement members in their midst.

Eventually, however, the situation became unsustainable. US President Richard Nixon's 'War on Drugs' raised the issue to a much higher bilateral priority for the US than had hitherto been the case. Saving American citizens from drugs cultivated abroad, and especially in the Middle East, became a central plank of American foreign policy in the 1970s and 1980s. With that in mind, the administration of President Jimmy Carter raised the issue more robustly with the Egyptian government. Initially, the Egyptian response was limited. After all, wasn't President Anwar Sadat, Egypt's great peace-maker, supposed to have smoked hash, and even chewed opium while delivering speeches? Moreover, Anwar Sadat's brother, Ismat, was head of the port of Alexandria, and hence able to control much of the trafficking of Egyptian contraband, drugs included.[15]

Eventually, the Americans prevailed, at least at an official level. From the early- to mid-1980s, access to El-Batniyyah was effectively closed to routine drug trading, according to one Egyptian famer who used to buy hashish in the area.[16] A dirty wasteland was temporarily left behind. The land covered roughly a mile square. The Agha Khan Foundation, a wealthy INGO based in the Islamic World, would help the cause of the Egyptian state by bearing some of the economic cost of subsequently redeveloping the area. In reality, the choking off of hashish production simply inflated demand for bango. El-Batniyyah's edgy aura continued for a brief period, for example, through the making and transmission of a feature film and a television drama series about the neighbourhood. The film in particular was claimed to be an accurate portrayal of a neighbourhood drugs economy in practice. However, that only proved to be a temporary respite for the drugs district of El-Batniyyah. Now, some two decades later, all that remains is narco-nostalgia.

Pre-Arab Spring drugs landscape

Bango

Bango has strong roots in Egyptian society and its neighbouring countries, such as Sudan. It has increasingly become the drug of choice or something comparable in Egypt for a mixed social grouping of intellectuals, students and members of the working class. It is primarily sold within the 50–100 gram weight range, but with marked fluctuations within these weight ranges reported. Bango is often cultivated by Bedouin tribes, for their own use and for exporting, especially in the east of Egypt. Bango has been placed in Category A (*alif*) in terms of the seriousness of illegal drug consumption, the same level as hashish. One of the great advantages of bango is the difficulty of adulterating the drug compared to cocaine, heroin and even hashish. The daily cost of consumption is around £E30–50 for both bango and hashish. See Table 1 for recent comparative prices for Bango and other drugs.

Part of the bango harvest is transported to the Gaza Strip, together with other high return contraband goods like small arms and drugs such as heroin. Prior to the summer 2014 Gaza war between Israel and the Palestinians, bango was trafficked to Israel via the extensive tunnel network, constructed informally by Palestinian criminals-cum-entrepreneurs. The Egyptian authorities tried to eradicate these tunnels through the use of water bombs. When this failed, they returned to the use of conventional ordinance.[17] It is unclear to what extent Israeli efforts to destroy the tunnels after July 2013 have succeeded in ending this double contraband of drugs and arms.

Hashish

There is a debate in Egypt about the dangers associated with hashish. There are broadly three positions held. Some maintain that hashish should not be viewed as an addictive drug, but one that has been part of the socio-cultural fabric of the country for as long as anyone can remember. As such, hashish should not be regarded as a drug at all, but as a culturally embedded substance and key part of an associated sub-culture, comparable to the warm beer of legend, consumed in England with an eye to the country's glorious past. In regional terms, this would make hashish analogous to the regular consumption of qat in countries such as Yemen, even more so now that the cloak of illegality has been extended to this narcotic. This view would be adamant in not seeing hashish as an addictive substance, and hence not as a gateway drug, leading to the possible consumption of other, more dangerous, substances. Those who fret about the risks of the consumption of hashish would tend to be

Table 1. Price of illegal drugs in Egypt, 1995–2012.

Drug Type:	Bango	Cocaine	Hashish	Heroin
Year				
1995	N/A	N/A	N/A	US$100/gram
2010	N/A	N/A	N/A	US$12.5–35/gram
2011	US$2.8/gram	US$160/gram	N/A	US$25/gram
2012	US$2.2/gram	N/A	US$15/gram	US$21/gram

Sources: Compiled by the author from separate sources, including Faisal Hegarzi, UNDOC (Interview with author, 30 October 2011).
Medhat Maher Kamel, Shubra Drop-In Centre (Interview with author, 7 February 2012).

dismissed by this tendency as being excessively 'bourgeois' according to Ahmed Fawzi, Secretary-General of the Social Democratic Party.[18]

A second view would be to see hashish, if not as addictive, then certainly as habit forming, a view held by Dr. Azmi Munir, Health spokesman for Free Egyptians Party, Salam Hospital, Muhandissin, Cairo.[19] It may be admitted that the 'odd smoke' might not do the consumer any harm. However, if hashish consumption really is a component of Egyptian national culture, as some of its proponents zestfully believe, then a life time's worth of consumption may well result in the exaggeration of some undesirable health and social traits prevalent in Egypt, such as lethargy and incoherence. This point of view underlines the ambiguity of the 'hash as culture camp'.

A third category of analysis would be to see hashish as altogether more pernicious. Hashish consumption would risk much more than a simple dalliance with a soft drug. It could result in a progression to drug addiction. This would be the traditional 'hash as gateway' approach, which would be wary of the drug from the outset.

Heroin

As with cocaine, Egypt had a major problem of addiction and of lethargy with heroin consumption in the 1920s and 1930s. While Egypt largely divested itself of the former, the latter proved more difficult to dislodge. By 2012, it was possible for the specialist NGO community to conclude that 'heroin is really big in Egypt'.[20] In the case of heroin, consumption in Egypt had rocketed not merely during the period of the revolution, but commencing beforehand. For instance, Essam Youssef's infamous reality novel entitled *A Quarter of a Gram* was first published in 2008 (English edition 2009),[21] crucially impacting Egypt before the first stirrings of the protests that would bring down Husni Mubarak. The book told the story of a group of upper middle class Egyptian university students, who go on an orgy of heroin-fuelled drug taking to alleviate their lives of boredom and worthlessness.

The heroin is alleged by the UN to come from Turkey according to Faisal Higazi of the UNODC in Cairo,[22] and before that Afghanistan. The Ministry of Health in Egypt has argued against the establishment of a methadone programme to help alleviate the impact of the drug. The primary argument against such a policy is that Egypt does not have the pharmaceutical system capable of administering such a programme and it will therefore run the risk of leaking onto the open market, with even larger numbers becoming drug dependent. This was the concern raised by Dr Nasser Loza of Behman Hospital, in Hilwan.[23]

Changes in patterns of drug consumption

There can be little doubt that drug consumption rose significantly during the period of the anti-Mubarak ouster and its immediate aftermath. This is certainly the overall conclusion of the managing-director of the addiction unit at the Ministry of Health, Dr Tamer al-Amroushy. This was established by extensive, evidence-led research, which covered not only Cairo, but some of the country's other governorates as well. Led by Professor Emed Hamdi, renowned Egyptian psychiatric physician, and funded by the Ministry of Health, 98,000 Egyptians were interviewed about their substance consumption habits over a five-year period. Of this figure, some 39,000 polled were resident in Cairo. The sample was as widely drawn as was feasible, with people of various ages, backgrounds and neighbourhoods being included, and with the survey conducted over two separate periods of time. Interviews were conducted with Cairenes in designated places, such as schools and clinics. If anything, the nature of the sample may have encouraged a higher level of conservatism in its responses, as people presumably would have displayed a reluctance to be interviewed, especially in close proximity to their peers.

Nevertheless, the polling turned up several unexpected conclusions. The main headline finding was that the prevalence of substance consumption in Cairo (that is including alcohol, but not tobacco) has achieved record levels, and hence was much higher than expected. In Egypt, the consumption of alcohol is not highly significant relative to other forms: in many governorates alcohol such as beer is not served, even though hashish may be. In short-hand cultural terms it is often said that in the Middle East alcohol is known as the drug of the infidel, while hashish is known as the drug of the Muslims.

In total, 5–7% of drug-takers were judged to be regular 'abusers' to the point of showing signs of having an addiction. This equates to 1–1.4 million members of the population. Professor Hamdi made it very clear that this figure did not apply to casual drugs use. When casual use is factored in, the rate rises sharply to 25–30% of the total: almost one-third of the adult population of Cairo is a regular consumer of drugs. Of this figure for casual use, 90% were identified as consumers of hashish, 35% alcohol, 32% opiates, 27% the abuse of pharmaceutical drugs, 25% solvent and related abuse, while 3% used cocaine and other types of amphetamines.

The size and extensive nature of the survey has also enabled us to fill some of the gaps relating to the abuse of illicit drugs in Cairo and elsewhere. For instance, the report found strong correlations between drug use, education and employment. Those with only a primary school education or less were more likely to become drug 'abusers'. The unemployed and those on modest earnings or with low status jobs were disproportionately likely to be represented among regular users. Moushira Khattab, head of the National Council for Childhood and Motherhood and close advisor to Suzanne Mubarak, the former president's wife, claimed in 2012 that drug dependency for Egyptian women was growing at an alarming rate, especially in the area of non-prescribed drugs, such as cough medicines.[24] The survey also showed that males were three times as likely to use these substances as females. The figure for females may have been exaggerated; Sleem estimates that 5% of drugs users are female in Lebanon, a country where one might have expected a larger proportion than in Egypt.[25] The youngest recorded age of drug consumption dropped to 10 years old, from 12 years old. Drug use among Bedouin was significantly higher. Religious background suggested that Christians were more likely to be casual users, while Muslim users were more likely to be problem users. Professor Hamdi ended this part of his survey by observing: 'Under the old regime, the relationship between work and success, and morals and values were stripped away, obviously leading the vulnerable – the young, poor and uneducated – to fall deep into addiction'.[26]

Emergence of Tramadol

Intriguing as the overall findings of the study were, the biggest surprise for Hamdi and NGOs like Freedom, was the sudden emergence of a synthetic, opioid drug, the use of which had rocketed during this time. Tramadol was nothing less than the big expansion drug of the post-revolutionary period. Drawing on his research data, Hamdi claimed that there was nothing less than 'an epidemic' of Tramadol taking place, especially among the young.

Tramadol was 'spreading like wildfire', especially within the category of urban drug users, among whom it was claimed to be 'as common as cannabis'.[27] The age-impact sensitivity connection between Tramadol and other psychotropic substances more generally seems in part explained by their only having come onto the Egyptian drugs scene over the preceding five or six years, according to Mustafa Bader, Deputy Director-General, Anti-Narcotics General Adminitration (ANGA) in Egypt,[28] and Mohamed Yahya, of the Amr Khalid organisation.[29]

Tramadol is a synthetic drug, an opioid painkiller. Chemically and pharmaceutically, Tramadol and heroin are the same thing. Tramadol increases the brain's serotonin levels. It also possesses some anti-depressant properties. This explains why Tramadol, as an opioid, makes the user feel highly energised. It strongly suggests that regular takers of Tramadol build up a resistance to the drug, this tolerance obliging a greater level of consumption in order to achieve the initial effects. The negative physical effects of Tramadol include depression, fatigue and stomach ailments. Other characteristics of chronic use include a reduction in empathy and, in extremis, epileptic fits. The treatment of Tramadol's side-effects was regarded as being difficult, attested one practicing professional, Abdul Rahman Al-Rashidy, Psychiatric Counsellor at the Maadi Rehabilitation Centre.[30] Meanwhile, there was also a claim that there had been an upsurge in domestic violence as a result of the use of the drug. Attacks on women had increased generally, owing to an apparent recklessness prompted by such consumption.

Origins

Tramadol was first introduced in Egypt as a medication for cancers and bone diseases. It was manufactured in Germany and then locally, in some of Egypt's pharmaceutical factories. The substance is best known within drugs circles in Egypt based on weight, the 220 mg and 225 mg tablets being known as 'the strawberry' and 'the apple', respectively.[31] Previously, Tramadol circulating in Egypt had invariably been manufactured in the country. From the anti-Mubarak revolution onwards, the control of drugs became much harder. Egyptian Tramadol no longer found itself operating in a closed market.

Increasingly, Egyptian Tramadol faced a globalisation of supply including competition with Tramadol made in China and India,[32] with the quality of production of a dubious standard. The psychotropic drugs were often routed through Jabal Ali Port in Dubai, one of the world's largest container ports and a haven for illicit trade. According to Mustafa Bader of ANGA, it is then delivered to Egypt through its main seaports, notably Alexandria.[33] For example, in 2010, Tareq Ismael of ANGA claimed the agency had seized 132 million tablets of Tramadol, which had passed through the free zone.[34] Even Syria became a significant source of supply of Tramadol, at least before the beginning of its vicious civil conflict from spring 2011 onwards.

But there were other factors at play. Chinese Tramadol in particular was far cheaper than other 'black market' supplies, especially in relation to the weight of the product. It quickly became evident that the Tramadol circulating was no longer confined to a single or dual source. Maher Kemal Mehdat, a drugs outreach worker at the Shubra Drop-in Centre, Freedom NGO, estimated that a strip of 10 Tramadol pills sold for roughly £E200 before the revolution was selling for £E20 a strip in October 2011, the cheaper Tramadol having been manufactured in China.[35] This seemed to indicate a complete collapse in the price of the product. With respect to weight, 200 mg of Tramadol produced in Egypt contrasted with

225 mg of the drug to be found in some Chinese products. This conclusion was challenged in relation to the safety of Tramadol from China.

Otherwise, in Egypt there were on balance fewer of the concerns that often accompany opioids, such as HIV, Hepatitis B and different forms of infection. In Egypt, the intra-venous consumption of drugs is still a relatively unusual method of intake. The preferred means of consumption is either to take the drug orally or through inhalation. The absence of a systematic programme of 'harm reduction', featuring such accoutrements as free syringes and shooting galleries, means that the mass injection of heroin and the like is not a reality in Egypt, or at least not yet. Professor Hamdi concluded that the relatively recent practice of younger, upper middle-class Egyptians using needles to inject themselves with amphetamines, notably those using the brand name of either 'Max' or 'Maxtone forte', may eventually result in the spread of learned behaviour among Egypt's drug consumers.[36]

Explaining the attraction

The best way to explain the rapid take-off in the circulation and consumption of Tramadol is through a combination of availability, versatility and desirability. Logically enough, the fact that the availability of the drug was limited, it being only available through the prescription system, should have restricted circulation at a critical time. In reality, the thinking behind access to the drug proved to be misconceived. In Egypt, the prescription system is not as extensive as it is in many other countries, admitted Professor Hamdi.[37] In 2009, the Egyptian authorities reclassified Tramadol as a Class A drug, as a warning to potential users. Previously, Tramadol had been categorised as a Class B drug, indicating that the drug regulatory authorities had initially been somewhat slow to respond to its rising threat.

Despite the good intentions behind the re-evaluation of the danger of such a move, specialists like Professor Hamdi argue that this in fact had a perverse effect on the drug market.[38] The reclassification process simply pushed the market out of the formal domain of regulatory scrutiny and onto the streets, where its transactions were effectively criminalised and hence obscured. Ironically, from a position of limited but tangible advantage through the prescription system, Egypt virtually overnight threw away its best chance of monitoring the emerging illicit drugs scene in Tramadol.

The loss of any system of quality control quickly had a visible impact upon the origins of the drug, its composition and the conditions in which it was used. With Tramadol cheap to purchase and easy to consume, the market was quickly flooded. Suddenly, a generation of poorer Egyptian males was able to afford the drug, and hence luxuriated in its versatility.[39] The fact that Tramadol quickly acquired a reputation for the enhancement of sexual performance, even though that is believed to be a transient side-effect of consumption, born more of urban legend than sustainable reality, helped to add to its aura, at least in the short term.

Appalled and mystified at the sudden and extreme swing in the price of Tramadol, some social commentators, like Maher Kemal Medhat and others, have tended to assume the existence of a hidden agenda, seeing such developments as best explained by a desire 'to anaesthetise our youth'.[40] The conspiracy theories were also extended to encompass macro-factors, as well as those affecting the individual. This view perceived Egypt to be under attack, 'at all gates', with respect to bringing illicit drugs into the country. With the surge in demand for Tramadol coinciding with the early phase of the revolution, there was already an enabling context in which drugs could be consumed and even celebrated at the same time. From open borders with Libya, through few internal controls, to a retreat of the public security from much of their policing functions, the constraints on the movement and consumption of drugs like Tramadol all but effectively disappeared.

The heightened impact of Tramadol, whether used on its own or as a component in drug cocktails, rapidly acquired a preference status, especially among males in their teens and early twenties. Tramadol could more easily be consumed as part of a poly-drug mix that suited the preferences of the consumer. In the case of Tramadol, a pain killer, the substance was often taken in conjunction with hashish, which could be used easily to generate a high.

Tramadol's new users appeared to display a disdain for the possible health impact of the drug on the nervous system. They appeared readily to consume the drug, in conjunction with other substances, which gave them a sense of bravura. In such a state of psychological diversion, drugs users appeared more willing to act recklessly, and were more likely to commit acts of violence or property crime when under the influence of such substances. Of course, less quality control combined with greater poly-drug use ran the risk of creating ever more unpredictable drugs, owing to the scale of ignorance as to what was contained within the drug as much as the directly harmful effects of the drugs used in such a situation.

Some state responses to drug consumption

The initial confrontation with the Mubarak regime over drugs, and focused on Tahrir Square, was surprisingly agnostic. Many Egyptians, especially those based in the countryside adopted a 'wait and see' posture, uncertain as to what would be the likely outcome. The forces of the state were in any case somewhat depleted, especially after it became plain that the military had no intention of taking sides, at least initially. In terms of resistance, it was only the police, the intelligence and the ruling National Democratic Party (NDP) that proved to be partisan actors. Even these were far from reliable elements for the state. The backlash against the police and the burning of the NDP headquarters in central Cairo weakened pro-regime forces. Instead, the national security warning seemed to be presented in another way. A failure to fall into line would be met by a wave of criminality which, for our purposes, would include those peddling illicit drugs.

From the outset, the police were only willing to choose the battles that they could win. In Upper Egypt, the police consciously avoided confrontations with those involved in drugs-related criminality. This included avoiding clashes in cities like Asiut and Sohag, as well as much of the desert areas, where drugs such as bango, hashish and opium were openly produced. The situation was even worse in the northern Sinai Peninsula compared to Upper Egypt and the capital, where the Bedouin tribes had decisively more firepower than elsewhere in the country. Their state of the art pick-ups could disappear into the interior at any time, outstripping military vehicles. According to one senior foreign diplomat, who had spent three years based in Cairo, Sinai in February 2012 was effectively out of control.[41]

The other main factor contributing to a sense of lawlessness in the Sinai was the provisions of the Egyptian–Israeli peace. A central stipulation of the treaty was that the Egyptian state should not be permitted to project power in the direction of Israel, to do so being considered a potential *casus bello*. With Israel now worrying much more about cross-border smuggling than inter-state war, this treaty requirement was quietly set aside as the impact of drugs trafficking became a bigger priority for the Jewish state in a context of evolving security threats.

Egypt did try to adopt a more uncompromising stance towards criminals, with the prison tariffs for robbery and drugs both being raised by the Presidential Council to 15 years in prison, acknowledged Dr Nasser Loza of Behman Hospital.[42] However, it proved hard to derive traction for a prison-oriented deterrence strategy. In practice, this seemed to have little impact. The absence of the police on the streets encouraged criminal gangs to attack potentially high profitability outlets, of which hospital pharmacies in poor and populated areas, such as Shubra, in the capital, was but one.

It was not only in the realm of the national security state that changes on the ground had implications for policy and hence drugs-related advocacy. In 2005 Egypt had adopted its first National Strategy for Drugs, in conjunction with the UNODC. The impact was a major one, not least because it was supported by First Lady Suzanne Mubarak. The engagement of Mrs Mubarak helped to galvanise political will for the strategy, not least in the difficult process of coordinating the necessary inter-agency activity. The involvement of Suzanne Mubarak would also have galvanised the prime minister's office, Ahmad Nazif, being a particular ally of the Mubarak family. Amr Osman, Manager of the Fund for Drug Control and Treatment of Addiction in Cairo, believes this would have ensured the necessary political will for the strategy, as long as the Mubarak political edifice remained in power.[43]

Conclusion

Egypt has long been a country that has consumed and even celebrated illicit drugs. At different times, various drugs have been embraced as the national drug of choice: hashish in the nineteenth century; the infamous 'white drugs' of cocaine and heroin in the 1920s and 1930s; hashish again after that; bango over the last couple of decades. Today, the synthetic opiate, Tramadol, largely appears to have taken over that role. Moreover, it has done so within a context of expanding drugs consumption, an apparent disregard for the potentially harmful effects of drugs, and with the revolutionary state poorly positioned to combat let alone reduce the existing impact of drugs on society.

The explosion in the consumption of Tramadol may be described as a perfect storm. It comprises: the collapse of a central regulatory authority in the context of the turmoil of the Egyptian revolution; the sudden affordability of such substances on the part of a stratum of young, otherwise impoverished, male Egyptians, who hitherto would have been unable to afford such substances; urban legends, covering such issues as the enhancement of sexual performance. Important though this narrative has been it has not been the whole story. Strong evidence, notably from the Hamdi report, has established that Tramadol came to dominate the drugs scene before the toppling of the Mubarak regime.

Is it likely that Tramadol will replace the likes of bango and hashish as the dominant drug of Egyptian culture? It will certainly take a long time before Tramadol can come close to making that claim. Cultures, whether drugs-related or other, do not shift overnight. A lot will depend on how long the acutely permissive society of drug taking in Egypt persists. If the authoritarian national security state effectively reasserts itself under the presidency of Abdul Fatah el-Sisi, then that tide of drugs may also recede. If, by contrast, drugs remain a visible and central part of economic occupation as well as youthful recreation, then persuading Egyptians to disavow such practices may prove to be as difficult as it has been at any other time since the country has tried to regularise such consumption.

Disclosure statement

No potential conflict of interest was reported by the author.

Notes

1. Russell, *Egyptian Service*.
2. Youssef, *Quarter of a Gram*, 429.
3. *Al Masry al Youm*, January 2012.
4. *Al Masry al Youm*, February 2012.
5. Interviews with author, 2011–2012.
6. Scott.
7. Interview with the author.
8. Davenport-Hines, *Pursuit of Oblivion*, 227.
9. Interview with author, 13 April 2011.
10. These include such functional areas as money laundering, international cooperation and the implementation of international agreements and conventions.
11. Krasner, *International Regimes*.
12. McAllister, *Drug Diplomacy*, 105.
13. For a further examination of some of the themes in this paper, see Chapter 4 in Robins, *Middle East Drugs Bazaar*.
14. Author participant observation, 18 November 2012.
15. Walter Armbrust, the well-known social anthropologist of Egypt and a colleague at St Antony's College, notes that the number of feature films being made during the Sadat period certainly gave the impression that drugs consumption was sharply increasing in Egypt. Conversation, 5 April 2011.
16. Confidential interview with author, 7 April 2011.
17. Al Tahrir, "Army Returns to Bombing."
18. Interview with author, 20 November 2012.
19. Interview with author, 19 November 2012.
20. Interview with author, 31 October 2012.
21. Youssef, *Quarter of a Gram*.
22. Interview with author, 5 April 2011.
23. Interview with author, 9 April 2011.
24. Interview with author, 5 February 2012.
25. Sleem, *Status Quo of Social Work*.
26. Interview with author, July 2011.
27. Interview with the author, April 2011.

28. Interview with author, 3 November 2011.
29. Interview with author, 11 July 2012.
30. Interview with author, 12 July 2012.
31. Nabil.
32. *International Herald Tribune*.
33. Interview with author, 3 November 2011.
34. Interview with author, April 2011.
35. Interview with author, 31 October 2012.
36. Interview with author, April 2011.
37. Interview with author, April 2012.
38. Interview with author, October 2011.
39. See Crabtree et al., *The Cup, the Gun*, 252–254, for more on poverty, demography and other contributory factors.
40. Interview with author, February 2012.
41. Confidential interview with author, 8 February 2012.
42. Interview with author, 9 April 2011.
43. Interview with author, 11 April 2011.

Bibliography

Al Tahrir. 2013. "Army Returns to Bombing Gazan Tunnels after failing to Eliminate Them with Water." *Al Tahrir*, 20 March.

Crabtree, S. Ashencaren, J. Parker, and A. Azman. *The Cup, the Gun and Civil Unrest in Muslim Societies*. Lndon: Whiting & Birch, 2012.

Davenport-Hines, Richard. *The Pursuit of Oblivion: A Global History of Narcotics, 1500–2000*. London: Weidenfeld & Nicholson, 2001.

International Herald Tribune. 2015. "Arrest Hints at China Role in Synthetic Drug Market." *International Herald Tribune*, 29 May. 10.

Krasner, Stephen D., ed. *International Regimes*. Ithaca: Cornell University Press, 1983.

McAllister, William B. *Drug Diplomacy in the Twentieth Century*. London: Routledge, 2000.

Nabil, Mahmoud. n.d. Accessed October 27, 2014. http://www.civicpole.net, http://www.civicpole.net/en/on-the-ground/egyptian-view/89-tranquiliser-abuse-in-egypt

Robins, P. J. 2016. *Middle East Drugs Bazaar. Production, Prevention and Consumption*. London: Hurst.

Russell, Thomas. *Egyptian Service, 1902–1946*. London: John Murray, 1948.

Scott. 1922. "F 879/151/10." Letter from Ambassador Scott, Cairo to Lord Curzon. Cairo, 18 February.

Sleem, Houda Nassim. "The Status Quo of Social Work Education and Its Impact on the Family and Children Services: Lebanon." See Chapter 7 in *Social Work in the Middle East*, edited by Hassan Soliman Hussein. Abingdon: Routledge, 2013.

Youssef, Essam. *A Quarter of a Gram*. Cairo: Montana Studios, 2009.

Al Maasry Al Youm. 2012, 11 February. Accessed February 2012. http://www.almasry-alyoum.com/article2.aspx?ArticleID=328550&IssueID=2413

Al Masry Al Youm. 2012, 29 January. Accessed January 2012. http://www.almasry-alyoum.com/article2.aspx?ArticleID=325896&ID=2391

ə OPEN ACCESS

Drug booms and busts: poverty and prosperity in a Nicaraguan narco-*barrio*

Dennis Rodgers

ABSTRACT
The income generated by the drug economy can often be substantial for the different parties involved, even at the lowest rung of this illicit trade. Yet the drugs trade is also a notoriously volatile activity, meaning that drug-related prosperity is highly prone to boom-and-bust cycles. Drawing on ongoing longitudinal ethnographic research in urban Nicaragua, this article explores the consequences of the cyclical nature of the drugs trade, tracing its unequal patterns of capital accumulation, as well as what happened to those who benefited from the drug economy when it became more exclusive and then subsequently moved on elsewhere.

Introduction

In contrast to findings in many other parts of the world, and most notably the US,[1] scholars have long noted how the income generated by drug economies in Latin America can often be substantial for many of the different parties involved, including at the local level, and even at the lowest rung of this illicit activity.[2] Perhaps not surprisingly, several studies have consequently highlighted the significant developmental impact that the drugs trade has had in local communities in Brazil, Mexico, or Central America, among others.[3] At the same time, however, the narcotics trade is also a notoriously volatile and contingent business, as production processes, the individuals and organisations involved, distribution routes, channels, and modus operandi, as well as sales and consumption patterns, change frequently, for reasons ranging from individual dealer attrition to competition between drug trafficking organisations, to law enforcement operations, to global economic downturns, to climatic events such as *el Niño*, to shifts in urban fashion, to the changes in transport timetables, to the introduction of particular forms of urban planning, among other factors.

While the effects of such changes can obviously be diverse, a generally under-considered aspect of the narcotics trade concerns what happens to those who benefited materially from the local drug economy once it has moved on elsewhere, become more exclusive, or been eradicated. Much of the existing literature tends to simply note that drug dealers and

---

This is an Open Access article distributed under the terms of the Creative Commons Attribution-NonCommercial-NoDerivatives License (http://creativecommons.org/licenses/by-nc-nd/4.0/), which permits non-commercial re-use, distribution, and reproduction in any medium, provided the original work is properly cited, and is not altered, transformed, or built upon in any way.

traffickers are often killed or incarcerated due to their involvement in the drugs trade,[4] both of which undoubtedly have negative impacts on their economic futures. However, many drug dealers also simply end up changing, reducing, or ceasing their involvement in the drug economy, and developing alternative occupational trajectories. Understanding how and why such choices are made, what constraints are endured, how options emerge, and why they are or are not taken up, is critical to getting to grips with the underlying nature of the narcotics trade.

Drawing on ongoing longitudinal ethnographic research in the poor Managua neighbourhood *barrio* Luis Fanor Hernández[5] begun in 1996, this article will first characterise the evolution of a local cocaine-based drug economy from its emergence in 1999 through to its significant decline by 2016, mapping out the reasons for its rise and fall, the nature of its transformation over time, the primary actors involved, as well as its socio-economic consequences. The second part of the paper then focuses on what might be termed the post-'downturn' lives of individuals who were involved as dealers in the drugs trade at different points in time, and whose trajectories respectively illustrate three typical pathways of former drug dealers: 'downsizing', 'destitution', and 'diversification'. Taken together, these provide a sense of the range of options open to former dealers in Nicaragua after drug 'booms' and 'busts', and exemplify how and why choices are made or imposed on individuals, as well as how drugs affect the lived experience of downward mobility.

The *barrio* Luis Fanor Hernández drug economy

Although drugs were by no means unknown in *barrio* Luis Fanor Hernández prior to 1999, cocaine was extremely rare, and those who consumed drugs mainly smoked marijuana, sniffed glue, or drank boiled *floripón* (a hallucinogenic flower native to Nicaragua).[6] The neighbourhood cocaine trade developed initially in an informal, ad hoc manner, around a single individual known as *el Indio Viejo* (the Old Indian), who had been a member of the first post-war local gang in the early 1990s.[7] After leaving the gang, he had started growing marijuana with his brother in a no-man's land near the *barrio*, selling the crop mainly to a regular clientele of local gang members, but also to a small number of individuals from outside the neighbourhood. Although he himself had lived in *barrio* Luis Fanor Hernández all his life, *el Indio Viejo*'s family was originally from the Caribbean coast of Nicaragua, and in 1999 a fisherman cousin from Bluefields, knowing of his involvement in the marijuana business, sent him a bale of cocaine – or '*langosta blanca*' ('white lobster') – that he had picked up at sea – presumably thrown overboard by drug traffickers as they sought to avoid arrest after being intercepted by the US or Nicaraguan Navy – and asked him to sell it for him. Through one of his non-neighbourhood clients, *el Indio Viejo* sold the cocaine to a drug dealer in another neighbourhood, and in doing so realised that the profit margins on cocaine were much higher than those on marijuana.

He consequently immediately set about actively organising his Caribbean networks of family and friends to send him any bales of cocaine they might find, initially offering to sell them on commission but rapidly simply buying them directly. He quickly found out, however, that he had to sell most of the cocaine in the form of crack – known in Nicaragua as '*la piedra*', or 'the stone' – due to local market conditions. Crack is made by boiling cocaine (cocaine hydrochloride) and sodium bicarbonate in water, and is much less expensive than cocaine, being obviously diluted and far less pure, to the extent that it is widely known as 'the poor man's cocaine', meaning that it was affordable in the generally impoverished context of *barrio* Luis Fanor Hernández. Making crack is, however, quite labour intensive, and *el Indio Viejo* decided to recruit collaborators in order to share the workload, and the *barrio* Luis Fanor Hernández drug economy became a three-tiered pyramid as a result. At the apex was *el Indio Viejo* – also known as the '*narco*' – who brought the cocaine into the neighbourhood and mainly wholesaled it, principally – but not exclusively – to half a dozen '*púsheres*' in the neighbourhood. *Púsheres* 'cooked' the cocaine they bought from the *narco* into crack which they then sold from their houses –'*expendios*' – to a regular clientele which included '*muleros*', the bottom rung of the drug-dealing pyramid. *Muleros* sold crack in small doses to all comers on *barrio* street corners, generally in the form of '*paquetes*' containing two 'fixes', known as '*tuquitos*'.

In total, then, by 2002 the *barrio* Luis Fanor Hernández drug economy directly involved 29 individuals: one *narco*, nine *púsheres*, and 19 *muleros*. The *narco*, *púsheres*, and *muleros* were all from the *barrio*, and were moreover all gang members or ex-gang members. The *narco* and *púsheres*, however, also often hired non-gang members – generally members of their household – to help them out, but a large number of *barrio* inhabitants were also indirectly involved in the drug economy by acting as '*bodegueros*', stashing drugs in their houses for the *narco* or for *púsheres* in exchange of payment, generally between US$15 and $70, depending on the quantity and the length of time it had to be stored. This constituted a substantial sum of money in a context where the median wage was around US$100, but paled in comparison to the sums earned by those more directly involved in the drugs trade. As I have described in more detail elsewhere,[8] in 2002 *muleros* in *barrio* Luis Fanor Hernández made US$350–600 per month from their drug dealing, while *púsheres* made between US$1050 and US$2400 per month. I have no direct information about the *narco*'s income, although this was clearly much higher. He owned two houses in *barrio* Luis Fanor Hernández – one of which had two stories, something that was relatively rare and a sign of conspicuous affluence in earthquake-prone Managua – two motorbikes, and a fleet of 10 cars, eight of which were taxis.

As many studies have highlighted, drug dealing is as much about status-generation as it is about income,[9] and all those involved in the *barrio* Luis Fanor Hernández drugs trade also engaged in various forms of 'conspicuous consumption' including wearing ostentatious jewellery, buying brand-name clothes, drinking imported alcohol, or shopping in supermarkets rather than the local market. Most striking, perhaps, was the infrastructural manifestation of this behaviour, as drug dealers materially transformed their homes from the drab wooden shacks that were the characteristic neighbourhood dwellings into ostentatious, gaudily painted brick houses with extravagant fittings – in one case, crystal chandeliers! – and filled with exotic furniture such as full-length Louis XIV rococo mirrors and hand-made hardwood chairs and sofas, as well as luxurious home appliances such as widescreen televisions, mega-wattage sound systems, and Nintendo game consoles. At the same time, however, the financial benefits of the drugs trade also trickled beyond the 'narco-bourgeoisie' of those directly involved, as these shared their bounty with extended family, to the extent that about 40% of households in *barrio* Luis Fanor Hernández were visibly better off as a result of drug dealing compared to surrounding non-drug dealing neighbourhoods.

The political economy of the narcotics trade in *barrio* Luis Fanor Hernández began to change from 2003 onwards, however, as *el Indio Viejo* sought to professionalise his operations. On the one hand, this was due to most of the current gang members he'd recruited to be street dealers – and who also provided a ready-made security apparatus for the drug economy[10] – having become crack addicts and therefore being increasingly unreliable. On the other hand, the ad hoc nature of his supply meant that it was not always regular, something that obviously impacted negatively on dealing. Through his Caribbean coast networks, he consequently developed links with a Colombian drug cartel – the Norte del Valle cartel, according to two *púsheres* whom I interviewed in 2007 – that was regularly moving drugs from Colombia to Nicaragua, in order to ensure a more regular, less contingent supply of cocaine, and also began to be more selective in his choice of associates as a result. By 2005, *el Indio Viejo* was leading a rather shadowy, tight-knit group that was locally referred to as the *cartelito*, or 'little cartel', and was highly feared, partly because it was something of an unknown quantity, since it involved individuals from outside the neighbourhood, although *barrio* Luis Fanor Hernández remained their main dealing territory.

Although *el Indio Viejo* continued to supply some local *púsheres* – who effectively became members of the *cartelito* – he cut others off, and actively discouraged the latter from attempting to pursue any drug dealing activities by dramatically killing a *púsher* after he attempted to secure an alternative source of cocaine for himself. During this period members of the *cartelito* also increasingly clashed with the local *barrio* Luis Fanor Hernández gang, muscling them out of the street drug trade by generally intimidating them and sometimes shooting randomly at any gang members they saw hanging around in the streets. After a few months of enduring such acts, the *barrio* Luis Fanor Hernández gang decided to retaliate and attacked *el Indio Viejo*'s house one evening in mid-2006, which led to a shootout between the gang and members of the *cartelito*, during which a gang member called Charola was badly wounded. The other gang members fled, leaving him behind, and a member of the *cartelito* called Mayuyu went up to Charola and killed him, shooting him in the head, execution-style, 'as a warning to the others', as he put it during an interview a few years later.

Following this event, the *barrio* Luis Fanor Hernández gang effectively ceased to exist and local drug dealing was fully and exclusively controlled by the *cartelito*. The number of people involved from *barrio* Luis Fanor Hernández was clearly smaller than previously, and the material benefits of the trade consequently no longer trickled down into the non-drug dealing population as much, despite 2006–2007 clearly being the high point of drug dealing in the neighbourhood in terms of volume. From late 2007 onwards, however, the *barrio* Luis Fanor Hernández *cartelito* began to reduce its involvement in local drug-dealing activities and refocused on drug-trafficking – ie moving drugs across Nicaragua – instead. The initial impulse for this was *el Indio Viejo* being arrested and deciding this was linked to the visibility of his drug dealing (although in actual fact it seems to have been bad luck – he was arrested by transport police officers who detained him due to a traffic violation but subsequently discovered significant amounts of drugs in his car). At the same time, though, *el Indio Viejo* had begun to realise that the profit margins of drug trafficking were much higher than those associated with drug dealing, and so whilst in prison, he institutionalised his existing Colombian cartel links, brokering an agreement to become their exclusive 'man in Nicaragua' – so to speak – and the *barrio* Luis Fanor Hernández *cartelito* began to take charge of transporting regular shipments of cocaine from the Caribbean coast of the country to the Honduran border.

This further reduced the number of people benefiting from the drugs trade in *barrio* Luis Fanor Hernández as the *cartelito*'s operations became increasingly spread across the country, and there was less need for local *bodegueros* and other indirect workers. Members were rarely seen, however, even after *el Indio Viejo* was released from prison in 2010, although *barrio* Luis Fanor Hernández was the theatre of frequent acts of unpredictable and extreme violence, largely related to the increasing monopolisation of the narcotics trade in Nicaragua that took place during this period, whereby rival *cartelitos* fought each other for control over drug trafficking routes and shipment rights. Although at the height of its success, the *barrio* Luis Fanor Hernández *cartelito* by all accounts became one of the four most important native drug trafficking organisations in Nicaragua, in 2011 *el Indio Viejo* was arrested again along with most other members of the *cartelito*, reportedly at the behest of a rival *cartelito* which had developed close links to certain members of the Nicaraguan government.[11] Although what remained of the *barrio* Luis Fanor Hernández *cartelito* subsequently re-organised in a much-reduced manner around *el Indio Viejo*'s former number two, another ex-gang member from the first post-war generation known as 'Pac-Man' (due to his voracious appetite), they constituted little more than a loose group of local dealers sharing the benefits of economies of scale, and by 2014 had effectively dissipated as an organised concern.

Between 2014 and 2016, four individuals continued to operate in *barrio* Luis Fanor Hernández as low-level street dealers, buying their drugs from bigger dealers in other neighbourhoods. One of these was Pac-Man's daughter, another was a former *púsher* from the early 2000s who had subsequently integrated the *cartelito*, and the other two had been *muleros* in the early 2000s. All principally sold crack, although it should be noted that the neighbourhood drug market had by then shrunk substantially compared to the past. This was partly related to the fact that when the *barrio* Luis Fanor Hernández *cartelito* moved from dealing to trafficking in the late 2000s, they not only reduced the local supply of crack dramatically, but also cracked down (so to speak) on local addicts in order to avoid drawing police attention to the neighbourhood. By November 2016, marijuana had in fact supplanted crack cocaine as the main drug being sold in *barrio* Luis Fanor Hernández, and there were only two local dealers left – one of the former *muleros* died, while Pac-Man's daughter left the neighbourhood – although a growing number of local delinquent youths were dealing in an 'amateur' manner[12] – that is to say, they sold sporadically on an occasional basis, generally motivated by immediate financial desires, although it should be noted that these tended to remain modest (needing to buy a new pair of shoes or a formal shirt for a birthday party, for example).

After the drugs boom

Many individuals in *barrio* Luis Fanor Hernández have clearly benefitted materially from the drugs trade over the course of the past two decades, whether directly, as dealers, or indirectly, employed as helpers or *bodegueros*, or as extended family members benefiting from the largesse of drug dealers. The particular trajectory of the *barrio* Luis Fanor Hernández drugs trade, however, clearly begs the question of what happens after a drug 'boom', once the drugs trade has changed or moved on. Or, put another way, what happens when things go 'bust'? I am particularly interested here in the consequences for the *barrio* Luis Fanor Hernández drug dealers who in the early and mid-2000s constituted what could plausibly be considered a nascent local 'narco-bourgeoisie', (primitively) accumulating unprecedented wealth within a local context historically associated with extreme poverty.[13] How do they cope with their central means of livelihood disappearing? Although those who benefitted indirectly from the drug economy have also frequently experienced a significant downturn in their material circumstances, in most cases this was clearly not as dramatic as for those who were directly involved, partly because the former's participation often did not constitute their sole or even primary economic activity.

The question of what happens to unemployed drug dealers is not considered very much in the existing literature on the drugs trade, but Sudhir Venkatesh's study of 'the underground economy of the urban poor' in 1990s Chicago,[14] and Randol Contreras' study of the South Bronx drugs trade during the 1990s and 2000s,[15] constitute two partial exceptions. The former describes how the demise of the crack economy in the Chicago neighbourhood of Maquis Park in the early 1990s led to the local drug gang turning to extortion of local businesses in order to replace its crack-related income, while the latter describes how the end of the so-called 'Crack Era' led to a group of previously successful drug dealers becoming 'stickup kids', moving from selling drugs to violently robbing drug dealers instead. Both of these patterns of behaviour are clearly quite contingent and context specific, and nothing analogous has come to the fore in *barrio* Luis Fanor Hernández. Although a couple of former local drug dealers have become violent delinquents since ceasing to be involved in the drugs trade, and (sometimes) prey on the local neighbourhood community, they do so on an individual basis rather than as a part of a group, while the professionalisation and exclusive monopolisation of the contemporary drugs trade in Nicaragua means that there is little chance of small-time delinquents successfully targeting drug dealers today.

At the same time, however, of the 29 individuals involved in drug dealing in *barrio* Luis Fanor Hernández in early 2002, 11 were locally economically active (whether formally or informally), six were incarcerated, five had died, four had emigrated, and three were unemployed, as of November 2016. This suggests that a range of options beyond the two described by Venkatesh and Contreras were open to former drug dealers in the neighbourhood. If we ignore death and incarceration,[16] the single most common trajectory was for former drug dealers to simply take up new occupations that more often than not had little to do with drug dealing, whether in Nicaragua or elsewhere. Chucki, for example, ceased dealing after the conflagration with the *cartelito* in 2006 that resulted in Charola's death, and started working as a car mechanic in *barrio* Luis Fanor Hernández instead. Similarly, Mondul – who was Charola's cousin – left the neighbourhood for Costa Rica, where he has since combined seasonal work as a rural coffee picker with construction work in San José. Neither the number of economically active former drug dealers nor their occupations were particularly exceptional compared to non-drug dealers, but the particular history of former drug dealers meant that their post-dealing occupational trajectories can potentially be distinguished as corresponding to three typical pathways: 'downsizing', 'destitution', and 'diversification'. Of the three, 'destitution' was the most common, followed by 'diversification', and then 'downsizing', although it should be noted that these different pathways to a certain extent overlap and combine.

Downsizing

'Downsizing' only applied to the handful of individuals who had previously participated in the *barrio* Luis Fanor Hernández drug economy and who continued to deal drugs, but on a much smaller scale, and therefore making much less. *El Gordo Sucio*, for example, had been one of the neighbourhood's most successful *muleros* in 2002, regularly making a profit of about US$600 per month, but in 2014 he was making no more than about $100 per month. This significant revenue shrinkage was first and foremost due to a decline in the volume of drugs that he sold, but another important reason was that *el Gordo Sucio* had become a serious crack addict; indeed, he told me during an interview in 2014 that this was the principal reason he had taken up drug dealing again after the fall of the *cartelito*, in order to ensure that he always had access to crack, and he admitted to frequently smoking his stocks rather than selling them.

The ramifications of downsizing were not only financial but also symbolic. During the early years of the *barrio* Luis Fanor Hernández drug economy, when it was organised pyramidally, the distinction between *púsheres* – who sold from their homes – and *muleros* – who sold on the streets – went beyond their separate roles in the crack production and sales process, and also involved their having different social statuses. *Púsheres* looked down on *muleros*, something that was reinforced by the fact that there was no mobility between distinct levels of the drug pyramid, ie a *mulero* could not aspire to becoming a *púsher*, and there was obviously no question of a *púsher* aspiring to replace the *narco*. Two of the individuals who continued to deal drugs post 2014 had both been *púsheres* previously, and they clearly perceived their low-level street dealing as a humiliating social demotion, as *el Negro* explained during an interview in 2014, responding to my questions about whether the rumours I'd heard that he had taken up drug dealing again were true or not:

el Negro: '*Si, si*, I'm still dealing drugs, but not like before, you know …'

Dennis Rodgers: 'What do you mean? Like you're independent now that *el Indio Viejo* is in prison and there's no longer a *cartelito*?'

eN: '*Pues, eso si*, but no, it's more than that …'

DR: 'You mean like you're not making as much money as before? Because you're selling less drugs? Or because it's more difficult to source drugs?'

eN: '*Si, eso también* [Yes, that too], but it's not that, Dennis … I mean, you remember how I used to sell before, yes?'

DR: 'Sure, you explained everything to me in several interviews over the years, I can't remember exactly how much you were making when, but you gave me a pretty good idea each time, which was very useful for my work'.

eN: '*Dale*, but I'm not talking about that … You remember how I had my own *expendio*, I sold from my house, *si*? Well, now I'm selling on street corners, hanging around, waiting for people to pass by, like a dirty *mulero* … Before my clients came to me, to my home – I was a *púsher!*'[17]

Destitution

While 'downsizing' meant a reduction in revenue, it nevertheless still involved earning a viable income. A little later during the course of the same interview mentioned above, *el Negro* made a throwaway comment that '*no me gusta vender asi* [I don't like to sell this way], but at least it means that I can afford to maintain my house and I don't have to sell all the nice things I bought when things were better'. When I asked him what he meant by this, *el Negro* commented that many former dealers in *barrio* Luis Fanor Hernández were now destitute. To a certain extent, this was due to the general lack of employment opportunities for poor, uneducated young men within Managua's broader labour market, as several former drug dealers were unemployed, and most of the locally economically active ones were in fact underemployed or earned very low incomes. At the same time, though, their destitution was also a function of the particular spending habits that they had developed when drug dealing, as many attempted to maintain public patterns of 'conspicuous consumption' in the face of unemployment, underemployment, or low income streams by the unsustainable means of pawning off the luxury furniture, electronic appliances, white goods, motorbikes, etc they had bought when dealing drugs. This, added to the lack of maintenance to their previously immaculately and gaudily painted houses, meant that many former drug dealers lived in conditions of 'faded grandeur', rattling about in crumbling, empty houses, dreaming nostalgically of the past, as became clear in 2012 when I visited Jasmil, a former *púsher* from the early and mid-2000s. He had been one of the first drug dealers to convert his wood shack into a brick house, which he would proudly have repainted a different colour every year, and it was a shock to see it washed out and the paint peeling.

'*Oye*, Jasmil, *que onda* [What's up]? I haven't seen you for ages! But what the fuck has happened to your house, why haven't you re-painted it?', I exclaimed.

'*Ya no tengo para eso ahora, maje* [I don't have any money for that now, mate]', he answered balefully, before going on to explain: 'I don't have a job anymore, there's no more drug dealing here, so how am I supposed to earn enough to live, let alone paint my house?'

DR: 'Yeah, I'm sorry, *maje*, shit happens ... But at least it's still nice inside, no?'

Jasmil: 'There's nothing inside, I've had to sell everything'.

DR: 'What? You mean all your furniture and stuff? But why?'

J: '*Pues*, how else am I supposed to survive? There's no more drug dealing, I've told you ... *No hay nada* [There's nothing] ...'

This mix of material and psychological consequences to the demise of the drugs trade in *barrio* Luis Fanor Hernández is not necessarily surprising. Certainly, it bears comparison to James Ferguson's famous study of economic decay and downward mobility among Zambian Copperbelt mineworkers, where he also points out that, in many ways, it is worse to have enjoyed economic prosperity and to have thought of oneself as being at the centre of progress and modernity before being cast aside, than to have always been poor and excluded.[18] Indeed, this was very much the tenor of my last conversation with *el Gordo Sucio* in 2014, when he even went so far as to bitterly wish that he had never got involved in drug dealing, something that is all the more poignant in view of the fact that he died of an overdose in February 2016. Having said this, as I have described elsewhere,[19] local neighbourhood inhabitants – both drug dealers and non-drug dealers – frequently displayed patterns of 'instant gratification' in their socio-economic behaviour,[20] and I suspect that most of the former *barrio* Luis Fanor Hernández drug dealers would probably disagree with both Ferguson and *el Gordo Sucio*, even though they were no longer able to maintain their previous living standards. Certainly, this was the general tenor of the conversation I had with a former *púsher* called Espinaca in November 2016, for example, who responded to my queries about his destitution with a rather philosophical '*Cuando hay, hay, y se tiene que disfrutar, y cuando no hay, no hay, y se tiene que aguantar* ...' [When you have money, you've got to enjoy it, and when you don't, you've just got to make do ...].

Diversification

Espinaca's discourse very much echoes that of Topi, a 'stickup kid' whom Contreras discusses in his study of South Bronx drug dealers who turned to robbery after the collapse of the local crack economy, describing him as a 'high lifer', living 'a roller-coaster ride of material and drug consumption, spending money as though it had no end' after a successful robbery.[21] He contrasts 'high lifers' with 'venturers', who 'invest robbery earnings in legal pursuits',[22] citing the example of Tukee, who invested in a pet store. Such diversification could also be observed in *barrio* Luis Fanor Hernández, although it only involved a very small number of former drug dealers. Some of these, such as Bismarck, had diversified while the neighbourhood drug economy was in full swing, while others, such as Kalia, developed a new economic activity after the end of the drugs boom. In both cases, however, their diversification was based on the strategic reinvestment of their narcotics trade profits. Kalia, who was a former *mulero* from the early 2000s, bought a plot of land and built a house in a new urban settlement in another part of Managua, moving there with his wife and daughters in 2012, and setting up a successful *fritanga* (outdoor fry-up). Although clearly a major step-down in terms of his revenue, in an interview in 2014 he professed to being much happier, and was in fact thinking of opening another *fritanga* in another part of this new neighbourhood, musing rather drolly that 'I could be *el poderoso de las fritangas*, like a *narco*, but for food!'

But perhaps the most striking exemplification of diversification in *barrio* Luis Fanor Hernández was a former *púsher* called Bismarck, who ceased dealing drugs in early 2007, partly at my urgings, and partly due to a growing sense of familial responsibility following fatherhood. As he explained during the following exchange in late 2007, where I questioned him about his new activities:[23]

DR: 'So, what are you doing now if you're not dealing drugs?'

Bismarck: 'I've got these new businesses which I've set up with the money I made from selling drugs – I've diversified, Dennis!'

DR: 'Uh-huh, and to what?'

B: 'Well, like a year ago I bought a *ranchón* [night club], but the stupid place didn't make any money, so I sold it a few days ago to some sucker who thinks he can make it work. Good luck to him, I say!'

DR: 'How much did you get for it?'

B: 'US$40,000'

DR: 'Hey, that's a good sum of money! What are you going to do with it?'

B: 'I don't know yet, I'm thinking that I might buy a *pulpería* [corner store], here in the *barrio*, at least I know how this place works, and what people want. With that amount of money, I could buy one that already exists in a good location, with nobody else around it. Or I might expand my shop at the Huembes market instead. I haven't decided yet'.

DR: 'You have a shop at the Huembes? What does it sell? Is it a proper shop or is it a stall?'

B: 'No, no, it's a proper shop, and it sells secondhand clothes'.

DR: 'Wow, that's something different! ... So how did you go about setting up your shop? Have you bought it or do you rent it? And why did you set it up in the Huembes?'

B: 'Well, the Huembes market is a good place to have a shop because it's nearby, you save on transport costs, and I know the place well, because I used to hang around there all the time when I was in the gang. So what I did was that I went to the market authorities and told them that I wanted to buy a shop, and they offered me this one, which was in a good location, and so I said yes'.

[…]

DR: 'So this is all legal and official?'

B: 'Yes, it's all authorised by COMMEMA [the *Corporación Municipal de los Mercados de Managua*, or Municipal Managua Markets Corporation]. I have a property title, and authorisation to sell, and I pay a monthly business tax of 200 *córdobas*[24] to COMMEMA. I've also just finished remodelling it, to make it look modern and all. I spent 5000 *córdobas*,[25] and it looks really good now, like a real store in one of the commercial malls. It's got to have the right *onda*, you know, otherwise it won't work, people won't come …'

[…]

DR: 'It sounds like you've got it all worked out!'

B: 'Yes, and God willing, if this works, I'll be able to expand, and this way my kids will have a whole chain of stores to help them survive in the future, once I'm gone'.

DR: 'Well, I suspect that you're not likely to die for some time, Bismarck, especially now that you've got out of drug dealing. Selling secondhand clothes is a much less dangerous occupation!'

B: 'Heh, heh! That it is, Dennis, that it is …'

The shop at the Huembes was the first item of a burgeoning property portfolio that Bismarck set about constituting after leaving the drugs trade behind. Part of the impulse for this strategy was a conversation that we'd had in 2003 when he responded to my nagging urgings to stop drug dealing and take up a less dangerous occupation by saying that he'd be willing to take a cut in his not inconsiderable earnings so long as he could secure a regular revenue, and then asked me what I thought he should invest his money in. I responded that the only type of investment I knew that yielded a positive rate of return over the long term was property. Bismarck later told me that he had taken this piece of advice to heart, although after a disagreement with the COMMEMA in 2009, Bismarck decided to focus exclusively on buying property in *barrio* Luis Fanor Hernández. He sold his shop at the Huembes market in 2010 and bought a *pulpería* (cornerstore) in the neighbourhood, where he also set up a motorcycle mechanic's workshop, and bought three adjacent houses which he joined together and converted into rental accommodation, renting out rooms on an individual basis, and two years later he bought another couple of houses which he also rented out, to two families.

As I have described elsewhere, the means through which he purchased his properties were often quite dubious, and he frequently secured his tenants' rent through violent means.[26] Bismarck's 'slum lordship', however, ensured that he had a monthly revenue of around US$600, equivalent to a little more than 50% of what he'd earned per month when drug dealing, and in interviews in 2012 and 2014 he professed himself happy with this, emphasising over and over that he was much less at risk of being killed or imprisoned. On my last visit to Nicaragua in November 2016, however, I was surprised to observe that

Bismarck's property empire had fallen apart. Firstly, his *pulpería* went bust, for reasons that were not completely clear to me. Secondly, his rental accommodation suffered an arson attack, most likely by disgruntled tenants seeking revenge for being humiliated by Bismarck. Then his motorcycle workshop was closed by the police, ostensibly because it had been set up on communal land (which was true), but in fact because Bismarck decided to stop paying them bribes to leave him alone – the arrangement was a leftover from his drug-dealing days – as a cost-saving measure following the loss of revenue resulting from the arson attack. This, however, prompted the families renting the two individual houses he had bought to stop paying their rent. Feeling that Bismarck no longer had police protection, the two families – which were linked by marriage – banded together to effectively 'expropriate' the houses, and after being badly beaten up when he tried to intimidate them, Bismarck now considers the houses 'lost'. Since the middle of 2016, he has worked as a personal chauffeur for the director of a Taiwanese clothing company operating in one of Managua's Free Trade Zones, earning US$180 a month, about 15% of what he earned a month as a drug dealer.

Conclusion

This article has explored what might be termed the local 'boom-and-bust' cycle of drug economies. It is well established that the global narcotics trade is a highly volatile business, but less considered is the way this macro instability is mirrored at the micro level, as local drug economies inevitably mutate and evolve over time, to the extent that they are always contingent and time-bound in nature. Certainly, the example of the *barrio* Luis Fanor Hernández drug economy highlights how while drugs can generate significant material benefits at the local level, these are generally unevenly distributed, something that moreover also applies afterwards, insofar as the long-term effects of being centrally involved in the drugs trade are by no means guaranteed. These issues are sometimes explored from a macro and aggregate perspective,[27] but the question of what happens to the individuals involved in a drug economy after it ceases to exist is rarely considered. Although death and imprisonment clearly often accompany such processes, they generally only affect a minority of those affected by the drugs trade, and most former drug dealers turn to alternative economic activities. While some manage to capitalise on the exceptional capital accumulation opportunity offered by drug dealing, others do not, however, and it is critical that we understand why this might be the case.

The question, then, is what happens to the majority who effectively find themselves out of a job – or, put another way, what do unemployed drug dealers do? How do they cope with the disappearance of an activity that provided them with contextually extraordinary levels of wealth? Does involvement in drug-related capital accumulation, even if only for a while, provide a comparative advantage to individuals after they have ceased dealing? Or do they face a situation like the one described by James Ferguson in his study of former mineworkers in the Zambian Copperbelt, where downward economic mobility had profoundly demoralising effects in the form of a widespread sense of 'abjection'?[28] The latter situation was certainly observable in *barrio* Luis Fanor Hernández, with many former drug dealers frequently waxing nostalgically about the past in interviews, and expressing feelings of loss and sometimes even humiliation about their new status, although others had no regrets, and philosophically accepted the contingent nature of their drug-dealing wealth. Such discourses were, however, associated variably with the three different possible pathways for former drug dealers' post-dealing occupational trajectories in *barrio* Luis Fanor Hernández that I have laid out in this article, namely 'downsizing', 'destitution', and 'diversification'.

The first effectively represented a desperate attempt to continue dealing drugs, albeit inevitably on a reduced scale because the neighbourhood was no longer a central geographical node of the drugs trade. In the long run this downsizing is clearly unsustainable, and moreover has diminishing returns, something that generated an undercurrent of anxiety among those engaged in this activity. The second pathway, destitution, was the lot of most drug dealers in *barrio* Luis Fanor Hernández. This was partly due to broader contextual factors, insofar as the Nicaraguan labour market offers few opportunities to uneducated young men,[29] but there was also a clear symbolic dimension to this condition, insofar as many drug dealers accelerate their impoverishment by persisting with forms of conspicuous consumption after they have lost the means to sustain these. This highlights the important symbolic elements surrounding the drugs trade, and which often drive some of its internal logic as well. It is interesting to note that although conceptually destitution might be considered particularly humiliating for former drug dealers, the levels of anxiety and feelings of humiliation were clearly not as high as those associated with downsizing, perhaps because the fact of 'faded grandeur' that applied infrastructurally to many former drug dealers' homes still offered a sense of symbolic hierarchy, but also due to the widespread indulgence in forms of instant gratification which meant that there existed a general sense in *barrio* Luis Fanor Hernández of 'easy come, easy go' in relation to wealth, and past success was often mythologised and provided enduring kudos.

The final pathway is that of diversification, which in many ways was the most unusual. This only concerned a small group of former drug dealers in *barrio* Luis Fanor Hernández, for reasons that most likely relate to idiosyncratic personality traits, although in the case of Bismarck, having an external agent – me – provide him with investment advice may also have played a role. What is interesting about the two examples of diversification that I discuss is that both Kalia and Bismarck explicitly drew on skills acquired while drug dealing to successfully carry out their new activities. This raises the issue of whether having been a drug dealer provides individuals with any transferrable advantages after they have ceased dealing. At first glance, the fact that Kalia and Bismarck belong to a minority group of former dealers suggests that this is not the case, but it might well be that their drug-dealing past is what allowed them to successfully diversify, in the same way that having been a gang member often provides individuals in *barrio* Luis Fanor Hernández with a 'violence dividend' that pays off for certain occupational trajectories – but not others – after leaving the gang. Certainly, it is striking that the overwhelming majority of economically active former gang members in *barrio* Luis Fanor Hernández seem to be earning significantly higher incomes compared to their employed non-ex-gang member peers in the neighbourhood.[30] This was not as clearly the case for former drug dealers in general, but certain individual former drug dealers such as Bismarck were among the richest individuals in the neighbourhood, although his subsequent impoverishment highlights how this was a very volatile position.

In general terms, then, while there is little doubt that the drugs trade can generate significant material benefits at the local level, these are often quite contingent. This applies not only while drug dealing takes place, but also afterwards, insofar as the long-term effects of being centrally involved in the drugs trade are by no means guaranteed. While some individuals manage to capitalise on the exceptional capital accumulation opportunity offered by drug dealing, others do not, and even those that do are by no means guaranteed to continue enjoying the fruits of their investments over the *longue durée*. The research presented in this article suggests that different trajectories occur for idiosyncratic reasons linked to individual personality or contingent externalities, but this picture may also be the result of the inevitably contextually specific nature of my case study. At the same time, however, even if this is the case, the research presented in this article also raises a number of broader issues about the drugs trade, including for example concerning the way that micro-level specificities can condition the development and articulation of macro-level processes rather than simply reflect the latter; how different types of drug-related activities generate very different forms of spatial, economic, symbolic, and political configurations; and, more generally, showcases the fundamentally embedded nature of the narcotics business, which rather than just being considered from a singular health or security angle clearly needs to be considered holistically in order to be properly understood in all its dimensions, whether positive or negative.

Disclosure statement

No potential conflict of interest was reported by the author.

Acknowledgements

The author is grateful to Desmond Arias, Thomas Grisaffi, Javier Auyero, Maziyar Ghiabi, and two anonymous referees for constructive comments on early drafts of this article.

Notes

1. Bourgois, *In Search of Respect*; Contreras, *Stickup Kids*; Levitt and Dubner, *Freakonomics*; Levitt and Venkatesh, "Economic Analysis of a Drug-Selling Gang"; Padilla, *Gang as an American Enterprise*; and Venkatesh and Levitt, "Are We a Family or a Business?"
2. Malkin, "Narcotrafficking, Migration, and Modernity"; Rodgers, "Critique of Urban Violence"; and Rodgers, "Why Do Drug Dealers."
3. Arias, *Drugs and Democracy in Rio de Janeiro*; McDonald, "Narcoeconomy and Small-Town Mexico"; and Rodgers, "Managua."
4. Brownstein et al. "Relationship of Drugs, Drug Trafficking"; Reuter, "Systemic Violence in Drug Markets"; Stanton and Galbraith, "Drug Trafficking among African-American Early Adolescents."
5. This name is a pseudonym, as are the names of all the individuals mentioned in this article.
6. Due to its proximity to the Colombian island of San Andrés, Nicaragua is geographically a natural trans-shipment point for drugs moving from South to North America. It was under-

exploited as such until the turn of the century because of the patchy nature of its transport infrastructure, including in particular the lack of connection between the Caribbean and Pacific coasts of the country. In late 1998, however, Nicaragua was devastated by Hurricane Mitch, suffering major infrastructure damage and resource drainage. This negatively affected the (already limited) capabilities of local law enforcement institutions, thereby facilitating the importation of drugs; and at the same time, post-Mitch reconstruction efforts focused largely on rebuilding transport links, including building a road between the Caribbean and Pacific coasts, and generally improving the whole network, which had a knock-on effect of increasing the volume of traffic and making moving drug shipments easier. A sizeable proportion of the Western hemisphere's South–North drugs trade has consequently been transiting through Nicaragua since the early 2000s.

7. Rodgers, "Living in the Shadow of Death"; and Rodgers, "When Vigilantes Turn Bad."
8. Rodgers, "Living in the Shadow of Death"; Rodgers, "When Vigilantes Turn Bad"; Rodgers, "Managua"; Rodgers, "Critique of Urban Violence"; and Rodgers, "Why Do Drug Dealers."
9. Baird, "*Duros* and Gangland Girlfriends"; Bourgois, *In Search of Respect*; and Contreras, *Stickup Kids*.
10. Rodgers, "When Vigilantes Turn Bad."
11. The latter subsequently consolidated monopoly control over the country's narcotics trade, to the extent that we can plausibly talk of Nicaragua now being a 'narco-state' – see Rodgers and Rocha, "Myth of Nicaraguan Exceptionalism."
12. Kessler, *Sociología del Delito Amateur*.
13. Rodgers, "Managua"; and Rodgers, "Symptom called Managua."
14. Venkatesh, *Off the Books*.
15. Contreras, *Stickup Kids*.
16. The deaths occurred primarily because of the reconfiguration of the drug economy in *barrio* Luis Fanor Hernández rather than its demise, and dying can thus be seen as a cause rather than an outcome of ceasing to deal drugs. The same was also true of imprisonment, as the example of Mungo highlights well. He was a former *mulero* from the early 2000s who due to his personal links to *el Indio Viejo* was exceptionally allowed to take up drug dealing in 2009 when the *cartelito* refocused on trafficking, despite not being a member of the *cartelito*. Mungo was, however, arrested in 2010, and his prison experiences led him to put an end to his drug dealing, albeit for reasons that had little to do with drug dealing per se and more the traumatic experience of being incarcerated (see Rodgers, "I've Seen Things").
17. At the same time, *el Negro*'s sense of humiliation clearly also stemmed from the fact that – due to his close personal friendship with *el Indio Viejo* – he had been one of the few original neighbourhood *púsheres* to integrate the *cartelito* once it became dominant, and then became one of two 'authorised' local dealers in *barrio* Luis Fanor Hernández once the *cartelito* had turned to trafficking rather than dealing, and he was easily the longest-standing of all the local drug dealers there have been in the neighbourhood.
18. Ferguson, *Expectations of Modernity*.
19. Rodgers, "Each to Their Own."
20. Lewis, *La Vida*.
21. Contreras, *Stickup Kids*, 194.
22. Ibid.
23. The following is an abridged extract from an exchange presented in fuller form in Rodgers, "Critique of Urban Violence," 99–102.
24. Approximately US$10 at the time.
25. Approximately US$250 at the time.
26. Rodgers, "Critique of Urban Violence."
27. Thoumi, *Illegal Drugs, Economy, and Society*.
28. Ferguson, *Expectations of Modernity*.
29. Rodgers, "Slum Wars of the 21st Century."
30. Rodgers, "After the Gang."

Bibliography

Arias, Enrique Desmond. *Drugs and Democracy in Rio De Janeiro: Trafficking, Social Networks, and Public Security*. Chapel Hill: University of North Carolina Press, 2006.

Baird, Adam. "*Duros* and Gangland Girlfriends: Male Identity, Gang Socialisation and Rape in Medellín." In *Violence at the Urban Margins*, edited by Javier Auyero, Philippe Bourgois and Nancy Scheper-Hughes, 112–132. Oxford: Oxford University Press, 2015.

Bourgois, Philippe. *In Search of Respect: Selling Crack in El Barrio*. Cambridge: Cambridge University Press, 1995.

Brownstein, Henry, Hari Shiledar Baxi, Paul Goldstein, and Patrick Ryan. "The Relationship of Drugs, Drug Trafficking, and Drug Traffickers to Homicide." *Journal of Crime and Justice* 15, no. 1 (1992): 25–44.

Contreras, Randol. *The Stickup Kids: Race, Drugs, Violence, and the American Dream*. Berkeley: University of California Press, 2013.

Ferguson, James. *Expectations of Modernity: Myths and Meanings of Urban Life on the Zambian Copperbelt*. Berkeley: University of California Press, 1999.

Kessler, Gabriel. *Sociología Del Delito Amateur*. Buenos Aires: Editorial Paidos, 2004.

Levitt, Steven, and Stephen Dubner. *Freakonomics: A Rogue Economist Explores the Hidden Side of Everything*. London: Penguin, 2005.

Levitt, Steven, and Sudhir Venkatesh. "An Economic Analysis of a Drug-Selling Gang's Finances." *The Quarterly Journal of Economics* 115, no. 3 (2000): 755–789.

Lewis, Oscar. *La Vida: A Puerto Rican Family in the Culture of Poverty – San Juan & New York*. London: Panther Books, 1967.

Malkin, Victoria. "Narcotrafficking, Migration, and Modernity in Rural Mexico." *Latin American Perspectives* 28, no. 4 (2001): 101–128.

McDonald, James. "The Narcoeconomy and Small-Town, Rural Mexico." *Human Organization* 64, no. 2 (2005): 115–125.

Padilla, Felix. *The Gang as an American Enterprise*. New Brunswick: Rutgers University Press, 1992.

Reuter, Peter. "Systemic Violence in Drug Markets." *Crime, Law and Social Change* 52, no. 3 (2009): 275–284.

Rodgers, Dennis. "Living in the Shadow of Death: Gangs, Violence and Social Order in Urban Nicaragua, 1996–2002." *Journal of Latin American Studies* 38, no. 2 (2006): 267–292.

Rodgers, Dennis. "Each to Their Own: Ethnographic Notes on the Economic Organisation of Poor Households in Urban Nicaragua." *Journal of Development Studies* 43, no. 3 (2007): 391–419.

Rodgers, Dennis. "Managua." In *Fractured Cities: Social Exclusion, Urban Violence and Contested Spaces in Latin America*, edited by Kees Koonings and Dirk Kruijt, 71–85. London: Zed, 2007.

Rodgers, Dennis. "When Vigilantes Turn Bad: Gangs, Violence, and Social Change in Urban Nicaragua." In *Global Vigilantes*, edited by David Pratten and Atreyee Sen, 349–370. London: Hurst, 2007.

Rodgers, Dennis. "A Symptom Called Managua." *New Left Review* 49 (2008): 103–120.

Rodgers, Dennis. "Slum Wars of the 21st Century: Gangs, *Mano Dura*, and the New Urban Geography of Conflict in Central America." *Development and Change* 40, no. 5 (2009): 949–976.

Rodgers, Dennis. "After the Gang: Pathways of De-Socialization from Violence in Nicaragua." Paper presented at the 2nd 'Socialization and Organized Political Violence' workshop, Yale University, October 17–18, 2014.

Rodgers, Dennis. "'I've Seen Things You Wouldn't Believe…': The Changing Experience of Incarceration in Nicaragua." Paper presented at the 2015 LASA Annual Congress, San Juan, Puerto Rico, May 27–30, 2015.

Rodgers, Dennis. "Critique of Urban Violence: Bismarckian Transformations in Contemporary Nicaragua." *Theory, Culture, and Society* 33, no. 7–8 (2016): 85–109.

Rodgers, Dennis. "Why Do Drug Dealers Live with Their Moms? Contrasting Views from Chicago and Managua." *Focaal – Journal of Global and Historical Anthropology* 78, (2017): 102–114.

Rodgers, Dennis, and José-Luis Rocha. "The Myth of Nicaraguan Exceptionalism: Gangs, Crime, and the Political Economy of Violence." In *Crime and Violence in Latin America*, edited by David Smilde, Veronica Zubillaga, and Rebecca Hanson. Boulder: Lynne Rienner, forthcoming.

Stanton, Bonita, and Jennifer Galbraith. "Drug Trafficking among African-American Early Adolescents: Prevalence, Consequences, and Associated Behaviors and Beliefs." *Pediatrics* 93, no. 6 (1994): 1039–1043.

Thoumi, Francisco. *Illegal Drugs, Economy, and Society in the Andes*. Washington, DC: Woodrow Wilson Center Press, 2003.

Venkatesh, Sudhir. *Off the Books: The Underground Economy of the Urban Poor*. Cambridge: Harvard University Press, 2006.

Venkatesh, Sudhir, and Steven Levitt. "'Are We a Family or a Business?' History and Disjuncture in the Urban American Street Gang." *Theory and Society* 29, no. 4 (2000): 427–462.

ə OPEN ACCESS

Maintaining disorder: the micropolitics of drugs policy in Iran

Maziyar Ghiabi

ABSTRACT
This article analyses the ways in which the state 'treats' addiction among precarious drug (ab)users in Iran. While most Muslim-majority as well as some Western states have been reluctant to adopt harm reduction measures, the Islamic Republic of Iran has done so on a nationwide scale and through a sophisticated system of welfare intervention. Additionally, it has introduced devices of management of 'addiction' (the 'camps') that defy statist modes of punishment and private violence. What legal and ethical framework has this new situation engendered? And what does this new situation tell us about the governmentality of the state? Through a combination of historical analysis and ethnographic fieldwork, the article analyses the paradigm of government of the Iranian state with regard to disorder as embodied by the lives of poor drug (ab)users.

'I call the camps if someone calls me!'

Police Officer in Arak, September 2014.

I have the feeling we are crying on a grave which is empty.[1] How many people, arrested for drug addiction and sent to compulsory camps, have actually been in front of a judge? And, if this has happened, had the judge said anything to them about treatment? I doubt that we can find ten people in the whole country who have met a judge before going to a camp, so I think the question here is something else and it is not related to compulsory treatment. … The problem, it seems to me, is that the question is not medical and therapeutic, but one of social and political control.

Professor Emran Razzaghi, International Addiction Studies Conference, Tehran, 10 September 2014.

Introduction: ethnography of a policy

In the southern district of Tehran's Bazaar, between Mowlavi Street and Shoosh Street, there are four public gardens. The biggest and most popular of these is Harandi Park, which stands at the heart of the old neighbourhood of Darvazeh Ghar. Since 2014, Harandi Park and, to a similar extent, the others have been *lieux* of encounter of large groups of drug users who

http://orcid.org/0000-0002-2171-2811

This is an Open Access article distributed under the terms of the Creative Commons Attribution License (http://creativecommons.org/licenses/by/4.0/), which permits unrestricted use, distribution, and reproduction in any medium, provided the original work is properly cited.

camp there with tents, sleeping bags, bonfires and piles of cardboard on the ground. Over the warm seasons – between March and November – the number of street drug users residing within the perimeter of the parks and the connecting alleys reaches three to four thousand, with additional visitors towards the evening spleen.[2]

While on a late-morning stroll across the lawn, I encountered waste collectors and gardeners working their way between groups of drug users, chatting or just passing through their circles. Every now and then, a police motorbike would ride on the main road circumscribing the park or in the middle of it, with not much preoccupation with the people smoking heroin or *shisheh*, the word for methamphetamine (crystal meth) in Iran. The entrance of a bigger tent, close to a smelly empty pool that served as an open-air loo, was animated by the bustling of a dozen people. I was told later that the tent is where the main distribution of *gart* (heroin) and *shisheh* in the Harandi area takes place and that it is the centre of gravity of the park. This is not an underground, hidden site of criminality or an unseen zone of crisis/disorder; the park stands in the middle of one of Tehran's most popular neighbourhoods, which has a symbiotic relation to its great bazaar and is located close to the main metro line (Line 1) connecting the wealthy north with the city's poorer southern districts. In contrast to the ever-lasting declarations of the 'War on Drugs' and the ever-increasing number of drug arrests, the situation in Harandi casts light on a different approach based on limited tolerance of public drug use and the tacit acceptance of street hustling, more or less.

Activism among civil society groups and non-governmental organisations (NGOs) has attracted public attention to this place, which by 2015 had become a leitmotif of debate around drugs policy in Tehran. The city municipality and the mayor of the district denied their acceptance of the situation and reiterated that there is no plan to transform Harandi into a social experiment of de facto drug decriminalisation.[3] A temporary alternative to the plans for collection of drug (ab)users, it refrains from the incarceration or forced treatment of the compulsory camps, which I will discuss in detail in this article. Instead, by having large gatherings of so-called 'risky' drug (ab)users concentrated in specific areas such as Harandi Park, social workers and medical personnel can intervene with harm reduction services (eg needle exchange, condom distribution, etc.) and attempt to introduce them into the cycle of treatment, notably methadone maintenance, even though many of these drug (ab)users are meth smokers or polydrug users, for whom methadone, a pharmacological opiate substitute, is not effective. The 'dispersion of risk' is reduced, according to public officials, who imply that without Harandi the whole of Tehran would be a scene of open-air drug use and drug hustling, with the spectre of HIV epidemics looming all too large over the populace. It would be *uncontrollable*.

This ethnographic vignette casts light on the routines and connections of everyday drugs policy in Iran. This article, similarly, analyses the micropolitics of 'addiction' policies and the way Iranians and the Iranian state treat drug (ab)users. (Ab)user, here, suggests the ambiguity that rules the definition of 'addiction' as a social artefact and the addict as its primary actor. The limit between using and abusing drugs, indeed, rests ultimately upon a judgement on the status of the addict; it is the outcome of legal prosecution, economic degradation and policing practices. While most Muslim-majority as well as some Western states have been reluctant to adopt welfare-oriented measures (eg harm reduction) towards drug users, the Islamic Republic of Iran has done so on a nationwide scale enshrined in the 2010 drug law reform. The article asks: What legal and ethical framework has this new situation engendered?

And what does this tell us about state practices with regard to zones of social disorder and crisis? The article does question whether Iran is a theocracy, a republic or just another authoritarian state as it has been the subject of endless scholarly work. The article is not interested in 'what is the nature of power'. Rather I discuss, following Deleuze's incitement, 'in what ways power is exercised, in what place it is formed and why it is everywhere'.[4] In this way the article shows how power works in the micropolitical dimension and how it defies top-down expositions of politics in the Islamic Republic.

Based on ethnographic research (immersion in the field) and more than 50 semi-structured interviews carried out between 2012 and 2016, the article analyses the grassroots dimension of drugs policy in Iran.[5] Ultimately, what governs the lives of precarious addicts is not the state's imposition of order through disciplinary mechanisms or Islamising principles. Instead, it is an assemblage of public and private means aimed at *maintaining disorder*.[6]

What is a 'camp' in Iran?

Known formally as short-term and medium-term in-patient treatment centres, these places are popularly known as *camps*. The word, rather than recalling the heinous reference to the Nazi concentration camps, refers to the expression *camp-e tabestani*, meaning 'summer camps' or 'holiday camps', that had become very much à *la mode* among middle-class Iranians in the 1990s.[7] When the camps soon became publicly known for their dehumanising conditions, the label 'camp' proved that destiny may sometimes be in one's name. As the Latin speakers would have said, *nomen omen*: 'name is destiny'.[8]

Adapted after the philosophy of recovery of Narcotics Anonymous (NA), the equivalent of Alcoholics Anonymous for drugs, the camps are based on a detoxification process, usually lasting for one 21- to 28-day session.[9] As charitable institutions, they are under the supervision of the Welfare Organisation – the state institution (formerly a ministry) charged with social assistance programmes – but they cultivate a close relationship with the police. In fact, the private rehab camps are regularly contacted by the police in order 'to accommodate' arrested drug users for rehab programmes, whenever the state-run compulsory camps are overwhelmed.[10] While people referred by the police to the compulsory camps are treated free of charge, those referred to the rehab camps are expected to pay the fees, at least partially. In some cases, the Welfare Organisation covers the cost of in-patient treatment (but the bureaucratic process is time consuming, and its outcome uncertain). The camp owners admit that in no case have they demanded the full amount. They accept any monetary contribution the addict, or his family, is capable of making. Most of the time, however, people referred to private camps by the police refuse to pay and, consequently, as a camp owner explained me, 'addicts are arrested by the police on Monday, and released by us [the camp owners] on Tuesday, because they don't have money [to pay the fees]'.[11] This has triggered criticism of the police, especially in view of the 2010 law reform that puts emphasis on 'the judicial supervision of the arrest, treatment and release process', which would require a judicial dossier to be opened for every referral. The camps are not legally required to keep the drug users against their will, so in the case of escape they do not take further action. Plus, there are no guards or police at their gates. The conservative newspaper *Keyhan* reminded the police that 'the [private] camps have no right to maintain the addicts without a ruling of the judiciary; similarly they cannot let the addict leave the camp without approval of the judicial authorities'.[12] Both practices are the rule rather than the exception. The dossier, alas, is missing.

With a drug-using population which has been described as among the largest worldwide, counting an estimated one and a half million out of a population of 80 million, the place of drugs is central to Iranian politics.[13] Rooted in the cultural practice of people (ie opium use), Iranians have also acquired a new taste for drugs as exemplified by the popularity of heroin and methamphetamines (*shisheh*). More importantly, governance of the drug question has resulted in the adoption of progressive, forward-looking policies, starting from the early 2000s, despite the Islamic Republic's uncompromising pledge to the War on Drugs. By 2005, the reformist government of Mohammad Khatami had introduced, under the pressure of an expanding HIV epidemic in prisons, a comprehensive set of 'harm reduction' measures. These included policies that remain often controversial in Europe and North America, such as needle exchange and distribution programmes, including in prisons (up to 2009), methadone maintenance and legitimisation of rehabilitation throughout the country.[14] By 2017, two safe injection rooms for drug users operated in Tehran (nearby the opening scene' parks) as part of a pilot project aimed at gathering evidence of this alternative model of drugs policy. This has put Iran ahead of most countries in the world in terms of drugs policy experimentation, despite a lack of reference to the Iranian case in international policy circles.

The institutions involved in the management of drugs policy are many: the Ministry of Public Heath oversees the work of methadone clinics; the Welfare Organisation is in charge of supervising the rehabilitation centres for drug addiction; and the police (*Niru-ye Entezami-ye Jomhuri-ye Eslami*, The Law Enforcement of the Islamic Republic, NAJA). Iran's law enforcement, besides their duty of countering drug dealing, have also been involved in compulsory treatment programmes for drug addiction. All these institutions partake in the governance of Iran's umbrella organisation for illicit drugs, the Drug Control Headquarters (DCHQ), which operates under the mandate of the president of the republic (Figure 1).

The coexistence of multiple visions of the drug phenomenon among these institutions has produced a contradictory set of responses. This ambiguity is enshrined in the legal framework of the drugs laws, which, in light of the emergence of crystal meth, were reformed in 2010.

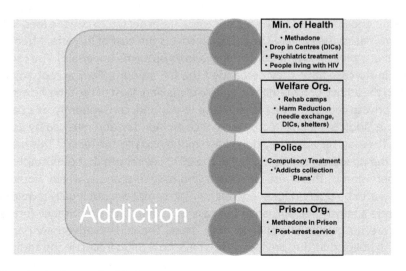

Figure 1. State institutions and addiction.

The oxymoronic laws

The 2010 drug laws reform, approved after complex negotiations within the Council for the Discernment of the Expediency of the State (aka Expediency Council),[15] displayed the political and legal situation of drug (ab)use, following the approval of the harm reduction policy. Under the populist presidency of Mahmud Ahmadinejad (2005–2013), observers expected a setback for the harm reduction system. However, practices of support to drug (ab)users continued and effectively widened their quantitative scope after 2005. By 2007, there were 51 government facilities, 457 private outpatient centres and an additional 26 transition centres.[16] By 2009, there were already 1569 treatment centres, 337 government centres and 1232 non-government centres operational throughout the country, providing services to 643,516 persons.[17] Why and how this occurred is a question that goes beyond the scope of this article, but, in summary, one can tell that the expansion of public health measures under Ahmadinejad followed the logic of privatisation, which remained a driving principle during his mandate in all socioeconomic fields. In addition to this, one should mention the influence that the medical community and the NGOs had acquired over the late 2000s. Both contributed to the legitimisation of this approach during the post-reformist period. The fact that harm reduction and treatment of drug abuse had been included in the text of the General Policies of the Islamic Republic of Iran, emanating from the Expediency Council and approved directly by the Supreme Jurist Ali Khamenei, surely contributed to this process.[18]

The 2010 law reform materialised also the idiosyncrasies of the politics of drugs in the twenty-first century. The law itself provides a localised example of the paradigm of government with regard to the crises of drug (ab)use that the post-reformist government had faced. Firstly, the 2010-reformed law legitimised harm reduction practices that had been practiced since the early 2000s, by including them into an institutional order. Secondly, the law instituted specific centres for the implementation of harm reduction and rehab centres; these include state-run centres and private clinics as well as charitable and grassroots organisations. More crucially, the 2010 law established a distinction between those drug (ab)users who are willing to seek treatment and, indeed, to refer to a recognised institution (eg clinic, camp), and those who do not seek treatment, who therefore can be subjected to arrest. It also introduced the death penalty for people carrying more than 30 g of amphetamine-type stimulants (ATS). The line that divides the status of the categories remained thin and highly ambiguous. The reform produced an oxymoronic law.

The provisions of the 2010 law seemed to respond, in fact, to the necessities materialised by the expanding crisis of methamphetamine that had surfaced in public spaces. Public officials during the late 2000s agreed that people addicted to meth could not be cured, or that a cure for them was either unavailable or too expensive to be provided on a large scale.[19] Meth users tend to be more mobile compared to people using heroin, who tend to 'chill' in a quiet place in contemplation of the spell of time. Iranian meth users had therefore a visible presence in the city, which caused concern among the law and order cadres as well as the public (Figure 2).[20]

This persuasion may have convinced the cadres of the state to seek mechanisms of intervention that were not necessarily coherent with each other, but which, from a state perspective, responded to the imperatives of public order. Pharmacological substitution programmes

Figure 2. Meanwhile on the Tehran Metro: a shisheh smoker.
Note: This photograph circulated widely in September 2015 among Telegram App users. I received it in the drugs policy group (which includes leading members of the drugs policy community) 'The Challenges of Addiction'.

(methadone) and harm reduction practices (needle exchange) were inadequate to respond to the treatment of meth users. The medical community had expressed its impotency regarding the wave of meth use over the early 2010s, a fact that had implications also for the way the police needed to counter the issue. A lack of medicalised solutions implied that the practice of isolation and confinement became the primary response. This time, however, it was not through incarceration in state prisons, as had been the case since 1979, but through the work of different agents: state-run compulsory centres, private rehab and informal treatment camps.

Humanitarian security

Since the implementation of the 2010 reform, the state had regularly intervened to collect street addicts and had confined them to compulsory camps, much to the astonishment of those who had worked towards the legitimation of harm reduction.[21] The category of people targeted by these operations are the unemployed proletariat, a wageless class of mendicants, petty robbers, petty dealers, garbage collectors and ex-prisoners who fall outside the moral order of modern society and its political economy.[22] In reality, part of the medical community and NGO sector had supported the text of the 2010 law on the basis that it legitimised harm reduction and proceeded towards a decriminalisation of addiction. The compulsory treatment camps, supporters of the 2010 law argued, were the necessary venue to medicalise addiction among those categories of (ab)users who could not be persuaded to seek treatment. It would be, they added, the safest way to introduce the addict into the cycle of treatment, thus facilitating his/her recovery.[23] Yet the state-run camps often exposed situations of degradation, which prompted several officials to express publicly their opposition to this model, on the grounds that it neither brought results nor offered humanitarian support.

The origins of this institutional model can be traced back to the early years of the Ahmadinejad government. In 2007, already, the new head of the Drug Control Headquarters, Commander-in-Chief Ahmad-Moghaddam, announced that 'the addict must be considered a *patient-criminal* who, if he is not under treatment, the court will rule for him compulsory treatment and the police will be the executor of a police-based treatment'. He then added, 'we have to build *maintenance* camps; the police has already built camps for the homeless addicts and vagrants, which in the opinion of treatment officials can be used as maintenance camps for addicts for a certain period (emphasis added)'.[24] This announcement can be considered an *ante tempore* elucidation of the 2010 law model. The continuity among homelessness, vagrancy and addiction is exemplified in the circumstances preceding Tehran's Non-Alignment Summit in summer 2012. Ahead of the official visit of 120 state representatives, the police rounded up several thousand homeless people through the 'addict collection programme'.[25] Regardless of whether they were also drug users, the status of homelessness triggered the intervention of the police in cleansing the public space.

The fact that, genealogically, the compulsory treatment camps were formerly camps for the internment of vagrants and homeless people revealed the primary concern of the state with regard to the management of the public (dis)order and the lumpen classes of the cities.[26] Much like in the 1980s, the officials adopted a language that emphasised the need to 'quarantine' problematic drug (ab)users, which had previously been addressed to the street vagrants.[27] Yet this rhetoric did not anticipate a return to past forms of intervention; the post-reformist 'quarantine', instead, envisaged the presence and 'supervision of doctors, psychologists, psychiatrists and infection experts as well as social workers' and the referral, after the period of mandatory treatment, *of maintenance*, to 'the non-state sector, NGOs and treatment camps'.[28] This was largely discussed and never fully implemented. The rationale, it was argued, was to introduce 'dangerous addicts' and risky groups into the cycle of treatment, the first of which were managed by the state, through the 'therapeutic police', the law enforcement in charge of addiction treatment in the state-run camps.

After the approval of the 2010 law, large budgetary allocations were made by the government to the police in furtherance to the construction of compulsory camps. In 2011, ca.

USD 8 million was allocated to the Ministry of Interior,[29] with the objective to build a major compulsory treatment camp in Fashapuyieh, in the southern area of the capital Tehran. This first camp was designed to intern in the first phase around 4000 addicts (with no clear criteria of inclusion), with the number going up to 40,000 when the entire camp had been completed.[30] Other camps were expected to operate in Iran's major regions, including Khorasan, Markazi, Fars and Mazandaran.[31] The deputy director of the DCHQ, Tah Taheri, announced that 'about 250,000 people needed to be sent to the compulsory treatment camps by the end of the year' as part of the governmental effort to curb the new dynamics of addiction.[32] The ambitious plan had the objective, among other things, of unburdening the Prison Organisation from the mounting number of drug offenders, a move likely to benefit also the finances of the judiciary and the police, always overwhelmed by drug dossiers.

Yet the nature of the compulsory treatment camps resembles that of the prisons. After all, Iran's drug legislation included a provision that required the separation of drug-related criminals from the rest of the prison population.[33] This plan, which had been given support over the years, had never materialised on a large scale, leaving the prisons filled with drug offenders.[34] By 2010, the prison population in Iran had increased to 250,000 inmates,[35] equivalent to ca. 312 prisoners for every 100,000 people. The rate of incarceration remained significantly lower than that of the US and Russia, the top incarcerators worldwide, which counted 716 inmates per 100,000 and 415 per 100,000, respectively.[36] But given that drug offences constituted the prime cause of incarceration in Iran, around 50 to 70%,[37] the ratio speaks of the centrality of incarceration within the national drugs strategy.

Mostafa Purmohammadi, a prominent Iranian prosecutor,[38] identified 'addicted prisoners' as one of the main concerns of the national prisons, and advised that the country needed to implement the mandatory treatment camps in order to alleviate the dangers and troubles of the prison system.[39] Consequently, for the first time in many decades, Iran's prison population had decreased by some 40,000 people in 2012, reaching the still-cumbersome number of 210,000 inmates. This datum, heralded as evidence of success by the post-reformist government, could be actually traced back to the introduction, on a massive scale, of the compulsory camps for drug addicts. In light of this consideration, the population confined in state institutions for charges of criminal behaviour (including public addiction) had actually mounted to almost double the number in prisons prior to 2010s.

Since the establishment of the Islamic Republic, the overall number of prisoners had multiplied by six times, and the number of those incarcerated for drug-related charges by 14 times, with one in three court cases allegedly being drug related in 2009.[40] If during the reformist period the introduction of harm reduction had been prompted, among other things, from the HIV epidemic in prisons,[41] the post-reformist government reacted with public outrage against the waste of money that the incarceration of drug addicts represented. In 2010, an official from the Prison Organisation outlined that maintenance costs were ca. US$1 per day per person, equivalent to 1.5 million per day, *ca.* 0.058% of the national budget (2009/2010).[42] Researchers from state institutions demonstrated that treating drug addicts would cost an average of 15 times less than incarcerating them.[43] In view of the number of drug (ab)users in prison, the creation of the compulsory treatment camps provided an alternative device for the maintenance and management of this population. The head of the judiciary, Ayatollah Sadegh Ardeshir Amoli Larijani, echoed these results, asking for a swift re-settling of addicted prisoners in the compulsory camps for treatment, which, instead of being under the supervision of the Prison Organisation, are managed by the DCHQ.[44]

At the same time, the government proceeded towards a significant expansion of methadone treatment, bringing treatment to more than 40,000 prisoners by 2014. Methadone, in this regard, represented an acceptable solution, as it was produced and controlled by the state, it was readily available through private and public clinics, and it greatly facilitated – by virtue of its pharmacological effects – the management of unruly subjects, such as drug addicts, in the contexts of prisons. Inspired by the relative success of these methadone programmes (in prisons, as much as outside), methadone treatment programmes were introduced inside some of the compulsory treatment camps supervised by the police. This, it seems, was identified as a productive way to introduce the highest numbers of drug abusers into the cycle of treatment, via allegedly less harmful drugs such as methadone. By familiarising arrested drug (ab)users with methadone, and by referring them to public methadone clinics, the authorities sought *to keep them off* more dangerous drugs, such as heroin.

Compulsory camps have also been part of the political economy of addiction in the Islamic Republic. By collecting, on a regular basis, street addicts from across the cities' hotspots, especially in the capital Tehran, the police benefit from a substantial financial flow, justified by the expenses that it putatively incurs in managing the camps. Given that most of the state-run camps are known for their Spartan and down-to-earth conditions and services, it is implied that considerable amounts of money are filling the coffers of the police. This also implies that the police has a stake in the continuation of the activities of the compulsory camps and in the seasonal intervention aimed at gathering so-called 'dangerous drug addicts'. The rationale behind this system is similar to that behind the instrumental arrests by the French police of 'illegal migrants' and 'potheads', or in the bonus/arrest cycle governing local policing in the US.[45] Similar procedures operate in these different contexts, where the public presence of drug users justifies budgetary expansion for the police, out of the politics of police arrest numbers.

The camps embody a new mode of law enforcement, one which, instead of contesting public health interventions (eg harm reduction), uses its rhetoric and for reasons that are not ultimately humanitarian. It is a form of humanitarian security, or, using Didier Fassin's oxymoron, 'compassionate repression'.[46] This strategy emphasised a management and maintenance of disorderly populations through coercive mechanisms, while leaving the larger group of drug (ab)users unbothered. But only a tiny portion of social disorder is targeted through the compulsory camps and the police.

'I can check on the girls when I am not here!'

The mechanisms of intervention in the field of addiction have been more multifaceted than that of state-run camps. In fact, state-run camps entered this field alongside societal organisations that had set foot in the period preceding 2010. Rehabilitation centres have been operating legally or informally since the mid-1980s, although their extraordinary expansion can be traced back to the early 2000s and the new politico-medical atmosphere brought in by the reformists.[47] Despite the promise of monetary subsidies from the state, most of the camps exist within an economy of subsistence based on donations from local communities, recovered addicts and mosques, and government cheques.

Official statistics reported in newspapers in the last decade reveal that one in 10 addicts in Iran is female.[48] Yet there are also strong indications that a growing number of women are using crystal meth, which would logically imply that the percentage of female users has increased in the last decade. Women represent only 5% of all referrals to state institutions providing service for drug abuse, but a much higher presence is revealed in formal and informal treatment camps.[49] The stigma for women is also more pervasive and, in several cases, female treatment camps have been set on fire because these camps were deemed immoral and 'nest[s] of sexual vice'.[50] Most of these places operate at the margins of the city, or inside apartments in popular neighbourhoods, in order to avoid being recognised as camps. No outdoor indication or explicit address is provided and the referrals occur through the state line of enquiry – ie the police – or through informal connections, via the family. Thence, the female treatment camps operate along those margins in which state intervention is rendered more problematic by the sensibility of gender issues, while popular resentment and stigma against them menaces their public presence. The state, for that matter, is reticent to allocate sufficient licences for the female camps, out of concern that the mushrooming of these institutions – once formally recognised by the state – would stipulate a less ambiguous datum of female drug (ab)use, one which might refute the static officialdom to which the government has hitherto pledged. In this way, it also secures flexibility in its cooperation with civil society. This condition marks more explicitly female drug (ab)users, but it also affects the phenomenon of treatment as a whole.

In 2011, the government approved the construction of one compulsory treatment camp for female addicts, to be located in the Persian Gulf region of Hormozgan. The site would host multiple categories of ab(users) whose common feature is their relation to the street (and the moral order): runaway girls trapped in drug abuse, streetwalkers, sex workers, female mendicants, and petty drug dealers and users. All these categories blur into each other, at least if one *sees like a state*.[51] The location itself indicated that the site of this camp had to be peripheral; south along the coast of Hormozgan, the camp would work half as a public exile and half as a refuge from the public gaze. Hormozgan itself, however, had historically been characterised by heavy drug (ab)use, including among women, a fact that perhaps further justified the location of the camp there. The particularity of this project was also its nature as a joint venture between the state and a private organisation expected to manage the centre, an exception both to the 2010 law and to the practice in other camps.[52] Given the ethical challenges of running a state-run treatment camp for women, the authorities partly disengaged from its routine administration and partly took advantage of the existing expertise and activism of NGOs dedicated for precarious women's affairs.[53] Yet a single female camp, located at the very periphery of Iran, could not comply with the necessities dictated by growing meth use among women. This void had been already filled by the establishment of female treatment camps, managed by private individuals or charities. I shall refer to one of them in particular, to which I was given repeated access over the course of my ethnographic fieldwork in 2014: the women's camp situated in the city of Arak.

Operating as a sister branch of a male camp, the female camp could hardly be described as a camp. In reality, it was an apartment inside a four-storey building in a formerly middle-class area (mostly inhabited by public employees), today referred to generally as *pay-in-shahr*, 'downtown' (in Persian, it indicates 'a popular periphery'). The apartment has three rooms and a small kitchen, with a long corridor used by the girls as a lounge to watch satellite TV (which is formally banned in Iran). The director had a number of close-circuit TV (CCTV) cameras installed in the apartment and has access to the video on her laptop; she could control the three rooms of 'the camp' from the desk of her office, or when she was at home, via an online application to which the CCTV cameras are connected. 'In this way', she explained, 'I can check on the girls when I am not here'. She argued that the camp is self-managed by the girls themselves, who cook, clean and take care of the daily management of the place. They have a friendly, intimate relationship, she held, and she would like the place to be as comfortable and welcoming as possible for them. The door at the entrance of the apartment, nonetheless, has to remain locked at all times when she is not in; 'otherwise the girls might run away and might go back to use drugs'. When I asked her 'What if a person inside the apartment feels sick or needs urgent help?' she justified this by saying that she can be reached at any time via mobile phone and that she checks on them regularly via the CCTV. She also relied on one of the girl in particular, Samira, who helped her by doing the grocery shopping and checking on the other girls while the director is away. Samira had been in the camp for a year and a half, since she was referred there by the female prison organisation. She had spent time in prison on several occasions for meth possession, aggression, armed robbery and 'moral crimes' (a euphemism for alleged sex work). Whether institutionalisation in this private camp had produced positive effects on her life is hard to say; certainly, she and I had the perception that her existence was suspended and that, despite the fact that she had stopped using drugs, addiction was still very much present in her life. In a way, this was nothing extraordinary: 'I do not smoke anymore', like 'I do not drink anymore', is part of the experience of people suffering from addiction, of the eternally 'recovering addict'.[54]

The fee for a 21-day period is ca. US$110, which is one third of Iranians' average monthly salary (ca. US$470).[55] The people coming to the camp, as I discovered, did not live in Arak but usually came from other cities, since they wanted to avoid being recognised by their communities. This small apartment in particular had two girls from Khorramabad, a Kurdish woman from Kermanshah and another from Khuzistan. Three of the girls were interned in the camp as part of a compulsory treatment programme and were sent to the camp by the police. Since there is just one compulsory treatment camp for women – located at ca. 120 km from Arak – the authorities rely on private camps to accommodate these women, in which case they also pay the fees for their treatment. Generally, the director explains, the women referred by the police are more problematic, some of whom manifest serious health issues, while others have several criminal charges pending in their dossiers. One of them confided to me that the doctor had diagnosed her with *skizofreni* ('schizophrenia') and asked me whether it was curable or not. It is not rare for these camps to refuse to take people referred by the police, out of fear of health contagion or in order to preserve their reputation.

The maintenance of order in the camp can indeed be troublesome. In the past, one of the women assaulted the director and threatened her with a knife. She was able to react, get a hold of the situation, and beat the woman, who had threatened her, under her feet. The director was condemned by the judge for her violent behaviour towards women interned in the camp. The camp was closed down for few months, before obtaining another licence under her husband's organisation, which, I came to discover, is also a rehab camp for male addicts.[56] The camp guaranteed a venue for 'treatment' and 'control' of female (ab)users who would otherwise be imprisoned. This does not imply that there is a statist strategy of covert manipulation through these organisations. Instead, this and other rehab centres operated as rhizomes of the state, a form of 'government at distance' of the drug phenomenon – a management of disorder.[57]

State of camouflage and subterfuge

It has become common knowledge – if not a joke! – that contemporary Iranian society offers a wide range of informal, illegal centres for the provision of services (eg retirement houses, pharmacies, education centres), and that despite the government's repetitive calls for their closure, these enterprises continue a lucrative existence.[58] But the sheer quantitative dimension of the illegal addiction camps – nine out 10 rehab camps – signifies that this category affects more largely and, perhaps, categorically the phenomenon itself. Indeed, one could say that legal treatment camps in Iran are marginalia within the page of treatment. The phenomenon of camps suggests that these institutions, regardless of their public/private, legal/illegal status, exist in a continuum. Together they constitute a primary means of intervention – or mode of government – of addiction. Already in 2007, the government warned against the mushrooming of illegal camps and gave an ultimatum of three months to all camp managers to register for a licence at the Welfare Organisation.[59] The DCHQ announced that 'by the end of the year, the problem of the camps will be solved',[60] yet in 2014, the number of these institutions was higher than ever, with a veritable burgeoning across the country.

In Tehran alone, there were more than 400 illegal camps,[61] while in Isfahan, out of 300 camps, only 16 had a licence.[62] In the city of Arak, where I conducted part of my fieldwork, there were about 50 illegal camps, located near villages or main routes, or in private houses.[63] These camps provide the opportunity for treatment for people and their families whose economic possibilities are limited. With the burden of economic sanctions being trickled down to popular strata, treatment in these institutions represented a more affordable and down-to-earth solution. Given the rootedness of the illegal camps, public officials started to change their approach, describing the camps as 'a positive sign, because it implies that many people in Iran seek treatment'.[64] As the country's treatment capacity could not exhaust the demand for treatment, the officials hold, the camps are instrumental in this endeavour, even when they operate illegally.[65]

In the management of addiction, however, their role bypasses the logic of treatment and service provision. One could define the illegal camps using a Persian idiomatic expression: 'the hand that captures the snake [*dast-e mar-gir*]'. Exclusively legal, bureaucratic or administrative means are deemed, according to the post-reformist govern*mentality*, insufficient and ineffective. To 'treat' addiction, hence, the state exploits the extra-legal function of the camps in areas from which the state itself had progressively disengaged, or has dissimulated its presence. The workings of the illegal camps can be sketched as such. In a situation when someone acts violently and volatilely, usually under the influence of meth, the family of the subject usually opts for the intervention of the camp personnel. This is regarded as a preferable option to the intervention of the police. By calling the illegal camp, the family avoids criminal charges, which could produce incarceration and time-consuming lawsuits, all of which cause greater economic burden to the family itself. Similarly, the intervention of the camp 'thugs' guarantees a lower profile for the family than that of the police, which, especially in popular neighbourhoods, can cause rumours and reputation damage (aka *aberurizi*).[66]

The police, too, seem to support the illegal camp system and, at times, inform the personnel of the camps about the location of the complaint. In this way, the camps take on the duties of the police, with regard to drug (ab)use.[67] A police officer confirmed this informally during a conversation:

> I am really happy that these camps exist; if a family calls us, instead of sending a soldier or a policeman, we call one of the people from the camps. So, if someone gets beaten, that's the camp people, which also means that, if someone has to beat someone else, it's always the camp people [and not the police]. Instead of taking the addict here to the police station, where he might vomit, feel sick and make the entire place dirty, he goes to the camp. Instead of coming here to shout and beat up people, or to bring diseases, HIV, he goes there. I call the camp if someone calls me.[68]

The camps are, thus, an apparatus of management of social crises and maintenance of disorder in the guise of addiction. *De facto*, many of the illegal treatment camps operate as compulsory treatment camps, because those secluded in them, for periods varying between 21 days and one year, have been forced into the camps. They have been forced not by the police, but by their local communities – usually their family members. The police play the part of the observer or the informant; they inform the camps, on some occasions, of the location and situation of a complaint, but no formal undertaking is initiated.

Inside the camps – several personal stories disclose – the managers adopt 'alternative techniques' for the treatment of addiction, the most infamous ones being 'beating-treatment', 'water-treatment', 'dog-treatment' and 'chain-treatment'.[69] Although there is generally a propensity towards sensationalising these accounts, the horrid accounts from inside the camps are telling about the lack of humanitarian purpose behind the workings of the camps. As in the case of the state-run *Shafaq* camp, which became the focus of a scandal in the 2010s, the deaths of interned addicts is the public signature of the camps' practice.[70] In 2016, all women were dismissed from the Shafaq centre, amidst allegations of violence.[71]

The liability for the crime remains exclusively with the camp managers, as noted in the statement of the police officer mentioned above. Camp managers are punished severely for casualties within the illegal camps. The state authorities have resorted, according to Islamic law, to *qesas*, retributive justice ('an eye for an eye'), envisaging the death penalty for the camp managers (specifically in case the family of the victim refuses to accept the 'blood money').[72] Although there are no clear data on the rate of deaths within the illegal camps, the reports in the newspapers suggest that these events have not been only sporadic between 2012 and 2016.

Among street drug (ab)users, the narratives of some of these camps gained mythological dimensions and instil vivid fear, a sentiment that is somehow reminiscent of a persecution. In this way, the camps fulfil a double promise: on the one hand, they intervene along the problematic margins of Iranian society (its 'uncivil' society), through the creation of extra-legal, unaccountable and, in view of their quantitative dimension, omnipresent institutions. They reduce the work of the police, while receiving nothing in exchange from the state. On the other hand, the camps are managed by former drug users, whose place within normative society remains unsettled. They struggle to find employment in regular businesses, and their housing status remains uncertain, and they often rely on temporary family accommodation; the camp, hence, becomes the only stable unit within their life, functioning as both occupation and residence. The post-reformist government succeeded in its quest 'to socialise the war on drugs' and to mobilise, by other means, civil society for statist ends.[73] It is not, however, a co-option of civil society, which remains autonomous and unburdened by governmental diktats. In fact, this mobilisation does not prop up, as a grand strategy, any macropolitical agenda. With the camps providing motivation and an ecosystem in which to find their place within society, the camp owners rehearse a system in which the phenomenon of drug (ab) use dissolves into the machinery of treatment. Former (ab)users are employed in them and, whether willingly or involuntarily, mistreat other 'addicts', along the lines of previous securitising policies against drug users. This phenomenon is a form of 'grassroots authoritarianism',[74] whereby social elements belonging to societal milieux of diverse nature partake in mechanisms of control, discipline and treatment fundamentally *maintaining disorder*. The camps' relationship with the state remains ambiguous, based on rhetorical condemnation by public officials, haphazard prosecution by the judiciary, and clandestine connections, for instance in the referral of complaints by the police to the illegal camps.

The multitude of illegal treatment camps hints at another statist rationale. Licences for these camps can be provided by the state through the Welfare Organisation; but in order to do so, the government needs to guarantee minimum financial support, which given the large number of these centres would drain the budget from other treatment programmes, notably the compulsory treatment camps. 'The closure of the illegal treatment camps is not part of the main policy of the state', declared a public official in a conference, adding that 'the existence of these camps is better than their non-existence, because their closure would mean disorder among the dangerous addicts'.[75] In view of their indirect connection to the police, which sees them as a useful complement vis-à-vis problematic users, these institutions can be interpreted as part of the state effect. Despite their private and unrecognised status, they perform a public, state-sanctioned role.[76]

Despite almost a decade of reiterated calls to close the doors of the illegal treatment camps, these institutions maintain solid roots and operate, *qua* rhizomes, across the margins of rural and urban Iran. Their ubiquity has given rise to the phenomenon of *kamp-gardi*, 'camp-touring', which refers to the unending journey of the addict from camp to camp, a circumnavigation that rarely has a way out and often leads to the destitution of the individual, or to their incorporation in the activities of a particular camp.[77] Those whose experiences have been more telling are often called by the rest of the community of the camps the 'Marco Polo', because they have visited as many camps as the Venetian traveller had done during his travels of the *Milione*.

There is no spelled-out policy about the role of illicit rehab camps, but the daily routines of drugs policy reproduce what works as a maintenance assemblage. It is at the level of micropolitics that this condition is best captured, as illustrated above. The camps operate as a rhizome of the state, which instead of reproducing vertical lines of control and discipline, becomes diffused and horizontal – similar to the grassroots (rhizomes) of a tree. When societal control is practiced, this is cropped out through the rhizomes that stem from the horizontal roots of the state itself, camouflaged as other forms of intervention, the illegal world of treatment dealing with the illegal life of drugs users. This forms what I define as *maintaining disorder* (Figure 3).[78]

Conclusions: maintaining disorder

There is no fundamental rupture, or watershed, among the state-run compulsory camps, the informal, illegal camps and the Harandi Park model (Table 1). Together they fulfil an

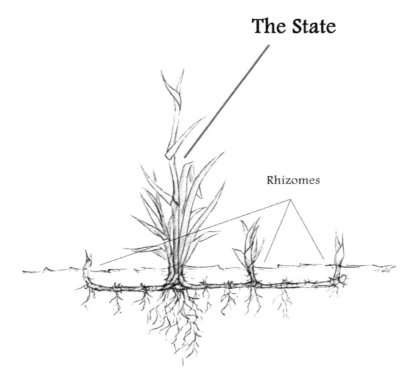

Figure 3. The state and its rhizomes.
Note: Drawing courtesy of Italian artist *Fruk* (aka Federica Di Violante).

ultimately political objective in reaction to a phenomenon that has permanently been framed as a crisis. Because of that, the rehab camps enter a field of interest to the state – one could say an expediency – in which the underlying rule is the *maintenance of disorder*, the management of a permanent crisis, an ordinary emergency embodied in the presence of drugs users. It is not, as one would expect in the Islamic Republic, a matter of moral evaluation, religious justification or variation in (post-)Islamist change. Islam and theological considerations do not have a place in this matter and, in fact, found no place in the narratives described in this article.

There are other social fields where what the article demonstrated for drugs can be similarly ascertained. Here are a few cursory examples: Iranian authorities, based on religious interpretation, allow and actively sponsor so-called 'temporary marriages' (*sigheh* in Farsi), while *de jure* punishing premarital sex. Temporary marriage is a contractual agreement (as all marriage is according to Islamic jurisprudence) in which the two parties determine beforehand the duration of the marital bond. In practice, temporary marriage has resulted in the tolerance of sex work, especially in sites of religious pilgrimage (Qom, Mashhad), but has also become an expedient for people not willing to engage in a permanent union.[79]

Similarly, since the late 1980s, the authorities have legislated in favour of gender reassignment surgery (sex change), legalising and providing welfare support for people who want to change gender, while denying legal status to homosexuals.[80] This has gained the Islamic Republic a reputation as a leading centre for sex change surgery worldwide.

Table 1. Rehabilitation 'camps'.

	State run	Private	Illegal
Legal status	Legislated under Article 16 of the 2010 drug law.	Legislated under Article 15 of the 2010 drug law.	Illegal.
Management	Managed by the NAJA, with support from the Welfare Organisation, Ministry of Health.	Managed by private organisations, charities, associations, etc.	Managed by private individuals, or group of people.
Funding	Receive direct state funding, through DCHQ.	No direct funding from the state. Fees are applied for treatment periods of ca. 21 days. Donations from families. Subsidies from Welfare Organisation per treated addict.	No subsidies or governmental funding. Fees apply per person. Donations from local communities. Negotiations for poor families.
Personnel	Social workers, police officers, medical professionals (on paper). In practice, police and local aides.	Former drug users; NA members; social workers and volunteers.	Former and current users.
Methods	Detoxification; in some facilities, methadone substitution is provided. *Narcotics Anonymous* (NA) support potentially available.	Detoxification, mostly based on NA 12 steps; some organisations adopt specific therapies, eg music therapy, meditation.	Detoxification, also through violent means and coercion.
Target group	Street drug users; homeless drug users; *Patoqs*. Polydrug users.	Depends on the organisation; mostly, lowermiddle-class drug users, both urban and rural. In specific cases, upper-class people.	Poor drug users, young people, men under psychotic attacks; mostly *shisheh* and polydrug users.
Means of referral	Arrests. Police operations, drug addicts' round-up plans. Coercive.	Voluntary referral, through advertisement, word of mouth.	Family, community referral; police referral. Mostly coercive.
Fees	Free.	Set fees (government decree); often negotiated.	Flexible fees, based on status, negotiation.

In its ethical dilemma and political incongruence, the drugs and addiction question resembles the above-mentioned cases, for the Islamic Republic has systematically criminalised drug offenders and punished them with draconian measures, while it has also provided one of the most progressive and controversial sets of public health programmes for drug (ab) users. In quantitative scope, however, the drugs case is far more conspicuous and mainstream than the issues of sex work and sex change. As seen in the narratives of the article, maintaining disorder, instead of imposing order, had governed the logics of public interventions on drugs. This approach prompts limited tolerance of public drugs use – and the life of 'addicts' – in the case of Harandi Park as well as in the existence of illegal treatment camps, where their life is subject to informal control. The contradictions and articulations of this assemblage ultimately show the primacy of political prerogatives over ideological lineages.

This frame of analysis may prove useful for the understanding of political processes at large: in the tolerance of opposition and dissent within ambiguous limits of institutional politics; in the dynamics of clerical opposition within the Islamic Republic; and in the enforcement of public codes of conduct, as related to the *hijab*. In this article, maintaining disorder defined the governmental approach to the drug crisis but also the state's ideology of practice.

This art operates at the level of fabrication, make-believe and execution, confuting the notional existence of law and the state, as seen in the case of the camps and the park. In intervening on the phenomenon of drug (ab)use, the Islamic Republic envisioned its modus operandi as one based on secular pillars of management. The result has been a paradigm of government that deals with social crisis and ethical disorder without the objective of solving it, or of imposing a strict script on it. Instead, what is distinctive is the engendering grey area of state control/repression/compassion in dealing with precarious lives. This grey area situates Iran's case in the global grey areas of the immigration detention centres, the homeless shelters, the terrorist detainees' camps. Seen this perspective, maintaining disorder is not specific to Iran, but is a paradigm of government in the current epoch.

Disclosure statement

No potential conflict of interest was reported by the author.

Funding

This work was supported by the Wellcome Trust Society & Ethics Doctoral Scholarship [Grant No. WT101988MA]. The symposium where the paper was first presented was made possible by Wellcome Trust Small Grants [Grant No. 202095/Z/16/Z].

Acknowledgements

I would like to acknowledge the comments and advice of the participants of the Symposium 'Drugs, Politics and Society in the Global South' held in Oxford in October 2016. My gratitude goes also to the Wellcome Trust which enabled this research to take place. Moreover, I would like to thank Dennis Rodgers, Rasmus Christian Elling, Pablo Howard Seward Delaporte, Stephanie Cronin, Mitra Asfari, Jim Mills, Billie Jeanne Brownlee, Rafa Gude and Fariba Adelkhah, for their critical comments on parts of and ideas discussed in this article. Special thanks also the United Nations Office on Drugs and Crime, particularly to Gelareh Mostahshari, who provided very useful comments on a draft of this article. I am also grateful to Sean Rothman and Shahid Qader for their editorial assistance in the preparation of the Special Issue. All errors are my sole responsibility.

Notes

1. A Persian proverb equivalent to 'Don't count your chickens before they hatch'.
2. Accounts of Harandi Parks also appeared in newspapers. See *Iran*, October 5, 2015.
3. This model could potentially develop into something similar to Sao Paulo's *De Braços Abertos* project in *Crackolandia*; see Prefertura da Cidade de São Paulo, 'O Programa do Braços Abertos', available at https://www.prefeitura.sp.gov.br/cidade/secretarias/upload/saude/DBAAGO2015.pdf
4. Deleuze, *Due Regimi di Folli e Altri Scritti*, 3.
5. See Garcia, *Pastoral Clinic*; Zigon, *HIV Is God's Blessing*; Raikhel and Garriott, *Addiction Trajectories*.
6. Similarly, a police officer during the Great 8 (G8) in Genoa in 2001 asserted that the government did not want the police to establish order, but *to maintain the disorder*. Reported by Agamben, "Comment l'Obsession Sécuritaire Fait Muter."
7. I am grateful to Fariba Adelkhah for pointing out this aspect.
8. This is different from the French case described by Fassin, where activists as well as Sarkozy himself who opposed these places used the word 'camp' instead of 'centre' to delegitimise them. In Fassin, *Humanitarian Reason*, 133–4.
9. Rehabilitation in these centres follows the 12-step process established by NA. Most of the camp managers and assistants are also members of NA and the camps often have logos and banners indicating their affiliation to the NA superstructure. Based on ethnographic observations in rehab camps in several Iranian cities, 2012–2016.
10. Interview with the manager of a camp in the village around Arak, 2 April 2014.
11. Interview in Hasanabad, April 3, 2014.
12. *Keyhan*, June 10, 2012.
13. This is the official government data and it has been stable over the last few decades, despite significant changes in the drug market and evidence of a rise in drugs use. There are other estimates, at times declared by government officials themselves, which refer to higher numbers, eg 2–5 million; see United Nations Office of Drugs and Crime (UNODC), "Drug Prevention Treatment and HIV AIDS," https://www.unodc.org/islamicrepublicofiran/drug-prevention-treatment-and-hiv-aids.html
14. Ghiabi, "Drugs, Addiction and the State," chapter 6.
15. All Iranian legislations are discussed in Parliament with the exception of drug laws, which are legislated exclusively in the Expediency Council.
16. Calabrese, "Iran's War on Drugs."
17. DCHQ, "Drug Control in 2009."
18. The text of the General Policies can be found on the website of the Expediency Council, available at https://maslahat.ir/DocLib2/Approved%20Policies/Offered%20General%20Policies.aspx
19. Interview with Tahernokhost, Tehran, September 2012; and interview with Emran Razzaghi, Tehran, September 2012.
20. For instance, the increase of reckless driving and lunatic behaviour in public, described in journalistic pieces, hints at this. See *Aftab-e Yazd*, August 30, 2008. For stories about *shisheh*, which went viral, see *Mehr*, December 22, 2012, available at https://www.mehrnews.com/news/1770270/; and *Sharq*, November 3, 2013, available at https://sharghdaily.ir/1392/08/14/Files/PDF/13920814-1874-22-12.pdf
21. These operations are usually called *nejat*, 'salvation', and prior to 2010 they contemplated incarceration for short periods.
22. In the presidential election of May 2017, the issue of marginalisation became a central theme. Addiction was a key category of this debate; for a discussion of the category of 'lumpen', see Denning, "Wageless Life." One could see how the addiction camps are the postmodern equivalent of the *lazzaretti* and *lazzaroni*, the leper hospital and leper.
23. *Mehr*, September 26, 2012, available at https://www.mehrnews.com/news/1608510/
24. *Iran*, May 12, 2007.

25. Ethnographic observation while working as a research intern at the United Nations Office on Drugs and Crime, September 2012. Accounts available also in *Tabnak,* September 12, 2012, available at https://www.tabnak.ir/fa/news/272411
26. A similarity that is reminiscent of the 1980s approach; see Ghiabi, "Drugs and Revolution in Iran."
27. *Hamshahri*, April 30, 2008.
28. Ibid.
29. After 2009, incidentally, the head of the DCHQ was Mostafa Najjar, then Interior Minister.
30. *Jam-e Jam*, February 28, 2011, available at https://www1.jamejamonline.ir/papertext.aspx?newsnum=100836959206
31. Ibid.
32. *Jam-e Jam*, May 16, 2011.
33. In Article 42 of the Reformed 2010 Drugs Law; the text is available at https://rc.majlis.ir/fa/law/show/99642
34. *Salamat News*, May 8, 2012.
35. *Tabnak*, February 8, 2013 available at https://www.tabnak.ir/fa/news/301709
36. International Center for Prison Studies, *World Prison Population List*, 2013, available at https://www.apcca.org/uploads/10th_Edition_2013.pdf
37. *Eqtesad News*, February 11, 2017, available at https://www.eghtesadnews.com; It is said that up to 80% of death sentences are due to drug trafficking charges. See *Sharq*, August 8, 2010.
38. He was Minister of Interior between 2005 and 2008, and is the Minister of Justice in Rouhani's current government.
39. *Ruzegar-e Ma*, August 27, 2011.
40. *Hamshahri*, January 22, 2009.
41. Behrouzan, "Epidemic of Meanings."
42. *Jam-e Jam*, April 11, 2010; The equivalent of ca. US$150,000 per day.
43. *Hamshahri*, April 30, 2009.
44. *Aftab News*, June 16, 2011, available at https://aftabnews.ir/prtb89b8wrhb5fp.uiur.html
45. For the Iranian case, see *Mardomsalari*, September 22, 2012; For an ethnographic study of French police strategies and governmentality, see Fassin, *La Force de l'Ordre*. A discussion of morality and the police instead can be found in Fassin, "Maintaining Order".
46. Fassin, *Humanitarian Reason*, 135.
47. Christensen, *Drugs, Deviancy and Democracy*.
48. In a decade, the number of female drug 'addicts' has almost doubled, according to the DCHQ; see *Fararu*, August 2, 2016, available at https://fararu.com/fa/news/283802/
49. *Hamshahri*, June 24, 2009.
50. *Sharq*, July 24, 2012.
51. Scott, James C. *Seeing like a State*.
52. *Khabaronline*, June 10, 2011, available at https://www.khabaronline.ir/print/156388/
53. A good example is *Khaneh-ye Khorshid*, which had collaborated with the state in providing welfare services to sex workers in Tehran.
54. On this oxymoronic figure, see the 'detoxified addicted' in Deleuze, *Due Regimi di Folli e Altri Scritti*, 119.
55. Statistical Center of Iran, available at https://www.amar.org.ir
56. I later came to learn that this story was also widely reported in the news. See *Sharq*, September 24, 2012.
57. For a discussion of 'government at distance', see Hibou, *Privatizing the State*, 15.
58. *Hamshahri*, May 4, 2008.
59. *Hamshahri*, March 9, 2010. The Welfare Organisation has an ad hoc office for drug addiction, which issues these licences.
60. Ibid.
61. Ibid.
62. Interview with Hamid-Reza Tahernokhost, Drug Demand Reduction, UNODC, Tehran, September 2012.
63. Interview with Hasan Solhi, head of a state-run clinic in Arak, March 2014.

64. *Jam-e Jam*, May 16, 2011.
65. *Hamshahri*, January 25, 2010.
66. Ethnographic notes in popular neighbourhoods of Shush, Dowlatabad, in Tehran; and Futbal, Cheshm-e Mushak, in Arak. See also *Jam-e Jam*, April 16, 2012.
67. Interview with Tahernokhost, September 2012.
68. Interview with a former police officer in Arak, September 2014. There is a telling comparison with the work of the Red Cross in the French migration centre of Sangette (later the 'Jungle'), where the aid workers are found policing the centre instead of the police who have an 'almost benevolent attitude'. See Fassin, *Humanitarian Reason*, 139.
69. *Andisheh-ye Nou*, October 12, 20009; *Salamat* News, October 22, 2013, available at https://www.salamatnews.com/news/85137/
70. For an overview, see *Tabnak*, December 25, 2013, available at https://www.tabnak.ir/fa/news/366881
71. The public diatribe can be read here: *Azad News Agency*, April 25, 2016, available at https://www.ana.ir/news/98756
72. *Etemad-e Melli*, June 11, 2009.
73. Intervention by DCHQ official Hami Sarrami at the Addiction Studies Conference, Tehran, September 2015.
74. Shore, Wright, and Però, *Policy Worlds*, 114.
75. *Jam-e Jam*, December 19, 2010.
76. Shore, Wright, and Però, *Policy Worlds*, 14, 114.
77. See also *Jam-e Jam*, December 19, 2010.
78. Navaro-Yashin, *Faces of the State*, 119 and 134.
79. Haeri, *Law of Desire*.
80. Najmabadi, *Professing Selves*. The cost of the entire process is covered by the Welfare Organisation.

Bibliography

Agamben, Giorgio. "Comment l'obsession sécuritaire fait muter la démocratie [How the Securitising Obsession Transforms Democracy]." *Le Monde Diplomatique* January, 2014. Accessed February 3, 2017. https://www.monde-diplomatique.fr/2014/01/AGAMBEN/49997

Behrouzan, Orkideh. "An Epidemic of Meanings: HIV and AIDS in Iran and the Significance of History, Language and Gender." In *The Fourth Wave: Violence, Gender, Culture and HIV in the 21st Century*, edited by V. K. Nguyen and J. F. Klot. Paris: UNESCO, 2011.

Calabrese, John. "Iran's War on Drugs: Holding the Line." *The Middle East Institute*, December 3, 2007.

Christensen, Janne Bjerre. *Drugs, Deviancy and Democracy in Iran: The Interaction of State and Civil Society*. London: IB Tauris, 2011.

DCHQ (Drug Control Headquarters). "Drug Control in 2009." Accessed February 1, 2017. www.dchq.ir

Deleuze, Gille. *Due Regimi di Folli e Altri Scritti: Testi e Interviste 1975–1995* [Two Regimes of Fools and Other Writings: Texts and Interviews]. Torino: Einaudi, 2010.

Denning, Michael. "Wageless Life." *New Left Review* 66 (2010): 79–97.

Fassin, Didier. *Humanitarian Reason: A Moral History of the Present*. Berkeley: University of California Press, 2011.

Fassin, Didier. *La force de l'ordre: une anthropologie de la police des quartiers*. Paris: Editions du Seuil, 2011.

Fassin, Didier, ed. "Maintaining Order." In *At the Heart of the State*. London: Pluto Press, 2015.

Garcia, Angela. *The Pastoral Clinic: Addiction and Dispossession along the Rio Grande*. Berkeley: University of California Press, 2010.

Ghiabi, Maziyar. "Drugs and Revolution in Iran: Islamic Devotion, Revolutionary Zeal and Republican Means." *Iranian Studies* 48, no. 2 (2015): 139–163.

Ghiabi, Maziyar. "Drugs, Addiction and the State in Iran: The Art of Managing Disorder." DPhil diss., University of Oxford, 2017.

Haeri, Shahla. *Law of Desire: Temporary Marriage in Shi'i Iran*. Syracuse: Syracuse University Press, 2014.

Hibou, Béatrice. *Privatizing the State*. New York: Columbia University Press, 2004.

Najmabadi, Afsaneh. *Professing Selves: Transsexuality and Same-Sex Desire in Contemporary Iran*. Durham, NC: Duke University Press, 2013.

Navaro-Yashin, Yael. *Faces of the state: Secularism and Public life in Turkey*. Princeton, NJ: Princeton University Press, 2002.

Raikhel, Eugene, and William Garriott, eds. *Addiction Trajectories*. Durham, NC: Duke University Press, 2013.

Scott, James C. *Seeing like a State: How Certain Schemes to Improve the Human Condition have Failed*. New Haven, CT: Yale University Press, 1998.

Shore, Cris, Susan Wright, and Davide Però, eds. *Policy Worlds: Anthropology and the Analysis of Contemporary Power*. 14 vols. London: Berghahn Books, 2011.

Zigon, Jarrett. *"HIV is God's blessing": Rehabilitating Morality in Neoliberal Russia*. Berkeley: University of California Press, 2011.

'We Will Revive': addiction, spiritual warfare, and recovery in Latin America's cocaine production zone

Pablo Seward Delaporte

ABSTRACT
Once a key site in the War on Drugs against cocaine, the Upper Amazon in northeastern Peru has lately seen an increase in addiction to coca paste, a toxic by-product of the cocaine manufacturing process. Unregulated and coercive Pentecostal ministries, founded and administered by recovered pastors, constitute the main form of addiction treatment in the Upper Amazon today. Based on ethnographic research in nine ministries and using the example of the ministry 'We Will Revive,' this article suggests that Pentecostal ministries re-articulate addiction as demonic possession. Accordingly, ministries treat addiction through spiritual warfare against the Devil. In so doing, Pentecostal ministries change the locus of the War on Drugs from trade networks to sinful bodies.

'We Will Revive' (*Reviviremos*) is an unregulated, coercive Pentecostal ministry that treats addiction to coca paste, a smokable by-product of the cocaine manufacturing process. It is located in Golondrina, an informal settlement (*asentamiento humano*) at the edge of a mid-sized city in northeastern Peru's Upper Amazon, an area infamous for being the region that has historically produced most of the world's crude cocaine.[1] When I first visited Golondrina, in July 2016, no single wood panel fibre shanty looked distinctive. I was eventually able to locate 'We Will Revive' by tracking Evangelical rock music and what seemed to be military drills – '1, 2, 3, 4 … 1, 2, 3, 4' – coming from inside one shanty. I knocked on the door and a joyful man wearing a suit, sweat pouring down his temples, cracked it open. The shanty opened to an empty room, leading to what appeared be a gaol cell, set apart by a makeshift metallic bar structure. Inside the 'cell' there were 20 young men, their heads shaved. They sat around a crowded plastic table reading the Bible. Behind the cell, four eight-square-metre rooms, each lined with old torn cots scattered on the floor, and a narrow hallway leading to two doorless bathrooms, completed this enclosed but open-air space where residents at 'We Will Revive' are kept against their will.

Alex, the man who let me in to 'We Will Revive,' is a Pentecostal pastor in his mid-forties. Alex was raised in the city where Golondrina is located. As a teenager, he developed an

---

All interviews took place in Spanish. The name of research subjects has been changed for anonymity purposes. The name 'We Will Revive' is also a pseudonym. I intentionally do not disclose the exact location of 'We Will Revive' or any other ministries I studied.

addiction to coca paste. Alex promised Jesus Christ he would dedicate his life to 'saving' others if He 'saved' him, which He did. After recovering at an institution similar to 'We Will Revive' in his home city, Alex founded 'We Will Revive' in Golondrina, where 'help was most needed.' Today, he lives with his wife and daughter in a backroom of his church, located three blocks away from 'We Will Revive.' Most of his congregants are Golondrina locals, family members of the youth interned. Alex tells me many of his congregants knew him when he was *un adicto* (an addict). They witnessed his change, from the lowly to the holy. His congregants, many of whom formed part of Alex's church before interning their relatives in 'We Will Revive,' trust Alex. They gave him informal consent on behalf of their interned relatives and pay Alex a US$40 monthly fee in order to cover the ministry's expenses. Alex tells me he does not profit from the ministry and, in fact, sometimes must offset costs with his own meagre income as an auto rickshaw puller.

Every Sunday, Alex walks interns to his nearby church for cult service – the only occasion when they are allowed to exit the ministry. I attended Alex's cult service on the Sunday after first visiting 'We Will Revive.' The service started, as Pentecostal services so often do, with a fervent praising session, but soon led to a fiery tirade by Alex. 'Do you know what is wrong (*mal*) with your children?' Alex cried. 'They are possessed (*poseídos*).' Drugs, Alex argued, are Satan's (*Satanás*) new medium to make a generation of Christians 'slaves' once again. Alex figured Satan, a term he used interchangeably with the Devil (*el Diablo*), as an external, material but elusive being. The Devil uses 'addiction' (*adicción*) to lodge himself into Christian 'hearts,' hardening them with 'hate,' thus breeding violence in an otherwise peaceful 'Christian nation.' The solution to the 'problem of drugs,' Alex concluded, is to war (*luchar*) against the Devil by converting those whose hearts the Devil has colonised to Pentecostalism.

Pentecostal addiction treatment ministries in Peru's Upper Amazon, where 'We Will Revive' is located, arrived from Lima and other coastal cities in Peru in the early 2000s. These institutions are part of a larger movement Latin America of unregulated faith-based addiction treatment centres, usually founded and administered by recovered pastors. These centres have become the primary mode of addiction treatment in many Latin American countries.[2] They are based on the therapeutic community model, a common form of residential addiction treatment based on mutual aid.[3] Like Alex, locals in the Upper Amazon who recovered at these institutions, however, then created their own, where they formed a novel assemblage between the imported therapeutic community model and Pentecostal faith healing traditions. Beginning in the 1960s and persisting to this day, Latin America in general has seen an explosive growth of so-called neo-Pentecostalism, an Evangelical religious form that emphasises gifts from the Holy Spirit, such as glossolalia, divine healing, and, most importantly, born-again experiences. Although imported into Latin America, neo-Pentecostal institutions grew by means of local movements, like the movement of Pentecostal addiction treatment ministries in the Upper Amazon.[4]

Based on three months of ethnographic research in nine Pentecostal addiction treatment ministries located in mid-sized cities of Peru's Upper Amazon, this article seeks to understand the form that recovery from coca paste addiction takes in these ministries, using 'We Will Revive' as an example. I argue that, drawing from a lived experience of addiction that is particular to the Upper Amazon's history with the illicit cocaine industry, Pentecostal ministries re-articulate addiction as demonic possession and the possessed body as a sinful vessel. After an instantaneous conversion, the body as sinful vessel gradually becomes a sacred body, the privileged subject of the miraculous healing powers of the Holy Spirit.

Throughout this process, I argue, recovery from coca paste addiction takes the form of spiritual warfare. The concept of spiritual warfare is generally used in the literature on the globalisation of Pentecostalism to refer to 'ritualised practices' by which (predominantly indigenous) 'communities' that have converted to Pentecostalism 'attempt to rid themselves of territorial spirits they engaged with in the past.'[5] In contrast, here I refer to spiritual warfare as an articulation of Pentecostal spiritual practices – including prayer, praising, and preaching – with practices commonly associated with military warfare, such as abductions, confinement, drills, and a hierarchical institutional structure. This article suggests that in the Upper Amazon, and likely other parts of Latin America, we are seeing the emergence of another War on Drugs, one that fights a moral economy of coca paste addiction that is in many ways a product of the more conventional, economic, and geopolitical war on cocaine production.

In what follows, I start by narrating the life story of Alex, whose experience with addiction and recovery cannot be disentangled from the Upper Amazon's history with the illicit cocaine industry and the War on Drugs against cocaine. I then proceed to show how addiction in the Upper Amazon has a particular signification. As a phenomenon that emerged at a particular historical juncture, it has come to signify more a social condition of the person than a biological state of the body. Third, I specify how, in the therapeutic space of 'We Will Revive,' addiction is re-articulated as demonic possession and recovery as conversion. I then provide a vignette of life inside 'We Will Revive,' showing how, in the long-term, recovery as conversion in Pentecostal addiction treatment ministries in the Upper Amazon takes the form of spiritual warfare.

Alex's life story

After World War II, too economically dependent on the post-war commodity circuits the United States came to hegemonise, the Peruvian state was forced to begin complying with anticocaine economic and political sanctions. Out of vested interests in the formerly legal Peruvian cocaine economy, the Peruvian state had historically flouted these sanctions.[6] The War on Drugs against cocaine became official in Peru with the criminalisation of coca leaf and cocaine production in 1949.[7] Far from stifling the once legal global cocaine trade networks between Peru and the United States, however, the War on Drugs created incentives for their proliferation.[8]

The Peruvian state, undergoing a process of internal expansion and state-building, had sponsored a special development programme in the 1940s that provided subsidies and credits for Andean peasants to settle the Upper Amazon. By the 1960s, facing economic and political instability, the Peruvian state abandoned the Upper Amazon to its own means. The few farmers that stayed in the region, including Alex's father, decided to use the deserted infrastructure for coca leaf production.[9] By the mid-1980s, farmers from the Upper Amazon had monopolised the illicit crude cocaine market in Peru. Villages turned into outlaw towns offering everything 'from retail sales of food and agricultural supplies to musical entertainment and sexual services.'[10] With the growth of the cocaine industry in the Upper Amazon, the region, in particular the Upper Huallaga valley, became home to an all-encompassing cocaine boom. The boom extended from around 1984 to 1997. Locals remember the boom era as one of unprecedented wealth but also generalised insecurity. The boom era resulted in as many as 11,000 deaths, as the first of Latin American *narcos*, a United States-sponsored corrupt Peruvian army, and the insurgent groups the Shining Path and the Tupac Amaru Revolutionary Movement (MRTA) fought over the drug trade.[11]

Alex's father decided to send Alex – an illegitimate child he did not appreciate and who was, in any case, too young to work – to the city as the boom started. Living in the city, isolated from the cocaine production zones, Alex became caught in a coca paste consumption market that emerged with the boom era. When Alex was 13 years old, he developed an addiction to coca paste. In order to overcome his addiction, when Alex turned 16 years old he enrolled in the army. He was eventually posted to the epicentre of the war in the late 1980s. Alex's assignment consisted in protecting outbound *narco*-flights from 'terrorists' in exchange for coca paste, which he would then distribute to the army.

After suffering a psychotic breakdown induced, Alex claims, by excessive violence coupled with coca paste use, he was released from the army. Alex returned to the streets of his home city and began stealing from his own family to sustain his addiction. His brothers sometimes 'threw the dogs on me,' but usually, instead of calling the police, his family would 'sympathise' and drive Alex somewhere far from home and 'deposit' him there. On two occasions, the city police transported Alex and 'hundreds' of other coca paste users to the countryside, where the Shining Path, which had an explicit extermination policy against *fumones* (coca paste smokers),[12] ruled. Alex increasingly became hopeless. When tuberculosis did not kill him, he tried to commit suicide:

> A psychologist once told me, you will never change; drugs are your life sentence. That is what psychology, medicine, society says: we are a scourge (*lacra*) of humanity, we are useless. But I am a living testimony that this is not true.

In the late 1990s, international and national drug eradication efforts disarticulated the illicit global cocaine networks on which the Upper Amazon had prospered. A 'more subdued, less extreme, if depressed present' came to define life in the region.[13] As the Upper Amazon underwent conversion, so did Alex. This is how Alex narrated his conversion experience to me:

> One day I was smoking coca paste at 10 am. I could no more; I was so unwell … I lived in a hollow (*hueco*), on a hill by the street: there I smoked, there I sat all day, my bathroom was there, I slept there … And at 10 am a person, a *changed* person, with a tie and a book under his arm that was the Bible appeared … 'My crazy friend (*loquito*),' he tells me, 'do you remember me? I am Floiber' … He was a friend that would go along with me when I was into drugs … For me it was revealing to see Floiber: a *changed* man, with his Bible. And he tells me, 'I want to take you to Lima … Let's go,' he tells me, 'I will introduce you to someone who can change your life. His name is Jesus Christ.'

Today Alex has a family and a job. He is always clean-shaven and his hair always looks slick. In short, he is what by Pentecostal standards is an exemplary human, the flipside of that former self he preserves in a photograph that he is quick to show me: unkempt, emaciated, vexed, with tattered clothes, sitting on a street corner.

Addiction in the Upper Amazon

According to municipality officials, Golondrina, the informal settlement where 'We Will Revive' is located, emerged in the late 1990s. The state reclaimed a drug lord's territory and donated the land to a local university, which was unable to stop poor migrants from the war-torn countryside from 'invading' the territory. Many of the parents whose children are today interned at 'We Will Revive' were once employed as low-level workers in the illicit cocaine industry, like Alex's father himself. In this capacity, many dealt directly with crude cocaine, but, they claim, they never smoked it. Some feared the Shining Path. Others feared drug lords interested in maintaining a sober workforce. But, in most cases, smoking crude cocaine was just out of the question. As far as they were concerned, it was toxic stuff meant for *gringos*.

Alex's generation was the first to begin consuming coca paste in the Upper Amazon, which in turn is the first place where coca paste was consumed before it spread throughout South America.[14] The shift from a zone of cocaine production to cocaine consumption is part of a broader trend in Latin America. According to official statistics, the annual prevalence of cocaine use, including coca paste use, in South America increased from 1.84 million users in 2010 to 3.35 million in 2012, 'three times the global estimated average level of consumption.'[15] Scholars have attributed this shift to increased enforcement of the drug trade and structural adjustment policies. While enforcement pushed Latin American drug trafficking organisations to 'create alternative income by entering, and sometimes promoting, local drug markets,'[16] structural adjustment policies granted them more purchase on unfettered global trading networks.[17] According to the local police, following eradication campaigns those who once produced crude cocaine for export in the Upper Amazon now import crude cocaine and sell it locally in the form of coca paste. This new coca paste consumption market has affected marginalised men the most.[18]

Unlike their parents, this new generation found themselves living in peripheral urban settings like Golondrina, jobless and vulnerable to this emergent coca paste market. Informal auto rickshaw pulling, as in many slums in the global South, became the main source of employment for young men in Alex's generation.[19] Addiction became a symptom of this general economic transition.

The prototype of the *adicto*, as interviews with 'We Will Revive' interns and Alex made clear to me, is the young man who, finding himself in a new urban setting, loses his sense of duty and his place in society, and succumbs to drugs. When asked directly about *adicción* as a biological condition of the body, interns referenced standard features of the biomedical category of coca paste addiction, including intense craving, drug tolerance, and withdrawal symptoms (termed locally *chiri chiri* or *dengue*).[20] But, when asked in an open-ended manner about *adicción* in general, interns, much like Alex in his narrative above, tended to speak about a social condition of the person and not a biological condition of the body. Interns usually described the *adicto* as a *lacra*. In a Christian context, the term *lacra* refers to a body out of place in a pre-ordained social order. *Lacra*, a Biblical scourge, is a person who cannot control his body, whose carnal pleasures violate the sacredness of the human body. The term, indeed, is also used to refer to homosexuals and prostitutes.

Consistent with the *lacra* construct, 'addicts' in the Upper Amazon are often imagined as living in what fieldwork pastors, residents and their relatives, as well as acquaintances not affiliated with addiction ministries, generally termed a *hueco* (hollow). *Hueco* is a category that encompasses a set of locations in urban space where 'everyone knows' addicts gather: sewer canals, the underside of bridges, alleys, parks, and the like. From an anthropological perspective, addicts as *lacras* are 'matter out of place.' In anthropologist Mary Douglas' classic cross-cultural analysis, she shows that such 'dirt' constructs refer to objects which disrupt taxonomies, produce anxieties about contamination, and provoke rejection.[21]

As *lacras* young men suffering from addiction are often criminalized. As anthropologist Teresa Caldeira has observed in another Latin American urban context, consistent a Christian political theology, crime is often construed as the manifestation of evil. Caldeira argues that evil is thought to '*infiltrate*, *infest*, and *contaminate*' subjects positioned in 'improper spaces or lacking the proper attributes of a member of society.' Evil reigns in particular in 'the streets,' as drug use renders subjects 'easy targets for the forces of evil.'[22]

In what follows I will argue that residents and pastors in Pentecostal ministries internalise their stigmatised condition as *lacras* using the language of sin. At the same time, however, they re-articulate it, through spiritual warfare, into demonic possession. I argue that this re-articulation works toward their own empowerment.

Addiction as possession, recovery through conversion

Christianity is based on the foundational belief that 'the apparent loser may be the real winner unrecognised.'[23] The mystery of Christianity, indeed, is that an ordinary man considered killable during his time was a divine being. As such, Christian discourse provides a powerful means for the stigmatised or marginalised to redeem their social condition. I argue that ministries use Christian discourse to re-frame the addicted body, colloquially considered a *lacra*, as, symmetrically, a sinful vessel. This sinful vessel is particularly prone to demonic possession. As anthropologist Thomas Blom Hansen points out, the Pentecostal soul as an empty vessel is open to what is thought to be the good influence of Jesus.[24] Indeed, as with Alex's story above, the 'near social and physical death and resurrection and social rebirth of a man' is a common 'myth of origin' for many Pentecostal institutions.[25] Because demonic possession and its solution – conversion – are the domain of pastoral rather than biomedical care, by re-framing addiction as possession addicts reclaim the authority of treating themselves.

As with the notion of *lacra* as matter out of place, the notion of possession as a weapon of the weak has a long anthropological pedigree. In an influential cross-cultural analysis, for instance, anthropologist I. M. Lewis argued that those possessed, including in the Christian tradition, are often oppressed women and men who come from lowly origins. According to Lewis, 'peripheral cults' – and Pentecostalism in the context of a predominantly Catholic country would certainly qualify as such – are used by women and 'downtrodden categories of men' for venting 'pent-up animosity.'[26] Possession, in this account, works as an 'apotheosis,' whereby 'pain and suffering' are re-framed as signs of 'divine favour,' with the result of a temporary subversion of power.[27]

During my fieldwork, pastors and residents constantly referred to *adicción* as the product of hate (*ira*) bred by the Devil in the heart or soul of the addict. Interns at 'We Will Revive' explained to me that the Devil gets hold of the hate that a child feels when he is excluded, as Alex did when his father rejected and abandoned him. That hate then grows inside the child and manifests itself through sin, including carnal pleasure in the form of addiction. A representative case in this regard is that of Gary, who at the time of my research was 10 months into the 'We Will Revive' programme. After fleeing his father's coca leaf plantation when he was 12 years old, following a genocidal eradication campaign and losing track of his family, Gary ended up in the streets. He started consuming coca paste, he claims, as a 'refuge' from the hate he felt for his mother for abandoning him. His hate led Gary to a severe addiction. He ended up living in a ravine, 'without shoes, without anything.' He believes he truly recovered only upon re-uniting and forgiving his mother. It was then that he was able to purge the hate of the Devil from his heart. In this sense, following anthropologist Michael Taussig's well-known argument about the work of the imaginary of the Devil among proletarianised plantation workers and miners in Colombia,[28] one way of interpreting the discourse of the Devil in Pentecostal ministries is as a representation of the societal abandonment and economic change that, for people suffering from addiction in the Upper Amazon, seems to be at the root of addiction.

According to pastors and residents in the ministries I studied, recovery from addiction takes the form of a sudden rupture of the 'yoke' between the addict and God through the Holy Spirit of Christ. What the yoke represents is precisely the internalised hate the Devil breeds inside the addicted body. During a three-day national conference of 'Clamor en el Barrio,' a neo-Pentecostal church for addiction treatment with one location in the Upper Amazon, this moment of breaking the yoke was re-enacted. At the climax of an Evangelical rock song during the conference, the lead singer broke with the lyrics and started murmuring to the microphone: 'Expose yourself to the presence of God. Your chains will break.' The singer gradually increased the tone of his voice as he repeated these words. The instrumentals became louder and louder and the lighting effects more intense until, finally, everyone broke through together in ecstasy, singing: 'I love you! I need you!' Many residents then rushed to the front of the stage, where pastors blessed each resident by touching their foreheads, praying for them, and releasing them to the ground, whereupon residents remained for some time before waking up again. 'God just gave you a hug,' the lead singer declared at this point, 'and by means of that hug he has told you, my son that was dead has revived.'

Each resident in 'We Will Revive,' some sooner than others, underwent this event of sudden recovery during one of Alex's Sunday cult services. Pastors and residents in general described recovery to me as an unmistakable feeling of warmth inside their bodies. Most of them could tell you the exact day and year when they recovered. This form of recovery as conversion is consistent with Pentecostal liturgy more generally. As Latin American televangelist Luis Palau claims, whereas under Roman Catholicism, Latin America was 'oriented to a dead Christ,' a reference to the prominence of Crucifixion in Catholic liturgy, 'our emphasis is that he is alive. He can touch your life now, revolutionise your home, make you a different person.'[29] Rather than the Crucifixion, it is the Pentecost that is glorified: the raining down of miracles on the faithful after the Ascension of Christ.

However, recovery is never eternally guaranteed. Many pastors and converted residents did not doubt that in the 'blink of an eye,' as a 'Clamor en el Barrio' pastor once put it, you can become repossessed and relapse into addiction. According to the Pentecostal worldview, 'the Holy Spirit does not enter and permanently stay in a person.'[30] Measures to stave off the Devil's return to the heart of the convert are necessary. This is where spiritual warfare, as a practice for staving off the Devil of addiction, comes in.

The practice of spiritual warfare in 'We Will Revive': a vignette

When I returned to 'We Will Revive' the day after first visiting it at 6 am, James, Alex's assistant who sleeps outside the cell by the main entrance, was waking everyone. James came of age in an informal settlement near Golondrina. He claims he works as an assistant for Alex because that way he can recover from addiction at 'We Will Revive' without asking his mother to pay the monthly fee Alex charges – but also because he has gang rivals outside the ministry whom he rather avoid. After James had woken everyone, Jonatan, one of two 'elder brothers' (*hermanos mayores*) in the ministry, patrolled the four rooms, approaching each half-dressed resident and reproaching those who had not yet taken a shower. As residents bathed, dressed, and tidied their rooms, they proceeded to the dining room, where they sat on stools around the table and read the Bible, not without first asking permission from James to enter the room, as they always did whenever they exited a room and entered another throughout the day.

James then entered the cell and visited each room. He called Jonatan over and pointed out that one of the rooms was untidy and criticised his lack of leadership. Jonatan, concerned that his position as elder brother was in jeopardy, interrupted Yerson – a recent admit who slept in the room in question – from his Bible study and punished him with 30 push-ups. After Yerson completed his push-ups, Jonatan readied everyone for the chant that he was to lead that morning, 'Come … come … come the spirit of Jesus, overpower me (*apo-dé-rate*), overpower me, overpower my being … There is no God that can do things like you do – not with a sword or an army but with your Holy Spirit.' The 20 residents stood with their eyes closed, clapping and chanting in beat with Jonatan. When Jonatan stopped singing, all residents bent over, as if by default. With their knees on the ground and elbows over their stools, they began praying.

Ten minutes went by before James tapped Jonatan's shoulder and Jonatan ordered everyone to stop praying and stand up. The 'Structure Group' (*Grupo Estructura*), as James referred to them – two residents who were on their way to becoming elder brothers – stood simultaneously and, with their arms firmly against their sides, asked James for permission to go and 'meditate.' James approved the request and the Structure Group, who went by Structure One (*Estructura Uno*) and Structure Two (*Estructura Dos*), marched to the hallway. There they proceeded to stand, with their faces pressed against the wall and their hands held behind their backs.

When Alex returned from his morning shift as an auto rickshaw puller it was around 11 am. As residents worked on their respective assignments – making crafts for sale, mopping the floors, washing dishes – Alex lectured them from the room outside the cell on the five virtues the programme teaches residents to follow: honesty, acceptance, tolerance, humility, and discipline. He then subjected the Structure Group to strenuous exercise, claiming that they had to be agile for a 'rescue operation' a family of an addict had scheduled for the following day: the future resident was large and stubborn; capturing him was going to require physical and spiritual discipline.[31]

Pastors and residents after conversion: self-sustaining recovery

As is evident from the vignette of 'We Will Revive' above, residents at different stages of treatment are subjected to different forms of discipline that, together, work toward producing a ministry where the recovery of each depends on the recovery of the other. Those at the bottom, like Yerson, are subjected to a set of practices thought to induce conversion. Those at the top, converted elder brothers like Jonatan and assistants (*asistentes*) like James, enforce these practices. Those at the middle, represented here by the Structure Group, have already been converted, but have not yet been disciplined as elder brothers. This structure offers a method to combat the stealthy ways of the Devil. Unlike Catholic monastic practice, as Thomas Blom Hansen has observed, in a Pentecostal context fighting the Devil is not a 'constant, interior battle with [one's] own innate sinfulness,' but a 'collective work of mutual surveillance in the congregation.'[32]

The Devil is thought to be endlessly planning to infiltrate the ministry, conceived as a new family of fellow born-again Christians. This vigilance requires an attuned heart that can detect the resurgence of hate inside the person. Pastors regularly use photos to show residents how they were when they first arrived at the ministry, reminding them that each is a product of the presence of the Holy Spirit in their hearts, which they must continue fostering. Dramatic displays of forgiveness among residents and between residents and pastors are common as a way to purge the hate that the Devil continuously implants in the hearts of residents.

Having an attuned heart, in turn, requires having a constant relation with God through a strict regimen of spiritual practices.[33] The production of a vigilant ethic in residents is commonly achieved through physical discipline. Alex once explained his therapeutic practice to me in the following manner:

> The directors of the ministry where I was interned as a young man were recovered addicts like me now, and they disciplined me strongly: they would require I meditate all night … And the sun would rise and my feet would be swollen … from standing all night. But it was for my own good. It was there that I first found myself asking God for help … and fighting the Devil who works against God.

This understanding of the therapeutic practice of the (sometimes violent) discipline practiced in ministries I visited was perhaps most clearly expressed to me by Jeremy. Jeremy escaped from Alex's ministry some three months into his first internment. Back on the streets, he started stealing from his father to buy coca paste and his father had him committed to Alex's ministry a second time. At this point of his story, Jeremy turned his back on me and lifted his shirt. He showed me a set of superficial scars. 'This second time I had problems with violence.' There was a mutiny and even though 'I was not part of it … they did not care and hit me with sticks.' Jeremy claims that at the moment he developed a deep resentment against Alex, but retrospectively, he believes, 'it did me well.' 'Out of being 100% intolerant and proud' when he arrived at Alex's ministry the first time, Jeremy claims he is now '20%.' For Jeremy, in short, violent practices progressively opened his body to the love of God. It was God, through his love, which then purged and continues to purge the demonic hate that was at the root of his addiction.

The interpretation of life in Pentecostal ministries after conversion that I am proposing here is consistent with a framework provided by Alain Badiou for Saint Paul's conversion, which anthropologist Joel Robbins has applied to conversion to Pentecostalism.[34] In Badiou's language, ministries offer the structure for an event – conversion – to occur. But, in order for the event to become what Badiou terms a 'situation' and have any 'impact on social life,' 'postevental subjects' must force the 'situational unfolding' of the event over time.[35] Pastors and converted residents must continuously unfold the event of conversion through the very structure of the ministry for conversion to translate into sustained recovery from addiction.

Historically, in Latin America as elsewhere, scholars of religion have understood conversion to Pentecostalism as a radical break with the past. This is precisely the way Pentecostals themselves frame conversion. However, scholars of religion have since come to appreciate the many ways in which religious conversion is instead an ongoing creative process, which often spans an entire pastoral career.[36] Yet, it seems most precise to me to think of conversion as a dialectical process involving both a break (in the form of an event) and a continuation with the past (in the form of a situation).

By seeing others evangelised, converted pastors and residents are able to secure their faith in the miraculous healing powers of the Holy Spirit on which their recovery depends. The making of a victorious, sacred space from which evangelisation campaigns can depart ultimately allows residents not only to recover from addiction in the short-term but also to overcome their stigmatised social condition as *lacras* in the long-term. Because the space is sacred, although located in poor areas, ministries are always clean and tidy. When they attain the level of growth of 'Clamor en el Barrio' – the most successful Pentecostal addiction treatment ministry I studied – the very 'architecture, dress styles, music, books, [and] audiovisual material' of the Pentecostal church, as anthropologist Birgit Meyer has observed in Africa, become 'signs of good life'.[37] When I left 'We Will Revive,' which was one of the most precarious of the ministries I studied, Alex informed me that he had found a place in a building that was much larger and in better conditions where he would relocate.

Concluding remarks

In way of conclusion, I outline the theoretical implications of my argument, as well as some limitations of the argument and considerations for future work. One body of literature this article contributes to is that on the globalisation of Pentecostalism, specifically as it relates to the phenomenon of the growth of Pentecostalism in urban peripheries throughout the global South.[38] Pushed to depressed cities by the drug war, Alex's generation in the Upper Amazon formed part of a global trend of growth in mid-sized cities that, paradoxically, had little capacity for labour absorption.[39] This trend has been particularly dramatic in the Amazon at large, where shantytowns accounted for approximately 80% of city growth in the later part of the twentieth century.[40]

The key question for this literature is why has this new Protestant ethic appealed so dramatically particularly to those dispossessed and excluded by the spirit of late capitalism? Identity and recognition, order, health, prosperity, social support, and social mobility have all been proposed as explanations.[41] The assumption is that conversion to Christianity involves conversion to modernity. In this article, I have attended to one form in which Pentecostalism has entered the everyday lives of the urban poor in a particular context: as addiction treatment ministries. This article also provides an interesting case of forced conversion, a phenomenon that has not received enough attention in the literature on Pentecostalism.[42]

A second body of literature this article contributes to is that on faith-based addiction treatment, including in the form of Pentecostal ministries. This body of literature is significantly smaller than that on biomedical approaches to addiction, despite the fact that the majority of people suffering from addiction in Latin America receive treatment in faith-based institutions.[43] The literature that does exist on faith-based addiction treatment institutions is largely quantitative. Most of the qualitative literature, in turn, is denunciatory in scope, foreclosing the space of engagement and critique prematurely.[44] This article joins a recent wave of scholars in anthropology who have begun thinking more openly about Christian rehabilitation centres in the Americas. On the basis of patient ethnographic attention to these emergent therapeutic spaces, these scholars have, for instance, challenged inherited assumptions about the role of violence in addiction recovery, and deconstructed the false dichotomy between captivity and freedom.[45] This literature has offered a richly textured picture of Christian rehabilitation centres, which works against functionalist interpretations. It is certainly the case, as anthropologist Helena Hansen argues in reference to Evangelical ministries in Puerto Rico, that Pentecostal ministries in the Upper Amazon provide disempowered men with an 'alternative quasi-economic system involving its own forms of labour, professional identity, and rewards.'[46] It is certainly the case, as religious studies scholar Andrew Chesnut argues in reference to Pentecostalism in Brazil, that Pentecostal institutions provide health services for disenfranchised populations.[47] Yet, ministries' *raison d'être* cannot be reduced to the needs they fulfil alone.

A third body of literature this article contributes to is the anthropological literature on social abandonment. This framework describes abandonment in contexts of urban poverty as residual spaces where those excluded from society are left to die.[48] Instead, following critiques of this literature that emphasise the relational character of urban poverty,[49] in this article I have argued that informal settlements in the Upper Amazon have designed novel institutional arrangements that – far from abandoning people suffering from coca paste addiction – subject those considered ill to a particular mode of recovery. This interpretation on my part is consistent with how pastors and interns themselves think about ministries. Pentecostalism presumes that all people, including the faithful, are sinners, and that those considered addicts are, in this sense, far from exceptional. Rather than abandoned, the addict, like everyone, must be saved.[50]

One alternative to the abandonment framework is provided Michel Foucault's institutional analysis of power. Indeed, much of the abandonment literature is inspired on Giorgio Agamben's critique of Foucault.[51] Yet, Pentecostal ministries do not, as disciplinary institutions within a Foucauldian framework, intervene into the biological life of the body – or the population, for that matter. A more appropriate Foucauldian framework is that of pastoral power, as the power dynamics in Pentecostal ministries are indeed of the pastoral type – emanating from the self-sacrificial office of the pastor, who is interested in providing salvation for each and all of the souls under his care.[52] Yet, that populations suffering from addiction in the Upper Amazon are not abandoned does not necessarily mean that they are subjected to power apparatuses – be them apparatuses that foster biological or spiritual life.

The final body of literature this article contributes to is that on the War on Drugs in Latin America. Too often, the War on Drugs – as an economic and geopolitical war on drug production and a punitive strategy against drug consumption – is purified from the social contexts in which it is embedded. One social context in which the War on Drugs is embedded is Christianity. For instance, Latin Americanist literary critic Jean Franco documents in detail how Mexican cartels use Christian death cults to give meaning to cruel violence.[53] Likewise, Hermann Herlinghaus argues that the contemporary drug war in Latin America is not entirely about 'economic struggles'; it also involves 'fantasies related to original sin,' 'guilty territories and populations,' and a propaganda machine that is 'charged with elements of a sacred war.'[54]

To what extent the other War on Drugs I have traced in this article, that of spiritual warfare, will change the terms of the conventional War on Drugs in Latin America – especially as a consensus that the War on Drugs has only led to more violence in Latin America grows stronger – is an open question. Anthropologist Kevin O'Neill, writing about Pentecostal ministries for gang prevention and addiction treatment in Guatemala, has found that Pentecostal ministries form part of a larger industry of state-sponsored social programmes that target violence, through conversion, before it starts.[55] However, there are no such direct connections between Pentecostal ministries in the Upper Amazon as instruments of securitisation and the sovereign Peruvian state, at least for now. In this sense, although embedded in a significantly different religious milieu, the ministries I study are more similar to the Mexican *anexos* anthropologist Angela Garcia studies, which are spaces at the border of the state, where recovery also takes the form of exposure rather than containment.[56]

Having pointed to potential theoretical contributions of this article, for future considerations it is important to also point out the argument's limitations. First, the article has left aside the experiences of coca paste users who do not identify or are not identified by others as male. A 1999 study found that out of a sample of 93 therapeutic communities in Peru, only one accepted females, despite an ongoing 'feminisation' of drug use in Peru.[57] A second limitation concerns the fact that the cases presented in this article, in particular Alex's, all, roughly, follow an ideal trajectory. In fact, many coca paste users never make it to ministries; many others escape or are withdrawn from ministries before completing their programmes; and many transition from ministry to ministry, in a chronic cycle of relapse. One effect of this latter limitation is that this article portrays Pentecostal ministries in a positive light. I consider this to be a healthy antidote to most depictions of informal faith-based addiction treatment centres in Peru, which – especially after the deaths of 43 interns following two fire incidents in Lima in 2012[58] – are portrayed negatively as, in one renowned Peruvian psychiatrist's words, 'centres of usury, mistreatment, and death.'[59] On the other hand, my argument should not be interpreted as absolving the retrenched Peruvian state of responsibility for the treatment of addiction, or the United States and its War on Drugs against cocaine for overdetermining the emergence of addiction in the Upper Amazon.

In closing this article, I would like to point out that I have also left aside the fraught ethics involved in the coercive practices that many ministries, including 'We Will Revive,' engage in. How similar or different is the logic of reforming through captivity as it is enacted in coercive Christian centres, on the one hand, and prisons, on the other? Can we condemn the one, as a repressive state apparatus, and defend the other, as a laudable (if always imperfect) grassroots initiative, without falling into a double standard? By allowing people to identify as addicted as a way to recognise sin and achieve salvation, do the discourses such programmes propagate reproduce or reduce the stigma of being addicted? These are important questions, which, given the scale of this phenomenon, must be pondered. In good anthropological fashion, however, I would insist that we should not rush to conclusions, and immediately adopt the moralist stance of reforming these centres, as if they did not know what they are doing, or worse, contributing to ongoing efforts of shutting them down. Perhaps what we are witnessing is a new Protestant ethic that places what decolonial scholar Sylvia Wynter might call the 'postcolonial variant of Fanon's category of *les damnés*' at the cusps of new formations of globalised capitalist warfare.[60]

Disclosure statement

No potential conflict of interest was reported by the author.

Funding

This research was supported by the Society for Psychological Anthropology / Robert Lemelson Foundation Fellowship, made possible by a generous donation from The Robert

Lemelson Foundation. This research was also supported by the Department of Anthropology at Stanford University. The training for this research was supported by the National Science Foundation's Graduate Research Fellowship Programme under Grant DGE-1656518.

Acknowledgments

First and foremost, I thank the pastors and residents of Pentecostal addiction treatment ministries in Peru's Upper Amazon for sharing their stories with me and welcoming me into their lives. Writing this article would not have been possible without the exceptional mentorship of Angela Garcia. I also give my sincere thanks to Thomas Blom Hansen, James Ferguson, Tanya Luhrmann, Liisa Malkki, Duana Fullwiley, Sharika Thiranagama, and Matthew Kohrman for their excellent and generous mentorship. The two anonymous reviewers for this article were incredibly helpful with their comments. I thank Ian Whitmarsh, Mauricio Najarro, Ellen Kozelka, Claudia Rafful, and Timothy Nest for valuable feedback on a paper presented on the basis of this article. Finally, my deepest appreciation goes to Maziyar Ghiabi for organising the Special Issue of which this article is part.

Notes

1. Gootenberg, *Andean Cocaine*.
2. For Mexico, see Garcia, "Serenity," 456. For Peru, see Becerra and Bazo, *Diagnóstico situacional*. For Latin America, see IDPC, "Compulsory Rehabilitation in Latin America."
3. De Leon, *The Therapeutic Community*.
4. Hartch, *Rebirth of Latin American Christianity*.
5. Robbins, "The Globalisation of Pentecostalism," 128.
6. Gootenberg, *Andean Cocaine*, 136–7, 190, 206–8, 214.
7. Ibid., 228.
8. Ibid., 255–89.
9. Kernaghan, *Coca's Gone*, 10.
10. Ibid., 11.
11. Páucar, *La guerra oculta*, 6.
12. CVR, *Informe final*, Volume V, Chapter 2. For an example of non-state armed groups targeting drug users in Latin America, see Zeiderman, *Endangered City*, 85.
13. Kernaghan, *Coca's Gone*, 1, 4.
14. UNODC, *Pasta básica de cocaína*, 37–9.
15. UNODC, *World Drug Report*, 51–4.
16. Durán-Martínez, "Drugs Around the Corner," 124–9.
17. CIDDH, "El Éxito."
18. UNODC, *Pasta básica de cocaína*, 27–40.
19. For a discussion of rickshaw pulling and informal labour, see Davis, *Planet of Slums*, 189.
20. UNODC, *Pasta básica de cocaína*, 83–118.
21. Douglas, *Purity and Danger*.
22. Caldeira, *City of Walls*, 91. For a review of the anthropology of evil, see Csordas, "Morality as a Cultural System?"
23. Miles, *Crisis*, 4.
24. Hansen, *Melancholia of Freedom*, 267.

25. Ibid., 269–70.
26. Lewis, *Ecstatic Religion*, 26–8.
27. Ibid., 61–3.
28. Taussig, *Devil and Commodity Fetishism*.
29. Hartch, *Rebirth of Latin American Christianity*, 93.
30. Meyer, "Aesthetics of Persuasion," 753.
31. For a discussion of the capturing of drug users by Christian vigilante groups in Guatemala City, see O'Neill, "On Hunting."
32. Hansen, *Melancholia of Freedom*, 266–7.
33. For a description of such practices, see Luhrmann, *When God Talks Back*, 101–32.
34. Robbins, "Anthropology, Pentecostalism, and the New Paul."
35. Ibid., 639–40.
36. Gooren, "Anthropology of Religious Conversion," 99–100.
37. Meyer, "Aesthetics of Persuasion," 751.
38. Davis, *Planet of Slums*, 195–8.
39. Ibid., 8–19.
40. Browder and Godfrey, *Rainforest Cities*.
41. Robbins, "Anthropology of Religion."
42. Kling, "Conversion to Christianity."
43. IDPC, "Compulsory Rehabilitation in Latin America."
44. Jürgens and Csete, "In the Name of Treatment"; Wilkinson, "Sin sanidad."
45. Garcia, "Serenity"; O'Neill, "On Liberation."
46. Hansen, "The New 'Masculinity,'" 3.
47. Chesnut, *Born Again in Brazil*.
48. Biehl, *Vita*.
49. Han, *Life in Debt*.
50. I thank an anonymous reviewer for pointing this out.
51. Agamben, *Homo Sacer*.
52. Foucault, *Security, Territory, Population*, 125–30.
53. Franco, *Cruel Modernity*, 214–46.
54. Herlinghaus, *Violence Without Guilt*, 10.
55. O'Neill, *Secure the Soul*, 9–10.
56. Garcia, "Serenity," 462.
57. Becerra and Bazo, *Diágnostico situacional*, 68; UNODC, *Pasta básica de cocaína*, 119–24.
58. Mangelinckx, "Comunidades Terapéuticas en Perú."
59. Galli, "¿Centros de rehabilitación?"
60. Wynter, "Unsettling the Coloniality of Being," 261.

Bibliography

Agamben, Giorgio. *Homo Sacer: Sovereign Power and Bare Life*. Translated by Daniel Heller-Roazen. Palo Alto, Calif: Stanford University Press, [1995] 1998.

Becerra, Beatriz and Jorge Young Bazo. *Diágnostico situacional de las comunidades terapéuticas Peruanas* [Situational Diagnosis of Peruvian Therapeutic Communities]. Lima: Contradrogas, 1999.

Biehl, João. *Vita: Life in a Zone of Social Abandonment*. Berkeley: University of California Press, 2005.

Browder, John and Brian Godfrey. *Rainforest Cities*. New York: Columbia University Press, 1997.

Caldeira, Teresa. *City of Walls: Crime, Segregation, and Citizenship in São Paulo*. Berkeley: University of California Press, 2001.

Chesnut, Andrew. *Born Again in Brazil: The Pentecostal Boom and the Pathogens of Poverty*. New Brunswick, NJ: Rutgers University Press, 1997.

CIDDH. *El Éxito del Modelo Económico Peruano: A cambio, el fortalecimiento del Narcotráfico* [The Success of the Peruvian Economic Model: In Return, the Consolidation of Drug Trafficking]. Lima: Centro de Investigación Drogas y Derechos Humanos, 2010.

Csordas, Thomas. "Morality as a Cultural System?" *Current Anthropology* 54, no. 5 (2013): 523–546.

CVR. *Informe final* [Final report]. Lima: Comisión de la Verdad y Reconciliación, 2003.

Davis, Mike. *Planet of Slums.* New York: Verso, 2006.

De Leon, George. *The Therapeutic Community: Theory, Model, and Method.* New York: Springer Publishing Company, 2000.

Douglas, Mary. *Purity and Danger: An Analysis of Concepts of Pollution and Taboo.* London: Routledge, 1966.

Foucault, Michel. *Security, Territory, Population: Lectures at the Collège de France, 1977–1978.* Translated by Graham Burchell. New York: Palgrave Macmillan, 2007.

Franco, Jean. *Cruel Modernity.* Durham, NC: Duke University Press, 2013.

Galli, Enrique. "¿Centros de rehabilitación o centros de usura, maltrato y muerte?" ["Rehabilitation centers or centers of usury, mistreatment, and death?"] *Ideele Revista*, June, 2012. Accessed October 25, 2016. http://revistaideele.com/ideele/content/%C2%BFcentros-de-rehabilitaci%C3%B3n-o-centros-de-usura-maltrato-y-muerte

Garcia, Angela. "Serenity: Violence, Inequality, and Recovery on the Edge of Mexico City." *Medical Anthropology Quarterly* 29, no. 4 (2015): 455–472.

Gooren, Henri. "Anthropology of Religious Conversion." Chap. 4 in *The Oxford Handbook of Religious Conversion.* Oxford: Oxford University Press, 2014.

Gootenberg, Paul. *Andean Cocaine: The Making of a Global Drug.* Chapel Hill: University of North Carolina Press, 2008.

Han, Clara. *Life in Debt: Times of Care and Violence in Neoliberal Chile.* Berkeley: University of California Press, 2012.

Hansen, Helena. "The 'New Masculinity': Addiction Treatment as a Reconstruction of Gender in Puerto Rican Evangelist Street Ministries." *Social Science and Medicine* 74, no. 11 (2012): 1721–1728.

Hansen, Thomas. *Melancholia of Freedom: Social Life in an Indian Township in South Africa.* Princeton: Princeton University Press, 2012.

Hartch, Todd. *The Rebirth of Latin American Christianity.* Oxford: Oxford University Press, 2014.

Herlinghaus, Hermann. *Violence without Guilt: Ethical Narratives from the Global South.* London: Palgrave Macmillan, 2009.

IDPC. "Compulsory Rehabilitation in Latin America: An Unethical, Inhumane and Ineffective Practice." *International Drug Policy Consortium*, February, 2014. Accessed October 30, 2016. http://idhdp.com/media/1236/idpc-advocacy-note_compulsory-rehabilitation-latin-america_english.pdf

Jürgens, Ralf, and Joanne Csete. "In the Name of Treatment: Ending Abuses in Compulsory Drug Detention Centers." *Addiction* 107 (2012): 689–691.

Kernaghan, Richard. *Coca's Gone: Of Might and Right in the Huallaga Post-Boom.* Palo Alto, Calif: Stanford University Press, 2009.

Kling, David. "Conversion to Christianity." Chap. 26 in *The Oxford Handbook of Religious Conversion.* Oxford: Oxford University Press, 2014.

Lewis, I. M. *Ecstatic Religion: A Study of Shamanism and Spirit Possession.* London: Routledge, [1971] 2003.

Luhrmann, Tanya. *When God Talks Back: Understanding the American Evangelical Relationship with God.* New York: Vintage Books, 2012.

Mangelinckx, Jerome. "Comunidades terapéuticas en Perú: La historia se repite" [Therapeutic Communities in Peru: History Repeats Itself]. *International Drug Policy Consortium*, 6 September. 2013. Accessed October 22, 2016. http://idpc.net/es/blog/2013/09/comunidades-terapeuticas-en-peru-la-historia-se-repite

Meyer, Birgit. "Aesthetics of Persuasion: Global Christianity and Pentecostalism's Sensational Forms." *South Atlantic Quarterly* 109, no. 4 (2010): 741–763.

Miles, Jack. *Christ: A Crisis in the Life of God.* New York: Vintage Books, 2002.

O'Neill, Kevin. "On Liberation: Crack, Christianity, and Captivity in Postwar Guatemala City." *Social Text 120* 32, no. 3 (2014), 11–28.

O'Neill, Kevin Lewis. "On Hunting." *Critical Inquiry* 43, no. 3 (2017): 697–718.

O'Neill, Kevin. *Secure the Soul: Christian Piety and Gang Prevention in Guatemala.* Berkeley: University of California Press, 2015.

Páucar, Felipe Mariluz. *La guerra oculta en el Huallaga, Monzón y Aguaytía* [The Hidden War of the Huallaga, Monzón, and Aguaytía]. Tingo María, Perú: CEDAI, 2006.

Robbins, Joel. "Anthropology of Religion." Chap. 8 in *Studying Global Pentecostalism: Theories and Methods*. Berkeley: University of California Press, 2010.

Robbins, Joel. "Anthropology, Pentecostalism, and the New Paul: Conversion, Event, and Social Transformation." *South Atlantic Quarterly* 109, no. 4 (2010): 633–652.

Robbins, Joel. "The Globalization of Pentecostal and Charismatic Christianity." *Annual Review of Anthropology* 33 (2004): 117–143.

Taussig, Michael. *The Devil and Commodity Fetishism in South America*. Chapel Hill: University of North Carolina Press, 1980.

UNODC. *Pasta básica de cocaína: Cuatro décadas de historia, actualidad, desafíos* [Coca Paste: Four Decades of History, Actuality, challenges]. Lima: United Nations Office on Drugs and Crime, 2013.

UNODC. *World Drug Report 2015*. New York: United Nations, 2015.

Wilkinson, Annie Kathryn. "'Sin sanidad, no hay santidad': Las prácticas reparativas en Ecuador ['Without sanity, there is no sanctity': Reparative practices in Ecuador]." MA Thesis, FLACSO, 2013.

Wynter, Sylvia. "Unsettling the Coloniality of Being/Power/Truth/Freedom: Towards the Human, After Man, Its Overrepresentation – An Argument." *CR: The New Centennial Review* 3, no. 3 (2003), 257–337.

Zeiderman, Austin. *The Endangered City: The Politics of Security and Risk in Bogot?*. Durham, NC: Duke University Press, 2016.

Fighting crime and maintaining order: shared worldviews of civilian and military elites in Brazil and Mexico

Anaís M. Passos

ABSTRACT
Domestic internal security missions have become a centrepiece of Brazil and Mexico's counter-narcotic efforts. Relying on a set of interviews, this article addresses narratives of elites engaged in the decision-making process and implementation of military operations to counter drug trafficking crimes in Rio de Janeiro and Tijuana. In spite of different levels of drug trafficking organisation and international ramification, this article points out the existence of shared narratives of growing insecurity and criminal strength in Brazil and Mexico, justifying state military reaction against a perceived national security threat. The article thus suggests the relevance of civil–military elites' perception in defining public policies' instruments and, ultimately, in upholding the militarisation of security in democratic regimes.

Introduction

Both Brazil and Mexico have high homicide rates for countries in peacetime.[1] Though violence is not only explained by drug trafficking, analysts contend the particular dynamics acquired by illegal drug and arms markets in these regions, in which non-state armed groups and state agents participate, contribute to the state of affairs.[2] Wherein Mexico is identified as a major supplier of drugs to the US, Brazil is a renowned traffic hub in Latin America for the US, Canada and Western and Central Europe.[3] In this article, I analyse two military operations that were deployed in the cities of Rio de Janeiro and Tijuana in 2007–2015 as a means to combat 'organised crime and drug trafficking'. I seek to identify commonalities between the narratives of narcotics-fighting civilian and military elites justifying state reaction, despite the fundamental differences in how non-state armed groups operate in each country. To capture these accounts, I rely on a qualitative study of 65 in-person interviews conducted in February–August 2016 in Rio de Janeiro, Mexico DF, Tijuana and Paris with major civilian and military authorities in close proximity to the military operations as well as residents living in areas of military incursion. For safety concerns, I anonymise some interviewees' names and other related information.

I split the article in three parts. In the first section, I identify basic differences in terms of criminal groups' activities and affiliation traits which deconstruct the perspective of homogeneity supposedly constituting the 'transnational unitary threat' of drug trafficking.[4] In the second part, I rely on interviews to analyse the discourses of key civilian and military figures regarding their perceptions of severity of violence provoked by illegal groups and the objectives of the deployed military missions. According to these narratives, the state was responding to a 'security crisis' and spiral of violence perpetrated by non-state armed groups. As we will see, this verification is not a pragmatic one, as it is grounded on shifting categories of what pertains to the realm of police and military functions. It is also based on a subjective perception – fear of crime – which is shared by sectors of society, including businessmen and middle classes, depending on when and where crime is located. The third section will focus on comparing dynamics adopted in the course of militarisation and the consequences these brought for criminality reduction in short and long terms. Lastly, I conclude by arguing that elite perceptions of insecurity reify the notion of organisation of crime as the hegemonic explanation for violence. Moreover, it is a constituting part of the process of militarisation itself and, ultimately, shapes the domestic role ascribed to military forces in democratic regimes.

Section 1: The military's role in counter-narcotic policies in Brazil and Mexico

In Mexico, during the administration of Felipe Calderón (2006–2012), *operativos conjuntos* (joint operations) were launched in regions with a high percentage of drug-related crimes with the aim of curbing and undermining criminal groups activities.[5] In parallel, in late 2010, former Brazilian President Lula authorised the deployment of armed forces to 'restore law and order' (GLO operations; *operação para garantia da lei e da ordem*) in *Complexo do Alemão* and *Penha*, two favelas located in the northern region marked by the lowest levels of human development in Rio de Janeiro.[6] There are some structural differences to be emphasised here. In terms of civilian control over domestic missions, the Brazilian armed forces are subordinated to a civilian Minister of Defence; in Mexico the two ministries, i.e. the Secretariat of Defence (*Secretaría de la Defensa*, Sedena), comprising the Army and the Air Force and the Secretariat of Navy (*Secretaría de la Marina*, Semar) are directly linked to the president. Thus, in striking difference to most Latin American countries, Mexico has no civilian Minister of Defence.[7] Secondly, intervention of Brazilian armed forces in domestic affairs is understood by most scholars to be in decline post-1985 democratic transition.[8] Counter-narcotics military operations are episodic, limited in time and space. This contrasts with the case of Mexico, in which democratic alternation at the Federal Executive level in 2000 paradoxically coincided with a dramatic expansion of military participation in intelligence agencies and police departments.[9] Another difference lies in the character of drug trafficking organisations (DTO) that operate at a local level. In Rio de Janeiro, criminal groups are largely restricted to drug retailing in socio-economically deprived areas; in Tijuana, DTOs have operated across the US–Mexico border with a greater level of organisational complexity, developing colluded ties with state bureaucracies.[10]

Rio de Janeiro and Tijuana share the pervading trait of inequality along the cities' geography. Be it the double fence with stadium like illumination to prevent unintended flows of Latin Americans from entering San Diego territory, or privatised complexes of buildings separating those who inhabit *asfalto* (asphalt) and *favela* in the Marvellous City, dichotomy is manifest in everyday life. In the state of Rio de Janeiro, the number of people living in favelas grew at a rate of 34% from 1980s to 1990s, partially due to the lack of state housing policies and a growing number of people facing poverty and unemployment linked to economic stagnation, passing from a total of 717,066 residents living in 165,275 domiciles (1980) to 962,793 residents living in 239,678 houses (1991).[11] Today about 23% of the entire population of the city of Rio de Janeiro lives in favelas, which is approximately 1,443,773 people out of 6,320,446.[12] It is inside some of these poor areas where drug retailing takes place.[13]

CV is the oldest criminal group operating in the state of Rio de Janeiro.[14] Its origin dates back to 1979, when inmates rioted over poor conditions in the maximum-security prison *Penitenciária Cândido Mendes* on *Ilha Grande*. Between 1982 and 1985, CV members expanded their control over former cannabis sell points, replacing it by the more profitable cocaine.[15] The press, in early 1990s, depicted CV as a top-down hierarchical organisation that was trained by political prisoners. Yet, according to scholarly research, local bosses today in some favelas that lie within CV territorial presence maintain a degree of autonomy and lack solid organisational ties.[16] In 2008, the expansion of *milícias* and the instalment of local police stations inside favelas, as part of the UPP (Unities of Pacifying Police) programme launched by the State Public Security Secretary, largely curtailed CV activities.[17] Although favelas were characterised as 'stateless' areas by key authorities and residents during fieldwork, a refined explanation seems to fall in a less dualistic reading of reality. For instance, Desmond Arias has suggested criminal networks operating in Rio have used 'cross-institutional ties' (with the police and politicians) to achieve their group goals.[18] Another indicator of the blurred boundaries between legal and illicit affaires is found in the inquiry conducted by Congress in 2006 on arms trafficking. It reported that around 18% of apprehended guns with criminals were actually diverted from domestic security forces.[19] Steady corruption and unjustified violent behaviour are possible explanatory variables. The residents I spoke to in Alemão, Penha and Maré commonly preferred the deployment of military forces over police even though it meant the application of a war-like device along urban landscape. In interviews in Maré, another favela occupied by military forces during the World Cup Games in 2014, residents emphasised the practice of *arrego*, a bribe given by drug dealers to police officers from the *Batalhão* (local police headquarters).[20] A young student living in the area since childhood attributes the very low level of police operations in her hill (*morro*) to *arrego*. For her, police actions are nothing more than a 'show', instead of a true commitment to ensure the safety of her community.[21]

> So, as I told you, here operations are less frequent because there is bribe. Police officers come, shoot and leave. They arrive in the morning or in the end of the afternoon, just to say: we are here.

In Tijuana, unlike Rio, DTOs are not territorially based in specific neighbourhoods. Instead, they are involved in colluded relations with officials operating across the borders.[22] The city represents one of the busiest land ports of entry into the United States and holds one of the highest population growth rates in Mexico. As such, it's known to be an informal transit point for migrants coming from Central America, dreaming of the American passport, migrants deported from USA for criminal convictions, along with menial workers looking for jobs in Machilladoras.[23] Due to changing urban dynamics and state incapacity to respond to social needs, about 53% of residents in Tijuana live in irregular settlements (*asentamiento iregulares*), often lacking proper conditions of water and sanitation.[24] According to the official data, about 50,000 vehicles and 25,000 pedestrians cross San Ysidro port of entry each day.[25] Neighbouring San Diego, Tijuana is a key transit route for the US market where major sums of drugs and money are processed. Though opium smuggling in Baja California can be identified as early as 1916, the contemporary dominance of AFO dates back to 1980s and is the unintended consequence of the policies of the US Drug Enforcement Agency (DEA).[26] In 1980, estimates indicate that 80% of cocaine arrived through Dade County in Florida; in 1990, 90% of US supplied cocaine entered though the US–Mexican border.[27]

As Shirk points out, AFO members cultivated 'critical links to law enforcement and government officials' across the borders to ensure the thriving of their illicit drug trade from Central Mexico to US through Baja California.[28] AFO has recurrently used violence and murder to intimidate those denouncing their illicit activities.[29] The former Municipal Police Chief in Tijuana, Julian Leyzaola, known for his *mano dura* (tough hand) policy with crime, stated in an interview that when he took office, he refused a weekly payment of US$18,000 in the form of bribe from *El Chapo*. During his tenure in Tijuana, he emphasised, that he had survived five assassination attempts ordered by organised crime, before the last one in *Ciudad Juárez* in 2015 which left him paralysed. Leyzaola is a retired military officer who has recently pursued a political career at *Partido Encuentro Social*. He was trained in counter-insurgency operations in France, and had worked in different security-office positions in Baja California. He has also been denounced by human rights groups while heading the Municipal Police in Tijuana. Leyzaola was accused of having personally tortured police officers to investigate if they were colluding with organised crime groups. According to Leyzaola, *el problema* (the criminal issue) was located in Tijuana which was divided among AFO and Sinaloa cartel. He stated he could not defeat the crime in Tijuana as the Municipal police offered them immunity. According to him, police officers warned criminals from AFO and Sinaloa cartel when he was in town:[30]

> As a state police officer, I worked in all Baja California state. But I've realized that (…) the Baja California's criminal issue was in Tijuana. So I started to attack the criminal issue in Tijuana with the state police. I realized I couldn't as a state police officer arrive at Tijuana and defeat the criminals' resistance to state authorities. Because in Tijuana two criminal groups were operating, Chapo Guzmán and Arellano Félix.(….). But the municipal police in Tijuana was offering them immunity. One group from the police was protecting los Arellano, and the other protecting los Chapos. And when I entered in Tijuana willing to fight these criminal groups, I couldn't because the police let them know beforehand about my plan. So I couldn't do anything against them. There was no way. They were 'bulletproof'. The police sheltered the criminal groups, and did not let me attack them.

Although Leyzaola stressed how entrenched was the organised crime while he was heading the State Police of Baja California, it should be noted that since early to mid-2000s, the activities of the organisation were disrupted with the arrest or murder of its key leaders. Researchers depict AFO as an amalgamation of cells faithful to the family, but keeping a degree of operational independence.[31] The leader of one cell, Eduardo Teodoro García Simental, 'El Teo', who for a long time had worked with Arellano Félix, challenged the family's leadership and allied himself with *Cartel de Sinaloa* who was longing to expand its network in Baja California. This has provoked an internecine conflict among DTOs, particularly in Tijuana, which coincided with the deployment of *Operativo Conjunto* in the region. Similarly, *Comando Vermelho* presence in favelas was declining in 2010 as a result of UPPs instalment in the locality. This is in spite of the official narrative according to which the state was mainly reacting to violent actions perpetrated by the 'organised crime', which signalised criminals' strength vis-à-vis the state. In the next section, I will explore these narratives in detail.

Section 2: Countering drug-trafficking: shared worldviews of civilian and military authorities

GLO operation in Rio de Janeiro

In 2010, Rio de Janeiro enjoyed peaceful times. Governor Sergio Cabral had been re-elected in the first round of elections with 66.08% of votes and was a political ally of the federal government.[32] UPPs were largely approved by citizens living in favelas, as homicide rates had been in decline since 2008.[33] Despite these comforting figures, Rio remained a 'split city' where social inequality was present in daily state action and inaction.[34] As research has exhaustively demonstrated, *favelados*[35] are vulnerable to the lethal violence of drug dealers and police officers who do not receive proper training to counter drug-related crimes.[36] In 2016 in the city of Rio de Janeiro, official accounts report that 492 people were killed during police action, and 18 police officers died while performing their duty.[37] In 2007, a police operation in Alemão led to the deaths of about 19 young men, who were presented by the press as drug dealers.[38] As such, armed forces intervention in favelas, far from being an external interruption in a peaceful state of affairs, is better interpreted as the continuation of a violent approach to tackle the problem of drug retailing.

Planned initially to last until October 2011, the first GLO operation was extended until June 2012. A considerable number of military personnel was deployed to combat what was interpreted as an *evolving threat* from organised crime.[39] Military forces performed functions of patrolling, searching and arresting suspects.[40] According to public officials I interviewed, what triggered the deployment of this military operation were a series of criminal actions in late November, including attacks on police stations and the death of a driver after he was assaulted at the highway Rio-Magé on 21 November 2011, in the city of Duque de Caxias.[41] In six days, a local news article states, about 96 buses and cars '[had] been burned-out in arson attacks'.[42] A former top-level military official involved in the decision-making at the time stressed that Rio was in 'a total crisis'. He states that citizens were living in fear, and were confined to their houses because of the criminal acts: [43]

> Me – Sir, how do you evaluate the media's reaction to the Alemão and Maré operations?
>
> How do I evaluate the media's reaction? I think in Alemão the action was a bit different than in Maré. In Alemão, Rio was in a total crisis, the population could not leave their houses. Criminals burning cars, actions like that. So it was … There was the need [to deploy the armed forces].

CV was accused of sponsoring these arson attacks as they were in decline due to the expansion of the UPP programme. Burned-out cars appeared on the front page main newspapers such as *Folha de São Paulo*, *O Globo* and *O Dia* to communicate the 'audacity' and 'cruelty' of criminals. According to another former top military official, violence reached 'an unbearable level'. He explained how there was a lack of state 'authority' in the area and criminals were 'showing off' their guns, which was not usually the case. Also he argues the commitment of patrimonial crimes (burning of cars and buses) pushed the governor to take decisive actions to restore law and order in the region. In this case, criminal actions outside favelas were considered as 'visible' and thus 'ostensive' for authorities:[44]

> (…) So there was a point that was considered by the state governor and not only by the government, but also by the population, as unbearable.
>
> Me – But when did the governor consider it was unbearable? Was it because of the attacks?
>
> Show of force, criminals circulating with arms every hour, car thefts everywhere inside the area, but ostensive. Many times there is the owner of the area, but no one is seeing him. That is, it's

not ostensive. It doesn't mean it should be allowed. But the problem was [the] population there had no authority, [if the] authority cannot contain, how … how is it going to be?

State presence in this case was defined by virtue of authority, preventing criminals from disposing guns in an ostensive way outside favelas perimeters, but not necessarily disarming them permanently. The former Minister of Defence, Celso Amorin, who assumed office at the end of operation in Alemão and Penha, emphasised domestic security operations should be regarded as a secondary mission, as they were activated under 'exceptional circumstances whether it be (…) failure of security, failure of law and order or the lack of domination in an area, as Alemão and Maré, taken by criminals'.[45] The discourse conveyed by these three officials makes reference to the legal framework in which GLO operations are embedded. Since 1891, the Armed Forces in Brazil are constitutionally equipped to 'ensure law and order', which in the period of Old Republic (1889–1930) meant repressing regional rebellions and maintaining territorial unity.[46] Military forces are considered the last resort in extraordinary circumstances wherever public security forces are deemed less likely to succeed in their tasked mission to *maintain order*. In this case, the officials' narratives not only justify their action, but also frame it according to the existing constitutional clauses pertaining to the domestic roles of the armed forces which are constituted by the Federal Constitution (article 142), presidential decrees (3897/2001) and complimentary laws (97/1999). The aforementioned set of laws determines that the president is equipped to authorise the deployment of armed forces to guarantee law and order whenever the police forces are not available or are considered by state governors inadequate to counter crime.[47] This legal framework also stipulates GLO operations should happen on a temporary basis, in a pre-defined area with the shortest possible duration.[48] 'To maintain order' is, evidently, an open-ended definition with great modicum of ambiguity, thereby providing opportunity to state governors to adapt it according to the political agenda at stake.

In Brazil, the military doctrine has evolved towards a more detailed and comprehensive definition concerning the military roles in domestic security. For example, in comparison to the previous 1997 version, the recent Brazilian Army Field Manual for Operations (2014) was expanded to include a new category to the set of basic military missions and operations in support of civil authorities, which comprises GLO operations.[49] Yet some high-ranking authorities in Brazil reported to me there was an internal divergence regarding their support for these kinds of missions as they in the long-term, if not attending the requisites of time and space limitation, tended to divert the Army from its main mission of external defence. A retired officer added state governors faced high incentives for demanding military support for maintaining security in their states, as costs were entirely federal responsibility and they could use their limited police contingent in other areas with thinner policing.[50]

Operativo Conjunto in Tijuana

The narrative of a 'security crisis' in Rio can be seen in Mexico at the national and local levels. In September 2006, a group of armed masked men burst into a crowded dance club in Uruapán, Michoacán, and threw down five human heads leaving a note saying this was carried out in the name of *La Familia*.[51] This episode received attention from mainstream media due to its brutality. On December 2006, just 10 days after taking office, President Calderón, attending a request made by the state governor Lázaro Cárdenas (*Partido de la Revolución Democrática*, PRD), authorised the first of several military operations in Mexico.

In his new year's message, he stated: 'we will steadily intensify our fight against crime, against drug dealing'.[52] On 2 January 2007 a joint operation was launched, as formally requested by Governor Eugenio Elorduy Walther (*Partido Acción Nacional*, PAN), in Tijuana, as well as in its surrounding areas in Baja California and Baja California Sur.

After the 9/11 terrorist attacks in the US, border surveillance was reinforced by US law enforcement agencies, hindering the traffic of drugs to US, which led some elements of AFO to diversify their activities to other criminal acts such as kidnappings.[53] Business leaders pressured the governor to request military support in the state due to their fears of the prevalence of kidnapping and crime against the business and middle classes.[54] According to the former head of Anti-Organised Crime Unit of the Mexican Federal Attorney General's Office (SEIDO), AFO was the first drug trafficking organisation to steadily rely on kidnapping prior to President Calderón's war against drugs in December 2006. Furthermore, AFO cells colluded with anti-kidnapping teams which are part of the Municipal Police (*Grupo Anti-Secuestros*) to kidnap citizens.[55] In 2006, a 15-day March (*Marcha contra la Inseguridad*) was held in the state, organised by *Consejo Ciudadano de Seguridad* (Baja California Public Security Citizen Council) seeking to draw attention to the severity of the security problems in the region.[56] In an interview, a businessman who has lived in Tijuana since 1958 told about his activities in *Consejo Ciudano*, which he joined after being a victim of kidnapping in 2004. He organised a series of marches which were held in Baja California between 2004 and 2006 to protest against the lack of attention given by the governor to their demands. This businessman questioned the unwillingness of the governor to take decisive actions to improve the security conditions. For him, this could be understood as a sign of compliance with crime or governor's fear of a possible retaliation from the organised crime in case he decided to fight 'them':[57]

> The objective was to put pressure over the authorities because we did not see things changing. When we reached Mexicali the governor joined us and finally decided to do something. He said everything that was happening was only a matter of citizens' perceptions, it was not really happening. Of course it was happening! Well, you ask yourself many questions and many of them were of course happening. The corruption ... they were ... I even said in a meeting directly to the governor. I said: 'Mister President [bang over the table] here is nothing more than two things. Or you are afraid and that's why you don't fight them, or you are working with them. You are colluded with them'.

Although statistics about crimes occurrence are under-reported in Mexico and should be viewed with caution, criminal statistics from 2005 to 2008 indicate an increase in kidnapping rates along with citizens' growing fear of being kidnapped. The average of monthly kidnapping in Baja California (SSP) increased from nine in 2005 to 38 in 2006. This number increased to 115 in 2008 due to the internecine war in CAF organisation. *El Teo* started to work for Cartel de Sinaloa and relied on kidnapping to diversify his revenue sources at the time.[58] A businessman, who was born and raised in Tijuana, reported he had moved to San Diego in 2006 due to insecurity. He praised Leyzaola's action towards ensuring the safety of the citizens, in contrast to the politicians who would be entangled in blame games:[59]

> I moved to San Diego because it was very insecure here.
>
> Me – What kind of threats? Not being able to go outside?
>
> Well, kidnappings, everyday there were kidnappings of businessmen. Indeed many people in drug trafficking died.(...) there were many fightings, too much, a lot. A dark time for Tijuana. Very very dark. There was no leadership from politicians, from government. They all blame each

other and were really irresponsible, no need to point out one. They were irresponsible because at the end they were elected and are responsible for ensuring security. It's the minimum, right?

About 3296 federal forces, including officers from Sedena, Semar and Polícia Federal, were deployed in Baja California, part of them in Tijuana. This striking number is illustrative of the scope of the conducted military missions.[60] At that time, General Guillermo Galván, the Secretary of Defence stated they would: '(…) conduct aerial reconnaissance activities and checkpoints settings to drain drug trafficking in seven areas'.[61] Federal Deputy Jorge Ramos, former mayor at Tijuana (2008–2010) from PAN and today heading the Security Bicameral Commission at the National Congress stated that the crime had 'overtaken the city' prior to *Operativo Conjunto* and was defining the community's life, being the de facto power in Tijuana. Ramos said 'the state' had been surpassed by Cartel de Sinaloa and AFO with the complicity of many municipal officers:[62]

> Me – So, Mister Deputy, from your experience as mayor how would you describe the situation in Tijuana at the beginning of your administration?
>
> Ok … [I'd frame it] In a context where the Mexican state institutions had been surpassed by the organized crime. Crime had taken the city and it was actually the de facto element defining business', governments' and even the community's lives and that with extreme levels of government complicity. Local police officers were involved with the organized crime, working for them. So it was a challenge, [that] the conception of the Mexican state was surpassed by outlaw groups.

Yet, as I pointed in the above sections, this feature has been present since the early establishment of AFO in Baja California in mid 1980s. Besides the co-optation of municipal police by the organised crime, another element in the official narrative is the lack of adequate policing firepower vis-a-vis DTO. A former head of intelligence services at the time (CISEN) stated local policing forces did not have the required military power to combat organised crime (*grupos delincuenciales*). The deployment of armed forces was seen as the only viable option to counteract what was defined as the high level of lethal violence used by them:[63]

> Me – Sir, were you present when operativos conjuntos were announced? Could you tell me a little bit how the process was?
>
> I'll go back to something I have already said. When one realizes the presence of powerful organized crime groups, with the weaponries we made reference to, and realized that state and municipal corporations did not have the firepower that these groups had, it was necessary to go to the federal level. And the federal police still is in the beginning, had 6000 elements, nothing more. Why the decision was taken to deploy the Armed Forces? First, and this is fundamental, we assume that the presence of organized crime is a threat to *internal security*. That is, not as a *public security issue* but as an *internal security problem* within the realm of armed forces missions. According to this logic, we speak in terms of their firepower, and indeed the ones who had the capacity to resist them were the armed forces.[64]

This official in Mexico alluded that the threat the state was facing was an internal security issue, which is assumed to belong to the realm of military forces. The parameters to establish this differentiation are rather ambiguous, as it can be interpreted from analysing the legal framework under which the military operates in domestic security. The latter includes article 89 of the Federal Constitution (1917), the General Law for the Army and Air Force, the Defence Plan II (DN-II) and the jurisprudential thesis issued in April 2000.[65] The jurisprudential thesis has been one of the most important legal documents orienting the counter-narcotics policy conducted by Felipe Calderon administration (2006–2012). According to the General Law for the Army and Air Force (26/12/1986), the military forces have, among their main missions, to safeguard internal security and provide external defence (art.1). There is no clear legal definition on the meaning of internal security; Mexican laws vaguely refer to it as a constitutional function ascribed to the military forces, without properly defining a time framework, as in Brazil.[66] In 2014 the Manual for the Use of Force by the Mexican Armed Forces was edited precisely to adapt force proportionality to domestic missions and internal security. Policy makers have taken public and internal security as equivalent terms. This has raised critics from civil society with regards to expansion of the domestic roles ascribed to military forces, especially when human rights violations were denounced. A major source of hasty debate in Congress lately has been Mexico's law on internal security. Deputies from PRI, PAN and PRD presented different law initiatives to further define the conditions in which armed forces should be deployed in internal security. These law proposals vary regarding the scope of missions ascribed to the Armed Forces, ranging from only executing apprehension orders or prisons in the act of committing an offence (as the PRD proposal) to broader functions of patrolling, establishing checkpoints on a permanent basis without prior Executive consent (PAN) and executing security public functions as receiving complaints and conducting investigations when local investigative bodies (Ministerio Publico) are not available (PRI). While the Secretary of Defence has publicly insisted on the necessity of regulating the Mexican Army's role in internal security, he also firmly stated that this should not lead to engaging officer corps in public security functions, since that may undermine military readiness in defending the nation.[67] As a research institute affiliated with Mexican Senate pointed out recently, there are provisions in the proposals going against constitutional principles laid out by the Constitution such as the definition of public security competent bodies (art. 21 FC) and principles as freedom of transit and not being the target of violence from any public agent (art. 11, 14 and 16 FC).[68]

Although the 'War on Drugs' has mainly been depicted as a foreign notion borrowed from the US, especially the Ronald Reagan administration that deemed narcotics a national security threat in the mid-1980s, the set of interviews with key military and civilian authorities have highlighted specific national and local trends. This article illustrates how decision-makers in our two cases used the existent legal framework to frame the perception of security threat emanating from drug-trafficking groups. In this case, the Brazilian elites stressed the need to enforce 'law and order' in stateless areas as it is contended by the Constitution. On the other hand, Mexican elites justified the extension of the domestic roles of the military forces as the right answer to the rising problem of internal security and the collusion of Municipal Forces by the organised crime, which would justify the resort to military forces. In Rio de Janeiro the commitment of criminal offences outside favelas nurtured the narrative of a security crisis in late 2010. In Tijuana it was the victimisation of middle and business classes which caused the main source of insecurity perception.

Section 3: Domestic military operations: a balance on figures

Concerning the level of organisation and crime in each city, there are some similarities in the operation dynamics that should be highlighted. In Tijuana, federal agents temporarily disarmed the municipal police to explore whether any of their guns were used in killings, mostly connected to AFO and Sinaloa Cartel for whom corrupted police officers worked at the time. In Rio de Janeiro, part of the strategy for 'cleaning the area' was to control police officers operating in Alemão and Penha, making sure they only belonged to the local Battalion that was subordinated to the military commander. For example, two active-duty military officers, part of contingents deployed in Alemão and Penha, described to me how police officers could only do patrols in the area during the GLO operation accompanied by the military and that they occasionally bumped into non-authorised patrolling – which was interpreted as collecting bribes from dealers – and expelled them.[69] Another similar feature was to establish secure hotlines for citizens to report crimes – Nosotros Sí Vamos in Tijuana, Disque Denúncia in Rio de Janeiro – acknowledging the general lack of citizens' confidence in law enforcement institutions. Julian Leyzaola reported how he asked the residents, after he shared with hem his personal phone number, to call him whenever they witness a police officer engaging in illegal activity.[70] However, since hotlines were run by local Military Districts in each city, it is not clear how in the medium-term they succeeded in communicating a better image of law enforcement services, who were not 'in the spotlight' in advertising such services. As Felbab-Brown highlighted, the quality of the anti-corruption campaign in Tijuana is questionable: of the 35 officials arrested 2009 for having ties with organised crime, all were released due to the lack of evidence.[71]

Leyzaola also changed the dynamics of patrolling by concentrating police patrols in the city centre. He increased the number of street patrols from 10 to 150 in attempting to choke crime in that locality. However, this left other parts of the city, namely in banlieue, with a smaller police patrol.[72] The strategy is similar to the military patrolling adopted in Rio de Janeiro. Regarding the latter, military officers highlighted to me how they patrolled the streets in much larger groups than police officers, who allegedly used to go in a group of two or three. The basic group was a combat group (*grupo de combate*, GC) of seven headed by a sergeant, and comprising two corporals and soldiers. It augmented the dissuasion effect and also reduced the possibility that one member could be tempted to accept bribes from police officers.[73] Regarding the consequences of these two operations, the balance is contradictory. *Operativo Conjunto* Tijuana was praised by some civilian officials part of Calderón staff for being a successful example of reducing drug related violence.[74] After the spike in homicide rates between 2008 and 2010, levels went back to slightly higher thresholds compared to 2006, but still much lower than during Tijuana dark period and, according to residents, the city 'went back to life' with a resurgence of cultural events and business activity.[75] However since 2013, homicide rates and thefts resumed increasing, partially attributable to an updated crime fragmentation post-*Operativo Conjunto* in the city as now cartel de Sinaloa, cells of AFO and the new arrival Cartel Jalisco Nueva Generación are reported to be disputing Plaza Tijuana.[76] Due to the change in Mexican criminal justice system for a centralised and uniform oral-trial accusatory model, many military arrests done during military operations were released, feeding the resurgence of AFO.[77] A business leader complained authorities underestimated their grievances regarding violence since most homicides are considered to be a 'settling of accounts' between drug dealers, as they happen in *colonias* (outskirt) far away from the city centre.[78] The business community is now pressuring the governor to solve the issue. Recently, the State Security Council president requested the return of military support.[79]

The situation in Rio de Janeiro is equally gloomy. While the GLO operation was praised for reducing crime incidence in the months following deployment, accounts report that while military troops were on ground the situation remained peaceful, it seems the situation deteriorated since the instalment of seven UPPs and withdraw of military troops in mid-2012. Shootings are frequent but rarely reported by the media, even when they cause fatalities.[80] Many local juvenile associations were created to report local protests and denounce daily violence. A group of young residents in Penha and Alemão created on Facebook a *pipoco* (slang for shooting) calendar where they mark the days when there was a shooting in one of the areas. Residents in Alemão and Penha describe being 'in the middle of a war' or 'in the crossfire', and having constant fear regarding their physical integrity.[81] Comando Vermelho is still the main criminal group operating in the region, though what seems to be broken is their dominance as residents report that criminals are now entering the community to rob or rape, not respecting 'CV dominance'.[82] Moreover other favelas located in the edge of Rio de Janeiro, such as Complexo do Chapadão, are depicted by the press as being the new 'CV headquarters' as drug dealers migrated to this region when military troops entered Alemão and Penha.[83] Recently a contingent of about 8500 soldiers was deployed in Rio de Janeiro to support police officers once in combating organised crime, this time along the main highways and Ipanema wealthy neighbourhood.[84] It should be noted that military officers question the efficacy of such policies in combatting drug trafficking. A military officer in Brazil, who had participated in the famous Rio Operation to establish law and order in favelas in Rio in 1994 and in Alemao said drug dealers played a 'cat and mouse' game with the police. For example, drug traffickers 'had an alarm system' which notified them about any military patrolling.[85] Leyzaola stated he was aware that 'while there is demand, there will be an offer'. Yet, he emphasised, 'I also believe that criminal organisations never can be above the law'.[86]

It is clear that public security policies adopted in parallel to military operations lack endurance, compromising a sustainable approach in reducing drug-related crimes. During the tenure of President Calderón, Tijuana received extra federal money through Subsemun (Municipal Public Security Subsidy) in exchange for submitting police officers to a series of requirements, including a vetting process (*controles de confianza*).[87] Newly elected in July 2012, president Enrique Peña Nieto from PRI downgraded the matter of public security in agenda and interrupted the programme. UPPs in Rio de Janeiro now face many difficulties, including the deterioration of training and quality standards initially applied at the programme outset as the state faces a severe fiscal and political crisis.[88] During the operation in Alemão and Penha, an attorney general local office was installed to register criminal reports with alacrity and endure trust in communities regarding law enforcement services.[89] The service was paused when military troops left the area.

Conclusion

This article has examined the 'War on Drugs' in Brazil and Mexico by focusing on two specific military operations to counter drug trafficking crimes. I have examined the narratives of key military and civilian authorities regarding their policies. In spite of unequal drug trafficking characteristics in Rio de Janeiro and Tijuana, I have highlighted the existence of a common security crisis narrative to justify the deployment of armed forces, conveying the image of strength and unity among criminal groups that would urge a military response. I also compared similar dynamics adopted in the course of militarisation processes and finally attempted to measure the consequences of this operation regarding the proclaimed first objective of curtailing organised crime and drug trafficking activities that would provoke violence. Though military presence on ground succeeded in reducing crime rates during the course of operations, being praised by mainstream media, civil authorities and some security officials, it failed to generate an institutionalised long term solution for more effective police and law enforcement services. The accentuation of violence in both cities after the retreat of military forces signals the limits within short-term perspectives assenting over exclusively military dissuasion for preventing criminals from committing a crime, without being combined with institutional changes in police and law enforcement services. Meanwhile, Rio de Janeiro and Tijuana continue to be cities delineated by huge traits of urban disparity and social inequality in which drug trafficking or retailing provides a satisfactory, albeit illegal, shortcut for income resources.[90] A long-lasting solution should also focus on that side of the equation.

Disclosure statement

No potential conflict of interest was reported by the author.

Funding

This work was supported by Coordenação de Aperfeiçoamento de Pessoal de Nível Superior [grant number 0436-14-3].

Acknowledgements

This work was initially developed for the workshop 'Drugs, Politics and Society' at Oxford University in October 2016, organised by Maziyar Ghiabi. The author is grateful to the support of Olivier Dabène, her current dissertation adviser, to Asma Faiz, Maria Teresa Martinez-Trujillo, Hussein Abou Saleh, Laura Matte and the anonymous reviewers for the valuable feedback and comments on this article. Finally the author would like to thank the Capes Foundation in Brazil (Coordenação de Aperfeiçoamento de Pessoal de Nível Superior) [0436-14-3] and Sciences Po Doctoral School in France for having funded the dissertation fieldwork in Tijuana and Rio de Janeiro.

Notes

1. In 2015, Mexico had an intentional homicide rate of 17.15 per 100,000 people (Inegi/Conapo 2015) while Brazil was 28.9 per 100,000 (Ministry of Health-SIM/Ibge, 2015). Both percentages are much higher than the average world intentional homicide rate the World Bank estimated for 2015 of 5 per 100,000. https://data.worldbank.org/indicator/VC.IHR.PSRC.P5.
2. Desmonds Arias and Goldstein, "Violent Pluralism," 17.
3. About 40–50% of heroin apprehended in US comes from Mexico, also a major clandestine producer of methamphetamine for US consumption. https://www.dea.gov/docs/2015%20NDTA%20Report.pdf. According to the last World Drug Report, Brazil was reported 1747 times by 56 recipient countries in 2005–2014. Together with Argentina, Brazil is the 'most frequently mentioned in major individual drug seizures'. UNODC, *World Drugs Report*, 39.
4. In this sense, Peter Andreas criticises the characterisation of organised crime as 'a crime syndicate that acts globally' since crime organisation ranges from self-smugglers to independent small-scale entrepreneurs and loose transnational gangs; Andreas, *Border Games*, 20.
5. Calderon Hinojosa, "Estrategia Nacional de Seguridad," 41–42.

6. Cavallieri and Lopes, "Índice de Desenvolvimento Social," 7.
7. As the literature highlights, Ministries of Defence, headed by a civilian minister and ideally advised by a non-exclusively military staff, are a fundamental vehicle for ensuring civilian control over armed forces and thus for sustaining a more democratic pattern of civil–military relations; Bruneau, *Ministries of Defence and Democratic Control*, 5.
8. Hunter, *Eroding Military Influence*, chapter 1; Bruneau and Tollefson, "Civil–military Relations in Brazil," 108; Call, "War Transitions and the New Civilian," 12.
9. López González, *Presidencialismo y Fuerzas Armadas*, 18.
10. While *Comando Vermelho* (CV) uses walkie talkies to operate in favelas, Arellano Felix organisation (AFO) had a secure radio system used in the border area of Tijuana in the early 2000s; Jones, *Mexico's Illicit Drug Networks*, 55. In San Diego, AFO worked with gangs as Los Angeles based 18th street gang, San Diego Barrio Logan street and the so-called Mexican Mafia prison gang; Shirk, "Tale of Two Mexican Border," 487.
11. Resende, *Operação Rio*, 40.
12. Cavallieri and Vial, "Favelas Na Cidade Do Rio," 2.
13. Research on illegal drug markets in Rio de Janeiro relies mostly on ethnographic research conducted in favelas. There are few (almost none) empirical studies on the dynamics of international drug trafficking and the connection with *matutos*, the ones bringing cocaine from Peru, Bolivia, Paraguay and Colombia to Brazil. Rafael, Um Abraço Para Todos, 84–85; Zaluar, "Juventude Violenta," 347.
14. Besides CV, three other criminal groups are known to operate in the state of Rio de Janeiro: *Terceiro Comando Puro* (TCP), *Amigo dos Amigos* (ADA), both originated from internal splits within CV, and the *milícia*, which gathers corrupted police officers. In December 2007 city councilman Josinaldo Francisco da Cruz (*Nadinho*) was accused of leading the milícia at Rio das Pedras, in the Western part of Rio, being arrested with other public officials who were equally part of this criminal organisation, such as the state deputy Natalino Guimarães and the councilman *Jerominho*. Comissão Parlamentar de Inquérito, *Relatório Final Da Comissão Parlamentar de Inquérito*, 34.
15. Ibid.
16. Misse, "Les Organisations Criminelles Au Brésil," 51.
17. Zaluar and Barcellos, "Mortes Prematuras e Conflito," 25.
18. Desmonds Arias, *Drugs and Democracy*, 189–190.
19. See Report of the Special Rapporteur on Industry, Commerce and CAC, 2006, National Congress, Brazil. https://www.comunidadesegura.org/files/active/0/Reatorio%20subrelatoria%20de%20industria%20comercio%20e%20cac.pdf.
20. Interviews with residents in Complexo da Maré, Rio de Janeiro: student 04/13/2016, high school teacher 04/22/2016 and taxi driver 05/12/2016.
21. Interview with student from Complexo da Maré, 04/13/2016:
22. Though CV members have been reported to pay bribes to police officers, during my fieldwork, residents in Alemão and Penha related the increase of police operations inside favelas to insufficient payment as CV lost drug related profits with UPP expansion. As CV did not engage in diverse activities as AFO, this suggest the relation between the group and police officers was rather asymmetric favouring the latter. This does not seem to be the case in Tijuana, where police officers worked for cartel de Sinaloa or AFO, a deeper level of collusion in contrast to Rio, and could monitor police operations, regularly making threats through unsecured police radios. In early 2009, two mid police officers in Tijuana confessed that they earned 'US$500 and US$700 a month to facilitate criminal operations'; Sabet, "Confrontation, Collusion and Tolerance," 19, 22 and see note 28.
23. Between 1995 and 2010, the population growth rate in Tijuana was 57.5%, well above the rates in Puebla (25.94%) and Ecatepec de Morelos (13.5%); Reynoso, "¿Qué Cuenta El Rancho Tijuana?," 53.
24. Alegría Olazabal and Ordoñez Barba, *Legalizando La Ciudad*, 53.
25. US General Administration. https://www.gsa.gov/portal/content/104,872.

26. Astorga analysed General Records of the US Department to document illicit drug trade activities at the beginning of the twentieth century; Astorga, *Drogas Sin Fronteras*, 27–31.
27. Morton, "War on Drugs in Mexico," 1638.
28. Shirk, "Tale of Two Mexican Border Cities," 493.
29. Zeta is an investigative newspaper created in 1980 in Tijuana whose offices were attacked in March 1987. In 1997, its co-founder and prize-winner Jesus Blancornelas was ambushed and attacked by 10 gunmen in his way to the airport. After that, Zeta offices were daily secured by a military tank; Jesus Blancornelas. 1999. "Hace dos años." *Zeta*. November 19–25.
30. Interview with Julian Leyzaola 09/29/2016.
31. Sabet, "Confrontation, Collusion and Tolerance," 17.
32. https://www.tre-rj.jus.br/site/eleicoes/2010/index.jsp#.
33. For homicide rates at the state and capital levels in Rio de Janeiro, please consult the data from ISP/RJ (*Instituto de Segurança Pública*). https://www.isp.rj.gov.br/dadosoficiais.asp. According to a survey applied by IBPS (*Instituto Brasileiro de Pesquisa Social*), 92% of residents in favelas with UPPs and 77% of residents in favelas with no UPPs approved the project in 2010. https://oglobo.globo.com/rio/pesquisa-mostra-alta-aprovacao-das-upps-em-favelas-sejam-pacificadas-ou-nao-2911694.
34. The term was dubbed by Ventura, *Cidade Partida*.
35. Favelados are those who live in favelas.
36. Moreira Alves and Evanson, *Vivendo No Fogo Cruzado*; Lees, "Cocaine and Parallel Polities," 50–52; Zaluar and Alvito, *Um Século de Favela*, Introduction. Some police stations installed as part of the UPP programme are made of containers, which are unsafe and unsanitary for police officers. Interview with police officer, 04/18/2016.
37. Data from Instituto de Segurança Pública/State Public Security Secretary, Rio de Janeiro. https://www.isp.rj.gov.br/dadosoficiais.asp.
38. Interview with social activist from Complexo do Alemão, 04/14/2016. Interview with Isabel Santos, NGO Justiça Global, 05/10/2016.
39. According to official statements and documents, 1937 army soldiers were engaged in the mission, besides 120 police officers and 25 law enforcement agents, all subordinated to the Military Commander during the entire operation. The Army provided 50 lightweight vehicles, 40 transport vehicles, 20 motorcycles, six armoured vehicles, two ambulances and two helicopters. Seven different Army Infantry Divisions were deployed, staying an average of three months on the ground, in order to avoid a long exposure to the environment that could eventually lead to corruption and discipline break.
40. The Armed Forces were authorised to arrest people only when a suspect was caught in the act of committing an offence; only police officers were legally authorised to detain suspects.
41. Interviews with former Ministers of Defence in Brazil Nelson Jobim and Celso Amorim (22/03/2016, 23/03/2016). Regarding the drivers' death, please consult https://www1.folha.uol.com.br/cotidiano/2010/11/833,834-motorista-morre-em-tentativa-de-assalto-na-br-116-em-duque-de-caxias-rj.shtml.
42. Folha de São Paulo 11/21/2011. https://www1.folha.uol.com.br/cotidiano/2010/11/836,598-armed-forces-willstrengthen-security-in-rio-where-six-days-of-attacks-have-left-43-dead.shtml.
43. Interview with retired military officer, 05/04/2016.
44. Interview with retired military officer, 03/30/2016.
45. Interview with former Ministry of Defence, Celso Amorim, 03/23/2016.
46. Carvalho, *Forças Armadas e Política*, chap. 1.
47. Decree no. 3897/2001, art. 2, para. 2.
48. Decree no. 3897/2001, art. 5.
49. Brazilian Army, Manual de Fundamentos de Operações, EB20-MF10.103.
50. See note 46.
51. La Jornada 09/07/2016. https://www.jornada.unam.mx/2006/09/07/index.php?section==estados&article==037n1est and BBC 09/07/2016. https://news.bbc.co.uk/2/hi/5,322,160.stm.
52. See note 7.

53. Interview with former Director of Kidnapping Unit, Ministério Público, 08/03/2016.
54. Interview with business leader 06/29/2016; interview with resident 08/03/2016; interview with businessman 08/02/2016; interview with business leader 08/03/2016.
55. El Mexicano, El cártel de Tijuana, número uno en secuestros http://www.el-mexicano.com.mx/informacion/noticias/1/3/estatal/2008/05/31/272020/el-cartel-de-tijuana-numero-uno-en-secuestros.aspx. 05/31/2008; Jones, "The Unitended Consequences," 158.
56. Sabet, "Confrontation, Collusion and Tolerance," 15.
57. Interview with business leader 08/08/2016.
58. Interview with former Tijuana resident 07/01/2016; interview with civic association leaders 08/01/2016.
59. Interview with businessman 02/08/2016.
60. In comparison, during the Condor Operation in 1976, conducted to eradicate pavot and cannabis crops in three states (Sinaloa, Chihuahua and Durango), 10,000 soldiers were deployed; Astorga, "Géopolitique Des Drogues Au Mexique," 56.
61. Joaquin López Doriga TV news show, 01/02/2007. Consulted at Videoteca Televisa, México City.
62. Interview with congressman Jorge Ramos, 06/17/2016.
63. Interview 05/26/2016.
64. The emphasis is mine.
65. Semanario Judicial y su Gaceta Novena Época. Instancia: pleno, tomo XI, 2000 April, Tesis P.J./36/2000, p.552.
66. Interview with military officer, 07/13/2016.
67. El Universal, Cienfuegos: no confundir seguridad interior con seguridad pública, 12/05/2016. https://www.eluniversal.com.mx/articulo/nacion/seguridad/2016/12/5/cienfuegos-no-confundir-seguridad-interior-con-seguridad-publica.
68. Galindo, Gómez and Castellanos, Seguridad Interior: Elementos para El Debate, 14-25.
69. Interview with active-duty military 04/14/2016; interview with active-duty military 04/07/2016.
70. Felbab-Brown, "Calderón's Caldron," 2–3; interview with Julian Leyzaola 09/26/2016.
71. Felbab-Brown, "Calderón's Caldron," 5.
72. See note 70.
73. Interview with active-duty military 08/04/2016.
74. Interview with former head of intelligence services 05/26/2016; Interview with former security member during Calderón tenure 07/26/2016.
75. Data on crime rates is based on complaints made to the attorney general office; SENSP (2016).
76. See note 57 above and author interview with journalist from Zeta Tijuana, 08/01/2016.
77. Jones, *Mexico's Illicit Drug Networks*, 89.
78. Interview with business leader 06/29/2016.
79. See https://zetatijuana.com/2017/05/22/empresarios-reclaman-por-inseguridad-kiko-y-el-patas-evaden-asumir-liderazgo/.
80. In April 2015, when a boy named Eduardo de Jesús was killed by a police officer while playing in front of his house, the local newspaper "Voz das Comunidades" edited an issue to mark 100 days of daily shootings inside the community; Voz das Comunidades, 100 dias sem Paz.
81. Interview with social activist from Complexo do Alemão, 04/14/2016; painter from Complexo do Alemão 04/28/2016; student and funk MC (singer) from Complexo da Penha 04/12/2016; health employee working in Alemão 04/26/2016.
82. Interview with journalist from Complexo do Alemão, 04/15/2016.
83. See https://epoca.globo.com/tempo/noticia/2015/05/complexo-do-chapadao-nova-fortaleza-do-trafico.html and https://odia.ig.com.br/noticia/rio-de-janeiro/2015-052015-05-03/na-hierarquia-da-violencia-chapadao-e-o-novo-alemao.html.
84. See: https://g1.globo.com/jornal-nacional/noticia/2017/07/mais-de-10-mil-militares-e-policiais-reforcam-seguranca-no-rio-de-janeiro.html.
85. Interview with military officer, 04/07/2016.
86. See note 30 above.
87. Tijuana received about US$8.2 million in 2008 ($104 million pesos) and a marginally reduced amount in 2009 and 2010; Sabet, "Confrontation, Collusion and Tolerance," 25.

88. Interview with police officer 04/18/2016 , Interview with police officer 04/19/2016, Interview with retired police officer 05/14/2016.
89. Interview with former Ministry of Defence, Nelsonn Jobim, 03/22/2016.
90. Rolnik develops an index through which she demonstrates the correlation between territorial exclusion and violence in urbanised landscapes. See Rolnik, Exclusão territorial e violencia.

Bibliography

Alegría Olazabal, Tito, Ordoñez Barba, Gerardo. *Legalizando La Ciudad. Asentamientos Informales Y Procesos de Regularización En Tijuana* [Legalizing the City: Informal Settlements and Regularization Processes in Tijuana]. Tijuana, BC: El Colegio de la Frontera Norte, 2015.

Andreas, Peter. *Border Games. Policing the US–Mexico Divide*. Ithaca and London: Cornell University Press, 2000.

Astorga, Luis. *Drogas Sin Fronteras* [Drugs Without Borders]. 1st ed. Mexico DF: De Bolsillo, 2015.

Astorga, Luis. "Géopolitique Des Drogues Au Mexique." [Geopolitics of Drugs in Mexico.] *Hérodote* 112, no. 1 (2004): 49. doi:10.3917/her.112.0049.

Bruneau, Thomas C. *Ministries of Defense and Democratic Civil–military Relations, Occasional Paper*. Occasional Paper. Monterey, California, 2001.

Bruneau, Thomas Charles, and D. Scott. "Tollefson. "Civil–military Relations in Brazil: A Reassessment." *Journal of Politics in Latin America* 6, no. 2 (2014): 107–138.

Calderon Hinojosa, Felipe. "Estrategia Nacional de Seguridad." In *Los Retos Que Enfrentamos. Los Problemas de México Y Las Politicas Publicas Para Resolverlos (2006–2012)* [The Challenges We Face: Security Problems in Mexico and the Public Policies to Address Them], 1st ed., 19–76. Mexico, DF: Debate ed, 2014.

Call, Charles T. "War Transitions and the New Civilian Security in Latin America." *Comparative Politics* 35, no. 1 (2002): 1–20.

Carvalho, José Murilo de. *Forças Armadas E Política No Brasil* [Armed Forces and Politics in Brazil]. Rio de Janeiro: Jorge Zahar ed., 2005.

Cavallieri, Fernando, and Gustavo Peres Lopes. "Índice de Desenvolvimento Social (IDS) Da Cidade do Rio de Janeiro." [Social Development Index (IDS) in the City of Rio de Janeiro.] *Coleção Estudos Cariocas* April, no. 20080401 (2008): 1–12.

Cavallieri, Fernando, Adriana Vial, and IPP/Prefeitura da Cidade do Rio de Janeiro. "Favelas Na Cidade Do Rio de Janeiro: O Quadro Populacional Com Base No Censo 2010." [Favelas in the City of Rio de Janeiro: Figures on Population Based on 2010 Census.] *Coleção Estudos Cariocas* May, no. 20120501 (2012): 1–18.

Comissão Parlamentar de Inquérito. *Relatório Final Da Comissão Parlamentar de Inquérito Destinada a Investigar a Ação de Milícias No Âmbito Do Estado Do Rio de Janeiro* [Final Report from the Parliamentary Commission to Investigate the Action of Paramilitary Groups in the State of Rio de Janeiro]. Rio de Janeiro: Legislative Assembly of the state of Rio de Janeiro, 2008.

Desmonds Arias, Enrique. *Drugs and Democracy in Rio de Janeiro: Trafficking, Social Networks, and Public Security*. Chapel Hill, NC: University of North Carolina Press, 2006.

Desmonds Arias, Enrique, and Daniel M. Goldstein. "Violent Pluralism. Understanding the New Democracies of Latin America." In *Violent Democracies in Latin America*, edited by Enrique Desmonds Arias and Daniel M. Goldstein, 1–34. Duke: Duke University Press, 2010.

Felbab-Brown, Vanda. "Calderón's Caldron: Lessons from Mexico's Battle Against Organized Crime and Drug Trafficking in Tijuana, Ciudad Juárez, and Michoacán." *Latin America Initiative at Brookings*, September (2011): 1–54.

Galindo C., C. M. Gómez, R. Y. Sepeda, and R. Castellanos. "Seguridad Interior: Elementos Para El Debate." [Internal Security: Issues to Discuss.] *Temas Estratégicos* January, no. 39 (2017): 1–36.

Hunter, Wendy. *Eroding Military Influence in Brazil. Politicians Against Soldiers*. Chapel Hill and London: The University of North Carolina Press, 1997.

Jones, Nathan. *Mexico's Illicit Drug Networks and the State Reaction*. Washington, DC: Georgetown University Press, 2016.

Jones, Nathan. "The Unintended Consequences of Kingpin Strategies: Kidnap Rates and the Arellano-Felix Organization." *Trends in Organized Crime* 16, no. 2 (2013): 156–176. doi:10.1007/s12117-012-9185-x.

Lees, Elizabeth. "Cocaine and Parallel Polities in the Brazilian Urban Periphery: Constraints on Local-Level Democratization." *Latin American Research Review* 31, no. 3 (1996): 47–83.

López, Gonzalez, and Jesus Alberto. *Presidencialismo y Fuerzas Armadas en México, 1876-2012: Una Relación de Contrastes* [Presidentialism and Armed Forces in Mexico, 1876–2012: A Relation of Contrasts]. Mexico, DF: Ediciones Gernika, 2012.

Misse, Michel. "Les Organisations Criminelles Au Brésil : La Complexité Des Marchés Illégaux En Millieu Urbain." [Criminal Organizations in Brazil: The Complexity of Illegal Markets in an Urban Landscape.] *Problèmes d'Amérique latine* 76, no. 2 (2010): 43. doi:10.3917/pal.076.0043.

Moreira Alves, Maria Helena, and Philip Evanson. *Vivendo No Fogo Cruzado. Moradores de Favela, Traficantes de Droga E Violência Policial No Rio de Janeiro* [Living in the Crossfire: Favela Residents, Drug Traffickers and Police Violence in Rio de Janeiro]. São Paulo: UNESP, 2012.

Morton, Adam David. "The War on Drugs in Mexico: A Failed State?" *Third World Quarterly* 33, no. 9 (2012): 1631–1645.

Rafael, Antônio. *Um Abraço Para Todos os Amigos: algumas considerações sobre o tráfico de drogas no Rio de Janeiro*. Niterói: EDUFF, 1998.

Resende, Juliana. *Operação Rio. Relatos de Uma Guerra Brasileira* [Rio Operation. Testimonies of a Brazilian War]. 1st ed. Rio de Janeiro: Editora Página Aberta, 1995.

Reynoso, Zulia Yanzadig Orozco. "¿Qué Cuenta El Rancho Tijuana? Desde Su Fundación Y Más Allá." [What Rancho Tijuana Tell Us? From Its Origins and Beyond.] *Revista de Direito Da Cidade* 8, no. 4 (2016): 1516–1542. doi:10.12957/rdc.2016.26031.

Rolnik, Raquel. "Exclusão territorial e violência." *São Paulo em Perspectiva* 13, no. 4 (1999): 100–111.

Sabet, Daniel. "Confrontation, Collusion and Tolerance: The Relationship Between Law Enforcement and Organized Crime in Tijuana." *Mexican Law Review* 2, no. 2 (2009): 3–29.

Shirk, David A. "A Tale of Two Mexican Border Cities: The Rise and Decline of Drug Violence in Juárez and Tijuana." *Journal of Borderlands Studies* 29, no. 4 (2014): 481–502. doi:10.1080/08865655.2014.982470.

UNODC. *World Drug Report 2015*. Vienna: United Nations Publication. 53 vols, 2015. doi:10.1017/CBO9781107415324.004.

Ventura, Zuenir. *Cidade Partida* [Splitted City]. 6th ed. Rio de Janeiro: Companhia das Letras, 1996.

Zaluar, Alba. "Juventude Violenta: Processos, Retrocessos E Novos Percursos." [Violent Youth: Processes, Setbacks and New Paths.] *Dados* 55, no. 2 (2012): 327–365. doi:10.1590/S0011-52582012000200003.

Zaluar, Alba, and Marcos Alvito. *Um Século de Favela* [A Century of Favela]. 5th ed. Rio de Janeiro: Editora FGV, 2006.

Zaluar, Alba, and Christovam Barcellos. "Mortes Prematuras E Conflito Armado Pelo Domínio Das Favelas No Rio de Janeiro." [Premature Deaths and Armed Conflict for Favelas Control in Rio de Janeiro.] *Revista Brasileira de Ciências Sociais* 28, no. 81 (2013): 17–31. doi:10.1590/S0102-69092013000100002.

Turning deserts into flowers: settlement and poppy cultivation in southwest Afghanistan

David Mansfield

ABSTRACT
Supply-side interventions are often criticised for reducing illicit drug crop cultivation in one location only for it to rise in another: the balloon effect. The balloon effect is generally seen as an inevitable consequence of attempts to reduce opium and coca cultivation. In Afghanistan, there is little evidence of this causal relationship and limited acknowledgement of the socio-economic, political and environmental processes that govern access to the factors of production such as land and labour. This paper examines the settlement of former desert areas in southwestern Afghanistan. It shows how the encroachment on this land and the rapid expansion of opium production since 2003 were supported by affordable deep-well technology, collapsed controls on the use of what is officially government land and the relatively high price of opium that endured long after the demise of the Taliban prohibition of 2000–2001. Finally, it reveals that the rate of settlement of these areas was affected by an opium ban imposed across the Helmand Food Zone from 2008 to 2011 and shows how this drug control effort ultimately helped transform the province, bringing new land under permanent settlement and thereby increasing Helmand's capacity to cultivate more opium poppy than ever before.

1. Introduction

Balloon effect is widely used as shorthand to question the cost-effectiveness of drug control efforts. Squeezing a balloon (a metaphor for drug control efforts) in one area only for the balloon to expand elsewhere is seen as an exercise in futility. Law enforcement, eradication, alternative development – each is dismissed as ineffective because the problem will be displaced and move to a new location.[1]

Two arguments support the balloon effect. The first, based on economics, proposes that with a given demand and diminished short-term supply, prices will rise, attracting new providers to the market and leading to a resurgent supply. Assuming an inelastic demand for drugs, any action to suppress production recovery in the supply of coca and opium is inevitable. The second argument draws on the fact that aggregate levels of drug crop cultivation have remained largely uninterrupted or even expanded over the four decades of the drugs war.[2]

Beyond the question of how the net benefits, or costs, of supply-side interventions are distributed, there is also the question of causality: whether a shift in cultivation is a direct effect of drug control efforts or a function of wider socio-economic processes that predate and are unrelated to those efforts.[3] The assumption is typically that expanded production is a direct consequence of a drug control intervention that has reduced supply. That expansion into other areas may have started before any efforts to reduce supply may be linked to migration from areas where there has been no attempt to reduce supply, or may be inaccurate or incomplete.

Empirical evidence of the balloon effect tends to be limited, often anecdotal and lacking in rigour.[4] There is a tendency to overlook the quality of data, the timing and sequencing of displacement,[5] and the failure to document how economic and social processes that resulted from reduced cultivation led to increased production elsewhere. Population or demographic data is rarely used to show the movement of people; there are no panel interviews of those who have been exposed to drug control efforts and relocated to produce coca or opium elsewhere. Data is lacking on the origins, history and composition of those cultivating drugs in 'new' areas of production. Instead, reduced cultivation in one area is viewed as inevitably followed by an increase in another, both linked to drug control measures.

This tendency to assume causality is indicative of the tendency of much of the drugs literature to focus exclusively on the efficacy of specific counternarcotics interventions.[6] Such an approach tends to miss the on-the-ground dynamics and local 'messiness' in drug crop-producing areas and to ignore wider socio-economic, political and environmental processes, including interventions that have no counternarcotics objectives but have profound effects on drug cultivation and prohibition. The focus on changes in production at national, provincial and regional levels, and the failure to analyse the processes that lead to cultivation shifting from one area to another, contribute little to understanding whether the limitations of supply reduction efforts are an inevitable function of economics or whether there are fundamental problems in the kind of interventions that are being pursued.

This paper examines whether the balloon effect offers an adequate explanation of changing patterns of cultivation in Afghanistan. It explores the dramatic expansion of settlement and opium poppy cultivation into two former desert areas in southwestern Afghanistan. Following this Introduction, the paper is divided into five further sections. Section 2 offers an overview of the methodology. Section 3 describes how the geographic distribution of opium poppy cultivation in Afghanistan has emerged, consolidated and adapted to statebuilding and to counternarcotics efforts. Section 4 presents case studies from two provinces where desert land has been brought under agriculture, much of it cultivated with opium poppy. Section 5 concludes that the expansion into the desert spaces of southwestern Afghanistan is only in part a function of efforts to reduce opium production in other areas (the balloon effect). It is also a consequence of rising opium prices and – most importantly – of affordable agricultural technology and limited domestic sovereignty, for a rural population exposed to conflict and limited livelihood opportunities.

2. Methodology

This paper is based on in-depth fieldwork and high-resolution imagery undertaken between 2011 and 2013 in 20 research sites in two former desert areas. Fieldwork consisted of 812 interviews with rural households and supplementary data collection among those providing services to these desert communities. A total of 602 interviews were conducted with farmers in eight research sites in the area north of the Boghra canal in Helmand Province and 170 interviews with farmers in 12 research sites in Bakwa in Farah Province. A further 40 interviews were conducted with individuals involved in the provision of services to the population in the former desert areas in the cities of Lashkar Gah, Gereshk, Farah and Delarem, including those trading solar panels, diesel, pesticides and the leasing of drilling equipment for sinking deep wells.

High-resolution, remote sensing imagery was integral to the research design. Geospatial data on vegetation was combined with high resolution imagery to examine the history of settlement in the former desert area. Research sites were then identified based on the duration of settlement, ranging from sites that showed evidence of agricultural production prior to 2003 to those settled in 2013. Remote sensing imagery was then used to verify that fieldworkers had been to the identified sites, and examine the results of primary data collection. The high-resolution imagery allowed further exploration of primary research findings: identification of crops under cultivation and of new or damaged physical infrastructure, and measurement of changes in the area under cultivation. Finally, geospatial analysis supports the extrapolation of research findings over a wider geographic beyond the research sites themselves.

Fieldwork was undertaken by a team of local researchers. The research addressed the inherent problems associated with primary data collection when researching an illegal or underground activity by focusing its enquiry on household livelihood strategies. The pressure to act against opium cultivation and trade has made illicit drugs a more sensitive topic for discussion with farmers and other stakeholders than was the case in the 1990s and early 2000s. However, the rural household remains the most accessible unit of analysis when looking at the opium economy in Afghanistan; it offers a basis for cross-referencing findings both with other work on rural livelihoods in Afghanistan, and with other research on the specific role of opium production in rural livelihood strategies in Afghanistan and elsewhere.

Discussions in the field focused on the direct experience of respondents and their households rather than on a wider geographic area, where answers become increasingly speculative.[7] Individual interviews with farming households were conducted in the field as farmers tended their crops, since holding interviews in the household compound can attract attention from others and become subject to repeated interruptions and biases. Group discussions with farmers were avoided, as they tend to be dominated by community elites, are inappropriate for discussing sensitive issues and, increasingly, represent a security threat in rural Afghanistan, particularly in the south.

3. Changing patterns of opium poppy cultivation in Afghanistan

The emergence of widespread poppy cultivation

Although opium poppy cultivation is thought to have a long history in Afghanistan, there is little evidence of significant production until the 1980s,[8] marked by the Iranian Revolution, the proclamation of the Hadd ordinance banning opium production in Pakistan and – most importantly – the civil war in Afghanistan. During the war years, Afghanistan emerged as global leader in opium production, based on what has been referred to as a 'triple comparative advantage of favourable physical, political and economic conditions'.[9] This growth in cultivation can be linked to the political and economic interests of warlords who built patronage networks by taxing cultivation and, in some cases, participating directly in the trade.

Opium production became an ideal agricultural commodity during the war years, in the absence of a functioning state that could neither support growth in the legal rural economy or use law enforcement to constrain cultivation. As a drought-resistant crop, a yield could be obtained despite damaged irrigation systems or inconsistent water supply; as a high-value/low-weight commodity, opium could be easily transported on poor roads or across porous borders. Skills involved in cultivation were easily learned and harvesting tools could be produced by local craftsmen or by farmers themselves. Market support was provided by local traders, avoiding long-range transport and transaction costs. Finally, during the war the use of opium increased significantly in Afghanistan and among the Afghan diaspora in Pakistan and Iran, thereby increasing the demand for opium production.[10]

As opium cultivation expanded from the higher valleys into larger landholdings in lower areas, its role in rural livelihoods and in the overall economy began to grow. The expansion of the crop meant that landowning households which did not meet the labour requirements could offer land on a sharecropping basis to land-poor, underemployed males. This practice led to a symbiotic relationship between the landed and the land-poor, fuelling socio-economic differentiation between and within rural areas.

Opium gave the land-poor access to land on which to grow a high-value cash crop and food crops, and to engage in the system of advance purchases on opium that provided liquidity for households during periods of food scarcity, family illness or life-cycle events such as births, marriages or deaths. Opium poppy also provided wage labour for those who could travel to neighbouring districts during the labour-intensive harvest period.

The multiplier effect created further economic opportunities through the service industries associated with the cultivation, trade and processing of opiates, as well as the resulting disposable income, some of which was reinvested in the local economy. Those with capital and access to the means of violence benefited from asset accumulation and political and military influence.

Given its widespread economic and social benefits, little was done to contain the opium economy during the 1980s and 1990s. Drug control efforts were rare and were largely for show, aimed at encouraging an increase in development assistance from foreign sponsors.[11] There are considerable doubts as to the effectiveness of campaigns, due to the challenges of estimating levels of cultivation and questions about territorial control.[12]

These earlier efforts at drug control offered only temporary lulls in production across limited geographic areas. They disrupted political arrangements with local commanders and possibly with drug traders and processors, and appear to have yielded little of the donor assistance and patronage that regional commanders were looking for.

Consolidation during the Taliban years

The Taliban's arrival in the southern provinces in 1994 did nothing to stop the growth in opium. Cultivation expanded significantly under their rule, facilitated by the removal of checkpoints and militias along the major roads and driven by limited economic opportunities in the legal rural economy.[13] The UN Office on Drugs and Crime (UNODC) estimated that the level of cultivation rose from 18,500 hectares in 1987[14] to 91,000 hectares in 1999.

During the 1990s, opium expanded beyond its traditional centres of production in the South, East and Northeast to parts of the North and Centre and more districts in the Eastern Region.[15] Those households with insufficient land in the core production areas sent family members to other provinces where they had ethnic or familial ties. There they leased or sharecropped land, sharing their skills in opium production with the local population.[16] These itinerant harvesters then returned to their own land and applied their new skills.[17]

There was growing experimentation by farmers who attempted to cultivate opium poppy for the first time, limiting production to small plots of land situated among crops like wheat and onion in case their poppy failed.[18] The proactive role of the rural population expanding cultivation, combined with what has been referred to as the 'footloose'[19] nature of the drugs economy, points to the degree of autonomy in rural areas and the economic opportunities that opium offered a wide range of actors.

During the Taliban's rule, the opium trade became consolidated within the Afghan economy. Before the ban in July 2000, the Taliban did little to hamper production or trade, beyond a few flurries of activity at the behest of the UN Drug Control Programme (UNDCP): closing some laboratories, small-scale eradication and proclamations prohibiting opium production.[20] Opium was dried and traded on the streets of district bazaars close to the highway. Marketing hubs in the East and South proliferated and moved closer to the arterial roads.[21] Heroin processing facilities were found in the main valleys, often near the district centre where Taliban soldiers were located.

Some viewed this expansion, coinciding with Taliban's territorial gains, as evidence of the Taliban's control of the trade. But the relationship was more complex, reflecting local political settlements and bargains. In some cases, local Taliban leadership tolerated drug production and trade, unwilling to challenge powerful local interests. In others, Taliban commanders were actively involved in opiate trade and taxation.

These local arrangements came undone with the imposition of the Taliban ban in July 2000. After numerous requests by the UN and international donors to act against the drugs trade, the Taliban imposed an effective ban on opium production in the 2000–2001 growing season, reducing cultivation from 82,000 hectares in 2000 to 8000 hectares in 2001 (see Figure 1). Although UN officials billed it as 'one of the most remarkable [drug control] successes ever',[22] it was an event that many would come to regret.

For the Taliban, the ban imposed hardships on the rural population that enabled Western military forces to encourage rebellion against the regime. For the Interim Administration and its successor, the Government of the Islamic Republic of Afghanistan, cessation of production led to a rapid rise in the price of opium that made cultivation profitable even in marginal areas. Combined with the return of the *mujahidin* leadership to provinces they had presided over in the 1980s and 1990s, opium became a mainstay of the Afghan economy and a metric by which both the Afghan government and the international project in Afghanistan came to be judged.

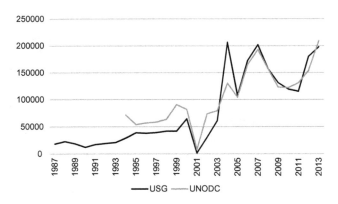

Figure 1. Opium poppy cultivation 1987–2013 (hectares).

Expansion and shifting patterns of cultivation under the statebuilding project

Giustozzi argues that for political entrepreneurs the drugs economy became a source of power during the initial years of the Karzai regime.[24] Members of Parliament, government ministers, regional power brokers and elements of the security apparatus were thought to be directly involved in the drugs trade or to have received payments for their role as 'security providers'.[25] Byrd and Jonglez reported growing market integration,[26] while others claimed that trafficking had become concentrated in the hands of a few key individuals, many with close links to the Ministry of Interior.[27]

Evidence of market concentration was less obvious in the provinces following the Taliban's collapse in 2001. In fact, cultivation expanded significantly in areas with few pre-existing market linkages and limited production experience.[28] This was prompted because high prices were sustained following the collapse of the ban and the launch of counternarcotics efforts. Increased cultivation was also seen in the traditional areas of production as farmers took advantage of high prices and the absence of government control to make up for the loss of income and rising debts that many had incurred under the Taliban ban.[29] By 2004, opium poppy could be found in 194 out of 364 districts and in all 34 provinces, compared to only 54 districts in eight provinces in 1994.[30]

After 2005, national opium poppy cultivation fluctuated widely, falling between 2008 and 2010, only to rise again in 2011. However, aggregate levels mask regional, provincial and district-level variations. Dramatic reductions in Helmand and Nangarhar Provinces had a significant impact on aggregate statistics: a fact that helped meet the demand of the UK and US governments.

Counternarcotics efforts are one factor in these reductions. Cultivation fell significantly in Nangarhar – a province that had been second only to Helmand as a major producer of opium – after the imposition of bans by two governors. The most striking example is Helmand itself where the Helmand Food Zone (HFZ) was introduced in 2008. With financial and logistical backing from the UK and US governments, this initiative consisted of three activities: a counternarcotics information campaign aimed at deterring planting, distribution of wheat seed and fertiliser, and eradication.[31] Within the HFZ, cultivation in 2009 fell from 103,590 to 69,833 hectares (see Figure 2). By spring 2011, there was a 40% reduction in cultivation compared to the 2007–2008 growing season.

A second factor in the downward trend in cultivation in 2008 and 2009 was the shift in terms of trade between wheat and opium.[32] The rapid rise in world cereal prices in late 2007, combined with insecurity in Pakistan following the assassination of Benazir Bhutto, restricted cross-border trade in Pakistani wheat flour and led to higher wheat prices in Afghanistan. High levels of opium production between 2002 and 2007 led to opium prices falling from US$700/kg in September 2001 to less than US$60/kg in the 2007–2008 growing season.[33]

With this shift in prices, farmers across Afghanistan became increasingly concerned about food security; many opted to cultivate wheat rather than cash crops. In the less fertile areas where opium had little tradition and the population lacked experience and skills, farmers realised that they could produce wheat on their own land rather than using opium profits to purchase wheat. Under these conditions, farmers did not need to be coerced to abandon opium production, although this did not stop the political leadership or counternarcotics community from taking credit for reduced cultivation.[34]

A third factor in reductions during this period was the growth of opportunities in the legal economy, particularly in the lower valleys where most development assistance had been provided. The World Bank estimated that between 2002 and 2012, US$55 billion of aid was given to Afghanistan, and the average annual growth rate in gross domestic product was 9%.[35] Major poppy-growing provinces like Helmand received an estimated US$600 million of development assistance between 2009 and 2011, the years in which the HFZ was implemented.[36]

As early as 2008, the areas around provincial centres in most opium-growing provinces showed increasing signs of agricultural diversification and more complex cropping systems that included high-value, short-season horticultural crops and the cultivation of a variety of crops on a single unit of land. This allowed farmers to better manage the risk of crop failure and increase on-farm income.[37] Households in these areas exploited wage-labour opportunities in the service sector and construction industry, further diversifying their income base.

A fourth reason for falling levels of cultivation was the rollout of national and international security forces to the regions. From 2004 on, communities began to mobilise through the establishment of Provincial Reconstruction Teams (PRTs). By 2008, the perceived failures of centralised statebuilding, the growing insurgency and the new counter-insurgency doctrine

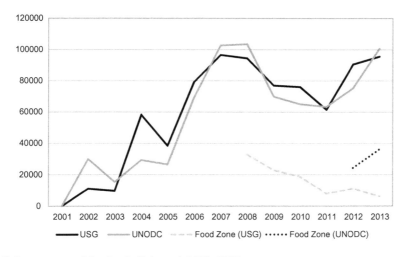

Figure 2. Opium poppy cultivation in Helmand, 2001–2013.

led to a shift towards bottom-up state building and devolution to the districts. A typical trajectory was for opium cultivation to fall in areas around the provincial centres. In provinces like Helmand where military presence extended into the districts, production was also deterred. The impact of military operations on levels of cultivation was most stark in Marjah District in Helmand Province where, following the deployment of 15,000 US Marines and the Afghan National Defence and Security Forces (ANDSF) in February 2010, the amount of land dedicated to opium poppy fell from 60% to less than 5% the following season.[38]

The combination of these factors – provincial drug control efforts, the shift in terms of trade between wheat and poppy, the uptake in economic opportunities within the legal economy and the deployment of military forces to key provinces – led to reduced opium production, even in provinces where the crop had a long history and was most concentrated. While initially lauded as the success of counternarcotics interventions and the statebuilding effort, reduced cultivation in some provinces in the south and southwest were offset by dramatic increases in production in more remote desert areas within the same provinces: areas that had not been under opium poppy cultivation before or, indeed, under any kind of agricultural production. The following case studies examine the expansion into two desert areas and explore the extent to which this was, or was not, a direct consequence of efforts to reduce opium production elsewhere: the balloon effect.

4. Case studies: turning deserts into flowers

Remote sensing indicates that between 2003 and 2013 the amount of farmed land in the southwest increased from 151,962 to 432,896 hectares. This section examines the expansion into two desert areas: the former desert area north of the Boghra canal in Helmand Province and Bakwa on the border between Farah and Nimroz Provinces.

Building a New Life north of the Boghra Canal

In 2002, the land north of the Boghra Canal in Helmand was desert, containing a few scattered communities that had arrived in the late 1990s. By 2013, there were about 35,500 hectares of farmland (see Figure 3); not isolated, scattered fields but contiguous fields reaching the outskirts of Camp Bastion/Leatherneck, and home to 160,000 people.[39]

Since 2003, many farmers in this area have seen their capital grow. Most came from the canal command area in central Helmand where they had no land and arrived in the desert with few possessions. By 2013, most of them owned a house, productive land, a motorbike, a generator and a solar panel for power. They had a regular supply of dried meat, and fresh meat and fruit 'once or twice a week'.

For the first wave of settlers before 2007, agriculture was back-breaking work. They had to remove the stones that littered the area, level the land, apply manure and fertiliser, and sink a deep well for irrigation. They lived in tents until they could build houses and bring their families. These settlers claimed traditional rights over the desert land.

For the next wave of settlers – sharecroppers and tenants who came after 2007 (see Figure 4) it was easier; land preparation was complete and many houses had been built. These settlers knew that it would be a difficult life; many had family and friends who had purchased or captured land, or had worked in the area during the opium poppy harvest. These

Figure 3. Expansion of agricultural land north of the Boghra canal in Helmand, 2002–2012.

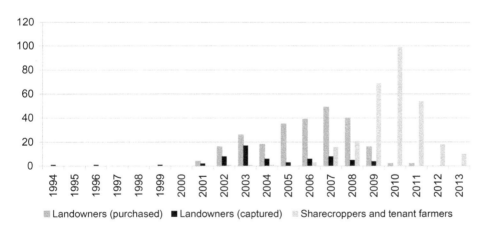

Figure 4. Year of settlement in area north of Boghra canal, by land tenure ($n = 602$).

settlers belonged to a wider variety of tribal groups but were still primarily indigenous to the southwest of Afghanistan.

After several years of eking out an existence, life in the former desert area became easier. The bazaars that sat astride the Boghra canal grew with the availability of disposable income, and a number of *melas* (weekly markets) began to emerge. When households earned enough money to purchase a motorbike, or even a car, they could travel to the capital, to other provinces, or to Pakistan to get treatment for the sick or to buy agricultural inputs and consumables.

Farmers responded to new technologies as they became affordable and made farming in a harsh terrain more manageable. Drilling equipment, cheap generators and water pumps were available, thus farmers were able to abandon shallow wells and make deep wells. They began to use herbicides to manage weeds and limit the use of family labour. They adopted solar technology, mobile phones and motorised transport.

Life had not been easy back in the canal command area. One farmer described his departure from his home and his attempts to escape the fighting: 'Because of this government I came from my village to the *dasht* [desert]. Always the government pushes the people. We have not seen any benefit from this government, only costs and losses. I am happy here to have poppy and no fighting'.

Many of the land-poor also came to escape the opium ban imposed by the '*kafir* [non-believer] government' and its foreign backers. For them, the ban and the uptake of less labour-intensive crops such as wheat had meant that landowners could farm their own land with family labour. Consequently, those who had relied on opium poppy cultivation to obtain land and a place to live found themselves dispossessed. Without jobs or development assistance, they had little choice but to resettle.

The high price of opium following the Taliban ban in 2000–2001 made agricultural cultivation in the desert an attractive proposition. At prices of more than US$200/kg, opium paid for the initial investments in land and expensive deep-well technology without which the land could not be cultivated. And the HFZ, with its emphasis on wheat and its banning of opium poppy, compelled many land-poor to leave the canal command area after 2008, settling in the desert lands where there was a demand for their services as sharecroppers and tenant farmers. Desperate for land, they accepted a smaller share of the opium crop than they had received in the canal command area before the ban.[40] Thus, a mobile population skilled in opium poppy cultivation settled in the former desert area, increasing the amount of land under agriculture and the percentage dedicated to opium poppy.

Order was established within the atomised communities. Familial and tribal links, patronage networks and the Taliban provided a stability that appealed to many who had fled what they saw as intrusive and inequitable governance in the canal command area. Without a government they considered legitimate and capable of improving their lives, they sought only a system that offered physical security and a fair way of resolving disputes, and that left them alone to earn a livelihood – including growing opium poppy. They found this in the former desert.

However, life remained difficult; many complained about summer heat, lack of shade and the fact that there was no schooling for their children. After 2012, their lives became even harder. Once the Taliban were subdued in two key districts of Helmand, the ANDSF and 'foreigners' brought the fight to the desert. Farmers described the fear that women and children felt during the night at the sound of 'choppers' hovering overhead. They told of incursions by members of the ANDSF and of attempts by the Afghan Local Police to seize their generators and water pumps and eradicate their opium crops (or to demand money for not doing so). In the 2013–2014 planting season, the farmers faced a new threat. Following violent resistance from the Taliban, district authorities established checkpoints along the Boghra canal and seized any vehicle transporting diesel, fertiliser or water pumps.

It was not these acts of 'interdiction' that most threatened the farmers. The more pressing concern was the repeated incidence of 'disease' that affected their opium crop and greatly reduced their yield. While it was most likely a consequence of monocropping and failure to rotate crops or rest the land, farmers viewed it as a campaign of crop destruction launched by the Americans. They talked of a spraying campaign that caused disease and 'burned' their crops.[41]

Even worse was the absence of the fivefold rise in prices that had accompanied the poor yields of 2010 and the inflow of military forces into central Helmand. Instead, prices fell after the 2013 harvest, as low as US$114/kg by summer.[42] These crop losses provoked considerable anger. Some farmers questioned the character of government officials and expressed resentment of the threat government posed to their way of life. Most farmers reported cutting back on meat and fruit and having trouble meeting the costs of health care. Those with land recognised the severity of their situation; one farmer said, 'If I move from this area I will lose my land because I don't have any ownership document'. Some resolved their immediate financial difficulties by selling their opium stocks or marrying off their daughters.

The situation for sharecroppers was even more challenging. While many wished to leave the area following the poor harvest, few found land elsewhere. Unless opium poppy returned to the canal command area, where were they to go? It was only because opium poppy was such a labour-intensive crop that they were needed in the first place.

However, despite the obvious problems, the population north of the Boghra canal kept growing. Even as late as 2013, farmers continued to arrive, reassuring themselves that a low yield of opium poppy was still better than wheat and hoping that opium yields would recover in 2014.

Bakwa: retaining ownership of the desert frontier

The area known as Bakwa[43] is located on the boundaries of the districts of Bakwa in Farah Province and Delarem in Nimroz Province. The initial desert settlement by the Noorzai tribe – 13 villages, each irrigated by an underground water system known as *karez* – is unrecognisable. The settlement of desert land between the villages started in the late 1990s, spurred by new agricultural technologies and the absence of controls to prevent the encroachment of government-owned land. Since then, opium cultivation has supported the rapid expansion of agricultural land, from 24,062 hectares in 2003 to 105,936 hectares in 2013 (see Figure 5) and an increase in population from 62,000 to 274,000 people.[44]

As in Helmand, shallow wells were first dug in response to repeated crop failure in the *karez*-irrigated areas, caused by severe ongoing drought. At the peak, there were an estimated 5000 shallow wells in the area. However, while the shallow wells supported agricultural production in the villages and some expansion into desert space, it was the introduction of deep-well technology that facilitated the dramatic encroachment of desert lands. This technology is said to have been introduced by non-governmental organisations and farmers who became aware of the equipment and its potential during their time as refugees in Pakistan. As in other southern provinces, expansion into the desert was also supported by low-cost Chinese water pumps and generators and the adoption of other improved agricultural techniques.

In Bakwa, the wells are almost twice as deep as those in the areas north of the Boghra canal. With a water table that is falling as much as one metre per year but still ranges from 25 to 30 metres deep, many farmers have invested in the desert area for the long term. While most wells have been drilled at the expense of the landowner, there are reports of a number of wells paid for by the US-led Farah PRT.[45]

Figure 5. Expansion in agricultural land in Bakwa, 2003–2013.

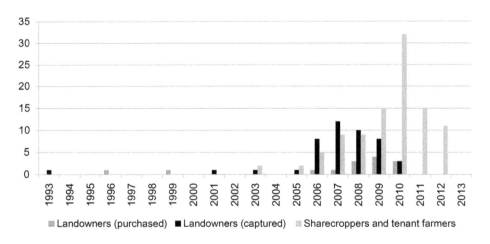

Figure 6. Year of settlement in Bakwa, by land tenure ($n = 170$).

The pattern of land settlement in Bakwa differs from the iterative process of moving further north in the desert areas of Helmand (see Figure 6). In Bakwa, the original *karez*-irrigated villages are the focal point for expansion into the desert lands; the population of each village is said to have moved into the desert lands that surround them, absorbing land some distance from their village. However, the population has been careful not to stray too far into the desert and encroach upon land that might be claimed by neighbouring villages. Disputes over desert land between villages are said to have been minimised by the large amount of land available, as well as the ethnic homogeneity of the rural population and their ability to resolve matters within the indigenous Noorzai tribe.

In each village, newly acquired desert land was distributed according to local traditions, with land allocated to each household according to the land they owned in the original *karez*-irrigated village. Thus, a household with five *jeribs* of land out of 400 *jeribs* in the village would get as much as 70 *jeribs* of the 5600 *jeribs* of desert land that the village absorbed. With thousands of *jeribs* of desert land available, and no government able to prevent the incursions, this first wave of settlers often received 80–100 *jeribs* to be divided among their family.

The original settlers looked for ways to fund the drilling of deep wells. Some sold parcels of their land to migrants from other parts of the south who faced population pressures and a shortage of land in their home villages and came to the area seeking a better quality of life. These land sales helped provide the capital required to bring new land under cultivation and produce opium that could be sold, with the money earned reinvested in more land. It is claimed that through this process some of the original settlers have acquired three or four deep wells, each of which irrigates 15–20 *jeribs* of land.

As in the desert spaces of Helmand, settlers would reside in a tent until they had drilled a well, prepared the land and built a house. However, land in Bakwa has not been commoditised and sold on a large scale as it has in the area north of the Boghra canal (see Figure 6). After an initial flurry of sales to help finance the development of their land, the Noorzai settlers have sought to retain ownership within the tribe. Instead of selling land, they have looked for tenant farmers and sharecroppers: a skilled labour force that has helped improve the land through their toil, and in some cases provided the capital investments required to bring the land permanently under cultivation. Landowners with sufficient capital offer sharecroppers and tenants four-fifths of the final crop, compared to two-thirds in other parts of the south. Landowners without sufficient capital may pay enough benefits to attract tenants who are unable to purchase land because they are not from the Noorzai tribe.

For example, in an increasingly common arrangement in Bakwa, the landowner provides a deep-well and generator at the start of a five-year tenancy, and the tenant covers the annual costs of production but pays the landowner only one-sixth or one-seventh of the crop. At the end of the tenancy, the tenant is required to ensure that the deep well is still operating. This arrangement is mutually convenient to both sides; the landowner is particularly grateful to be left with a fully productive farm on which he can then employ a sharecropper who will pay him one-fifth of the crop.

Opium poppy has been a significant enticement for both landowners and migrants in Bakwa, occupying on average two-thirds of the land cultivated in the 2012–2013 and 2013–2014 growing seasons. For the original Noorzai settlers it has been the means of investment in their land. It has financed turning vast expanses of the desert into productive agricultural land and provided a good income to those who now own it. For those who do not own land, the value of the crop and its labour-intensive nature have provided work opportunities and opportunities for the licit economy in nearby towns.

As in Helmand, all those who have migrated to Bakwa have pre-existing contacts – family or friends – in the area; the majority are from tribes indigenous to southwest Afghanistan. Most of tenant farmers or sharecroppers have come to Bakwa because they do not have sufficient land in their own villages or are looking to escape conflict. Many migrants arrived in Bakwa in 2006 and 2007 from the district of Farah, in direct response to an opium ban in those areas around the provincial centre. More recent migrants have come from central Helmand, escaping the opium poppy ban imposed by the HFZ. A few have come from more distant provinces, but even these have contacts in the area and initially work building mud brick houses before obtaining land to cultivate opium poppy.

The population of Bakwa is fortunate not to have seen the crop failures that farmers have experienced north of the Boghra canal. Most farmers attribute their higher yields to the quality of the soil in Bakwa as well as the large amount of household land. Those interviewed in Bakwa reported an average of 25 *jerib*s in contrast to an average of only 12 *jerib*s in Helmand. These larger holdings militate against the monocropping of opium poppy, allowing some wheat to be grown and supporting crop rotation. A few farmers were even supporting effective plant husbandry by leaving some land fallow each year. The economic conditions at the two sites were such that, at the start of the 2013–2014 growing season there were reports of farmers from north of the Boghra canal relocating to Bakwa in search of better opium yields.

Most of those interviewed in Bakwa saw their overall welfare as having improved over the last decade. The great majority of families – including those sharecropping the land – own at least one motorbike, a generator and a solar panel. Those who own large tracts of land have considerably more assets at their disposal, including motor vehicles and tractors. Households in Bakwa also reported a higher consumption of meat and fruit than typically found in other areas; even sharecroppers reported that they had 'rich food' once a week.

These improvements in welfare are considered a direct result of opium poppy cultivation, and farmers are acutely aware that they are vulnerable to the government's counternarcotics efforts. Most see the government in Bakwa as at best irrelevant, at worst a potential risk to their physical and economic wellbeing. Few government services are provided to the area; the district health centre destroyed by the Taliban in 2008 was still not repaired five years later.

Governance in Bakwa is dominated by the Noorzai tribe, but also by the Taliban. The Afghan government is rarely seen, even in the district centre of Bakwa. In comparison, the Taliban is viewed as providing a major service by preventing the government from destroying the opium crop. As in the desert areas of Helmand, the payment for this protection is seen as nominal.

Of course, none of these entities – the Noorzai, the Taliban or the government – is completely independent. Farmers cite Noorzai elders in government positions living in Farah city and Kabul. They claim that these individuals travel unmolested in Bakwa, as local Talibs are fearful of retribution if they injure or kill a fellow Noorzai. Thus, tribal homogeneity, familial connections and the concentration of landownership among the Noorzai ensure that all parties calibrate their actions and recognise political affiliation as only a temporary convenience. The result is relative peace, particularly compared to the areas north of the Boghra canal.

5. Conclusion

It is the case that efforts to reduce levels of opium poppy cultivation provided an impetus to the settlement of former desert space in southwestern Afghanistan. However, migration to these areas was already underway by the time that many of these interventions started.

This research has shown that the initial momentum behind the settlement of the desert areas was the tenfold increase in opium prices associated with the Taliban ban imposed in the 2000–2001 growing season. The ban raised the economic value of desert land; when combined with the collapse of the Taliban regime and access to affordable deep-well technology, there was little to prevent the encroachment of former desert land by those with a traditional claim over the land and sufficient force to impose their will. These three factors made agricultural production in the desert an economically viable activity for a burgeoning rural population.

It was only later that the balloon effect, as it is currently understood, really took effect. In late 2006, we saw the consequences of limited efforts to reduce opium poppy cultivation around provincial centres in Farah and Helmand and of escalating conflict associated with the deployment of Western military forces. By 2009, these factors led to the migration of greater numbers of people – in particular the land-poor – into the desert.

Many took up residency as tenants and sharecroppers under far less favourable conditions than in the better irrigated areas they had come from. They provided an added impetus to opium poppy cultivation in the former desert areas. They offered a relatively cheap and skilled labour force to those who had already captured or purchased land, further supporting the transformation of unproductive desert space and the consolidation of rural communities.

This research has, however, shown that settlement in these new areas is not available to all. There are strict rules defining who can take ownership over land and who can cultivate it on a temporary basis. Traditional land rights, the means of violence, and tribal and familial connections govern land use in these desert spaces. Therefore, reductions in one region of Afghanistan cannot simply lead to migration and the displacement of cultivation to the south or southwest of the country. There are clear barriers to accessing the land and water which shape the displacement of opium production in light of supply-side efforts.

Furthermore, while localised reductions in opium poppy cultivation have occurred in the better-resourced areas of south and southwestern Afghanistan, they have been more than offset by disproportionate increases in former desert lands. These increases suggest that more profound changes are occurring in the rural economy of Afghanistan than simply the displacement of cultivation from one area to another. Air has not simply been displaced from one part of the balloon to another; more air has been added. The pressure on existing land caused by a rapidly expanding rural population and fewer wage-labour opportunities in the urban economy, as well as the collapse of formal controls over the use of 'government land', has opened the floodgates for continued encroachment of the desert lands of the south and southwest.

Obviously, the inflationary impact of opium prohibition has facilitated this process. With further increases in opium prices following low yields in 2010, those leasing or sharecropping land began monocropping opium poppy in much greater numbers, hopeful that they too might take up permanent residency and purchase desert land. Even with lower opium prices, falling yields and the return of opium poppy to parts of the HFZ in 2014,[46] farmers continue to settle these former desert lands.

For proponents of poorly considered supply-side interventions, such as the HFZ, the continued settlement of these desert areas raises questions as to whether displacement can really be considered an unintended consequence of their efforts. Even the most basic understanding of land tenure arrangements in central Helmand, and the differing labour demands of opium poppy and wheat, would have indicated that a simple crop substitution would lead to the dispossession of those who provided the labour for opium poppy and encouraged them to search for new lands nearby.

For those who simply dismiss increased cultivation in the former desert areas as a function of market corrections and the balloon effect, there is an unanswered question: What is driving this unrivalled expansion of opium production in Afghanistan at a time when organisations such as UNODC and the European Monitoring Center for Drugs and Drug Addiction say that consumption in some of the major opiate-consuming nations of Europe, and North America is shrinking?[47]

Disclosure statement

No potential conflict of interest was reported by the author.

Funding

This work was supported by the European Commission under the EU FP7 Framework [grant number LINKSCH 285073] Research Project.

Acknowledgements

Thanks to Ann Bauxum for editorial inputs and to Jonathan Goodhand and John Collins for their comments.

Notes

1. Caulkins, Kulick and Kleiman, *Drug Production and Trafficking*; Reuter, "Production and Trafficking"; Thoumi, *Illegal Drugs*, 231–232.
2. Chouvy, *A Typology*, 16.
3. Chouvy, *A Typology*.
4. Ibid.
5. The academic literature on Afghanistan offers many examples of incorrect association between fluctuations in the reported number of hectares cultivated with opium and drug control efforts. The most obvious are the reports of the Taliban prohibiting opium in 1994 when they first swept to power in southern Afghanistan.
6. Mansfield, *A State Built on Sand*.
7. Swedish Committee for Afghanistan, "Farming Systems of Nad Ali District, Helmand Province," *Agricultural Survey of Afghanistan, Report 15* (Peshawar: SCA, 1992), 1.
8. Macdonald, *Drugs in Afghanistan*, 59.
9. Goodhand, *Contested Transitions*.

10. Macdonald, *Drugs in Afghanistan*.
11. Mansfield, *Failure of Quid Pro Quo*.
12. Martin, *An Intimate War*.
13. United Nations Drug Control Programme, *Strategic Study #1*.
14. United States Department of State, *International Narcotics Control Strategy Report*.
15. United Nations Drug Control Programme, *Strategic Study #1*.
16. United Nations Drug Control Programme, *Strategic Study #1*; United Nations Drug Control Programme, *Strategic Study #5*.
17. United Nations Drug Control Programme, *Strategic Study #1*.
18. Ibid.
19. Byrd, *Responding to Afghanistan*, 17.
20. Mansfield, *A State Built on Sand*.
21. United Nations Drug Control Programme, *Strategic Study #2*.
22. Jelsma, *Learning Lessons*, 1.
23. United Nations Office on Drugs and Crime, *The Opium Economy*; Mansfield, *What is Driving Opium*.
24. Giustozzi, *War and Peace*, 9.
25. Mankin, *Gaming the System*.
26. Byrd and Jonglez, *Afghanistan's Drug Industry*.
27. Buddenberg and Byrd, *Afghanistan's Drug Industry*, 201.
28. Mansfield, *Opium Poppy Cultivation in Nangahar*.
29. United Nations Office on Drugs and Crime, *Opium Economy in Afghanistan*; Mansfield, *What is Driving Opium*.
30. United Nations Office on Drugs and Crime/Ministry of Counter Narcotics, *United Nations Afghanistan Opium Survey 2004*.
31. Mansfield et al., *Managing Concurrent and Repeated Risks*.
32. Ibid., Mansfield and Pain, *Counter-Narcotics in Afghanistan*.
33. Mansfield and Pain, *Counter-Narcotics in Afghanistan*, 14.
34. Mansfield and Pain, *Counter-Narcotics in Afghanistan*; United Nations Office on Drugs and Crime/Ministry of Counter Narcotics, *United Nations Afghanistan Opium Survey 2008*, 2.
35. Goodhand, *Contested Transitions*.
36. United Nations Office on Drugs and Crime/Ministry of Counter Narcotics, *United Nations Afghanistan Opium Survey 2014*, 29.
37. Mansfield and Pain, *Counter-Narcotics in Afghanistan*; Mansfield, *Resurgence and Reductions*.
38. Mansfield, *Central Helmand in 2011/12*, 3.
39. This estimate is based on a population density of 0.9 persons per *jerib* of cultivated land.
40. Mansfield, *From Bad They Made It Worse*, 51.
41. Ibid., 79–83.
42. United Nations Office on Drugs and Crime/Ministry of Counter Narcotics, *Afghanistan Drug Price Monitoring Monthly Report 2013*, 3.
43. It is important to differentiate between the *district* of Bakwa in Farah Province and the *area* of Bakwa which encompasses the districts of Bakwa in Farah and Delarem in Nimroz.
44. This estimate is based on a population density of 0.51 persons per *jerib* of cultivated land ($n = 170$).
45. While none of those interviewed reported having their well paid for by the PRT, a member of the PRT reported in 2010 that the PRT 'could fund only 20 wells' and that 'farmers would be required to swear that they will not use the wells for opium production' http://theafghanplan.blogspot.com/2010/08/dust-and-soil-bakwa.html
46. United Nations Office on Drugs and Crime/Ministry of Counter Narcotics, *United Nations Afghanistan Opium Survey 2014*, 21.
47. European Monitoring Center for Drugs and Drug Addiction, *EU Drug Markets Report*, 26.

Bibliography

Buddenberg, D., and W. Byrd, eds. *Afghanistan's Drugs Industry*. Kabul, Afghanistan: UNODC, 2006.

Byrd, W. *Responding to Afghanistan's Opium Economy Challenge*. Policy Research Working Paper 45. Washington DC: World Bank, 2008.

Byrd, W., and O. Jonglez in *Afghanistan's Drug Industry UNODC and World Bank*, Washington DC: World Bank, 2006.

Caulkins, J. P., J. D. Kulick, and M. A. R. Kleiman. *Drug Production and Trafficking*. New York City: Center on International Cooperation, New York University, 2010.

Chouvy, P. "*A Typology of the Unintended Consequences of Drug Crop Reduction*." *Journal of Drug Issues* 43, no. 2 (2012): 216–230.

European Monitoring Center for Drugs and Drug Addiction. *EU Drug Markets Report*. Luxembourg: Publications Office of the European Union, 2013.

Felbab-Brown, V. "*Kicking the Opium Habit*." *Conflict, Security and Development* 6, no. 2 (2006): 127–149.

Giustozzi, A. "War and Peace." *International Peacekeeping* 14, no. 1 (2007): 75–89.

Goodhand, J. *Bandits, Borderlands and Opium Wars*. DIIS Working Paper. November, 2009.

Goodhand, J. *Contested Transitions*. Oslo: Norwegian Peacebuilding Resources Centre. November, 2012

Jelsma, M. "Learning Lessons from the Taliban Opium Ban." *International Journal of Drug Policy* 16 (2005): 98–103.

Macdonald, D. *Drugs in Afghanistan*. London: Pluto Press, 2007.

Mankin, J. "*Gaming the System*." *Journal of International Affairs* 63, no. 1 (2009): 195–209. New York City: Colombia University.

Mansfield, D. What is Driving Opium Poppy Cultivation? Paper for the UNODC/ONDCP Second Technical Conference on Drug Control Research, July 19-21, 2004.

Mansfield, D. *Opium Poppy Cultivation in the Provinces of Nangarhar and Ghor*. Kabul: AREU, 2006.

Mansfield, D. *Resurgence and Reductions*. Kabul: AREU, 2008.

Mansfield, D. *Central Helmand in the 2011/12 Growing Season*. Unpublished report for the British Embassy Kabul, January 2012.

Mansfield, D. *From Bad They Made It Worse*. Kabul: AREU, 2014.

Mansfield, D. *A State Built on Sand*. London: Hurst, 2016.

Mansfield, D. *The Failure of Quid Pro Quo*. Paper prepared for the International Conference on Alternative Development in Drug Control and Cooperation, Feldafing January 7-12, 2002.

Mansfield, D., and A. Pain. *Counter Narcotics in Afghanistan*. Kabul: AREU, 2008.

Mansfield, D., Alcis Ltd., and OSDR. *Managing Concurrent and Repeated Risks*. Kabul: AREU, 2011.

Martin, M. *An Intimate War*. London: Hurst, 2014.

Reuter, P. "Can Production and Trafficking of Illicit Drugs Be Reduced or Only Shifted?" In *Innocent Bystanders*, edited by P. Keefer and N. Loayza, 95–134. Washington, DC: Palgrave MacMillan and The World Bank, 2010.

Swedish Committee for Afghanistan, "Farming Systems of Nad Ali District, Helmand Province," *Agricultural Survey of Afghanistan, Report 15* SCA, 1992.

Thoumi, F. E. *Illegal Drugs, Economy, and Society in the Andes*. Washington DC: Woodrow Center Press, 2003.

United Nations Drug Control Programme. *Strategic Study #1: An Analysis of the Process of Expansion of Opium Poppy to New Districts in Afghanistan*. Islamabad: UNDCP, 1998.

United Nations Drug Control Programme. *Strategic Study #2: The Dynamics of the Farmgate Trade and the Coping Strategies of Opium Traders*. Islamabad: UNDCP, 1998.

United Nations Drug Control Programme. *Strategic Study #5: An Analysis of the Process of Expansion of Opium Poppy to New Districts in Afghanistan*. Islamabad: UNDCP, 1999.

United Nations Office on Drugs and Crime. *The Opium Economy in Afghanistan*. New York City: United Nations, 2003.

United Nations Office on Drugs and Crime/Ministry of Counter Narcotics. *United Nations Afghanistan Opium Survey*. Kabul: UNODC/MCN, 2004.

United Nations Office on Drugs and Crime /Ministry of Counter Narcotics. *United Nations Afghanistan Opium Survey*. Kabul: UNODC/MCN, 2008.

United Nations Office on Drugs and Crime /Ministry of Counter Narcotics. Afghanistan Drug Price Monitoring Monthly Report. Kabul, 2013.

United Nations Office on Drugs and Crime/Ministry of Counter Narcotics. *United Nations Afghanistan Opium Survey*. Kabul: UNODC/MCN, 2014.

United States Department of State. *Bureau of International Narcotics Matters*. International Narcotics Control Strategy Report. Washington DC: US Government Printing Office, 1997.

Quasilegality: khat, cannabis and Africa's drug laws

Neil Carrier and Gernot Klantschnig

ABSTRACT
This article explores the concept of 'quasilegality' in relation to two of Africa's drug crops: khat and cannabis. It argues that the concept is useful in understanding the two substances and their ambiguous relation to the statute books: khat being of varied and ever-changing legal status yet often treated with suspicion even where legal, while cannabis is illegal everywhere in Africa yet often seems de facto legal. The article argues that such quasilegality is socially significant and productive, raising the value of such crops for farmers and traders, but also allowing states to police or not police these substances as their interests and instincts dictate. It also argues that there is no clear link between the law on the statute book and the actual harm potential of these substances. Finally, it suggests that the concept has much wider use beyond these case studies of drugs in Africa in a world where global consensus on drug policy is cracking, and where many other objects of trade and activities find themselves in the blurred territory of the quasilegal.

Introduction

Anti-drug law has been a powerful force for more than 100 years, colonising statute books around the world. A complicated assemblage of good intentions, genuine concern, more dubious intentions and vested interests has brought many substances into the orbit of international and national legal frameworks, and continues to do so. There has been an almost inevitable pattern: if something gets classed as a drug, then soon enough the law will attempt to colonise it, generally through prohibition. Such a pattern has perhaps reached its heights in the UK, where recently an expansive ban on anything 'capable of producing a psychoactive effect in a person who consumes it' (aside from the socially sanctioned exceptions such as alcohol, tobacco, caffeine) has been introduced in an attempt to counter what had been termed 'legal highs'.[1]

This global force has encountered much friction, using the terminology of Anna Tsing in describing how universalising forces and grounded particularities meet in creative tension, often generating new social forms in the process.[2] In the case of global drug law, the apparently universal logic of the 'war on drugs' forms and unravels through interactions with particular locales or people. Such friction often results in traction, as pre-existing concerns about particular substances – or political motives only distantly related to drug eradication – make such logic attractive, while allowing repressive drug policy purchase. Sometimes this collision leads to excessively enthusiastic embrace of the 'war on drugs' as the recent extrajudicial killings in the Philippines make clear.[3] Yet, despite this traction, to state an obvious point, prohibition by law has proven no straightforward recipe for eradication. Indeed, even the strongest states lack capacity to enforce these laws effectively, while policing flows of smuggled commodities in a world built on global trade is incredibly difficult.[4]

Friction encountered by drug law can also generate resistance and certain substances are hard to definitively depict as legal or illegal. While law makers might try and fix their status under the law – and consequently fix their moral status as 'bad' – such substances refuse to comply, or only comply partially. These substances take on a 'quasilegal' quality where moral and legal ambiguity surround them. This paper explores the quasilegality of two substances in particular in relation to Africa: khat and cannabis. Their quasilegality differs: khat varies greatly in its relation to the statute books (being legal in Kenya and Ethiopia, but illegal in Tanzania and now much of the west), but is often tainted with illegality even when it is legal; cannabis, meanwhile, is universally illegal *de jure* in Africa, though often appears de facto legal.

Despite these differences, both show the social importance of quasilegality. Legal ambiguity matters: it can be socially and politically useful; it can be fraught with danger, yet also opportunity, for producers, traders and consumers; it can be something to resist, as some try and make the substance in question unambiguously illegal, others unambiguously legal. The quasilegality of these substances also raises critical questions about the future of drug law in Africa and beyond as the friction it encounters becomes ever more disruptive to the intention of bringing about a drug-free world.

This paper examines the quasilegality of khat and cannabis in turn, before demonstrating the political, economic and social salience of their legally ambiguous status in Africa. In the final section, the paper connects its case studies to the current flux in global drug laws where 'quasilegality' is becoming the norm in a number of ways. First, however, we look in more detail at the term 'quasilegality' and its ability to capture a key aspect of not just drugs like khat and cannabis, but other commodities, activities and even people whose relationship to the state and law is ambiguous.

Quasilegality

'Quasilegal' is a term with resonance in a number of fields, from the study of law and the state to the study of drugs and other such goods. The prefix 'quasi' adds the idea of ambiguity to the term 'legal' through its meaning of 'as if', 'almost' or 'seemingly'. Quasilegal can refer to procedures and rules within an organisation that are not supported directly by state law, but resemble them in form, while also referring to what might elsewhere be termed 'paralegal'. Oren Perez links the quasilegal to 'fuzzy law': 'soft law' that lies between the 'poles of lawlessness and complete legality'.[5] Such a definition is useful for our purposes, linking the term as it does to spaces where state law is often rivalled by 'semi-autonomous social fields' in the words of Sally Falk Moore; spaces that the substances we examine travel through while often regulated by relationships of trust more than legal contract.[6]

The term also hints at the vagueness of the law and its flexibility. In this regard, it links to debates in criminology regarding the concept of 'discretion', where there is much leeway in the interpretation and application of legal statutes.[7] This leeway is influenced more by social relationships than by reference to the law. The law is an imprecise tool so, in using discretion as to whether to charge someone with an offence or whether to apply a more or less lenient penalty, those who apply the law enter into an ambiguous – quasilegal – realm. The law and its vagueness is also capable of being corrupted by its protagonists, where discretion becomes a tool for indiscretion and discrimination.[8]

However, there is a small literature that has taken up the term in relation to the status of psychoactive substances. It refers to substances that are generally legal such as alcohol and tobacco, but whose trade and usage can become illegal, for example, where smuggled to evade tax or where consumed by minors or after licencing hours.[9] But it is in regard to one of the very substances we shall explore that the term quasilegal has become most associated: khat. In a contribution to Appadurai's seminal 1986 volume *The Social Life of Things: Commodities in Cultural Perspective*, Lee Cassanelli wrote about khat within northeast Africa, its commodity chains and its varying legal status. He argued that khat's quasilegality meant that it 'hovered on that indistinct boundary between legality and illegality' and lack of social consensus about its status made it 'susceptible to manipulation for political ends'.[10] As a substance with ambiguous harm potential – capable of being defined as either relatively harmful or relatively harmless – and one not under international control, its political economy spurred producer countries to defend its legality (though there are anti-khat voices within these producer countries too) and consumer countries (who benefit less economically from its trade) to outlaw it. This meant that in some jurisdictions khat was legal and in others khat was illegal.

Cassanelli's analysis of khat has had influence in wider conceptions of illicit flows through the work of van Schendel and Abraham.[11] They build on Cassanelli to argue that 'what determines legality and illegality at different points of the commodity chain is the particular regulatory scale an object finds itself in'.[12] These scales are not just those of the state, but include transnational and social regulatory scales. This approach is encapsulated by their distinction between the *il/legal* and the *il/licit*: il/legal referring to how states define these substances and il/licit referring to how societies view the substances as legitimate or otherwise items of trade and consumption. They argue that 'students of illicit practices need to begin by discarding the assumption that there is a clear line between illicitness and the laws of states'.[13] Thus, some substances or activities are socially viewed as licit even though by law they are illegal, and vice versa. Quasilegal can help capture this ambiguity and help break glib assumptions that legality maps cleanly onto the values of wider society.

Our focus is on 'quasilegality' as a quality that comes to coalesce in things, people or activities. Coming to possess such a quality certainly relies on the varying forms of social and legal regulatory relationships that Van Schendel and Abraham focus upon, but is something that can adhere to a substance through its associations and something that can be hard to shift however much resistance there may be to these associations. By focusing on quasilegality in this way, we suggest that legal ambiguity is not just something that emerges in specific regulatory regimes, but can be relevant even in contexts where it is either definitively legal or definitively illegal (as well as definitively licit or illicit). In a sense, in quasilegality, the precise wording of the statute books is only secondary – what matters is how these substances are treated by those tasked with upholding the law and by wider society. And far from simply being a mismatch between the law and its application, quasilegality has important implications, as we suggest through a case study of one quasilegal substance that is often legal but treated as illicit – khat – and another that is always officially illegal, yet treated as licit – cannabis.

Khat

Khat is the archetypal quasilegal substance, thanks to Cassanelli's 1986 analysis. It consists of the stimulant stems and leaves of the shrub *Catha edulis* (Forsk.) which is found from the Middle East down to the Eastern Cape, and is now cultivated intensively in Yemen, Ethiopia, Kenya, Uganda and Northern Madagascar, and consumed in that region, as well as globally through the region's diasporas. In Kenya the substance is more commonly known as *miraa*. The actual harvested commodity varies in what is considered edible: in Yemen, Ethiopia and Madagascar often just the leaves and tender stem tips are chewed, whereas in Kenya small leaves and bark of stems are chewed. Chemical analysis of khat has revealed several alkaloids, the most potent being *cathinone* which acts in a similar manner to amphetamine.[14] Generally, chewing khat renders one alert and acts as a euphoriant, making it popular in recreational and work contexts. A crucial factor is its perishability.[15] *Cathinone* rapidly degrades into a weaker alkaloid post-harvest, and once khat dries it loses potency and value (though there is a growing international trade in dried khat). Wherever it is used, therefore, consumers usually want it as fresh as possible.

Chewing khat is associated with some adverse health consequences, though the scale of these is disputed and the evidence ambiguous.[16] The most serious health concerns include a link between heavy consumption and cardiac problems, especially when chronic consumption is combined with other cardiovascular risk factors,[17] and an association with liver damage is supported by a small number of cases in the UK.[18] Khat is also said to be the cause of a number of social harms: it is linked with family breakups, as chewers – generally, but by no means exclusively, male – reportedly spend much time away from the home; and it is often cited as a cause of unemployment, as khat is associated with idleness. Income diversion is also seen as a major problem in countries such as Djibouti where a large proportion of household income is spent on khat. What evidence there is in respect to social harms suggests demonising khat as their source is simplistic, falling into the trap of 'pharmacological determinism', where all agency is given to the substance rather than the wider social context.[19]

Whether khat is a relatively harmless mild stimulant or an addictive curse on society is fervently debated, yet it is unrealistic to expect any conclusive assessment, as with most such substances – however mild – ambiguity reigns.[20] There are 'problem users' who chew at the expense of food (khat – like other stimulants – reduces appetite) and sleep, making it hard for them to hold down work; however, evidence suggests that many chew more moderately and with relatively few ill effects.[21] More positively, some point to its link to cultural identity and its role in bringing people together in peaceful gatherings where amity is generated and advice proffered. Going even further, some have even described khat as playing a contributory role in uniting people in the context of Somaliland's post-war path to peace.[22]

It is important to describe these debates about khat and its potential for medical or social harm or benefits, as its ambiguities in these regards matter for how states treat it under the law. As Cassanelli emphasised,[23] these ambiguities mean that policy makers have been able to argue both for banning it and not banning it, depending on their instincts or interests at any one time; ambiguity that has helped generate an extremely varied international legal situation. Although khat is not under international control, it has come to be prohibited in numerous countries throughout the world, but remains legal in others. The colonial government of Kenya attempted to prohibit it through what was known as the 'khat ordinance'.[24] This law was crippled from the start by khat's ambiguities. Debates raged among colonial officers about its addictiveness or otherwise (and which substance to best compare it to – opium, gin or tobacco), while a racialised view emerged of khat harming pastoralists such as the Somali, while being innocuous for agriculturalists such as the Meru of central Kenya who were and still are the main cultivators of the crop in Kenya. These ambiguities led to fuzzy and unworkable law: the trade of the substance was prohibited in the north while Meru cultivation and consumption was protected as a cultural right. Bans imposed in the postcolonial era, including in Somalia (which banned it in the 1980s), also failed through lack of legitimacy, ever-increasing demand and inability to police multiplying smuggling routes.[25]

Since Cassanelli's writing on khat, it has become yet more ambiguous legally. Khat went global in the 1990s and 2000s with the spread of the Somali diaspora and consequent demand for the crop in places like Minneapolis, encountering more illegality as several Western countries had banned it not so much because of its alleged harms, but because its individual compounds *cathinone* and *cathine* were scheduled internationally in 1988.[26] This scheduling applied only to the isolated compounds, and was not intended to subject khat itself to international control. Nevertheless, scheduling led to Sweden and Norway prohibiting the substance itself in 1989; the USA scheduled cathine (1988) and cathinone (1993), the Drug Enforcement Administration taking this scheduling to imply that khat itself is scheduled when it contains these substances. Canada scheduled the plant itself in 1997, while a number of other European countries soon also banned the substance.[27] However, khat's exact legal status and penalties for those caught with it in these territories is far from clear, especially in the US. There, defence lawyers often use the argument that fair warning of khat's illegality has not been provided as khat itself is not listed as a scheduled substance under Federal Law, or that defendants are unaware that khat contains cathinone and therefore do not understand its status.

The UK has been the most recent country to ban the substance, in 2014, after a long review process in which the chief body advising the government on drug policy – The Advisory Council on the Misuse of Drugs – recommended it not be banned, but the government, under pressure from UK-based Somali anti-khat activists and other European countries whose illegal khat imports were routed through the UK, banned it anyway.[28] Indeed, for the Conservative Home Secretary of the time – Theresa May – banning khat was a 'win-win' political move, appearing 'tough on drugs' yet sympathetic to the plight of an ethnic minority. Khat became a 'Class C' substance, a relatively low classification, but one that stopped the legal import of over 56 tonnes of khat that had been coming from Kenya and Ethiopia. There have since been seizures, although how actively policed the substance is remains in doubt as khat is unlikely to be high up the list of priorities for overstretched police forces. Obtaining khat is still reckoned reasonably straightforward, as some of Carrier's informants have confirmed, and a variety of dried khat called *graba* appears increasingly popular, being easier to smuggle and said to remain potent once rehydrated. While a standard retail bundle of khat sold for £3 in the UK when legal, now such a bundle retails from £15–45, reflecting how risk has affected pricing.

Thus, while its legal status still varies greatly, if anything khat is moving towards the more illegal side of the spectrum, certainly in the West. Yet in most producer countries back in Africa it remains *de jure* legal, although it is often treated as illegal. For example, its production has risen in recent decades in Uganda and Madagascar, where it is technically legal, yet there are continual rumours that the substance is banned or about to be banned such is its conflation with other drugs, and various local by-laws add further ambiguity as Beckerleg relates in regard to Uganda.[29] Indeed, as Beckerleg suggests for Uganda, there is often much conflation of khat and other drugs, including cannabis, that further muddy the waters concerning the legality of the substance.[30]

However, in one jurisdiction at least the situation appears to be clarifying: Kenya. The crop was long subject to ambiguity in Kenya as the government kept aloof from either encouraging or discouraging its production fearing international disapproval and, in Carrier's early research on the substance in the early 2000s, there was sufficient ambiguity about the substance for security officers to once threaten him with arrest in the hope of a bribe when they spotted him carrying some: they felt the substance sufficiently 'quasilegal' that a foreigner would believe them that it was in fact illegal. However, the recent ban in the UK has ironically made the substance if not 'respectable', then at least more unambiguously legal. This is because the Kenyan state came out in support of the crop under pressure from Meru growers and traders, now a powerful voting bloc since the introduction of devolution in 2013. Khat has been designated an official cash crop – for which Meru have campaigned for decades – while a task force has been established to see how its farmers can further benefit from the crop and be protected from the negative effects of the ban in the UK.[31] In the new era of Kenyan devolved politics, appealing to the important voting bloc of Meru County relies on politicians embracing khat: thus, Raila Odinga and William Ruto indulge in a little khat chewing at campaign rallies in the county. This would have been unthinkable in previous times. Thus, paradoxically, the UK ban on khat has meant that in Kenya khat is less quasilegal than it used to be.

Cannabis

Our other case study, *Cannabis sativa*, needs little introduction as a substance, though it is important to emphasise that, like khat, there is much ambiguity when it comes to its harmfulness or otherwise: medical opinion throughout history has been polarised,[32] and remains so today, especially in regard to mental health.[33] Like khat, this also allows rhetorically-strong arguments to be made for either restricting or liberalising its markets.

While not indigenous to Africa, cannabis has a long history on the continent, as cannabis traces on Ethiopian pottery from the fourteenth century reveal and research in southern Africa suggests cannabis was used well before 1500.[34] It was no doubt introduced through the Indian Ocean trade networks and Arabs who settled on the eastern African coast, from there percolating southwards and westwards. In Madagascar, its consumption is known from the mid-seventeenth century,[35] while in Central Africa, cannabis was integrated into a charismatic movement known as the *Bene Diamba* ('children of hemp' – *diamba* being a variant of a common term for cannabis), whose ceremonies suffused with cannabis smoke were bemusedly recorded by nineteenth century explorers.[36]

Throughout the region, cannabis was not just used for its intoxicating properties, but also as a medicine. Many traditional healers – such as the *sangoma* of southern Africa – still use all parts of the plant to cure various ailments. It was commonly reported in the literature of explorers that cannabis was smoked by warriors before raids, and its use by praise singers and those requiring deep thought to solve problems was also reported.[37] Despite the imposition of legal restrictions on cannabis production and consumption in Africa over the course of the twentieth century, it is as ubiquitous as ever and offers many farmers a livelihood.

In the course of the 1950s, cannabis use expanded in West Africa, where it has a much shorter history than on the rest of the continent, having been re-introduced by soldiers returning from South Asia after the Second World War. While initially associated with urban deviance, cannabis use and cultivation expanded to rural areas and other less marginal strata of society, such as students, and by the end of the 1970s cannabis had established itself as the favourite illegal drug across West Africa. In Nigeria – one of the latecomers to cannabis – the substance had entered the cultural mainstream by the 1980s, being used by a variety of social groups and in diverse social settings such as motor parks, university campuses and in bars. Cannabis was promoted – much to the dislike of military governments – by one of the country's musical giants, Fela Kuti.[38] In many places like Nigeria, cannabis kept its deviant reputation to some extent but also came to be a symbol of resistance to the state, not least in Fela's music.

Today, cannabis is by far the most widely consumed and traded substance deemed illegal by the state in Africa. The UNODC in its most recent large-scale study on cannabis on the continent estimates that there were 38.2 million cannabis users in 2005: 7.7% of 15–64-year-olds.[39] A 1999 UN report on drugs in Africa that surveyed 10 countries found cannabis sold much cheaper than bottled beer, making it highly accessible.[40] Large quantities are seized – especially in South Africa and Nigeria – as international concern has meant that cannabis consumers and farmers have been the easiest targets for drug enforcers, although supply appears unaffected.[41]

Social perceptions of cannabis and its potential harms in Africa are as polarised as those in the west between those who see it as a 'hard drug' strongly linked to 'madness', and those who extol its virtues as a 'herb'. In Ghana, Henry Bernstein reports of young consumers who eloquently defend cannabis as 'life-enhancing: good for ailments (asthma, appetite loss), reading, contemplation and sense of self – and sexual potency'.[42] These same consumers are very much influenced in their perceptions of cannabis by reggae culture and Rastafarianism, which is a major factor throughout the continent.[43]

Opposing views emanate from more 'respectable' segments of society. Doctors, in particular psychiatrists, were the first to write about the dangers of cannabis use in the 1950s and its impact on mental and social health, at times borrowing from western models and debates on addiction and substance abuse. Interestingly, the foremost medical experts on substance use on the continent had and still have an ambiguous idea of cannabis's harm potential.[44] While medical experts rarely simply condemned cannabis and its users, medical statements were nonetheless interpreted in a more negative light in the media and in government circles. For instance, while psychiatrists in Nigeria started to explore the mental health implications of cannabis in a relatively balanced and critical way, their concerns were often sensationalised in the media. Military governments since the 1960s knowingly ignored medical advice and instead initiated the most attention-generating and punitive legal and policy responses.[45]

Cannabis use is also strongly opposed by various religious groupings, such as Pentecostal Christian denominations, which also run some of the most well-funded drug treatment centres on the continent.⁴⁶ Even in contexts where cannabis has been smoked for centuries, its use by the younger generations is frowned upon, and the common discourse that substance use has degenerated as a result of the loss of power by African elders can be heard, as reported by the 1999 UN report from Mozambique.⁴⁷

Legally, cannabis should be much less ambiguous a substance than khat, as it is universally controlled under unified global drug conventions, while its prohibition is decreed by statute in all African countries and has been in some countries for over a century. In most countries, legislation was introduced alongside that against opium following the 1925 International Opium Convention (that also was concerned with cocaine and cannabis). These colonial ordinances were often based on imperial templates and responded to international treaties rather than to concerns about consumption within particular colonies.⁴⁸

South Africa is somewhat distinct in this respect, as concern over the consumption of 'dagga' (one of the local names for cannabis) has different historical roots. Already in the 1880s, use of dagga among workers in the Natal Colony became an important part of a government inquiry on Indian indentured labourers. In subsequent decades, South Africa became one of the leading proponents internationally to promote the prohibition of cannabis and its recognition as an internationally illegal drug in the 1920s. At the time, South African government concerns about dagga were intrinsically linked to racialised ideas about the control of labour and productivity on farms and mines.⁴⁹ This was quite different from most other parts of the continent, where there was little to no state concern about the substance until the 1950s.

Despite its overwhelming illegality since the 1920s, cannabis was increasingly commoditised, becoming deeply embedded in rural economies. In Lesotho, Laniel and Bloomer analysed its rise in rural significance in compensation for decreasing opportunities for migrant labour in South Africa.⁵⁰ In other countries, its importance was tied to the economic uncertainties of the neoliberal economic reforms and their often devastating effects on livelihoods.⁵¹ In Nigeria and other parts of West Africa, the rise of cannabis was linked to the decline in cocoa cultivation and first appeared as a means to compensate or diversify agricultural production.⁵² In recent decades, it has become a key produce of an area that used to be called Nigeria's 'cocoa belt' and in many ways it is now more than a 'compensation crop'.⁵³

In a context where cannabis plays such an important role in rural and urban economies, there are often few attempts made to enforce cannabis' *de jure* illegality. Nigeria's war on drugs since the 1990s is somewhat exceptional in this respect, although also its impact on the trade was at most marginal.⁵⁴ In countries especially reliant on the crop for rural economies, it is de facto legal. For example, in Lesotho and Malawi state enforcement is minimal, a state policy characterised by neglect. Of course, this neglect also comes about as few states have the capacity to police cannabis cultivation and trade effectively.⁵⁵

Furthermore, as a ubiquitous crop and item of consumption associated with medicine and tradition, as well as with popular figures like Fela Kuti, cannabis law meets much resistance on the continent as elsewhere in the world. Of course, there are local cultures of condemnation too, especially when the use of cannabis is linked to deviant and at times violent groups, such as insurgents in the Niger Delta, or when cannabis is debated in the context of mental health by doctors. These condemning discourses on cannabis in the media, state and medical circles, as well as in the general public, have given cannabis law and its enforcement some traction, as was the case in the Nigerian drug war in the 1990s.

Like khat, cannabis is a substance that for many in Africa has a social, economic and cultural legitimacy, and attempts to definitively fix it as 'bad' have often failed, especially if the main promoter of its illegality is a state that lacks legitimacy.[56] Cannabis may be illegal but, for many in Africa as elsewhere, it is far from universally condemned. In this context where some see it as a legitimate source of livelihood and relief, it is cannabis law that can seem illegitimate.

The social salience of quasilegality

Does this quasilegality matter? After all, these two substances flow freely in much of Africa and beyond despite what the statute books say: drug law is not only hard to police, especially for resource-poor states, it is also impossible to translate abstract law into definitive consensus about the production, trade and consumption of such substances. However, drug law still hangs over them, and their quasilegal and morally ambiguous statuses are socially and economically consequential in several respects.

While the trade and production of these commodities have expanded impressively, mostly without state input, quasilegality of course prevents governments from supporting these commodities in the way they can with other drug crops such as tea or tobacco. This situation has now somewhat changed in regard to khat in Kenya, but generally speaking producers of such crops have no legal support from the state. Meanwhile, underneath quasilegality, illegality often lies dormant and latent. For cannabis, its latent illegality can spring up to bite those who grow or trade such goods. For example, cannabis farmers and traders in Africa are often easy targets for law enforcers wanting to boost seizure statistics. Quasilegality cannot prevent many in Kenya, Nigeria and elsewhere from being charged and imprisoned for cannabis crimes.[57] These decisions are often made quite arbitrarily by the state and its police officers. Usually it is the small-scale producer and user who carries the can: as elsewhere, drug law disproportionately affects the poorest.

Quasilegality can also be useful for actors including the state. The state can be lenient in its implementation at times, or even become complicit in the trade, while it can be tough on these substances when politically convenient, for instance when increasing drug seizures will gain an African government western support, as was the case during Nigeria's war on drugs at the end of the 1990s.[58] As already alluded to by Cassanelli, lack of consensus about a substance's status makes it 'susceptible to manipulation for political ends'.[59] This is not only the case between states on the international level but also within states. Within the context of quasilegality, the implementation of drug law has often served as a means to extend state control, especially by expanding repressive law enforcement – often with donor-funded equipment.[60]

Meanwhile, for consumers and producers quasilegality is also useful in a number of ways, principally through enhancing economic and cultural value. In the case of cannabis, something freely sold in much of Africa and easy to grow, much of its economic value derives from illegality and the risk premium this adds to its sale price.[61] Quasilegality also gives khat a value boost, as its reputation as something not respectable in wider society can earn it respect among sub-cultures. In this way, khat becomes 'cool' and in demand as a commodity, especially among the young.[62] Cannabis gains appeal as its consumption is associated with defiance and counter-culture and is affiliated with famous smokers including Fela Kuti and Bob Marley.

In another geographical context, there are benefits to quasilegality, as Polson makes clear in relation to cannabis cultivation in California.[63] There cannabis' increasing legality for medicinal usage means it is far more tolerated as a 'licit' though not 'legal' crop, although producers can still be arrested and charged, making it still a risky occupation that attracts a premium. However, there are deep inequalities in who reaps rewards from this quasilegality, as it is those most able to distance themselves legally from the crop who benefit the most: Polson highlights how landowners who can distance themselves from what tenants were growing are those who benefit the most. Regarding cannabis in Africa, we see the same happening, with growers of cannabis being the easiest targets for law enforcers, yet also the ones benefitting the least from its trade.

However, growers in California value cannabis' licit yet illegal status as this can protect them from 'the predations of the regulated, competitive market'.[64] For farmers in Africa and other parts of the developing world too, the ability of drug crops to insulate them from predatory states is a key part of their appeal. In the case of khat in Kenya there are those who warn farmers to beware their longed-for government input, as with this might come less benevolent state attention including increased taxes. Indeed, khat and cannabis in much of Africa appear to offer producers and traders the benefits of a middle-ground between full licitness and legality and competition from corporate capitalism, and definitive illegality and the repressive consequences of consensus over their illicitness. Of course, this is a precarious middle-ground.

Importantly, quasilegality also spurs campaigns to definitively fix these substances as legal or illegal. For example, khat producers in Kenya have long campaigned to validate their commodity globally as a legal stimulant – not just to boost trade, but also out of pride in their khat heritage; on the other hand, Somalis campaigned to have it made illegal in Britain not just out of concern for social harms, but also because they reckoned a ban would give them validation from the UK government as a community to be treated seriously. Furthermore, in the latter case, we can see how illegality elsewhere in the world fed the notion among campaigners that khat must be harmful: why would it be illegal elsewhere, if not?[65] Here we see an instance of how drug law can help form public opinion. Meanwhile, in relation to cannabis there are numerous 'free the weed' campaigns in Africa, especially in South Africa, but also in Kenya, where recently a Member of Parliament – Ken Okoth – called for the substance to be legalised so farmers could profit from it as an export crop.[66]

In this way, quasilegality can be generative of social movements that seek to dispel this very quasilegality. Like the war on drugs and its universalising policy, legalisation and decriminalisation campaigns can be global and transnational in scale, and can also generate either traction or resistance in local contexts. As the next section discusses, in our current era such campaigns are apparently gaining traction.

Cracks in the system

Thus, the quasilegality of these substances and others like them matters. In this regard, quasilegality is becoming more common for drugs around the world as the global logic of the drug war both loses and gains traction depending on the substance and the jurisdiction. The experiments of Uruguay, Colorado and Washington in regard to cannabis legalisation suggest a loss of traction of the global drug policy regime, as do increasingly vocal international initiatives pushing for drug law reform. There was much optimism that the United

Nations General Assembly Special Session (UNGASS) on global drug policy in April 2016 would culminate in concrete change.[67] This session was pushed through by countries in the global south that have long suffered through more repressive drug policy, especially in Latin America where drug control has long been militarised.[68] However, the end result was disappointing for reformers, as more reactionary forces were able to promote hardly revolutionary recommendations.[69] Thus, the drug war is fighting back. Nonetheless, there are strong arguments that we are witnessing the fracturing of the international consensus on drug law that has been in place since the 1920s, particularly on such substances as cannabis.[70]

While repressive measures against drugs continue, and the recent horrors perpetrated in the Philippines show how anti-drug law remains a popular means of social control for autocratic leaders such as Duterte, perhaps the general tenor is towards more liberal policy. In Europe, Portugal is held as a case study of effective decriminalisation – another form of quasilegality. In the UK, a number of police forces have over the last few years retreated from active policing of small amounts of cannabis possession[71]: cannabis has thus become more quasilegal there too. In South America, coca also finds itself increasingly quasilegal as global anti-drug initiatives lose traction in a local context where many validate the crop and its consumption culturally and many depend on it economically.[72]

The drug war has perhaps gained traction in regard to khat, as witnessed by its increasing illegality in the west. While cannabis moves away from illegality, the arguably less harmful khat is pulled more towards it, and the story of other substances – including synthetic legal-highs and tobacco – suggest there remains a powerful impetus towards restrictive drug law. Of course, the situation is more nuanced than this suggests, as we have also seen khat becoming more licit in Kenya itself, and less quasilegal.

In regard to our two case-study substances, perhaps a wider generalisation can be made, in that khat has become illegal in western countries where it is used principally by minority populations,[73] while cannabis's illegality is ever more questioned as its use is so well ingrained into wider western society. As ever, there are far more powerful forces at work in the shaping of drug policy than simple evaluations of harmfulness or harmlessness. Some of these forces are economic in nature, and other states around the world will be monitoring the results of cannabis legalisation in places like Colorado and the apparent economic boosts to legal businesses and states that can come from such policy.[74]

Thus, global drug policy is itself increasingly ambiguous, and how this will play out in the African context remains to be seen. There is talk of legalising medical marijuana in Rwanda and the South African parliament has recently considered a similar proposal.[75] A less repressive drug policy is being seriously considered by the West Africa Commission on Drugs, although some countries remain wedded to harsher policies. There are of course many voices in Africa as elsewhere urging that, rather than making drugs like khat and cannabis more unambiguously legal, they should be made more unambiguously illegal.

Despite growing cracks in the landscape and logic of global drug policy, cannabis and khat are likely to remain decidedly ambiguous and quasilegal for the foreseeable future, on the African as well as the international level. Their quasilegality helps to understand the traction that drug laws and drugs more generally have in political and popular debates on the continent, as elsewhere – debates that are not simply about the pharmacological effects or the medical and social harms of psychoactive substances, but about their broader roles in helping to define inter-generational conflicts, the labelling of migrant communities or as a way to debate such contested ideas as development or national identity.[76]

As a concept, quasilegality is compelling as it captures the fluidity of the evolution, status and perceptions of these substances over time, helping to explore the extensive hidden spaces between the legal and illegal, where much drug-related activity and debate takes place. Yet it also has strong potential as a concept in analysing other areas of policy and law making characterised by ambiguity and fluidity. These include other aspects of society where the law attempts to stamp out things and activities deemed illegal yet regarded by many as 'licit', from sex work and migration to so-called 'radicalisation'. It is in this ambiguous space of the quasilegal where the law sometimes gains traction, but is ever susceptible to wider social values and desires.

Disclosure statement

No potential conflict of interest was reported by the authors.

Notes

1. UK Psychoactive Substances Act 2016.
2. Tsing, *Friction*.
3. See *The Guardian*, "Duterte Vows to Continue War on Drugs."
4. Nadelmann, "Global Prohibition Regimes."
5. Perez, "Fuzzy Law."
6. Moore, "Law and Social Change."
7. Gelsthorpe and Padfield, *Exercising Discretion*.
8. Ibid.
9. Okwumabua and Duryea, "Age of Onset."
10. Cassanelli, "Qat," 254.
11. Van Schendel and Abraham, *Illicit Flows and Criminal Things*.
12. Ibid. 17.
13. Ibid. 7.
14. Zaghloul et al., "Consequences of Khat Use," 80.
15. Carrier, "The Need for Speed."
16. Thomas and Williams, "Khat (*Catha edulis*)."
17. Graziani, Milella, and Nencini, "Khat Chewing from the Pharmacological Perspective," 772–773.

18. Chapman, "Severe, Acute Liver Injury and Khat Leaves."
19. Anderson and Carrier, *Khat: Social Harms*.
20. See Hansen, "The Ambiguity of Khat."
21. Anderson and Carrier, *Khat: Social Harms*.
22. Hansen, *Governing Khat*.
23. Cassanelli, "Qat."
24. Anderson and Carrier, "Khat in Colonial Kenya."
25. Ibid., 250. Khat is also illegal in Tanzania and Eritrea, although the reasons for these bans are unresearched.
26. Anderson and Carrier, *Khat: Social Harms*, 21ff.
27. Anderson and Carrier, *Khat: Social Harms*, 22–23.
28. Klein, "Khat Ban in the UK," 6–8.
29. Beckerleg, *Ethnic Identity and Development*.
30. Ibid., 169–171.
31. Carrier, "Khat and its Changing Politics."
32. Mills, *Cannabis Britannica*.
33. See, for example, the 2007 special issue of *The Lancet* on cannabis and mental health: "Editorial: Rehashing the Evidence."
34. Du Toit, "Dagga."
35. Ibid., 84.
36. Fabian, *Out of Our Minds*.
37. Du Toit, "Dagga," 96–97.
38. Klein, "Nigeria and the Drugs War," 60.
39. UNODC, *Cannabis in Africa*, 15.
40. UNDCP, *Drugs Nexus in Africa*.
41. Leggett, *Rainbow Vice*, 37; Klantschnig, "Politics of Drug Control."
42. Bernstein, "Ghana's Drug Economy," 18.
43. Savishinsky, "Baye Faal of Senegambia," 212.
44. Lambo, "Medical and Social Problems." Also see the work on cannabis by academics affiliated to Africa's major drug policy pressure group CRISA and its *African Journal of Drug and Alcohol Studies* for diverse medical views on the substance.
45. Klantschnig, "Histories of Cannabis Use."
46. Adelekan and Morakinyo, *Rapid Assessment of the Treatment*.
47. UNDCP, *Drugs Nexus in Africa*, 40.
48. Klantschnig, "Histories of Cannabis Use."
49. Government of the Colony of Natal, *Wragg Commission*; Crampton, *Dagga*.
50. Laniel, "Cannabis in Lesotho"; Bloomer, "Using a Political Ecology Framework."
51. Carrier and Klantschnig, "Illicit Livelihoods."
52. Klantschnig, *Crime, Drugs and the State*.
53. Laudati, "Out of the Shadows."
54. NDLEA, *Annual Report 2008*.
55. Carrier and Klantschnig, *Africa and the War on Drugs*, 106–129.
56. Ibid., chapter four.
57. NDLEA, *Annual Report 2008*.
58. Obot, "Assessing Nigeria's Drug Control Policy."
59. Cassanelli, "Qat," 254.
60. Carrier and Klantschnig, *Africa and the War on Drugs*.
61. Carrier and Klantschnig, *Africa and the War on Drugs*, 117.
62. Carrier, "Miraa is cool."
63. Polson, "Land and Law in Marijuana County."
64. Ibid., 226.
65. Although as discussed above, khat's path to illegality throughout the world was not a straightforward equation of harm generating law.
66. Ane-Loglo, *Decriminalising Drug Use*; *Nairobi News*, "Why this MP wants Bhang Legalised."

67. See UNGASS website.
68. On the push for new policy in Latin America, see *The Guardian*, "Leaked Paper Reveals UN Split."
69. For a critical report on UNGASS 2016, see International Drug Policy Consortium, *UNGASS on the World Drug Problem*.
70. Bewley-Taylor, *International Drug Control*.
71. *The Guardian*, "Durham Police Stop Targeting Pot Smokers."
72. *BBC News*, "Bolivia's Morales Boosts Legal Coca."
73. Carrier, "Strange Drug in a Strange Land."
74. On cannabis and tourist revenue in Colorado, see Kang, O'Leary, and Miller, "From Forbidden Fruit."
75. *BBC News*, "Afrique du Sud."
76. Carrier and Klantschnig, "Illicit Livelihoods."

Bibliography

Adelekan, M., and O. Morakinyo. *Rapid Assessment of the Treatment and Rehabilitation Facilities for Drug Dependent Persons in Nigeria*. Lagos: UNDCP, 2000.

"Afrique du Sud: 'égaliser le cannabis.'"*BBC News*, May 2017. Accessed May 7, 2016. http://www.bbc.com/afrique/region/2016/05/160507_afriquedusud-cannabis

Anderson, D. M., and N. Carrier. "Khat in Colonial Kenya: A History of Prohibition and Control." *Journal of African History* 50, no. 3 (2009): 377–397.

Anderson, D. M., and N. Carrier. *Khat: Social Harms and Legislation, a Literature Review*. London: Home Office Occasional Paper 95, 2011.

Ane-Loglo, M. *Decriminalising Drug Use: Why It Is Important for Ghana*. Accra: West Africa Civil Society Institute, 2016.

Beckerleg, S. *Ethnic Identity and Development: Khat and Social Change in Africa*. New York: Palgrave Macmillan, 2010.

Bernstein, H. "Ghana's Drug Economy: Some Preliminary Data." *Review of African Political Economy* 26 (1999): 13–32.

Bewley-Taylor, D. *International Drug Control: Consensus Fractured*. Cambridge: Cambridge University Press, 2012.

Bloomer, J. "Using a Political Ecology Framework to Examine Extra-Legal Livelihood Strategies: A Lesotho-Based Case Study of Cultivation of and Trade in Cannabis." *Journal of Political Ecology* 16 (2009): 49–69.

"Bolivia's Morales Boosts Legal Coca Production." *BBC News*, May 2017. Accessed March 9, 2017. http://www.bbc.co.uk/news/world-latin-america-39214085

Carrier, N. "A Strange Drug in a Strange Land." In *Travelling Cultures and Plants: The Ethnobiology and Ethnopharmacy of Migrations*, edited by A. Pieroni and I. Vandebroek, 186–203. Oxford: Berghahn, 2007.

Carrier, N. "Khat and its Changing Politics in Kenya and Somalia after UK Ban." *The Conversation*, May 2017. Accessed July 19, 2016. http://theconversation.com/khat-and-its-changing-politics-in-kenya-and-somalia-after-uk-ban-62119

Carrier, N. "'Miraa is Cool': The Cultural Importance of Miraa (khat) for Tigania and Igembe Youth in Kenya." *Journal of African Cultural Studies* 17, no. 2 (2005): 201–218.

Carrier, N. "The Need for Speed: Contrasting Timeframes in the Social Life of Kenyan Miraa." *Africa* 75 (2005): 539–558.

Carrier, N., and G. Klantschnig. *Africa and the War on Drugs*. London: Zed Books.

Carrier, N., and G. Klantschnig. "Illicit Livelihoods: Drug Crops and Development in Africa." *Review of African Political Economy* 43, no. 148 (2016): 174–189.

Cassanelli, L. V. "Qat: Changes in the Production and Consumption of a Quasilegal Commodity in Northeast Africa." In *The Social Life of Things: Commodities in Cultural Perspective*, edited by A. Appadurai, 236–258. Cambridge: University Press, 1986.

Chapman, M. H. "Severe, Acute Liver Injury and Khat Leaves." *New England Journal of Medicine* 362, no. 17 (2010): 1642–1644.

Crampton, H. *Dagga: A Short History*. Johannesburg: Jacana, 2015.

Du Toit, B. "Dagga: The History and Ethnographic Setting of *Cannabis Sativa* in Southern Africa." In *Cannabis and Culture*, edited by V. Rubin, and Mouton De Gruyter, 81–116. University Press, 1975.

"Durham Police Stop Targeting Pot Smokers and Small-Scale Growers." 2017. *The Guardian*, May. Accessed July 22, 2015. http://www.theguardian.com/society/2015/jul/22/durham-police-stop-targeting-pot-smokers-and-small-scale-growers

"Duterte Vows to Continue War on Drugs After Killing Confession." 2017. *The Guardian*, May. Accessed December 16, 2016. http://www.theguardian.com/world/2016/dec/16/duterte-vows-to-continue-war-on-drugs-after-killing-confession

"Editorial: Rehashing the Evidence on Psychosis and Cannabis." *The Lancet* 370, no. 9584 (2007): 292.

Fabian, J. *Out of Our Minds*. Berkeley: University of California Press, 2000.

Gelsthorpe, L., and N. Padfield. *Exercising Discretion: Decision-Making in the Criminal Justice System and Beyond*. London: Routledge, 2003.

Government of the Colony of Natal. *Report of the Indian Immigrants Commission 'Wragg Commission' 1885–7*. Pietermaritzburg: Davis and Sons, 1887.

Graziani, M., M. S. Milella, and P. Nencini. "Khat Chewing from the Pharmacological Perspective." *Substance Use and Misuse* 43, no. 6 (2008): 762–783.

Hansen, P. *Governing Khat: Drugs and Democracy in Somaliland*. Copenhagen: Danish Institute for International Studies Working Paper 24, 2009. May 2017. http://pure.diis.dk/ws/files/45269/WP2009_24_Governing_Khat_web.pdf.

Hansen, P. "The Ambiguity of Khat in Somaliland." *Journal of Ethnopharmacology* 132 (2010): 590–599.

International Drug Policy Consortium (IDPC). *The UNGASS on the World Drug Problem: Report of Proceedings*. September 2016. May 2017. http://idpc.net/publications/2016/09/the-ungass-on-the-world-drug-problem-report-of-proceedings.

Kang, S. K., J. O'Leary, and J. Miller. "From Forbidden Fruit to the Goose that Lays Golden Eggs: Marijuana Tourism in Colorado." *Sage Open October-December* (2016): 1–12.

Klantschnig, G. *Crime, Drugs and the State in Africa: The Nigerian Connection*. Leiden, Dordrecht: Brill, Republic of Letters, 2013.

Klantschnig, G. "The Politics of Drug Control in Nigeria: Exclusion, Repression and Obstacles to Policy Change." *International Journal of Drug Policy* 30 (2016): 132–139.

Klantschnig, G. "Histories of Cannabis Use and Control in Nigeria, 1927–1967." In *Drugs in Africa: Histories and Ethnographies of Use, Trade, and Control*, edited by G. Klantschnig, N. Carrier, and C. Ambler, 69–88. New York: Palgrave Macmillan, 2014.

Klein, A. "Nigeria & the Drugs War." *Review of African Political Economy* 26 (1999): 51–73.

Klein, A. "The Khat Ban in the UK: What about the Scientific Evidence?" *Anthropology Today* 29 (2013): 6–8.

Lambo, T. A. "Medical and Social Problems of Drug Addiction in West Africa." *Western African Medical Journal* 14 (1965): 236–254.

Laniel, L. "Cannabis in Lesotho: A Preliminary Survey." Paris: UNESCO Management of Social Transformations Discussion Paper 34, 1998.

Laudati, A. "Out of the Shadows: Negotiations and Networks in the Cannabis Trade in Eastern Democratic Republic of Congo." In *Drugs in Africa: Histories and Ethnographies of Use, Trade and Control*, edited by G. Klantschnig, N. Carrier, and C. Ambler, 161–181. New York: Palgrave, 2014.

"Leaked Paper Reveals UN Split Over War on Drugs." 2017. *The Guardian*, May. Accessed December 30, 2016. http://www.theguardian.com/politics/2013/nov/30/un-drugs-policy-split-leaked-paper

Leggett, T. *Rainbow Vice: The Drugs and Sex Industries in the New South Africa*. London: Zed Press, 2002.

Mills, J. *Cannabis Britannica: Empire, Trade, and Prohibition 1800–1928*. Oxford: Oxford University Press, 2003.

Moore, S. F. "Law and Social Change: The Semi-Autonomous Social Field as an Appropriate Subject of Study." *Law & Society Review* 7, no. 4 (1973): 719–746.

Nadelmann, E. "Global Prohibition Regimes: The Evolution of Norms in International Society." *International Organization* 44, no. 4 (1990): 479–526.

NDLEA. *NDLEA Annual Report 2008*. Lagos: NDLEA, 2008.

Obot, I. "Assessing Nigeria's Drug Control Policy, 1994–2000." *International Journal of Drug Policy* 15, no. 1 (2004): 17–26.

Okwumabua, J. O., and E. J. Duryea. "Age of Onset, Periods of Risk, and Patterns of Progression in Drug Use Among American Indian High School Students." *International Journal of Addiction* 22, no. 12 (1987): 1269–1276.

Perez, O. "Fuzzy Law: A Theory of Quasi-Legal Systems." *Canadian Journal of Law and Jurisprudence* 28, no. 2 (2015): 343–370.

Polson, M. "Land and Law in Marijuana County: Clean Capital, Dirty Money, and the Drug War's *Rentier* Nexus." *Political and Legal Anthropology Review* 36, no. 2 (2013): 215–230.

Savishinsky, N. T. "The Baye Faal of Senegambia: Muslim Rastas in the Promised Land?" *Africa* 64, no. 2 (1994): 211–219.

Thomas, S., and T. Williams. "Khat (*Catha edulis*): A Systematic Review of Evidence and Literature Pertaining to its Harms to UK Users and Society." *Drug Science, Policy and Law* 1 (2014): 1–25.

Tsing, A. L. *Friction: An Ethnography of Global Connection*. Princeton: University Press, 2004.

UK Psychoactive Substances Act 2016. 2017. May. http://www.legislation.gov.uk/ukpga/2016/2/contents/enacted.

UN Special Session of the General Assembly on the World Drug Problem (UNGASS). 2017. May http://www.unodc.org/ungass2016/.

UNDCP. *The Drugs Nexus in Africa*. Vienna: UNDCP, 1999.

UNODC. *Cannabis in Africa: An Overview*. Vienna: UNODC, 2007.

Van Schendel, W., and I. Abraham. *Illicit Flows and Criminal Things: States, Borders and the Other Side of Globalization*. Bloomington: Indiana University Press, 2005.

"Why this MP Wants Bhang Legalized in Kenya." 2017. *Nairobi News*, May. Accessed June 26, 2015. http://nairobinews.nation.co.ke/news/why-this-mp-wants-bhang-legalised-in-kenya/

Zaghloul, A., A. Abdalla, H. El-Gammal, and H. Moselhy. "The Consequences of Khat Use: A Review of Literature." *European Journal of Psychiatry* 17 (2003): 77–86.

Why do South-east Asian states choose to suppress opium? A cross-case comparison

James Windle

ABSTRACT
This paper compares the reasons given by three South-east Asian states (Laos, Thailand and Vietnam) for choosing to suppress opium production. While external pressure, often from the US or United Nations (UN)/League of Nations, is the most commonly identified reason in the literature, and was experienced in each case, it was not by itself sufficient to motivate states into action. All three cases were motivated by religious or ideological opposition to drug consumption or trade, rural development, state extension and concern for increasing domestic drug consumption. Apprehension about rising drug consumption often possessed racial or chauvinistic elements. The development of export commodities, environmental protection and national security were also identified in one or two cases. The paper concludes by hypothesising that economic and/or security considerations underlie all choices to suppress illicit drug crops.

Introduction

Opium has been consumed, in prepared form, for centuries in many regions of the world for recreational, religious, cultural and medicinal purposes. It is currently the primary ingredient in licit and illicit opioids, including heroin, and represents a valuable cash crop to some of the world's poorest farmers in some of the most impoverished regions of the Global South.

Many countries in both the Global West and South claim that eradication of opium at the source of production can remove the greatest quantity of heroin from global and national markets, and is easier and more cost effective than interdiction in transit.[1] Such theory and policy, however, conflict with decades of research demonstrating that not only can poorly designed interventions present significant negative consequences to farming communities and the state,[2] but interventions at the source are the least cost-effective means of controlling consumption or trade. The price of opium at the farm gate limits the global impact of source-country control policy: Because opium is produced in areas with low risk of eradication or arrest, and abundant cheap labour, traffickers can absorb farm-gate price increases with minimal effect on wholesale and retail profit. For example, Wilson and Stevens estimate the price mark-up for heroin between the Afghan farm gate and British streets as

---

http://orcid.org/0000-0001-8367-2926

approximately 15,800%.[3] Furthermore, markets in the Global West are often 'buffered' by markets closer to the source.[4] For example, Pietschmann demonstrates how sharply declining Afghan opium production in 2000 had a much greater impact on the neighboring countries of Iran and Pakistan than on Western Europe. This is because traffickers ensure that short-term reductions in supply are absorbed by reduced sales in (less profitable) local markets to maintain supply to (more profitable) Western markets.[5] International and national drug policy is, however, about more than stopping consumption in the Global West.

Indeed, the first step in any national intervention to suppress an illicit drug crop is an awareness by the government that suppression is in its best interest.[6] The current paper elaborates on a study of successful national opium suppression by further investigating why governments have viewed suppression as in their best interest. In the original study, success was defined as an excess of 90% reduction which brings potential national production below 20 metric tonnes.[7] Eight cases of national success were identified using this outcome measurement.[8] A process trace was then conducted on the case narratives to identify and examine the interplay of multiple causal factors[9] in the process of moving from a major source of illicit opium[10] to reaching the outcome measurement of success.

While it can be difficult to uncover what motivates governments to formulate drug policy, the original study identified eight reasons for national opium suppression:

1) State extension;
2) Ideology/religion;
3) National security;
4) Rural development;
5) Export commodities;
6) Environmental protection;
7) Domestic opium consumption;
8) External pressure.

The current paper will further explore these eight reasons. It will focus its enquiry on three South-east Asian cases (Laos, Thailand and Vietnam) in order to allow for a more contextualised discussion than would be permitted by using all eight cases. The current paper will provide greater space than was given in the original monograph, and explore a new hypothesis: that all eight reasons can be categorised as founded in political economy and/or security. The significance of racism and chauvinism will also be explored.

The purpose of this paper is to provide insight into how prohibitions on opium production and cultivation came to be, and the subsequent moves to suppress the crop. The paper is not concerned with prohibitions on consumption or trade, although there are overlaps in some cases. The following section will briefly introduce the three cases.

Case summaries

Lao PDR

During the nineteenth century, highland areas of Laos witnessed a significant increase in opium production and consumption, following migration flows of ethnic groups from China.[11] Highland peoples were permitted to produce opium for their own consumption by the French authorities during the colonial period. Production, however, remained minimal until the 1950s when farmers in Laos (and Thailand and Vietnam) increased their output in response to reductions in China, India and Iran. Production was further stimulated by the Second Indochina War[12] and, during the mid-1970s, reductions in Turkey and Thailand coupled with the government's encouragement of highland farmers to cultivate opium for the pharmaceutical industry; much of which was likely diverted.[13] It was during the mid-1970s that the opium trade shifted from 'a cottage industry … to a large industrial complex'.[14]

In 1987, the International Narcotics Control Board (INCB) visited Laos. This was followed a year later by the implementation of the first United Nations (UN)–Lao development project. In 1994, the 'Comprehensive Drug Control Programme' was rolled out to suppress opium production. Inspired by the Thai model,[15] the programme centred upon a 'gradual approach'[16] in which development was sequenced before law enforcement, and small-scale production was unofficially tolerated – a toleration partly motivated by the threat of violent opposition.[17] This said, 'voluntary' resettlement of highland peoples, including opium farmers, also began in 1994. Resettlement had multiple objectives, including state extension, and reducing opium production, swidden agriculture and poverty.[18]

Decree No. 14, in 2000, signalled a major shift in Laotian policy: The complete cessation of opium production was ordered within six years, later reduced to five. The 'Accelerated Rural Development Programme'[19] officially espoused a development-oriented approach.[20] In reality, however, the development–eradication sequence of the 'gradual approach' was reversed[21] and now centred upon 'coercive negotiations'.[22] That is, farmers had to sign contracts promising to cease opium production in exchange for developmental assistance before 'voluntarily' eradicating their own opium.[23] Reports suggest that contract signing was often preceded by intimidation from the military, and uncooperative farmers were threatened with imprisonment.[24] Laos was declared 'poppy-free' by United Nations Office of Drugs and Crime (UNODC) in 2006; its national production declined by 96% between 1989 and 2006.[25]

Thailand

Opium was first brought to the territory which constitutes present-day Thailand by Chinese merchants in 1282, and was first prohibited in 1360. The prohibition was repealed in 1851 to allow Chinese migrants to consume opium.[26] While Thailand had long profited from a state opium monopoly, and was central to regional traffic, opium production had remained a cottage industry until the 1950s[27] when farmers throughout South-east Asia responded to reduced output from China, India and Iran.[28] Production was officially prohibited in 1959; however, the state's lack of authority in highland areas coupled with significant corruption meant that production increased after the ban.[29]

During the 1960s, the Thai military engaged in a repressive militarised eradication campaign to suppress opium production in areas with high communist insurgent activity.[30] By 1968, however, politicians had begun to see coercion as counterproductive to counterinsurgency objectives[31] and Thailand began sequencing development before law enforcement. A large number of development projects were administered from the 1970s onwards, often in collaboration with members of the Thai Royal Family and, the UN and other foreign development agencies.[32]

In order to allow space for rural development, laws prohibiting opium were seldom enforced before 1983. Even after 1983, crops were only eradicated once farmers had access to alternative livelihoods, and few farmers were punished.[33] The majority of eradication resulted from negotiations with farming communities,[34] centred upon the use of levers, such as offering scholarships or favourable treatment when applying for Thai citizenship.[35] As schedules of development/eradication were often negotiated with communities at the beginning of development projects, communities tended to be pre-warned, often by several years, of forced eradication.[36] In 1999, the US Department of State removed Thailand from its major drug producers list, and UNODC declared Thailand 'poppy-free' in 2002. Thailand's national production declined by 98% between the peak of production in 1970 and 2010.[37]

Vietnam

Opium is believed to have first been introduced to Vietnam in 1665, and immediately prohibited. Like Laos and Thailand, some ethnic groups have cultivated opium poppies since migrating to the highlands from China in the early/mid-nineteenth century,[38] and highland production was accepted and sporadically supported during the colonial period. Between 1975 and 1985, the Vietnamese government bought opium from ethnic highland peoples for domestic and export medicinal purposes. While the state stopped buying opium in 1985, farmers did not stop producing it and the majority of the now enlarged highland opium output was sold on the black market.[39]

Highland opium production was, however, tolerated until its official prohibition in 1992.[40] State-administered crop substitution projects were established in the early 1990s. These projects were founded upon contracts whereby farmers agreed to immediately cease producing opium in exchange for compensation or rural development. Nonetheless, while drug control was later mainstreamed into national highland development programmes, the level of development support remained insufficient.[41]

Indeed, the core of the opium suppression effort was 'coercive negotiations'. From 1992, the official policy was to immediately eradicate opium poppies. So-called 'negotiated eradication' would begin with the distribution of propaganda on the harm of opium and promises of rural development assistance. As in Laos, after 2001, the military were involved in negotiations with farmers. While the presence of the military implied coercion, there are also reports of soldiers threatening farmers. Furthermore, general reports of widespread human rights abuses of highland peoples by the military and police may suggest that the intervention was far more repressive than is publicly acknowledged.[42] Within three years, opium production had declined by 99% from its 1990 peak.[43] The following section discusses each identified reason for suppressing opium production in turn. The three cases and eight factors are summarised in Table 1.

Table 1. Reasons for opium suppression.

	Thailand	Laos	Vietnam
External pressure	✓	✓	✓
State extension	✓	✓	✓
Rural development	✓	✓	✓
Export commodities	✓	✓	
Environmental protection	✓	✓	
National security	✓		
Ideology/religion	✓	✓	✓
Domestic opium consumption	✓	✓	✓

A cross-case comparison of opium suppression motivations

External pressure and international reputation

External pressure is the reason most often cited in, and explored by, the literature for choosing to suppress opium production. The US has notoriously applied pressure on many countries including Thailand (once the Vietnam War ended), and Laos in 1971 (once the Vietnam War ended).[44] Importantly, Thailand and the US have a longstanding, and strong, security and economic relationship, including the provision of military funding and preferential trade status to Thailand.[45] The experience of Turkey, another formerly significant opium producer with a close relationship to the US, may be instructive: During the 1960s the US threatened economic sanctions and withdrawal of aid and military funding, in order to force the government to suppress opium.[46] Similar mechanisms may have been at play in Thailand. External pressure does not, however, appear to be enough. Drug-producing countries have long resisted the often aggressive lobbying of the US, UN/League of Nations and others,[47] only to succumb when suppression is perceived as beneficial to the state or powerful groups within the state.

While there is no evidence of direct pressure being applied to Vietnam, the state had recently emerged from a period of isolation and wanted to demonstrate its credentials as an active member of the international community.[48] The government of Laos also believed that the opium trade made the country look backward, which they felt presented a barrier to the national goal of losing their Least Developed Nation classification. While Laos initially witnessed little direct foreign pressure[49] – notwithstanding the INCBs 1987 visit[50] – by the late 1990s pressure to accelerate opium eradication efforts was being applied by China, the UN, US and Vietnam.[51] This led to a shift from a development-orientated approach to a more coercive law-enforcement approach which sought the total eradication of opium within five years.[52]

State extension

All three cases sought to extend the state into isolated mountainous areas populated by ethnic minority groups. In each case, state extension was a separate policy objective which ultimately merged with opium suppression.

Indeed, the Thai intervention was essentially one of 'state extension through the administration of development-orientated projects' into isolated highland areas of Northern Thailand. In this case, after identifying the limitations of more coercive approaches, eradication and law enforcement were sequenced after the state had increased its authority in opium farming areas.[53] Furthermore, in 1967, the director-general of the Department of Public Welfare announced 'the Governments main objectives' in the Northern highlands included suppressing 'poppy growing, by promoting other means of livelihood' while 'instilling in [highland peoples] a sense of belonging and national loyalty to the nation'.[54]

State extension was a stated objective in several alternative development projects in Laos, including the Palavek Alternative Development Project, the Xieng Khouang Highland Development Programme and Nonghet Alternative Development Project Programme.[55] Furthermore, both Laos and Vietnam used opium suppression as a justification for expanding existing policies designed to further assimilate highland minorities within the dominant lowland culture and politics,[56] including the dovetailing of opium suppression with resettlement of highland peoples into lowland areas.[57] For example, a 1994 Laotian policy to resettle 60% of highlanders into new or existing lowland villages was justified by parallel objectives of extending the state into formerly isolated areas and, reducing poverty and opium production.[58]

Rural development, licit export commodity development and environmental protection

Opium suppression was connected to rural development in three cases, the development of licit export commodities was connected in two and environmental protection was connected in two. Rural development is closely associated with state extension: The integration of isolated peoples and areas can be supported by road building and extension of healthcare, education,[59] agricultural support and/or national or local markets. While environmental protection can be used to control nomadic peoples by excluding or controlling movement within environmental protection areas.[60]

By the early 1970s, Thailand viewed rural development as the primary means of both extending the state and suppressing opium production, as did some local Laotian alternative development projects.[61] The stated primary objectives of several alternative development projects in Laos (ie the Shifting Cultivation Stabilization Pilot Project) and Thailand (ie the Royal Northern Project) were development first and opium suppression second,[62] while dedicated development-orientated opium suppression projects were eventually mainstreamed into national development policy in Vietnam.[63]

There has been an emphasis on environmental protection in some Laotian and Thai alternative development projects. For example, in Laos, the pre-2000 Shifting Cultivation Stabilization Pilot Project prioritised watershed protection and poverty reduction above opium suppression, while the Thai Doi Tung Development Project stated the prevention of illegal logging as one of its key objectives.[64] There is some evidence that the governments of Laos and Thailand sought to use opium suppression as a means of establishing export commodities: coffee in Thailand[65] and various industrial crops in Laos.[66]

This said, rural development, development of export trade and environmental protection tend not to be primary motivations at the national level, but may rather maintain local interventions. That is, once interventions have begun, non-governmental organizations (NGOs), inter-governmental organisations and/or state agencies begin to identify opium suppression as useful in attaining their own institutional goals, and may later become important advocates of maintaining or increasing national efforts.

Security

Thailand is the only one of the three cases to have been motivated by traditional security threats, although (as will be discussed below) all three were motivated by security if a wider constructivist definition is applied. Thailand represents one of the most interesting and insightful cases regarding the intertwining of counter-narcotic and counter-insurgency policies.

Between the early 1950s and early 1980s, Thailand experienced a communist insurgency in the northern highlands. There was 'an atmosphere of panic' within the Thai government and military that the insurgency could further destabilise fragile border areas with antagonistic neighbouring states.⁶⁷ While the Thai military had long supported anti-communist insurgents involved in drug trafficking,⁶⁸ by the mid-1950s it was forcefully and repressively eradicating opium poppies to counter insurgent fundraising. Eradication techniques included napalming and planting landmines in poppy fields, and subcontracting allied anti-communist insurgents to attack farmers who resisted eradication efforts.⁶⁹ By the mid-1960s, however, the Border Patrol Police and some officials based in Northern provinces recognised that opium eradication inflated insurgent support bases in strategically important border areas,⁷⁰ most insurgents were motivated by the tangible support promised by insurgents rather than Communist ideology,⁷¹ and some local conflicts were responses to opium eradication with no political motivation.⁷² Indeed, Morey recalls the Thai Defence Minister telling King Bhumibol Adulyadej that violent counter-insurgency operations had failed. The King suggested that the insurgency could be ended by extending agricultural development, healthcare and education.⁷³ The discussion resulted in Prime Minister Tinsulanonda issuing two policy guidelines (Orders no. 66/2523 and 65/2525) stressing development as more effective than military force in suppressing the insurgency.⁷⁴

Ideology/religion

All three cases were founded upon perceptions that consumption and/or production and trade are contrary to ideological or religious norms and values. Many modern South-east Asian prohibitions are founded upon, or inherited from, long-established prohibitions on opium and/or other intoxicants, and reflect religious and/or cultural aversions to recreational drug consumption.⁷⁵ Laotian, Thai and Vietnamese societies are, for example, heavily influenced by philosophies/theologies which dictate that individuals should consider the needs of the country and family before their own – values often perceived as undermined by drug addiction and use.⁷⁶ Religious leaders of many early Buddhist societies, for example, lobbied for prohibition on the grounds that intoxicants obstructed concentration and thus impeded the primary goal of the monkhood,⁷⁷ while: 'From a Buddhist perspective addictive behaviour may be seen as a false refuge and a source of attachment which unwittingly, but inevitably, leads to suffering'.⁷⁸

It is for this reason that many Buddhist monks have actively engaged in anti-drug campaigns, often in the form of sermons to their congregation,⁷⁹ while Vietnam's labelling of drugs as 'social evils' is often seen as a response to the fear that creeping individualism was eroding Communist values. This concern was visualised by the 1996 poster of a red fist smashing drugs.⁸⁰

Domestic opium consumption

All cases specified increased consumption as a reason for prohibiting opium production. In all cases, anxiety surrounding consumption was coupled with chauvinism and/or racism.

South-east Asian states have often enforced dual prohibitions⁸¹: tolerance of highland production (consumption and trade), and strict prohibition in the lowlands. In 1851, for example, Thailand partly repealed a long-standing prohibition in order to allow Chinese immigrants to consume state-distributed opium.⁸² Full prohibition was reinstated in 1921 as officials felt that opium was negatively impacting Thai Buddhist culture,⁸³ and restated in 1959 amid concerns over increasing domestic lowland consumption.⁸⁴ This said, while prohibition was – and continues to be[85] – well implemented throughout lowland Thailand, consumption and trade were unofficially tolerated in highland areas for many years.[86]

Vietnam also tolerated highland opium consumption, until consumption increased in the lowlands. Not only was there a drastic increase in consumption during the early/mid-1990s but increased levels of intravenous heroin use contributed to one of Asia's worst HIV epidemics.[87] Laos's ultra-prohibitionist credentials date back to 1976 when it began incarcerating drug users in forced treatment camps.[88] Before 2000, however, small-scale highland opium production was tolerated for local consumption.[89] This changed after 2000 when a more coercive approach was taken: Laos was motivated not only by external pressure, as discussed above, but by concerns over rising lowland heroin consumption.[90] Furthermore, by the late 1990s, opium had become stigmatised as a 'key symbol of primitiveness and backwardness and into a fetishised cause of poverty'[91] at a time when the popularity of methamphetamines was rising.[92] Indeed, by the end of the century, many South-east Asian states had witnessed a switch from opium/heroin to methamphetamine – a drug perceived as modern and initially associated with increased labour productivity.[93]

Racism and chauvinism are common themes in the history of drug prohibitions. Drugs are the ultimate example of what criminologists refer to as alien conspiracies – moral panics surrounding drugs which are founded in stereotypical portrayals of 'foreign' criminals and 'foreign' drugs undermining 'our' way of life. South-east Asian states have long associated opium production and consumption with minorities of Chinese descent living in highland areas.[94] As such, many South-east Asian policies have been partly a response to the spread of a foreign (ie Chinese) drug in lowland areas. Opium also has an historical association with colonial France. For example, the Vietminh Declaration of Independence stated that the French had 'forced us to use opium'.[95]

Discussion

Drug policy is seldom the outcome of economically rational processes that weigh up evidence-based costs and benefits.[96] Rather, it is often the product of years, or even decades, of institutional learning, and[97] interaction and conflict between various bureaucratic, economic and moral entrepreneurs.[98] Conflicts may, for example, arise between humanitarian organisations and security contractors, the military and the exchequer, or foreign and domestic politicians responding to the needs and interests of their respective constituents. This section, however, proposes that all the reasons discussed above for suppressing illicit opium production are founded in political economy (Table 2) and/or security (Table 3) concerns. That is, economic and security considerations will ultimately take precedence over other

Table 2. Political economy reasons for opium suppression.

	Thailand	Laos	Vietnam
External pressure	✓	✓	✓
State extension	✓	✓	✓
Rural development	✓	✓	✓
Export commodities	✓	✓	
Environmental protection	✓	✓	
National security	✓		
Ideology/religion	✓	✓	✓
Domestic opium consumption	✓	✓	✓

Table 3. Security reasons for opium suppression.

	Thailand	Laos	Vietnam
External pressure	✓	✓	✓
State extension	✓	✓	✓
Rural development	✓	✓	✓
Export commodities	✓	✓	
Environmental protection	✓	✓	
National security	✓		
Ideology/religion	✓	✓	✓
Domestic opium consumption	✓	✓	✓

considerations in drug policy decision-making. Economic and security reasons are not mutually exclusive.[99] For example, both security and development contracting are profitable enterprises, while development can represent an effective long-term counter-insurgency strategy.

Economic considerations

Criminologists have long highlighted the influence of political economy on all aspects of criminal justice and drugs policy.[100] In terms of rural development and export commodities, the South-east Asian highlands have been, and still are, seen as untapped sources of labour, agricultural goods and tourism.[101] The Chinese government's Green Anti-Drug Project, for example, sought to suppress opium by enticing private agricultural companies to establish cash crop plantations in opium growing areas[102] – a 'drug policy' which should be viewed as part of the wider global land-grab phenomenon. Environmental protection also relates to political economy, with lowlanders often concerned that agricultural productivity will be reduced by highland slash-and-burn farming practices perceived as damaging flood defences or water quality and quantity.

All of the cases used opium suppression as a means of extending the state. From a political economy perspective, state extension may represent a means of integrating formerly isolated peoples into national economic systems – ensuring they buy from and sell to national markets, pay taxes, and produce exportable commodities. That is, state extension represents a process to both 'integrate and monetize the people'.[103] For example, in Vietnam, some Hmong farmers adapted to opium bans by producing black cardamom due to its 'increasing market demand',[104] while the Thai Department of Public Welfare was explicit that developing 'the economic and social conditions of hill tribes … may contribute to the national development'.[105] Furthermore, state extension in Laos, Thailand and Vietnam may have provided workforce expansion to keep pace with rapidly expanding national economies and increased agricultural output to feed growing urban populations.

Thailand is the guiding light of what can be achieved through alternative development. Not only has the country integrated highland peoples into lowland national markets, but both highland and lowland peoples have capitalised on Thailand's former status as a source of opium. For example, Doi Tung coffee shops – selling goods ranging from coffee to clothing and ornaments – are situated in prime locations, including Bangkok Airport and Jatujak Market, while opium tourism is big business in Thailand, as well as Laos and Vietnam: Tourists can trek into the jungle to gawk at former opium farmers, visit the opium museum and have their photo taken at the official 'Golden Triangle' (a sign at the Thai border overlooking Burma and Laos). Opium may no longer be a significant tradable commodity in the Thai highlands, but the myth of the trade certainly is.

Furthermore, the perception of the opium trade as backward and old fashioned, a theme running through the Laos narratives, links well to a political economy perspective. For example, Cohen suggests that the replacement of opium with industrial crops became symbolic 'of all that is modern and progressive, in contrast to the primitiveness and backwardness of opium'.[106] In some respects, these symbols of modernisation are designed to attract foreign investment.

Finally, Courtwright has shown how, in the UK and US, consumption of opium and opiates, which had been tolerated during the nineteenth century, gradually became viewed as deviant once their popularity declined with middle-/upper-class consumers and increased with working-class consumers.[107] Industrialists lobbied for prohibition amid concern that opium/opiate consumption by the working classes would reduce economic productivity.[108] It may be that, in South-east Asia, the state was willing to tolerate opium and opiate consumption in the highlands due to the perceived lack of integration into national economic systems. That is, if highlanders were living in self-contained economic bubbles, with little import or export to the lowlands, then opium consumption posed little threat to the national economy. Opium and opiates may, however, have begun to be perceived as a threat to the national economy when consumption by working-class lowlanders increased, and highlanders became viewed as an extension of the lowland workforce.

Security considerations

Policies to counter opium production may also follow Buzan and colleagues' securitisation process. In essence, security, as defined by Buzan and colleagues, is about the survival of 'referent objects', such as the state, or national sovereignty, religions or cultures. Securitisation is a response to existential threats to these referent objects. During the securitisation process an actor or actors – whether government, NGO or media – perform 'speech acts' in which an issue is presented as 'threatening the breakdown or ruin' of the referent object. Acceptance of the issue as a security threat by the audience elevates it and permits – indeed requires – the state to break its own norms of behaviour[109] or form new norms.[110] While confines of space limit an exploration into specific speech acts, we can identify where states were motivated by perceived existential threats.[111]

The opium trade has long been perceived as a traditional threat to national security. This is most well documented in China where, since the early nineteenth century, opium consumption has been believed to sap the strength of the military and thus limit the state's ability to defend itself against foreign and domestic threats. China was not alone in such fears. For example, the US has long held the same anxiety, dating back to the Civil War when opium addiction was referred to as the 'army disease'.[112] Thailand identified the opium trade as a source of revenue for insurgents, and it is likely that US military aid was used as leverage in negotiations.

Opium consumption has been seen as an existential threat to Buddhism, and Communism. Thailand, in 1921, was explicit in proclaiming opium a threat to Thai Buddhist culture.[113] In Vietnam, the portrayal of drugs as a 'social evil' was indicative of the government's perception of drug as a threat to Communism. Indeed, the 2000 'Law on Preventing and Combating Narcotic Drugs' explicitly states 'The drug problem poses a major threat to the entire society

… gravely affecting social order and safety and national security."[114] As Buddhism and Communism represent elements of the ideas which hold the state together,[115] threats to them can be seen as threats to the state itself.

Finally, the alien conspiracy perspective can be usefully combined with securitisation to further explore the issues of race and nationality.[116] The alien conspiracy perspective argues that states and the media often use racial or national stereotypes to identify 'foreign' criminals or objects as threats to societal values and interests.[117] This indicates that the threat has been imported from abroad, sparking a distinct form of moral panic centred upon the foreign actor or object. Such moral panics politicise the object. Securitisation is, in many respects, an extreme response to such moral panics. That is, an issue may take on alien conspiracy elements when the moral panic revolves around 'foreign' dealers or drugs, and becomes securitised when foreign actors or drugs are identified as posing an *existential* threat to a referent object. In all three cases opposition to opium was partly a response to the spread of a 'Chinese' drug, produced by isolated ethnic groups of Chinese descent, into lowland areas.

Securitisation can, and often does, result in more repressive policies.[118] Securitising *can*, however, result in more humane policy.[119] Indeed, very repressive drug crop suppression policies in politically unstable areas can have serious repercussions for national security. The most extreme example of this is the exceptionally repressive opium ban enforced in China during 1906–1917, which appears to have been a contributing factor in the fragmentation of the Chinese state.[120] Indeed, research on the psychology of terrorism suggests that perceived injustice – often an outcome of more repressive counter-terrorism policies – is a key motivation for engaging in political violence against the state.[121] And it is not difficult to see how removing a farmer's source of income can be perceived as unjust to those targeted by forced eradication and punishment. As such, repressive interventions can ignite traditional security threats, depending on local context. When Thailand identified the repressive suppression of opium as contributing to security threats during the mid-1960s it designed a humane development-orientated intervention which would extend the state into formerly isolated highland areas whilst pilfering political capital from insurgents.[122] That is, while most interventions are ignited by a combination of economic and (often racialised) security concerns, humane development-orientated policies can represent pragmatic approaches from both economic and security perspectives.

Conclusion

This paper was intended as a preliminary foray into why governments choose to suppress the production of illicit drug crops. While the complexity of drug policy decision-making is acknowledged, the comparison highlights how five factors featured in all three cases. While external pressure, often from the US or UN/League of Nations, is the most commonly identified reason in the literature, and was experienced in each case, it was not by itself sufficient to motivate states into action. All three cases were motivated by religious or ideological opposition to drug consumption or trade, rural development, state extension and concern for increasing domestic drug consumption. Apprehension about rising drug consumption often possessed racial or chauvinistic elements. The development of export commodities and environmental protection were identified in two cases, and traditional national security was identified as motivating factor in one case.

It is hypothesised that each of these factors, alone or, more likely, in combination, can be categorised as founded in political economy and/or (often racialised) security considerations. Identifying these underlying considerations highlights that illicit drug crops will only become a national priority when the issue is framed as a threat to the security of a referent object and/or the act of suppression is perceived as providing some economic benefit.

That drug crop suppression is founded in political economy and security draws from a long tradition of research into security and criminal justice policymaking,[123] yet in this context requires further investigation. Future research should address the following issues: (1) assess the chronological sequence for each case, in order to illuminate the processes towards suppression; (2) securitising speech acts (and actors), and reactions to such, should be systematically analysed to assess the extent and outcome of securitisation in source country drug control; and (3) analysis of a greater number of cases would provide insight into the generalisability of these findings.

Disclosure statement

No potential conflict of interest was reported by the author.

Acknowledgements

An early draft of this paper was presented at the symposium 'Drugs, Politics and Society in the Global South'. My thanks to Maziyar Ghiabi for organising the symposium, and the symposium members for thoughtful and constructive comments.

Notes

1. See Galeotti, *Narcotics and Nationalism*; US State Department, *International Narcotics Control Strategy*; Zhang and Chin, *A People's War*.
2. See Tullis, *Unintended Consequences*; Windle, "Harms Caused"; Windle, *Suppressing Illicit Opium Production*.
3. Wilson and Stevens, *Understanding Drug Markets*.
4. Caulkins and Hao, "Modelling Drug Market Supply Disruptions."
5. Pietschmann, "Price-Setting Behaviour."
6. Windle, *Suppressing Illicit Opium Production*.
7. Ibid.
8. The eight cases were China (Imperial/Republican), Iran, People's Republic of China, Turkey, Thailand, Pakistan, Laos and Vietnam.
9. George and Bennett, *Case Studies and Theory Development*.
10. To be included in the study the case had to have produced, at a minimum, an excess of 50 metric tonnes of opium per year for five years and be situated in the Asian/Middle Eastern 'opium zone'.

The intervention had to have taken place during the twentieth century. A full methodological discussion can be found in Windle, *Suppressing Illicit Opium Production*.
11. Culas, "Migrants, Runaways and Opium Growers"; also Culas and Michaud, "Contribution to the Study of Hmong."
12. See McCoy, *Politics of Heroin*; and Holiday, "Her Majesty's Ambassador's Visit."
13. G. Lee, "Minority Policies and the Hmong"; see also US State Department, "State Department Report to Congress."
14. Westermeyer, *Poppies, Pipes and People*, 274.
15. Windle, *Suppressing Illicit Opium Production*.
16. Boonwaat, "Balanced Approach to Opium Elimination"; Chansina, "Lao PDR's Experience."
17. Sirivong, "UN–Nonghet Alternative Development Project."
18. Baird and Shoemaker, "Unsettling Experiences."
19. Government of Laos, *Strategic Programme Framework*; UNODC, *Laos Opium Survey 2005*.
20. Boonwaat, "Balanced Approach to Opium Elimination."
21. Baird and Shoemaker, "Unsettling Experiences"; Kramer, Jelsma, and Blickman, *Withdrawal Symptoms in the Golden Triangle*.
22. Windle, "Suppression of Illicit Opium Production."
23. Boonwaat, "Balanced Approach to Opium Elimination"; US State Department, *International Narcotics Control Strategy Report* (2006 and 2009).
24. See Dze, "State Policies, Shifting Cultivation"; Kramer, Jelsma, and Blickman, *Withdrawal Symptoms in the Golden Triangle*; Lyttleton, "Relative Pleasures"; Pathan, "Opium Wars."
25. Windle, *Suppressing Illicit Opium Production*.
26. Windle, "How the East Influenced."
27. Morlock, "Limitation on the Production of Opium."
28. McCoy, *Politics of Heroin*; Renard, *Opium Reduction in Thailand*.
29. Windle, *Suppressing Illicit Opium Production*.
30. Economist, "Thailand: The Other Rebellions."
31. Ibid; Marks, "Meo Hill Tribe Problem."
32. Windle, *Suppressing Illicit Opium Production*.
33. Renard, *Opium Reduction in Thailand*.
34. Chotpimai, "Third Army Area Narcotics."
35. Renard, *Opium Reduction in Thailand*.
36. R. Lee, "Controlling Production of Opiates"; Renard, *Opium Reduction in Thailand*.
37. Windle, *Suppressing Illicit Opium Production*.
38. Culas and Michaud, "Contribution to the Study of Hmong."
39. Boonwaat, "Overview of Alternative Development."
40. Rapin et al., *Ethnic Minorities, Drug Use*.
41. Windle, "Suppression of Illicit Opium Production."
42. Ibid.
43. Windle, *Suppressing Illicit Opium Production*.
44. See McCoy, *Politics of Heroin*.
45. Chanlett-Avery, *Thailand: Background and US Relations*.
46. See Gingeras, *Heroin, Organized Crime*; Windle, "Very Gradual Suppression."
47. See Collins, *Regulations and Prohibitions*; Gingeras, *Heroin, Organized Crime*.
48. Cima, "Vietnam's Economic Reform"; Morey, *United Nations at Work*.
49. Cohen, "Symbolic Dimensions"; Lyttleton, "Relative Pleasures."
50. League of Nations and UN bodies have long played a significant role in lobbying states to enforce prohibitions and particular drug policies and strategies. For an in-depth discussion see Collins, *Regulations and Prohibitions*.
51. Kramer, Jelsma, and Blickman, *Withdrawal Symptoms in the Golden Triangle*.
52. Windle, *Suppressing Illicit Opium Production*.
53. Windle, *Suppressing Illicit Opium Production*, 97.
54. Cited in Keyes, "Buddhism and National Integration," 564.

55. See Bendiksen, "Marketing"; Sirivong, "UN–Nonghet Alternative Development Project"; UNDTCD, "Crop Substitution in Laotian Highlands."
56. See Corlin, "Hmong and the Land Question."
57. See Baird and Shoemaker, "Unsettling Experiences"; Bird, *'Voluntary' Migration*.
58. Baird and Shoemaker, "Unsettling Experiences."
59. Education has often been used as a means of cultural integration throughout South-east Asia: Michaud and Forsyth, *Moving Mountains*; Michaud, "Handling Mountain Minorities."
60. See Gilbert, *Nomadic Peoples and Human Rights*.
61. See Renard, *Opium Reduction in Thailand*; Windle, *Suppressing Illicit Opium Production*.
62. See Asian Development Bank, *Sector Assistance Program Evaluation*; Chareonpanich, "Integration of Crop Replacement Projects."
63. Rapin et al., *Ethnic Minorities, Drug Use*.
64. Asian Development Bank, *Sector Assistance Program Evaluation*; Nardone, "From Opium to Arabica."
65. Rosequist, "Narcotics and Agricultural Economics."
66. See Cohen, "Post-Opium Scenario"; Windle, *Suppressing Illicit Opium Production*.
67. Handley, *The King Never Smiles*, 185.
68. McCoy, *Politics of Heroin*.
69. See Chandola, "The Politics of Opium"; Economist, "Thailand: The Other Rebellions"; Gua, "Opium, Bombs and Trees."
70. Campbell, "Thais Hesitate to Wreck"; Economist, "Thailand: The Other Rebellions."
71. Girling, "Northeast Thailand: Tomorrow's Vietnam?"
72. Culas and Michaud, "Contribution to the Study of Hmong."
73. Morey, *United Nations at Work*, 73.
74. Thomas, "Communist Insurgency in Thailand."
75. Windle, "How the East."
76. Buddhism in Thailand, and a mixture of Communism, Confucianism and/or Buddhism in China, Laos and Vietnam.
77. Windle, "How the East."
78. Groves and Roger, "Buddhism and Addictions."
79. Ladwig, "Between Cultural Preservation."
80. McNally, "HIV in Contemporary Vietnam."
81. See Collins, *Regulations and Prohibitions*.
82. Windle, "How the East."
83. League of Nations, *Commission of Enquiry*.
84. Jinawat, "Thailand Country Paper."
85. Windle, "Security Trumps Drug Control." Contemporary Thailand's approach to lowland drug consumption may be termed 'ultra-prohibitionist', and zero-tolerance approaches often receive strong support from the general public.
86. Gibson, *Narcotics Trade in North Thailand*; McCoy, *Politics of Heroin*.
87. Windle, *Slow March from Social Evil*.
88. Daviau, "Integration of a Lineage Society."
89. Epprecht, "Blessing of the Poppy"; Kramer, Jelsma, and Blickman, *Withdrawal Symptoms in the Golden Triangle*.
90. Lyttleton et al., *Watermelons, Bars and Trucks*.
91. Cohen, "Symbolic Dimensions," 177.
92. Lyttleton, "Relative Pleasures."
93. See Chouvy and Meissonnier, *Yaa Baa*.
94. See Corlin, "Hmong and the Land Question."
95. The UK and US also associated opium with Chinese migrants during the late nineteenth and early twentieth centuries. Indeed, there were a number of moral panics regarding 'opium dens in Chinatowns' threatening 'to contaminate the West, with young white girls being ravished by sinister Orientals in these squalid places of sexual depravity and degenerate racial mixing'. The Chinese have, conversely, long portrayed opium in conspiratorial terms as a tool used by

their enemies (ie British, Japanese and later domestic class enemies) to weaken the state and its peoples: Dikötter, Laamann, and Xun, *Narcotic Culture*, 94; see also Kohn, "Dope Girls."
96. Monaghan, *Evidence versus Politics*.
97. Windle, "Very Gradual Suppression."
98. Collins, *Regulations and Prohibitions*; Windle, "How the East"; see also Becker, *Outsiders*.
99. See Buzan, Wæver, and de Wilde, *Security: A New Framework for Analysis*, 195.
100. See Reiner, "Political Economy, Crime and Criminal Justice."
101. See for example Delang, "Deforestation in Northern Thailand"; Scott, *The Art of Not Being Governed*; Quang, "Hmong and Forest Management."
102. Bendiksen, "Marketing"; Kramer, Jelsma, and Blickman, *Withdrawal Symptoms in the Golden Triangle*.
103. Scott, *The Art of Not Being Governed*, 4.
104. Tugault-Lafleur and Turner, "Of Rice and Spice," 112.
105. Cited in Keyes, "Buddhism and National Integration," 564.
106. Cohen, "Post-Opium Scenario," 248.
107. Courtwright, *Dark Paradise*.
108. Levine and Reinarman, "From Prohibition to Regulation."
109. Buzan, Wæver, and de Wilde, *Security: A New Framework for Analysis*, 23, 148.
110. Abrahamsen, *Blair's Africa*.
111. For examples of securitising speech acts on Asian drug policy, see Emmers, "ASEAN and the Securitization"; Windle "Security Trumps Drug Control"; and, under international law and in Russia, Crick, "Drugs as an Existential Threat."
112. Collins, 'Empire, War, Decolonisation'.
113. League of Nations, *Commission of Enquiry*.
114. Government of Vietnam, *Law on Preventing and Combating*.
115. Buzan, Wæver, and de Wilde, *Security: A New Framework for Analysis*.
116. Alien conspiracy and securitisation perspectives can both be traced to early constructivists, such as Howard Becker who analysed moral entrepreneurs lobbying for cannabis prohibition in the US, which resulted in 'the establishment of a new set of rules' (ie prohibition). Becker's original conception of moral entrepreneurs is, however, a little naïve in its belief that they seek 'to help those beneath them to achieve a better status', and thus ignores economic or political considerations. Becker, *Outsiders*, 149, 152.
117. Smith, *Mafia Mystique*.
118. See Crick, "Drugs as an Existential Threat."
119. Windle, "Security Trumps Drug Control."
120. Windle, "Harms Caused."
121. Silke, "Fire of Iolus."
122. Similarly, in the early 1970s, Turkey identified the threat suppression posed to political stability and implemented a strict regulated and taxable licit trade.
123. See Buzan, Wæver, and de Wilde, *Security: A New Framework for Analysis*; Reiner, "Political Economy, Crime and Criminal Justice."

Bibliography

Abrahamsen, R. "Blair's Africa: The Politics of Securitization and Fear." *Alternatives* 30, no. 1 (2005): 55–80.
Asian Development Bank. *Sector Assistance Program Evaluation for the Agriculture and Natural Resources Sector in the Lao People's Democratic Republic*. SAP: LAO 2005-17, 2005.
Baird, I., and B. Shoemaker. "Unsettling Experiences: Internal Resettlement and International Aid Agencies in Laos." *Development and Change* 38, no. 5 (2007): 865–888.
Becker, H. *Outsiders*. New York: Free Press, 1963.
Bendiksen, L. "Marketing – The Bottleneck of Opium Eradication? Experiences from East Asia in Marketing Alternative Development Products." In *Experiences from East Asia in Marketing Alternative Development Products Regional Seminar on Alternative Development, 12–16 March, 2001*. Bangkok: Thammada Press, 2002.

Bird, K. *Voluntary Migration in Lao People's Democratic Republic*. London: Overseas Development Institute, 2009. Accessed April 20, 2010. https://www.odi.org.uk/resources/download/2505.pdf.

Boonwaat, L. "An Overview of Alternative Development and Illicit Crop Eradication Policies, Strategies and Actions in the Region." In *Alternative Development: Sharing Good Practices Facing Common Problems*, UNDCP, 129–149. Myanmar: UNDCP, 2001.

Boonwaat, L. "The Balanced Approach to Opium Elimination in the Laos PDR." In *Poverty Reduction and Shifting Cultivation Stabilisation in the Uplands of Lao PDR*. Accessed March 14, 2010. https://www.nafri.org.la/document/uplandproceedings/TOC.pdf.

Buzan, B., O. Wæver, and J. de Wilde. *Security: A New Framework for Analysis*. London: Lynne Rienner, 1998.

Campbell, C. "Thais Hesitate to Wreck Opium Fields of Tribes." *New York Times*, February 20, 1983.

Caulkins, J. P., and H. Hao. "Modelling Drug Market Supply Disruptions: Where Do All the Drugs Not Go?" *Journal of Policy Modelling* 30, no. 2 (2009): 251–270.

Chandola, H. "The Politics of Opium." *Economic and Political Weekly* 11, no. 23 (1976): 832–833.

Chanlett-Avery, E. *Thailand: Background and US Relations. Congressional Research Service*, 2010. Accessed July 10, 2017. https://fas.org/sgp/crs/row/RL32593.pdf

Chansina, K. "Lao PDR's Experience of Sustainable Alternative Development and Opium Reduction." In *Sustaining Opium Reduction in Southeast Asia: Sharing Experiences on Alternative Development and beyond*, edited by UNODC, 37–49. Chiang Mai: UNODC, 2009.

Chareonpanich, C. "Integration of Crop Replacement Projects in National Rural Development Plan in Thailand." In *Regional Seminar on Replacement of Opium Poppy Cultivation, December 14–19, 1987*. Chiang Mai: UNDP, 1987.

Chotpimai, Y. "Third Army Area Narcotics Crops Cultivation Control Programme." *Regional Seminar on Replacement of Opium Poppy Cultivation, December 14–19, 1987*. Chiang Mai: UNDP, 1987.

Chouvy, P. A., and J. Meissonnier. *Yaa Baa: Production, Traffic, and Consumption of Methamphetamine in Mainland Southeast Asia*. Singapore: NUS, 2004.

Cima, R. J. "Vietnam's Economic Reform: Approaching the 1990s." *Asian Survey* 29, no. 8 (1989): 786–799.

Cohen, P. T. "The Post-Opium Scenario and Rubber in Northern Laos: Alternative Western and Chinese Models of Development." *International Journal of Drug Policy* 20, no. 5 (2009): 424–430.

Cohen, P. T. "Symbolic Dimensions of the Anti-Opium Campaign in Laos." *The Australian Journal of Anthropology* 24, no. 2 (2013): 177–192.

Collins, J. *Regulations and Prohibitions: Anglo-American Relations and International Drug Control, 1939–1964*. London: LSE, 2015.

Collins, J. "Empire, War, Decolonisation and the Birth of the Illicit Opium Trade in Burma, 1800–1961." In *Historical Perspectives on Organised Crime and Terrorism*, edited by J. Windle, J. F. Morrison, A. Winter, and A. Silke. Abingdon: Routledge, forthcoming.

Corlin, C. "Hmong and the Land Question in Vietnam: National Policy Concepts of the Environment." In *Hmong/Miao in Asia*, edited by N. Tapp, J. Michaud, C. Culas, and G. Lee, 295–320. Bangkok: Silkworm, 2004.

Courtwright, D. *Dark Paradise: Opiate Addiction in America before 1940*. Oxford Harvard University Press, 1982.

Crick, E. "Drugs as an Existential Threat: An Analysis of the International Securitization of Drugs." *International Journal of Drug Policy* 23, no. 5 (2012): 407–414.

Culas, C. "Migrants, Runaways and Opium Growers: Origins of the Hmong in Laos and Siam in the Nineteenth and Early Twentieth Century." In *Turbulent Times and Enduring Peoples: Mountain Minorities in the South-East Asian Massif*, edited by J. Michaud, 29–51. Surrey: Curzon, 2000.

Culas, C., and J. Michaud. "A Contribution to the Study of Hmong (Miao) Migrations and History." *Bijdragen Tot De Taal-, Land- En Volkenkunde* 153, no. 2 (1997): 211–243.

Daviau, S. "Integration of a Lineage Society on the Laos-Vietnam Border." In *Moving Mountains: Ethnicity and Livelihoods in Highland China, Vietnam and Laos*, edited by J. Michaud and T. Forsyth, 50–76. Vancouver: UBC, 2011.

Delang, C. O. "Deforestation in Northern Thailand: The Result of Hmong Farming Practices or Thai Development Strategies?" *Society and Natural Resources* 15, no. 6 (2002): 483–501.

Dikötter, F., L. Laamann, and Z. Xun. *Narcotic Culture: A History of Drugs in China*. London: Hurst, 2004.

Dze, M. "State Policies, Shifting Cultivation and Indigenous Peoples in Laos." *Indigenous Affairs* 2 (2005): 31–37.

Economist. "Thailand: The Other Rebellions." *The Economist*, March 29, 1969.

Emmers, R. "ASEAN and the Securitization of Transnational Crime in Southeast Asia." *The Pacific Review* 16, no. 3 (2003): 419–438.

Epprecht, M. "The Blessing of the Poppy: Opium and the Akha People of Northern Laos." *Indigenous Affairs* 4, no. 1 (2000): 17–25.

Galeotti, M. *Narcotics and Nationalism: Russian Drug Policies and Futures*. Brookings Institute, 2015. Accessed January 6, 2017. https://www.brookings.edu//media/Research/Files/Papers/2015/04/global-drug-policy/Galeotti-Russiafinal.pdf?la¼en.

George, A., and A. L. Bennett. *Case Studies and Theory Development in the Social Sciences*. London: MIT Press, 2005.

Gibson, D. J. *The Narcotics Trade in North Thailand*. Kew London: British National Archives: FO 371/186181, 1966.

Gilbert, J. *Nomadic Peoples and Human Rights*. Abingdon: Routledge, 2014.

Gingeras, R. *Heroin, Organized Crime, and the Making of Modern Turkey*. Oxford: Oxford University Press, 2014.

Girling, J. L. "Northeast Thailand: Tomorrow's Vietnam?" *Foreign Affairs* 46, no. 2 (1968): 388–397.

Government of Laos. *Strategic Programme Framework: Laos PDR 2006-2009*. Accessed April 3, 2008. https://www.unodc.org/pdf/laopdr/publications/lao_strategic_programme_framework_2006-2009.pdf.

Government of Vietnam. *The Law on Preventing and Combating Narcotic Drugs*, 2000. Accessed May 19, 2015. https://www.unodc.org/enl/showDocument.do?documentUid=2304&cuntry=VIE.

Groves, P., and F. Roger. "Buddhism and Addictions." *Addiction Research* 2, no. 2 (1994): 183–194.

Gua, B. "Opium, Bombs and Trees: The Future of H'mong Tribesmen in Northern Thailand." *Journal of Contemporary Asia* 5, no. 1 (1975): 70–81.

Handley, P. M. *The King Never Smiles: A Biography of Thailand's Bhumibol Adulyadej*. London: Yale University Press, 2006.

Holiday, L. G. *Her Majesty's Ambassador's Visit to Northern Laos*. Kew London: British National Archives: FO 371/137058. January 8, 1957.

Jinawat, P. "Thailand Country Paper." In *Alternative Development: Sharing Good Practices Facing Common Problems*, edited by UNDCP, 63–73. Myanmar: UNDCP, 2001.

Keyes, C. F. "Buddhism and National Integration in Thailand." *Journal of Asian Studies* 30, no. 3 (1971): 551–567.

Kohn, M. *Dope Girls: The Birth of the British Drug Underground*. London: Granta Books, 2013.

Kramer, T., M. Jelsma, and T. Blickman. *Withdrawal Symptoms in the Golden Triangle: A Drugs Market in Disarray*. Amsterdam: Transational Institute, 2009.

Ladwig, P. "Between Cultural Preservation and This-Worldly Commitment: Modernization, Social Activism and the Lao Buddhist Sangha." In *Nouvellesrecherchessur Le Laos*, edited by Y. Goudineau and M. Lorillard, 465–490. Vientiane: EFEO, 2008.

League of Nations. *Commission of Enquiry into the Control of Opium-Smoking in the Far East: Report to the Council*. C.635.M.254.1930, 1930.

Lee, G. "Minority Policies and the Hmong." In *Contemporary Laos: Studies in the Politics and Society of the Lao People's Democratic Republic*, edited by M. Stuart-Fox, 199–219. London: University of Queensland Press, 1982.

Lee, R. "Controlling Production of Opiates: The Case of Thailand." In *The Economics of the Narcotics Industry Conference*. Washington DC: US Department of State, 1994.

Levine, H. G., and C. Reinarman. "From Prohibition to Regulation: Lessons from Alcohol Policy for Drug Policy." *The Milbank Quarterly* 69, no. 3 (1991): 461–494.

Lyttleton, C. "Relative Pleasures: Drugs, Development and Modern Dependencies in Asia's Golden Triangle." *Development and Change* 35, no. 5 (2004): 909–935.

Lyttleton, C., P. Cohen, H. Rattanavong, B. Thongkhamhane, and S. Sisaengrat. *Watermelons, Bars and Trucks: Dangerous Intersection in Northwest Lao PDR*. Sydney: Rockefeller Foundation, 2004.

Marks, T. "The Meo Hill Tribe Problem in North Thailand." *Asian Survey* 13, no. 10 (1973): 929–944.

McCoy, A. *The Politics of Heroin: CIA Complicity in the Global Drug Trade*. Chicago, IL: Lawrence Hill, 2003.

McNally, S. P. "HIV in Contemporary Vietnam: An Anthropology of Development." PhD diss., The Australian National University, 2002.

Michaud, J. "Handling Mountain Minorities in China, Vietnam and Laos: From History to Current Concerns." *Asian Ethnicity* 10, no. 1 (2009): 25–49.

Michaud, J., and T. Forsyth. *Moving Mountains: Ethnicity and Livelihoods in Highland China, Vietnam and Laos*. Vancouver: UBC, 2011.

Monaghan, M. *Evidence Versus Politics: Exploiting Research in UK Drug Policy Making?* Bristol: Policy Press, 2011.

Morey, R. *The United Nations at Work: An Envoy's Account of Development in China, Vietnam, Thailand and the South Pacific*. Jefferson: McFarlane, 2014.

Morlock, G. A. "Limitation on the Production of Opium." *Department of State Bulletin*, 6 no. 285 (1944): 723–727.

Nardone, S. "From Opium to Arabica." *Bangkok Post*, June 15, 2008.

Pathan, D. "Opium Wars." *The Nation*, May 22, 2003.

Pietschmann, T. "Price-Setting Behaviour in the Heroin Market." *Bulletin of Narcotics* 56, no. 1 (2004): 105–139.

Quang, V. D. "The Hmong and Forest Management in Northern Vietnam's Mountainous Areas." In *Hmong/Miao in Asia*, edited by N. Tapp, J. Michaud, C. Culas, and G. Lee, 321–330. Bangkok: Silkworm, 2004.

Rapin, A., D. H. Khue, D. N. Duc, J. Eyres, V. C. Tran, P. Higgs, and N. V. Duan. *Ethnic Minorities, Drug Use and Harm in the Highlands of Northern Vietnam: A Contextual Analysis of the Situation in Six Communes from Son La, Lai Chau, and Lao Cai*. Bangkok: UNODC, 2003.

Reiner, R. "Political Economy, Crime and Criminal Justice." In *The Oxford Handbook of Criminology*, edited by M. Maguire, R. Morgan, and R. Reiner, 341–381. Oxford: Oxford University Press, 2007.

Renard, R. *Opium Reduction in Thailand 1970–2000: A Thirty Year Journey*. Chiang Mai: Silkworm, 2001.

Rosequist, E. "Narcotics and Agricultural Economics." In *Economics of the Narcotics Industry Conference*. Washington: US Department of State, 1994.

Scott, J. C. *The Art of Not Being Governed*. London: Yale University Press, 2009.

Silke, A. "Fire of Iolus: The Role of State Countermeasures in Causing Terrorism and What Needs to Be Done." In *Root Causes of Terrorism*, edited by T. Bjorgo, 241–255. Abingdon: Routledge, 2005.

Sirivong, B. "UN-Nonghet Alternative Development Project." In *Alternative Development: Sharing Good Practices Facing Common Problems*, edited by UNDCP, 19–23. Myanmar: UNDCP, 2001.

Smith, D. C. *The Mafia Mystique*. New York: Basic, 1975.

Thomas, M. L. "Communist Insurgency in Thailand: Factors Contributing to Its Decline." *Asian Affairs* 13, no. 1 (1986): 17–26.

Tugault-Lafleur, C., and S. Turner. "Of Rice and Spice: Hmong Livelihoods and Diversification in the Northern Vietnam Uplands." In *Moving Mountains: Ethnicity and Livelihoods in Highland China, Vietnam and Laos*, edited by J. Michaud and T. Forsyth, 100–123. Vancouver: UBC, 2011.

Tullis, L. *Unintended Consequences: Illegal Drugs and Drug Policies in Nine Countries*. London: Boulder, 1995.

UNDTCD (UN Department for Technical Cooperation and Development). "Crop Substitution in Laotian Highlands." *DTCD News* 4, no. 3 (1991): 1–2.

UNODC (UN Office of Drugs and Crime). *Laos Opium Survey* 2005. Bangkok: UNODC, 2005

US State Department. "State Department Report to Congress on: Narcotics in Laos, 1988." In *Laos: Beyond Revolution*, edited by J. Zasloff and L. Unger, 321–323. Hampshire: Macmillan, 1988.

US State Department. *International Narcotics Control Strategy Report*. Washington: US State Department, 2006.

US State Department. *International Narcotics Control Strategy Report*. Washington: US State Department, 2009.

Westermeyer, J. *Poppies, Pipes and People: Opium and Its Use in Laos*. Oxford: Oxford University Press, 1982.

Wilson, L., and A. Stevens. *Understanding Drug Markets and How to Influence Them*. Oxford: Beckley Foundation, 2008.

Windle, J. "The Suppression of Illicit Opium Production in Viet Nam: An Introductory Narrative." *Crime, Law and Social Change* 57, no. 4 (2012): 425–439.

Windle, J. "Harms Caused by China's 1906–17 Opium Suppression Intervention." *International Journal of Drug Policy* 24, no. 5 (2013): 498–505.

Windle, J. "How the East Influenced Drug Prohibition." *The International History Review* 35, no. 5 (2013): 1185–1199.

Windle, J. "A Very Gradual Suppression: A History of Turkish Opium Controls, 1933–1974." *European Journal of Criminology* 11, no. 2 (2014): 195–212.

Windle, J. "A Slow March from Social Evil to Harm Reduction: Drugs and Drug Policy in Vietnam." *Journal of Drug Policy Analysis* (2015). doi:10.1515/jdpa-2015-0011

Windle, J. "Security Trumps Drug Control: How Securitization Explains Drug Policy Paradoxes in Thailand and Vietnam." *Drugs: Education, Prevention and Policy* 23, no. 4 (2016): 344–354.

Windle, J. *Suppressing Illicit Opium Production: Successful Intervention in Asia and the Middle East*. London: IB Tauris, 2016.

Zhang, S., and K. Chin. *A People's War: China's Struggle to Contain Its Illicit Drug Problem*. Brookings Institute, 2015. Accessed January 6, 2017. https://www.brookings.edu/research/papers/2015/04/global-drug-policy.

Index

Note:
Page numbers in *italics* refer to figures
Page numbers in **bold** refer to tables
Page numbers followed by 'n' refer to notes

Abraham, I. 160
Accelerated Rural Development Programme (Laos) 176
Acevedo, Ramón 45
addiction markets 6, 7
addiction treatment *see* Upper Amazon (Peru), Pentecostal addiction treatment ministries in
Advisory Council on the Misuse of Drugs (UK) 162
Afghanistan (southwest), settlement and poppy cultivation in 22, 139–140; Bakwa 149–152, *150*; balloon effect 22, 139–140, 146, 153; Boghra Canal 146–149, *147*; case studies 146–152; consolidation during Taliban years 142–143; counternarcotics efforts 144, 152; cultivation between 1987 and 2013 *144*; cultivation in Hemland (2001–2013) *145*; emergence of widespread cultivation 141–142; expansion and shifting patterns of cultivation under statebuilding project 144–146; growth of opportunities in legal economy 145; research methodology 140–141; rollout of national/international security forces 145–146, 149; shift in trade between wheat and opium 145
Afghan National Defence and Security Forces (ANDSF) 146, 148
Africa, drug crops in 22, 158–159; cannabis 163–166; cracks in system 167–169; khat 161–163; quasilegality 159–161; social salience of quasilegality 166–167
Agamben, Giorgio 116
Agha Khan Foundation 59
Ahmadi-Moghaddam, Esmail 91
Ahmadinejad, Mahmud 89
Alcázar, Heberto 45, 50
alternative development projects 178, 179
Americas, predatory accumulation across 5–6

Amigo dos Amigos (ADA) 134n14
Amorin, Celso 127
al-Amroushy, Tamer 61
Andreas, Peter 133n4
Anslinger, Harry 43, 44, 45, 46, 47, 48, 49, 54n60
Anti-Narcotics General Administration (ANGA), Egypt 58
Appadurai, A. 160
Arab Spring, and Egypt 20; drugs landscape before 60–61; drugs landscape during 63, 65, 66
Arellano Felix organisation (AFO) 125, 128, 129, 130, 131, 134n10, 134n22
Arias, Desmond 124
Arlacchi, Pino 58
Armbrust, Walter 67n15
Astorga, Luis 135n26
Attewell, G. 27
authoritarianism, grassroots 21, 98

Bader, Mustafa 63
Badiou, Alain 114
Bakwa (Farah/Nimroz Provinces, Afghanistan), opium poppy cultivation in 149–152; expansion of agricultural land *150*; sharecroppers 152; year of settlement in *150*
balloon effect 22, 139–140, 146, 153
bango, consumption in Egypt 56–57, 60
barrio Luis Fanor Hernández (Nicaragua) 20–21, 69–70, 79–81; after drugs boom 73–79; destitution 75–76, 80; diversification 77–79, 80; downsizing 74–75, 80; drug economy 70–73; *el Indio Viejo* (the Old Indian) 70–73; gang violence 72; status of former drug dealers 74
Bassols, Francisco 45
Becker, Howard 188n116
Beckerleg, S. 162

INDEX

Bello, D. 27
Bene Diamba 163
Bernstein, Henry 164
Bhumibol Adulyadej 180
Big Food *see* food industry
Big Pharma *see* pharmaceutical multinational corporations
Big Tobacco *see* tobacco companies
biopower 3
Blancornelas, Jesus 135n29
Bloomer, J. 165
Boghra Canal (Hemland Province, Afghanistan), opium poppy cultivation in 146–149; expansion of agricultural land north of *147*; plant disease 148–149; sharecroppers 146, 149; year of settlement in area north of *147*
Booth, Martin 34
Bose, Chunilal 29
Bose, Kailas Chunder 28
Bourdieu, Pierre 5
Bourgois, Philippe 1, 15
Brazil, shared worldviews of civilian and military elites in 21–22, 122–123; domestic military operations 130–132; GLO operation (Rio de Janeiro) 126–127, 130–131; hotlines for citizens 131; legal framework 129–130; military's role in counter-narcotic policies 123–125; patrolling 131
Buddhism 181
Bulkley, J. W. 49
Bursley, Herbert S. 49, 50
Buzan, B. 183
Byrd, W. 144

Cabral, Sergio 126
Caldeira, Teresa 110
Calderón, Felipe 123, 127–128, 129, 132
California (United States), cannabis cultivation in 167
Campos, Isaac 4, 20, 40
camps, in Iran 21, 87–88, 91–92, 93, **100**; camp-touring 98; illegal 96–98; for women 93–96
Canada 49, 162
cannabis: in *barrio* Luis Fanor Hernández (Nicaragua) 73; cultivation in California (United States) 167; quasilegality of 22, 163–166, 167, 168; regulation 17, 18
capitalism 1, 4, 6
Cárdenas, Lázaro 40, 43, 49, 50, 52n8, 127
Caribbean 7
Carrier, Neil 21, 22, 158, 162, 163
cartels, drug 6, 7, 10, 72, 116, 125, 127–130, 131, 134n10, 134n22; *see also specific entries*
Carter, Jimmy 59
Cassanelli, Lee 22, 160, 161, 162, 166
Castillo Nájera, Francisco 44, 45, 48
cathine 162
cathinone 161, 162

Central America 4, 7, 124
Chakrabarti, P. 27
Chesnut, Andrew 116
China: Green Anti-Drug Project 182; -made Tramadol, in Egypt 63–64; migrants in West from 187–188n95; opium plague in 34, 183; repressive drug crop suppression policies 184
Christianity *see* Upper Amazon (Peru), Pentecostal addiction treatment ministries in
cocaine: coca paste *see* Upper Amazon (Peru), Pentecostal addiction treatment ministries in; consumption, in Egypt 61; crack 70–71; in India *see* colonial India, cocaine in; in Nicaragua *see barrio* Luis Fanor Hernández (Nicaragua); use, prevalence in South America 110
Cohen, P. T. 183
Colombia 7; disintoxication programme 44; drug cartels 72
colonial India, cocaine in 19, 26–27, 33–36; centralised monitoring system 32; consumption 28–30, 35; control and supply 30–33; Excise Acts 30; market 35; seizures 31–32, 33; smuggling 31–33, 34–35
colonialism 1; in Africa, and khat 162; medicines, flow of 27; opium plague, in China 34
Comando Vermelho (CV) 124, 125, 126, 132, 134n10, 134n22
Communism 181, 183
compassionate repression 93
Comprehensive Drug Control Programme 176
Consejo Ciudadano de Seguridad (Baja California Public Security Citizen Council) 128
conspicuous consumption 8, 71, 76, 80
Contreras, Randol 73, 77
Convention for Limiting the Manufacture and Regulating the Distribution of Narcotic Drugs (1931) 46
conversion, religious *see* Upper Amazon (Peru), Pentecostal addiction treatment ministries in
corrections corporations, for-profit 9
Courtwright, D. 183
crack cocaine 70–71
Creighton, Harold S. 44, 45
criminalisation, incremental 58–59
crystal methamphetamine *see* methamphetamine
cults, peripheral 111
cultural relativism 2
cultural values of drugs 23, 60, 61, 161, 164

dagga *see* cannabis
Dangerous Drugs Act (1920), UK 31
Daniels, Josephus 47
decriminalisation 4, 86, 91; camps 17; effective 168
Defence of the Realm Act 40B (UK) 31
Deleuze, Gille 87
demonic possession, addiction as 111–112

194

INDEX

destitution, in *barrio* Luis Fanor Hernández 75–76, 80
Dikötter, Frank 34
discretion, and quasilegality 159–160
diversification, in *barrio* Luis Fanor Hernández 77–79, 80
Doi Tung Development Project (Thailand) 179, 182
Dominican Republic 7
Douglas, Mary 110
downsizing, in *barrio* Luis Fanor Hernández 74–75, 80
Drug Control Headquarters (DCHQ), Iran 88, 96
drug decriminalisation camps 17
drug policy: micropolitics of *see* Islamic Republic of Iran, micropolitics of drugs policy in; militarisation of *see* militarisation of drugs policy
drug situation 17–19
drug studies 1–2; critical theoretical potential of 4–5; public health-dominated, intellectual poverty of 2–3
Duggan, Laurence 43–44
Duterte, Rodrigo 17–18, 168

economy: development, in producer nations 8; drug, *barrio* Luis Fanor Hernández (Nicaragua) 70–73; growth of opportunities in legal economy, in Afghanistan 145; illicit predatory economy 6–8; licit predatory economy (United States) 8–11; political economy, and opium suppression 181–183, **181**
education, and drug use in Egypt 62
effective decriminalisation 168
Egypt, drug consumption habits in 20, 56–57; anti-narcotics decrees 58; bango 60; changes in patterns 61–65; drug of choice 58–61; drugs landscape after Arab Spring 63, 65, 66; Egypt–Israel Peace Treaty 65; El-Batniyyah (Cairo) 59; hashish 20, 56, 57, 59, 60–61, 62; heroin 61; illicit drug consumption in modern Egypt 57–58; incremental criminalisation 58–59; open availability model 58; penal control model 58; pre-Arab Spring drugs landscape 60–61; price of illegal drugs (1995–2012) **60**; state responses 65–66; Tramadol 62–65; and war on drugs 59; white drugs epidemic 56, 57
Elorduy Walther, Eugenio 128
employment, and drug use in Egypt 62
entrepreneurs, moral 188n116
environmental protection, and opium suppression 179, 182
epidemics 1–2, 3, 9; pharmaceutical opiates 10; Tramadol *see* Tramadol, consumption in Egypt; white drugs, in Egypt 56, 57
ethnography 3, 4, 20, 85–87
European Monitoring Center for Drugs and Drug Addiction 154

evangelism *see* Upper Amazon (Peru), Pentecostal addiction treatment ministries in
Ewens, G. F. 29
Expediency Council (Iran) 89
export commodity development, and opium suppression 179, 182
external pressure, and opium suppression 178

Farah Province *see* Bakwa (Farah/Nimroz Provinces, Afghanistan), opium poppy cultivation in
Fassin, Didier 93, 102n8
favelas see Brazil, shared worldviews of civilian and military elites in
Fawzi, Ahmed 61
Fela Kuti 164, 165, 166
Felbab-Brown, Vanda 131
Ferguson, James 76, 79
financialisation 6
firearms 7–8
Flores Guevara, Mariana 48
food industry 10
Foucault, Michel 3, 5, 116
Franco, Jean 116
'free the weed' campaigns 167
Fuller, Stuart J. 43, 46, 49
fuzzy law 159

Galván, Guillermo 129
Garcia, Angela 117
gender, and drug use: in Egypt 62; in Iran 93–96
gender reassignment surgery, in Iran 99
geospatial analysis 141
Ghiabi, Maziyar 3, 5, 15, 21, 85
Giustozzi, A. 144
González Guzmán, Ignacio 45
graba 162
grassroots authoritarianism 21, 98
Green Anti-Drug Project (China) 182
Guatemala 116

Hamdi, Emad 57, 61, 62, 64
Hansen, Helena 116
Hansen, Thomas Blom 111, 113–114
harm reduction 2–3, 64, 88, 89, 90, 91
Harrison Narcotics Tax Act (1914), United States 31
hashish: consumption, in Egypt 20, 56, 57, 59, 60–61, 62; use in religious practices 23
Helmand Food Zone (HFZ) 144, 148, 152
Helmand Province (Afghanistan), opium poppy cultivation in 144, *145*, 146; Boghra Canal 146–149, *147*
heroin 10, 174–175; consumption, in Egypt 61; consumption, in Iran 86, 88
Higazi, Faisal 61
Honduras 7
humanitarian security, in Iran 91–93
hyper-incarceration 9

INDEX

ideology, and opium suppression 180
illicit predatory economy 6–8
imperialism 3–4
incarceration: and drug use 17; hyper-incarceration 9; rate, in Iran 92
India *see* colonial India, cocaine in
injustice, perceived 184
interdisciplinarity 16
internal security, Mexico 129–130
International Narcotics Control Board (INCB) 176, 178
International Opium Convention (1925) 165
international reputation, and opium suppression 178
Iran *see* Islamic Republic of Iran, micropolitics of drugs policy in
Islamic Republic of Iran, micropolitics of drugs policy in 17, 21; budgetary allocations 91–92; camps 87–88, 91–92, 93–98, **100**; Drug Control Headquarters (DCHQ) 88, 96; ethnography 85–87; Expediency Council 89; female addicts 93–96; humanitarian security 91–93; maintaining disorder 98–101, *99*; oxymoronic laws 89–90; prisons 92–93; state institutions *88*; state of camouflage and subterfuge 96–98
Ismael, Tareq 58

Jalisco Nueva Generación Cartel 131
Japan, cocaine supply to colonial India from 33
Jonglez, O. 144

karez irrigation 149, 150, 151
Kenya, legal status of khat in 161, 162, 163, 166, 167
Khamenei, Ali 89
khat, quasilegality of 22, 161–163, 166, 167, 168
Khatami, Mohammad 88
Khattab, Moushira 62
kidnapping, in Mexico 128–129
Kingsberg, M. 27
Klantschnig, Gernot 22, 158
Kolb, Lawrence 49

Laamann, Lars 34
Laniel, L. 165
Laos, opium suppression in 175–176; domestic opium consumption 181; environmental protection 179; export commodity development 179; external pressure and international reputation 178; ideology and religion 180; rural development 179; state extension 178–179, 182
Larijani, Sadegh Ardeshir Amoli 92–93
Latin America 7, 17; Brazil *see* Brazil, shared worldviews of civilian and military elites in; Mexico *see* Mexico; Mexico, shared worldviews of civilian and military elites in; *Reglamento Federal de Toxicomanías* (1940); Nicaragua *see barrio* Luis Fanor Hernández (Nicaragua); peace-time homicide in 8; Upper Amazon (Peru) *see* Upper Amazon (Peru), Pentecostal addiction treatment ministries in
League of Nations 58, 186n50; Opium Advisory Committee 26–27, 43, 48–49; Permanent Central Opium Board 27; and *Reglamento Federal de Toxicomanías* (1940) 43, 45, 46, 47, 48–49
legal highs 158
León, Alberto 45, 46–47, 50
Lewis, I. M. 111
Leyzaola, Julian 125, 128, 131, 132
licit predatory economy, in United States 8–11
López Lira, José 45
Loza, Nasser 61, 66
Luis Fanor Hernández (Nicaragua) *see barrio* Luis Fanor Hernández (Nicaragua)
Lula (Brazilian President) 123
lumpen populations 5, 6, 8, 11
Luxemburg, Rosa 6

McAllister, William B. 54n60
Madagascar 163
maintenance programmes 20, 48
Mansfield, David 21, 22, 139
maquiladora 6
marijuana *see* cannabis
Marley, Bob 166
marriages, temporary, in Iran 99
Marx, Karl 4, 5, 6
mass incarceration 9
May, Theresa 162
menthol cigarettes 10
methadone 61, 86, 93
methamphetamine 10, 86, 88, *90*, 94
Mexico 4, 7; drug cartels 10, 116, 125, 127–130, 131, 134n10, 134n22; maintenance programmes 20, 48; *Reglamento Federal de Toxicomanías see Reglamento Federal de Toxicomanías* (1940)
Mexico, shared worldviews of civilian and military elites in 21–22, 122–123; domestic military operations 130–132; hotlines for citizens 131; military's role in counter-narcotic policies 123–125; *Operativo Conjunto* (Tijuana) 127–130, 131; patrolling 131
Meyer, Birgit 115
micropolitics of drug policy *see* Islamic Republic of Iran, micropolitics of drugs policy in
milícia (criminal group) 134n14
militarisation of drugs policy 17–18; Thailand 176, 179–180; Vietnam 177; *see also* Brazil, shared worldviews of civilian and military elites in; Mexico, shared worldviews of civilian and military elites in
Mills, James H. 19, 26
money laundering 7

INDEX

Moore, Sally Falk 159
moral entrepreneurs 188n116
Morey, R. 180
Mubarak, Hosni 57, 61
Mubarak, Suzanne 62, 66
Mujica, Pepe 17
Munir, Azmi 61

Nangarhar Province (Afghanistan), opium poppy cultivation in 144
Narcotics Import–Export Act of 1922 (US) 44, 46
National Democratic Party (NDP), Egypt 65
National Institute of Mental Health (NIMH) 2
National Institute on Alcohol Abuse and Alcoholism (NIAAA) 2
National Institute on Drug Abuse (NIDA) 2
National Institutes of Health (NIH) 2
Nazif, Ahmad 66
neoliberal policies 5, 6
neo-Pentecostalism 107
Nicaragua 7, 16, 20; as trans-shipment point for drugs 81–82n6; see also barrio Luis Fanor Hernández (Nicaragua)
Nigeria, legal status of cannabis in 164, 165, 166
Nimroz Province see Bakwa (Farah/Nimroz Provinces, Afghanistan), opium poppy cultivation in
Nixon, Richard 17, 59
Noorzai tribe 148, 151, 152
Norte del Valle cartel 72

Odinga, Raila 163
Okoth, Ken 167
O'Neill, Kevin 116
open availability model, in Egypt 58
Operativo Conjunto (Tijuana) 127–130, 131
opioids 9–10; distribution, in Mexico see *Reglamento Federal de Toxicomanías* (1940); Tramadol see Tramadol, consumption in Egypt
opium 174; in China 34, 35; domestic consumption, in South-east Asian states 180–181, 183; plague, in China 34, 183; poppy see Afghanistan (southwest), settlement and poppy cultivation in; suppression see South-east Asian states, opium suppression in; external pressure, and opium suppression 178
organised crime 6, 8, 10, 122–133, 133n4; see also cartels, drug
Osman, Amr 66
Overbeck-Wright, A. W. 29–30
OxyContin 10

paan, and cocaine use 28, 30, 35
pain pills 9
Palau, Luis 112
Parran, Thomas 47
Passos, Anaís M. 21–22, 122

Pax, Francisco 46
penal control model 58
Peña Nieto, Enrique 132
Pentecostalism *see* Upper Amazon (Peru), Pentecostal addiction treatment ministries in
perceived injustice 184
Perez, Oren 159
Peru *see* Upper Amazon (Peru), Pentecostal addiction treatment ministries in
pharmaceutical multinational corporations 9–10, 11
pharmacological determinism 161
Philippines 159, 168; militarisation of drugs policy 17–18
Pietschmann, T. 175
policy, drugs 17, 22–23; in Egypt 61; global, cracks in 167–169; in Iran *see* Islamic Republic of Iran, micropolitics of drugs policy in; militarisation of 17–18; and securitisation 184; war on drugs 18, 59, 108, 116–117, 130, 132, 158, 159, 165
political economy, and opium suppression 181–183, **181**
Polson, M. 167
poppy *see* Afghanistan (southwest), settlement and poppy cultivation in
Portugal 17, 168
post-colonial studies 34
power 3–4, 21, 87, 111, 116, 144, 165
predatory accumulation: across Americas 5–6; illicit predatory economy 6–8; licit predatory economy 8–11
Prem Tinsulanonda 180
primitive accumulation 4, 5, 6, 7, 73
privatisation 89
process tracing 175
prohibitionism: and drug use 3–4; in Mexico 20; in South-east Asian states *see* Afghanistan (southwest), settlement and poppy cultivation in
Provincial Reconstruction Teams (PRTs) 145, 149
pseudoephedrine 9, 10
public health-dominated drug studies, intellectual poverty of 2–3
Puerto Rico 6
Purdue Pharma 10
Purmohammadi, Mostafa 92

quasilegality 22, 159–161; benefits of 167; cannabis 163–166; cracks in system 167–169; khat 161–163; social salience of 166–167
Quintanilla, Luis 44

Ramírez, Eliseo 45
Ramos, Jorge 129
Al-Rashidy, Abdul Rahman 63
Reagan, Ronald 5, 9, 17, 130
Reglamento Federal de Toxicomanías (1940) 20, 40–41; Article 3 45, 46–47; clarifications 47;

and Colombian disintoxication programme 44; communication breakdown 44, 46, 49; controversy 42; Convention for Limiting the Manufacture and Regulating the Distribution of Narcotic Drugs (1931) 46; crafting 42; embargo of United States 41, 44, 45–46, 47, 49; General Health Council 42, 43, 45, 48, 50; informal negotiations with United States 47–48, 49; and League of Nations 43, 45, 46, 47, 48–49; León 45, 46–47, 50; López Lira 45; Ministry of Foreign Relations 47, 48; officialization of 43; presidential politics 43; Siurob 44–45, 46, 47, 48, 49, 50, 245n34; suspension of 50; and United States 41, 43–45, 46–48; visit of Creighton to Mexico City 44–45
rehabilitation camps, in Iran *see* camps, in Iran
religion: conversion *see* Upper Amazon (Peru), Pentecostal addiction treatment ministries in; and drug use in Egypt 62; and opium suppression 180, 183; practices, use of drugs in 23
remote sensing 141, 146
Rio de Janeiro (Brazil) 123–124; GLO operation 126–127, 130–131
Robbins, Joel 114
Robins, Philip 20, 56
Rodgers, Dennis 3, 20–21, 69
Rolnik, Raquel 137n90
Roosevelt, Franklin 48, 50
rural development, and opium suppression 179, 182
Ruto, William 163

Sadat, Anwar 59
safe injection rooms 17, 88
Said, Edward 34
Salazar Viniegra, Leopoldo 20, 40–42, 43, 46, 49
scholarship, drug 16
Second World War, and Mexico 50
securitisation 183, 184, 188n116
security: humanitarian, in Iran 91–93; internal, in Mexico 129–130; and opium suppression 179–180, 181, **182**, 183–184
settlement, of opium poppy cultivators *see* Afghanistan (southwest), settlement and poppy cultivation in
Seward Delaporte, Pablo 21, 106
sex change surgery, in Iran 99
Shanghai Opium Conference (1909) 26
Shifting Cultivation Stabilization Pilot Project (Laos) 179
Shining Path 109, 110
Shirk, David A. 125
shisheh see methamphetamine
Sinaloa Cartel 125, 128, 129, 130, 131, 134n22
al-Sisi, Abdul Fatah 57, 66
Siurob, José 44–45, 46, 47, 48, 49, 50, 245n34
Sleem, Houda Nassim 62
social abandonment 116

social life, and drugs 23, 34, 60, 164
South Africa, legal status of cannabis in 165
South-east Asian states, opium suppression in 22, 174–175; alien conspiracies 181, 184, 188n116; domestic opium consumption 180–181, 183; economic considerations 181–183, **181**; environmental protection 179, 182; export commodity development 179, 182; external pressure and international reputation 178; ideology and religion 180, 183; Laos 175–176; modernisation 183; reasons **177**; rural development 179, 182; security 179–180, 181, **182**, 183–184; state extension 178–179, 182–183; Thailand 176–177; Vietnam 177
special interest groups, in United States 8–11
spiritual warfare 108, 112–113
state extension, and opium suppression 178–179, 182–183
stateless societies 4
Stevens, A. 174–175
Subaltern Studies project 34
substance-use-disorder prevention research 2

Taheri, Tah 92
Taliban, and opium poppy cultivation 142–143, 148, 152, 153
Taussig, Michael 112
Tello, Manuel 43
Teodoro García Simental, Eduardo (*El Teo*) 125, 128
Terceiro Comando Puro (TCP) 134n14
Thailand, opium suppression in 176–177; domestic opium consumption 180–181; environmental protection 179; export commodity development 179; external pressure and international reputation 178; ideology and religion 180, 183; rural development 179; security 179–180, 184; state extension 178, 182–183
Thatcher, Margaret 5
Thelwall, Reverend Algernon 33
therapeutic community model 107
Tijuana (Mexico) 123, 124–125; *Operativo Conjunto* 127–130, 131
tobacco companies 10–11
Tramadol, consumption in Egypt 20, 57, 66; attraction for 64–65; emergence of 62–63; origins of 63–64; reclassification 64
trans-shipment points 7, 81–82n6
Trocki, Carl 27, 34
Trump, Donald 9
Tsing, Anna 158
Tupac Amaru Revolutionary Movement (MRTA) 109
Turkey 178, 188n122

Uganda, legal status of khat in 162
United Kingdom (UK) 19, 158; Advisory Council on the Misuse of Drugs 162; ban

of khat 162, 167; Chinese migrants, and opium 187–188n95; control of cocaine in 31; legal status of cannabis in 168; opium/opiate consumption in 183; opium trade by 34

United Nations General Assembly Special Session (UNGASS) 167–168

United Nations International Drug Control Program (UNDCP) 143

United Nations Office on Drugs and Crime (UNODC) 17, 61, 66, 143, 154, 164, 176, 177

United States (US) 58; addiction market 7; army disease 183; cannabis cultivation in California 167; Chinese migrants, and opium 187–188n95; control of cocaine in 31; Harrison Narcotics Tax Act (1914) 31; licit predatory economies and special interest groups in 8–11; and Mexico 122, 124, 128; militarisation of drugs policy 17; National Institutes of Health 2; opium/opiate consumption in 183; and Peru 108; predatory accumulation in 5–6; pressure on opium-producing countries 178; prohibitionist drug policies in 3–4, 5–6; and *Reglamento Federal de Toxicomanías* (1940) 41, 43–45, 46–48; scheduling of cathinone/cathine 162; unemployed drug dealers in 73

Upper Amazon (Peru), Pentecostal addiction treatment ministries in 21, 106–108, 115–117; addiction in Upper Amazon 109–111; ethics 117; faith-based addiction treatment 21, 115–116; globalisation of Pentecostalism 115; *hueco* 110; *lacra* 110, 111; life story of Alex 108–109; pastors and residents after conversion 113–115; possession, addiction as 111–112; practice of spiritual warfare in 'We Will Revive' 112–113; recovery through conversion 111–112; social abandonment 116; study limitations 117; war on drugs 116–117

UPP (Unities of Pacifying Police) programme 124, 125, 126, 132

Uruguay 17

Van Schendel, W. 160
Venkatesh, Sudhir 73
Vietnam, opium suppression in 177; domestic opium consumption 181; external pressure and international reputation 178; ideology and religion 180, 183–184; rural development 179; state extension 178–179, 182
violence 7–8, 23; addiction-related 18; of criminal organisations and drug traffickers 18; gang 72; institutional, of state 18; *see also* Brazil, shared worldviews of civilian and military elites in; cartels, drug; Mexico, shared worldviews of civilian and military elites in

warfare *see* spiritual warfare
war on drugs 18, 59, 108, 116–117, 130, 132, 158, 159, 165
Welfare Organisation (Iran) 87, 98
West Africa Commission on Drugs 168
'We Will Revive' (*Reviviremos*) 106–108, 109–110, 111, 112, 115, 117; practice of spiritual warfare in 112–113
Wilson, L. 174–175
Windle, James 21, 22, 174
women, drug use: in Egypt 62; in Iran 93–96
World Drug Report (2017) 17
Wynter, Sylvia 117

Xun, Zhou 34

Yahya, Mohamed 63
Yangwen, Zheng 34
Youssef, Essam 61

Zeta (newspaper) 135n29
Zozaya, José 49

Printed in the USA
CPSIA information can be obtained
at www.ICGtesting.com
LVHW060548170924
791293LV00006B/644